A History of Fatigue

A HISTORY OF FATIGUE

From the Middle Ages to the Present

Georges Vigarello

Translated by Nancy Erber

polity

Originally published in French as *Histoire de la fatigue. Du Moyen Âge à nos jours*

This work received the French Voices Award for excellence in publication and translation. French Voices Award is a program of Villa Albertine and FACE Foundation, in partnership with the French Embassy in the United States.
French Voices logo designed by Serge Bloch.

Polity Press
65 Bridge Street
Cambridge CB2 1UR, UK

Polity Press
111 River Street
Hoboken, NJ 07030, USA

ISBN-13: 978-1-5095-4925-2 – hardback

A catalogue record for this book is available from the British Library.

Library of Congress Control Number: 2022930950

Typeset in 11.5 on 14 Adobe Garamond
by Fakenham Prepress Solutions, Fakenham, Norfolk NR21 8NL
Printed in Great Britain by TJ Books Ltd, Padstow, Cornwall

For further information on Polity, visit our website:
politybooks.com

To Thierry Pillon

Contents

Acknowledgements

I especially want to thank the friends and colleagues who offered advice and read and re-read my manuscript. Their help was priceless: Jean-Jacques Courtine, Yan Descamps, Claudine Haroche, Jean-Noël Jeanneney, Corine Maitte, Séverine Nikel, Thierry Pillon, Monique Quesne, André Rauch, Cécile Rey, Sylvie Roques, Marc Saraceno, Didier Terrier, François Vatin, Jocelyne Vaysse.

Foreword

Thomas W. Laqueur

This book is, at grandest, a history of what it is to be human. Fatigue is a condition of our species being, both in a materialist, physiological sense and as creatures in culture. We can speak of fatigue as the condition of our muscles when lactic acid builds up, as mental exhaustion from living in a world largely indifferent to our wellbeing, and as one of the signs in the body of the Fall. Weary unto Death. But it is also a condition that exists in time; old fatigues may persist but new ones come into being: the inner dramas of the post-Freudian world are not the same kind of fatigue as the fatigue of the mind that came into being with Descartes and the deepening of a sense of conscience; there was no burn out in the Middle Ages.

But let me step back. One way to read this book is as the third in a trilogy about the history of the body over the last thousand years. The first installment was *Concepts of Cleanliness: Changing Attitudes in France since the Middle Ages* (1988), a history of the clean and the dirty body, of matter out of place on a corporeal stage and what ought to be done to set it right. It traced how, at the end of the Middle Ages, the bathhouses of Europe – a legacy of classical antiquity – were closed on the grounds that they posed both a moral and a physical danger to the individual as well as the social body. Hygiene became an individual responsibility: oils, powders, good grooming put each body in order. Famously, Vigarello argues that water was not part of the program: experts claimed that, itself not clean, it could seep into the pores of a porous body and only make it dirtier. Louis XIV supposedly took only two baths, both supervised by doctors. Cleanliness by the eighteenth century equaled clean clothes, clean linen and good manners for those who could afford it. The rest were dirty. Modern regimes were born, on the one hand, of increasing individualism – deodorants, soaps of all kinds – and, on the other, state-mandated public health measures to clean up the poor and their surroundings. The AIDS crisis of the 1980s and the closing of bathhouses comes as an epilogue.

In 2013 *The Metamorphoses of Fat: A History of Obesity* was translated into English. It is a history of the meaning of a big or small, a fat or thin body – male and female; of the moral and more broadly cultural valences of such bodies; of the meaning of fat itself; and of the means of achieving what was taken to be a normative body. It is a history of size. (Vigarello wrote other books in between: *A History of Rape: Sexual Violence in France from the 16th to the 20th Century* in 2001 and a history of beauty in 2004 that has not been translated.)

Being fat was a sign of health and plenty in the Middle Ages, but it was never an unambiguously good thing. As Vigarello concludes, "The stigmatization of the fat person is strongly dominant in a history of obesity," but at the same time what constitutes a fat person and what it means to be fat – or thin – has changed dramatically. The undernourished working-class woman of the nineteenth century does not bear the same meaning as the slender woman of fashion magazines whose body witnesses to her leisure and self-care; the medieval glutton is not the same as the fat-cat capitalist, the buffoon of cruel comedy, or the failed dieter whose problem is not sin but a lack of willpower. To be fat today is to be weak. And, of course, what we know about fat itself as a substance has changed. Obesity a thousand years ago and obesity today may not quite be incommensurable categories, but translation between paradigms is the heavy historical lift that Vigarello's 2004 book takes on.

The new book you are about to read is in its method and structure very much like its predecessors. It is on a grand time scale: from medieval knights in battle to exhausted health-care and other "essential" workers during the Covid epidemic. Its trajectory is toward modernity, toward the autarchic self and the democracy of bodies:

> One hypothesis structuring this book is that the increased autonomy of people in Western societies (whether genuine or assumed), the positing of a more individualized "self," and the ever expanding ideal of independence and freedom have made it ever more difficult for us to withstand anything that constrains or limits us, even more so if we add to this equation an awareness of potential obstacles, weaknesses and vulnerabilities.

But this book is different from its predecessors because its subject – fatigue – is far more deeply and, consequently, broadly imbricated in the deep time of humanity than either cleanliness or obesity. Clean or dirty, fat or thin are contingent qualities of our species. Fatigue is not. It began, as I suggested, with the Fall, when Adam was condemned to earn his bread through the sweat of his brow and Eve to give birth in pain; it is coterminous with Death coming into the world. In each of us it announces this unavoidable appointment. Fatigue is intimately tied not only to moral and cultural norms of an era but to its physics. (That is also why steel girders under stress suffer from it.) We can speak in the nineteenth century of cleanliness and obesity without the categories of thermodynamics; not so of fatigue, which is another name for corporeal entropy. We can speak of cleanliness and obesity without speaking of time and decay, of human fragility, illness, old age and death: as Vigarello writes, "fatigue dwells inside us, in our very hearts ..."

This book is an account of changes over time – paradigm shifts, inventions of specific fatigues – but also of continuities. The old remains, still comprehensible in the age of the new. Theme and variations on understanding loss, incapacity and exhaustion that in each age produce new kinds, and new understandings, of an enormously freighted category. It is difficult for Vigarello to answer precisely "what is fatigue?" or "what causes it?" because of its vast and geologically layered landscape mirrored in the conceptual shifts he documents.

Consider causes. An eleventh-century source lists, among others, the following causes of fatigue: excessive thought, too much speculation, investigating things that are beyond comprehension, dehydration, despair, worry, anger, sleeplessness, heavy burdens, shrunken organs and digestive ailments.

A thousand years later there is very little that does not cause fatigue, although modernity will not speak of humors or shrunken organs. Most of the time, the Mayo Clinic reports, it can be traced to "lifestyle factors": too little or too much physical activity; not enough sleep; bad eating habits; drugs and alcohol. And there is a long list of underlying conditions – as well as the medications that are used to treat them – that might explain fatigue that is not caused by lifestyle, i.e., by life. From acute liver failure to traumatic brain injury; overactive and underactive thyroid; diabetes; heart and kidney disease; states of mind – depression, grief, stress; and, in between, conditions difficult to place – chronic fatigue syndrome, fibromyalgia. From the perspective of medicine, as from that of a medieval monk, fatigue is consequence of life, of the frailty of body and soul.

There are so many causes because the landscape of fatigue is and has always been so vast. There are historical nodes: the ideal medieval warrior was the man who was not exhausted by battle. The opposite of fatigue in his case was endurance. The medieval pilgrim or traveler experienced exhaustion on account of physical dangers but also because of disorientation and incomprehension. Fatigue of the mind as well of the body. There was redemptive fatigue: the pain of walking barefoot for long distances as a form of atonement. The more widespread use of clocks allowed the measurement of time at work and a more acute sense of physical exertion for particular trades and tasks: the fatigue of labor. In the Renaissance people came to evaluate fatigue: which galley slaves could work the longest and the hardest. "War fatigue" became a category. The opposite of fatigue became tirelessness. Exhaustion, to be avoided by the medieval warrior, became a badge of honor among the functionaries of court; and court fatigue – swollen legs – became a cause of concern among those who had to endure long visits, uncomfortable postures and boring conversations. "Fatigue of the mind" became a category in the seventeenth century.

But the major paradigm shift came in the eighteenth century, and we still live in its light. To some degree it was based on new theories of the etiology of fatigue – nervous exhaustion – and on a new materialist view of the body as an energy-using machine. But, more importantly, these theories meant that fatigue could be measured, moderated and treated sympathetically. The whole Enlightenment project might be construed as an effort, through technology and right thinking, to lift humanity out of the sough of fatigue. This is what Malthus parodies as an impossible dream.

Vigarello follows this paradigm shift into the next two centuries: the measurement and alleviation of worker fatigue in industry and measures taken to alleviate it; the rise of a model of mental fatigue and its remedies which morphs into today's worry about stress; the advent of "burn out" – with its ironic appropriation of a mechanical image for a state of mind. (The word seems to have entered English in the late 1970s to describe what happens to those in the "fast lane" – i.e., those who live hectic, pressured lives, rock star, jet-set lives. Today the glamor is gone.)

The conquest of fatigue is at the same time a utopian dream and an impossibility. The day I began writing this foreword the following paragraph began an article on the *Wall Street Journal*:

> Effortless power is a defining feature of what we began, roughly 150 years ago, to call "modern" life. In countless domains, technology has equipped human beings to vastly increase the sensation of strength while vastly reducing the sensation of effort. A world-class weightlifter is physically powerful, but anyone can see that performing an Olympic deadlift requires tremendous physical, mental and even emotional strain, prepared for by years of training. Someone operating a forklift, on the other hand, can lift far more weight than any athlete with almost no exertion at all.

The first and the last sentences offer the dream of effortlessness – inertia and gravity will go away – or, at best, "no exertion at all": the end of fatigue. They echo the views of one of the nineteenth century's most enthusiastic defenders of industrialization. Andrew Ure, in his *Philosophy of Manufactures* (1835), writes:

> The constant aim and effect of scientific improvement in manufactures are philanthropic, as they tend to relieve the workmen either from niceties of adjustment which exhaust his mind and fatigue his eyes, or from painful repetition of efforts which distort or wear out his frame … how vastly productive human industry would become, when no longer proportioned in its results to muscular effort, which is by its nature fitful and capricious, but when made to consist in the task of guiding the work of mechanical fingers and arms, regularly impelled with great velocity by some *indefatigable physical power* … The non-factory weaver, having everything to execute by muscular exertion, finds the labour irksome.

In other words, through machinery, the physical as well as the mental fatigue of work will be no more. Nonsense of course, but I leave open the obvious question of whether this is true or not. Ure's fantasy is, however – well perhaps not quite – the modern version of the medieval imagined Land of Cockaigne, where roasted pigs walk around with knives in their backs, houses are made of bread and pastry, sex is freely available, and youth is forever. Or a version of the world of plenty that Marx envisions at the end of *The German Ideology*.

But then there is the kicker: the weightlifter whose prodigious feats demand "tremendous physical, mental and emotional strain." If we understand this allegorically, we might substitute for weightlifting any creative act, all cultural work broadly understood. We are back in the landscapes Vigarello describes. No machine – neither analog nor digital – experiences fatigue. Humans do. This book might be read as a history of how we understand this condition of our species being.

Introduction

"Stress," "drudgery," "burn out" or "mental overload": we have seen an inescapable extension of the realm of fatigue in the twentieth and twenty-first centuries. The tentacles of exhaustion stretch from our workplaces into our homes, from leisure time to the daily grind. Almost one in eight employees chooses the word "stress" first to describe their work.[1] In 2017 over a third of office workers said they had already experienced "burn out."[2] One hypothesis structuring this book is that the increased autonomy of people in Western societies (whether genuine or assumed), the positing of a more individualized "self," and the ever expanding ideal of independence and freedom have made it ever more difficult for us to withstand anything that constrains or limits us, even more so if we add to this equation an awareness of potential obstacles, weaknesses and vulnerabilities. This painful, overwhelming contradiction causes weariness as well as dissatisfaction. At that point, fatigue only becomes even stronger, imperceptibly permeating everything, seeping into ordinary moments or unexpected places and heightening its "internal" aspect. Fatigue insinuates itself into society, at work, at home, in our relationships with friends and family, and into our innermost self.

How did this happen?

The Latin terms *fatigato* or *defatigato* reveal the ancient origin of the word "fatigue." These words imply a direct connection between past and present, and their etymology almost automatically suggests that nothing, seen from the vantage point of weariness and exhaustion, will change over time. Fatigue dwells inside us, in our very hearts, and such inevitable decay has its own "limit" as surely as do illness, old age or death. This endpoint reveals its fragility, its "lack," and identifies two almost universally experienced obstacles: an "internal" one, based on the limitations of a person's life; the other, "external," is rooted in the outside world, its constraints and contradictions. There is nothing pathological here; it's actually the most ordinary kind of inadequacy. As Guy de Maupassant observed prosaically: "An overwhelming fatigue, finally, overcame him. He fell asleep."[3]

Yet, everything changes. Everything has a history that is more complex than it seems and is still relatively little known, full of metamorphoses that set off others, influencing the actions of people, cultures and societies. In our field, the history of the West, our understanding of fatigue has changed from one historical period to the next. Our diagnoses have varied. The symptoms of fatigue are different, the words used to describe it change, and the explanations for it adapt and diverge. As we embark on this very long road exploring the history of fatigue, we will have to delve into several histories: the history of the body, its depictions and its hygienic practices, the history of being and doing, of social structures, of work, war, sports, and also of our psychology, including the structure of our most intimate self.

The "most important" kinds of fatigue, the ones that invite analysis and the ones generally deemed most significant, have evolved over time. They are thought to be "categorical"; they create new perceptual fields. They are influenced by social mores and reveal the trajectory of our collective lives. In the Middle Ages, where our research begins, a warrior's fatigue was the central concern of a civilization that prized military valor. The warrior's fatigue is celebrated and written about while that of the commoner is despised. Fatigue is even factored into jousting; in the fifteenth century a combatant's performance would be rated higher based on the number of blows credited to each side in the clash.

Everything changes again in the classical period, when the church hierarchy becomes prominent and administrative and ministerial functions gained prestige. La Fontaine's banker and La Bruyère's lawyer lead us toward new descriptions. They exemplified specific types of weariness and opened our eyes to heretofore unknown concerns. Everything changes yet again with workers' fatigue in the nineteenth century, when industrial production – its social benefits as well as its dangers – begins to dominate the economy. The toll of bodily incapacity is rising and the ever increasing pace of work is disturbing. Since the logic of the system is calibrated to yield ever increasing output, cost savings and efficiency, from that time on the modern industrial system is denounced by critics from Villermé to Marx. Now that we live in the "Quaternary period"[4] of computers and office work, our fatigue is muted and less visible; information overload has taken the place of physical overwork, and unexpected personal and group crises are on the rise, the result of a long chain of hidden pain and suffering.

Depictions of the body and their evolution also shape our perspectives on fatigue. The oldest image associates a "state" of fatigue with the loss of bodily humors. A tired body is a dehydrated body. Exhaustion is the loss of substance, a diminishing density. No doubt this is a "simple" image, originating in antiquity and grounded in a belief that our bodily fluids are precious, even the ones that seep out from wounds, boil up with fevers, and drain away after death. Dehydration and rehydration are thus linked to the outward signs of an exhausted and reinvigorated body. A pallid, bloodless body is the ultimate visible proof of the experience of fatigue.

During the Enlightenment, interlocking fibers, filaments, "currents" and nerves took the place of bodily humors, and they explained the presence of fatigue. New symptoms were detected and other indices were acknowledged. Exhaustion was associated with an excessive amount of stimulation that was overwhelming and hard to recover from. Weakness was caused by tension that assailed the body repeatedly or regularly. Insufficient energy was caused not by leaking fluids but by unregulated stimuli. New physical sensations were recognized that interacted with a feeling of emptiness, a lack of motivation, and the loss of spirit. Thus began the search for "tonics" and specific stimulants that were not simply replacements for lost liquids but remedies to enhance endurance.

The image of fatigue changes again when the organizing principle is energy and organic combustion is key, according to the mechanistic nineteenth-century model. Then, fatigue comes to mean also the loss of fire, of a diminished force understood as "output," of the feeling of vigor slipping away, along with the scientific conviction that chemical wastes deposited in our flesh cause pain and suffering. This leads to the search for "revivifying" remedies, for ways to store energy, increase caloric intake and eliminate harmful substances and toxins.

Nowadays fatigue is understood in digital terms that prioritize internal cues and sensations and feelings of connectedness and disconnection. Thus, the torrent of advice to relax and slow down. There is an entirely new focus on the psychological, the interpersonal, on the value of connections, of mobility, and also of emotions that are cautiously restored to full strength.

Distinctions and degrees of fatigue have become clearer over time. Our civilization has invented sensitivities, attended to nuances, and heightened our perception of types of fatigue that had not existed before, and, as the years pass, bringing to light conditions that had long been overlooked. New words are invented and new symptoms discerned. One of these, for instance, is "lethargy," which the wealthy used in the seventeenth century to complain of heretofore unknown weaknesses and vulnerabilities. Another is "aching," adopted by the sensitive culture of the eighteenth century to designate a feeling of stiffness or discomfort that, previously ignored, resulted from physical exertion undertaken without the proper preparation. Nineteenth-century laborers suffered from "wasting," an irreversible physical decline that spanned generations and was understood as the aftermath of deprivation as much as overwork. The boundaries of the meaning of fatigue were continually displaced, and new degrees of fatigue have taken hold that afflict both mind and body.

The twentieth and twenty-first centuries, the age of extreme psychologizing of human behavior and emotions, have introduced new distinctions. Physical pain, after a long and hard-fought battle for recognition, has certainly not gone away. But our attention is focused on so many other symptoms: unease, anxiety, dissatisfaction with one's self. For every fatigue inflicted by external forces, another arises from an internal struggle, a truly personal, even intimate fatigue. There are obstacles and feelings of inadequacy within each of us that cause weaknesses and failures too. All this is aggravated by modern business management principles that ignore the individual in favor of maximizing short-term profits, leading to a lack of job security, to precariousness and unwanted career changes. This in turn results in a distinct contemporary contradiction: "A consumer who has choices, an employee who loses them, and a citizen who demands them."[5] These are very personal frustrations whose reality has, till now, been constantly questioned.

This is precisely the challenge of this historical and genealogical study: to show how something that seems permanently centered in our bodies has also, over the course of centuries, been ingrained in our minds, our social structures and their depictions, in the end affecting us intimately.

PART I

THE MEDIEVAL WORLD AND THE CHALLENGE OF LANDMARKS

A perennial threat to our survival, fatigue was ever present in medieval daily life. It was captured in images of exhausted bodies, bent by toil. Commentaries, from medical treatises to historical chronicles, fables and novels, dwelled on it. The traditional model of fatigue explained it as a loss of bodily humors and a lack of the body's precious fluids. Fatigue was thought to be a deficiency of matter, a leaking away of the substance that nourishes flesh, thereby shrinking it. It was a "mysterious" phenomenon too, with no exact measurement, no way to describe it precisely, even though a word existed: "fatigue," derived from the Latin *fatigare*, *fatigatio*, *defatigario*, and "weariness" from the Latin *lassitudo*. There were no gradations to indicate which was "greater" and which "lesser," save for one's own subjective sense, along with measures such as the length of the day, the variety and type of activities, and the approximate distance between points. This gap in the lexicon, however, did not mean that crises, accidents, physical injuries and dangers were not acknowledged.

People also disseminated the concept of fatigue in ways that were linked to their identities in medieval society. Travelers and pilgrims seem to have been among the first to do so. Pharmacopeias pitched their wares to people "who want to travel"[1] or to "those who tire of the journey" – pilgrims, merchants, or knights embarking on risky expeditions in treacherous territory. Meanwhile, chronicles and novels colorfully depicted the fatigues of warriors who brought fame and honor to the strongholds they defended. At the same time, hagiographies emphasized the exhaustion of those who served for the good of all in monasteries and nunneries. These varieties of fatigue were not precisely cataloged, but they were undoubtedly experienced, and references to them reflected more accurately than other indices a medieval conception of the social, of space and time. One might say, then, that these fatigues were situated exclusively in opposition to things, in the resistance of the environment itself.

1

A Clear Picture with Cloudy Landmarks

One central image dominated the perception of fatigue in the past: that of loss. Weakness was associated with lack, a material deficit. Nothing could be more concrete or more visual than its symptoms: sweat, flaccid muscles, breathlessness. Each one was associated with the vision of a body no longer under our control, afflicted with an uncontrollable "leakage," a loss of the "humors" believed to "constitute" the body as the crucial building blocks of organic life. Fluids filled the body and also flowed between its parts. They oozed from the slightest wound or the most insignificant bruise and took shape as beads of sweat, thus demonstrating the metaphorical equivalence of humans' life essence to the sap of plants and all the other liquids that nourish life. Such an image attested to the association of fluids with vitality. The body's "vital essence" was found in fluids. Their presence enhanced our vigor; their absence caused weakness, exhaustion and even death. Fatigue arose from what we have lost.

Physical exertion was essential to this belief, held by doctors as well as lay people. Moving one's limbs was key; repetitive motions produced friction, which caused warmth that transformed humors into vapor, causing sweating and other releases of bodily fluids. This resulted in deficiencies, the shriveling of flesh and the diffusion of pain throughout a body that was first dehydrated abruptly and then chilled rapidly. The twelfth century romance of Tristan and Iseult demonstrated this admirably; their wandering afflicted them inevitably with "pale and withered"[1] bodies. In the same way, medical commentators warned of overexertion, the subsequent "leaking" of fluids and dwindling of flesh that would diffuse pain to the "noblest" parts of the body: "But do not exert yourself too greatly. This will do you harm by reducing your body's warmth or causing you pains, in your head, stomach or chest that will make you suffer."[2] The "deficit" was the root cause and the vital organic matter that was lost led to weakness. Sweat was therefore "a dangerous symptom."[3] Fever may ensue because of an excess of friction and its dangerous consequences, especially if exercise was undertaken in "very high temperatures."[4]

The presumed aftermath of exertion concerned physicians so greatly that it alarmed them. A substantial loss of fluids, they believed, cannot be "restored." This kind of leaking was dangerous and threatened "those who, by sweating too much, eat away their own flesh."[5] Weakness made "a person stiff and dry; both one's valor and one's judgment were dulled by such exertion."[6] Workers must therefore take care not to "sweat over much,"[7] since science had not yet considered perspiration to be a self-regulating bodily function. Moreover, the boundaries of fatigue were unclear, and its excesses were informed only by lived experience and intuition. The world was still one of impressions and sensations. It was not yet the realm of evidence and measurement.[8] "Loss" itself in this system wasn't quantifiable, and it was not yet possible to conceive of a straightforward assessment. The deleterious effects of many actions weren't quantified or calculated, nor were the exertions of laborers in many trades or the energy expended in games, journeys or battles. Some activities demonstrated this toll better than others. For instance, starting in the twelfth century, the "fish route" convoys in France transported the daily catch from the shores of the English Channel and the Atlantic Ocean to the central market in Paris. The speed at which they traveled and the length of the journey made the death of cart horses an ordinary occurrence. So too was the exhaustion of the purveyors and the competition among them. As a result, in the thirteenth century a special fund was established to replace the "animals perishing of fatigue"[9] or to compensate for the loss of fish that rotted along the way. Finally, in 1500 the provost of Paris issued an edict that further regulated the rigors of the journey and the operations of the market.[10]

What words should we use?

It is an imprecise marker, undoubtedly, but the word "fatigue" trumps all others starting in the Middle Ages. This quite ordinary word, derived from the Latin *fatigare*, enabled writers and texts to employ an authentically French noun, as we have seen, in phrases such as "animals dying of fatigue"[11] along the "fish route" in the thirteenth century or the description of Galahad, "the greatest knight in the world," who "never suffers from fatigue,"[12] or that of Fierabras' battle with the Muslim opponent who "quickly succumbed to fatigue."[13]

Many other words or phrases might have taken the place of "fatigue": "the weakness paralyzing all his limbs"[14] endured by Durmart le Gallois, the "overheating"[15] of arms and legs recalled by Aldebrandin of Siena, the "low spirits"[16] described by Arnaud de Villeneuve in the thirteenth century, the "inner turmoil"[17] or "mental torment"[18] of Bartholomew the Englishman, who complained of insomnia and dehydration. So many descriptions focused on "loss," the breakdown of the body and its consequences.

Another facet of the medieval use of the word "fatigue" was related to perception. Weariness could be detected "externally" as well as "internally." For example, the "seven brothers" challenged by Galahad were "so tired that they can no longer defend themselves,"[19] and their posture telegraphed their exhaustion. In another example, Messire Gauvin, in *Perlesvaux*, "suffers from the fatigue of long days traveling";[20] in this case, his feelings revealed his discomfort. We cannot claim that the two diagnostic methods were clearly differentiated and developed. Recognizing fatigue remained an intuitive act, easily grasped but hard to pin down specifically, as one might with an illness or a symptom. Fatigue was not a "condition" that could be investigated, studied or observed. It was instead a phase, a fellow traveler in all stages of one's life, as inescapable as it was easy to recognize and clandestinely, mutually experience. It was a "lack," a hollow and inevitable echo of human inadequacy.

How to describe its intensity?

We are still in the realm of the uncertain when medieval medicine tries to define, categorize and diagnose the limits of fatigue and exertion. In the thirteenth century Bartholomew the Englishman chose commonly understood adjectives to describe intensity that were nonetheless subjective: "effort is threefold," he claimed, "heavy, light and medium," without giving specific details. There were also two speeds, "rapid" or "slow," and two amounts, "big" or "small."[21] We find yet another "subjective" descriptor, "long," introduced by the physicians of the Salerno school of medicine, their dictum repeated faithfully from the twelfth century on: “Don’t exercise for long; it will do you wrong.”[22] There was still no fixed rule; everything was relative, and subjects were analyzed only in relation to each other, with no standard rate of speed or explanatory mechanical principle, no set parameters even though observation clearly distinguished between “more” and “less.” The “disorganized number of systems of divergent measurements that varies from town to town, from one village to the next,”[23] was the most striking illustration of this. The world was still a kaleidoscopic mass of perceptions, of physical sensations, of visual observation; in short, it was the “almost approximately,” described by Alexandre Koyré,[24] rather than a neat geometric calibration.

In the thirteenth century, Aldebrandin of Siena, however, proposed shape and color as diagnostic tools for fatigue. Without being overly precise he posited that overexertion results in redness, flushing and thinness, but occasionally also “thickening or swelling” – thought, in an age-old medical tradition, to indicate excesses of vapors and fluids inside the body.[25] One had to “abandon” exertion as soon as the aforementioned “symptoms” appeared. Another warning sign was “sluggishness,” the awkward feeling of a “heavy” body.[26] Moderation in all things was undoubtedly the doctors’ advice, though it was both vague and rarely heeded. It had theoretical weight but was far removed from the daily round of work and activity, inasmuch as “intense” exertion could also be deemed praiseworthy.

There remain fits of anger, worries, disappointments, regrets and illusions, whose aftereffects could also be linked to fatigue, though again the threshold was more often estimated than delimited precisely. Constantine the African in the eleventh century actually listed several different causes of fatigue, with, however, little explanation: “Excessive thought [*nimia cogitatio*], recollection [*memoria*], investigating inexplicable things [*investigatio rerum incomprehensibilium*], speculation [*suspitio*], hope [*spes*], imagination [*imaginatio*].[27] He also pointed to loss due to mental immobility, internal tightening or disturbances in bodily fluids, highlighting dehydration again: “You must avoid and reject heavy burdens and cares because excessive worrying dries out our bodies, leaches out our vital energies, fostering despair in our minds and sucking out the substance from our bones.”[28] “Damage” afflicted shrunken organs and “hearts painfully contracting,”[29] among other things, as a result of internal suffering that diluted bodily fluids, making them less dense or even stopping their flow. One could blame overheating caused by regret, resulting in repeated spasms, stabbing pains, and "uncontrollable mental vagaries" that disturb our minds unnecessarily. Thus, Arnaud de Villeneuve firmly advised us: "Men must refrain from anger because fury and recriminations most likely dry out the body as they overheat all our limbs. Excessive heat dehydrates bodies and turns them into skin and bones."[30] Certainly anger was at fault, as was despair that "burns" too. And too many sleepless nights were accompanied by "worries … that dehydrate the body, impede proper digestion and wholly degrade a person's essence."[31] This pre-psychological diagnosis viewed all stimulus as primarily physical, with its frictions and vulnerabilities.

Despite the relative absence of definition or quantification, the Middle Ages did, nevertheless, have a "landscape" of fatigue – one that is diverse, multifaceted and rich in its own right, revealing differences in ways of co-existing with and battling against fatigue, of resisting it and succumbing to it. Fatigue was understood primarily in terms of events and places, in external "perceptible" elements, as it reflected and illuminated several well-established aspects of the causes of loss and exhaustion.

2

The Renowned Fatigue of the Warrior

To go beyond conventional descriptions in the Middle Ages, certain circumstances were necessary. Specific conditions needed to be met, such as a clash between things or a confrontation between people. Even more was required, such as the depiction of prestigious activities to attract our attention, since other actions that were generally overlooked would remain virtually invisible. In other words, the ranking of types of fatigue was highly subjective. Medieval descriptions demonstrated this by emphasizing certain kinds of exhaustion and not others, thereby revealing a culture and a worldview. This was evident in the battle scenes that dominated narratives. Depictions of labor, however, were undoubtedly more commonplace but were often deemed mediocre and dull. The more "extreme" the clash of warriors' weapons, the more frequently were such combats "observed," especially since they affected combatants' careers, determining their positions in a hierarchy and gradually solidifying their status. One example is the life of William Marshal, first earl of Pembroke, who, between the twelfth and thirteenth centuries, rose from the rank of little-known knight to serve as English Regent,[1] thanks to his victories in combat and tournaments while in the service of Patrick of Salisbury and of Henry II. His exploits in battle were inevitably the center of attention, as were his tenacity and ability to withstand pain. One way to define fatigue was to highlight how a warrior ignored and defied it.

Another specific and time-bound aspect was the value placed on outward appearance over inner emotion, the perceived over the felt, and a preference for narrative exuberance and verbosity that directed the gaze toward actions, toward weapons and how they were used. For instance, Fierabras in the twelfth-century novel was exhausted by his battle with the "heathen": "the fist that is clenched to strike" lets "go of the sword that is as long as a lance."[2] In contrast, the count of Normandy in *The Conquest of Jerusalem* had an apparently different reaction, more fantastical than realistic, but clearly associated with the handling of his sword: "He could no longer let go of his sword; his hand was so tightly clamped around the hilt that he was able to loosen his grip only after sprinkling it with warm water and wine to relax the muscles."[3] Certainly, the inner life of emotions existed, as we have seen,[4] but they were hardly mentioned and rarely described, no doubt because they were too subjective to be explored. Thus, narratives focused on a specific kind of exhaustion that emphasized relations between things over relations with the self and highlighted the external rather than the internal.

Then, a multitude of signs revealed visible physical effects on the body caused by fatigue, such as the "spittle foaming around the mouth"[5] of the Franks exhausted in the desert or the invaders fainting at the end of the siege of Jerusalem, their clothing soiled, torn and scorched: "They were filthy and many fainted from exhaustion."[6] Or the feet, bleeding after long marches, and "footgear, splitting, falling apart, torn from the toes to the ankles."[7] All these virtually "extreme" symptoms provoked admiration and excitement.

The privilege of endurance

Another value was associated with combat, uniting the "organic" and the "spiritual," drawing on reserves of physical strength and mental fortitude. This was, of course, the battle itself. A battle must be "long and relentless"[8] to merit praise, or it should be characterized by "unusual violence, lasting a very long time."[9] The warrior too had to be tenacious and fight with no holds barred, like the count of Saint-Paul at Bouvines in 1214, who "fought for a very long time with all his strength and was already staggering from the number of blows he struck."[10] Or he had to be resolute like the hero of the thirteenth-century novel *Jehan and Blonde*, who "refused to rest at any time during the battle."[11] This worldview put a high value on effort. It reflected a past world where haste was less prized than patience and a slow pace was superior to a rapid one. With their "manly attributes of aggression and resistance to all attacks," warriors embodied an almost symbolic goal: to demonstrate physical prowess no matter the cost and to "show no weakness."[12]

The celebrated fatigue of the warrior

Two criteria could also reveal greatness in the context of combat and fatigue: one identified the warriors who were most capable of testing the absolute limit of their strength and the other identified the fighters most ready to ignore those limitations. Warriors in the first category proved themselves by showing that they could suffer; those in the second category made it plain that they ignored all pain. Endurance was the essential quality, demonstrating tenacity however long the battle lasted. Jacques de Lalaing, a renowned knight at the court of Burgundy, exemplified this with his own special talents: "More than any other man, in fact, he was tenacious, experienced, and he knew very well how to provoke his opponent."[13] Galahad, "the greatest knight in the world," had an icy impassivity; he was "resolute, tireless."[14] This characteristic was so important that it was even attributed to horses, such as Baudoin's valiant steed in the *Conquest of Jerusalem*, "Prinsault the Aragonese who is never winded,"[15] or Fabur, the Arab stallion "who could gallop for twenty leagues without slowing or tiring."[16]

This idea became ever more prominent in the Middle Ages and was adopted as a key criterion in jousting. Witnesses in the fifteenth century would count the number of strikes and assess their force and duration. An example is the contest on December 15, 1445, in Ghent, in which Jacques de Lalaing fought a Sicilian knight till night fell: "Honestly everyone who was present said they had never seen such a number of violent blows in such a large number of encounters."[17] The aggressor would announce the number of intended strikes in advance, a proof of his confidence, his tenacity and his courage. This was actually required by the rules of engagement for a contest on the banks of the Saône River on October 2, 1450: "The number of ax blows must be decided in advance."[18] Another example was the "eloquent" number of hits (sixty-three) that a man named Jean Pitois called for in his encounter with Jacques de Lalaing on October 15, 1450.[19] In the middle of the fifteenth century, it was an unusual and rather indirect way to use calculations in assessing and thereby evaluating fighters' prowess.

The frequency and significance of references to these criteria eventually influenced knights' training itself. Jean de Bueil, a comrade of Joan of Arc, claimed that one must know how "to patiently endure the torments and hardships one encounters at the beginning" in order to earn "honor and glory in war."[20] Jean Le Meingre de Boucicault, who was appointed Marshal of France in 1391 by Charles VI, described how he was tested as a young man in battle, repeating the words "long, for so long" like a leitmotif: "no hardship was too great" while running and "going for so long on foot," "becoming accustomed to holding on for a long time," doing his duty "for so long," swinging an ax "for a long time," strengthening his arms and legs "to strike for a long time," increasingly "engaging in war," and "never stopping."[21] A single rule applied: repetition. Only one point of view existed: continuity. This dedication to comprehensive and overpowering repetition was far removed from the modern preference for "gradual," "progressive" and punctuated efforts, and it revealed an older approach of becoming accustomed to fatigue and enduring long passages of time. Here, learning to overcome fatigue was not a matter of gradual accommodation but, instead, of resisting it totally and at all times and being committed to the situation immediately and absolutely.

This priority, however, was only for knights; it was different for the rest of the troops. For example, archers were not bound to it when in 1335 the English King Edward III recommended best practices for future fighters: "It is forbidden on pain of death in all parts of the kingdom to play any game except for throwing darts and shooting with bow and arrow."[22] Skill in handling a weapon was important, and not preparation for the long marches and physical exhaustion that were in store for non-knights as well. The French King Charles VII's decree of April 28, 1448, revealed the same expectation when it directed each parish to maintain archers for future combat.[23] This highlights a distinct social divide; training in endurance was reserved for the most prestigious members of the battle corps, represented by "the ponderous knight, a knight defined both technically and socially, armed with a great breast plate … of chain mail, equipped with a lance and a sword,"[24] a man clad in 25 kilos of iron whose ability to withstand fatigue and blows are impressive. This is clearly an important cultural sign: "At the end of the Middle Ages chivalry was still regarded as the essential currency, the lifeline of support, for armies."[25] Yet, the possible fatigue of underlings was not even considered.

3

The "Necessary" Suffering of the Traveler

Travel with its inconveniences and discomforts was the other realm of fatigue that is written about regularly in the Middle Ages. Travelers' suffering was less dramatic than that of warriors. It was acknowledged but not heralded, and, most of all, inevitable, feared and commented upon. Medieval culture came to the realization that journeys were difficult, marked by fatigue and weakness, but also by new experiences and discoveries.

A vision of space

Medieval conceptions of space were at the heart of this understanding of fatigue that in fact implicated the entire cosmos. A stable environment was abruptly in flux once distance was involved. Suffering began as soon as one set off "on the road." A journey put security at risk. In the medieval world, there was no vision of the Earth as a whole, just as there were no contiguous land masses as our modern minds might envision them.[1] This does not mean that there were no maps; early prints traced the outlines of frontiers and continents, but lines were their most prominent feature, demarcating journeys and sea crossings rather than presenting a view of the entire expanse that would enable the viewer to fully grasp the whole. The land space remained an "in-between, a void to fill,"[2] with poorly defined connections and paths littered with obstacles. Only places were important, such as those described by Marco Polo in the thirteenth century in his "legendary" voyage, where, although "he saw so many *Marvels*, he was impressed only by the gardens."[3] A journey intensified one's suffering as it charted one's forward progress. As a result, the distant horizon could delight as much as it threatened.

These commentaries were short since texts in the Middle Ages were not characterized by introspection or detailed revisiting of feelings. Like the fatigues of combat, the fatigues of travel were expressed mainly through descriptions of things, of visible effects and the attributes of places. Once again, an external geography conveyed the body's internal sensations by tracing travel conditions, features of the terrain and the weather. For instance, extremely strong winds repeatedly forced the papal envoy John of Pian de Carpini to lie flat on the ground as he crossed through "Tartary" in 1246.[4] And the desert expanses of the East, "sometimes rocky, sometimes sandy,"[5] reduced Jacopo da Verona to despair during his long trip in 1335.

Travelers' entire mental and material universe was at play in their observations of the area that surrounded them. They experienced each site in isolation, disconnected from all the others. As a result, each departure became a "confrontation." Thus, it is not surprising if the residents of Montaillou in the thirteenth century heaped praise on Pierre Maury when he crossed "a wide river surreptitiously, bearing on his shoulders [Guillaume] Bélibaste and then Arnaud Sicre to carry out an ambush."[6] The hazards of long distances and the encounters with ever present challenges formed travelers' first major hurdle.

The danger of "elsewhere," the anxiety stoked by unfamiliar lands and their unpredictable conditions was certainly one of the main themes of medieval literature. Brendan,[7] the Irish priest who set off with a dozen companions in search of an earthly paradise, encountered so many and such strange challenges that between the tenth and fifteenth centuries his journey was featured in 120 texts. Brendan suffered extreme exhaustion and confronted abysmal horrors. In addition to the rigors of the journey itself, he survived terrifying encounters with animals and grueling close calls with monsters, devils and demons. These types of fantastical visions were central to many novels, stimulating readers' imaginations and livening up the narrative.

Exhaustion, to be more specific, was at the heart of several notable medieval journeys; traveling along borders, on the sea, in the forest, in the desert and to the Holy Land, in particular, increased the risk of getting lost. During these seemingly endless expeditions on foot, exhaustion could be fatal. In 1419, Nompar of Caumont explained: "I set off in the middle of the night because of the extreme and dangerous heat in this land that has felled many people along the way."[8] Mountains and forests were understood to represent the threat of physical danger, and forests were especially feared because of the shadows within, the meandering paths and irregular woodland edges. Forests were given a number of literary epithets: felonious, adventurous, lost, invisible.[9] They were associated with wandering as well as danger not only because of the "traps, secret places, possible ambushes" concealed within but also on account of the "difficulties orienting oneself and finding a way out of the woods."[10] Anecdotes about exhaustion proliferated. King Lot and his son, having arrived at the forest warden's house in Northumberland, slept "deeply after the extreme effort and great pains they had experienced."[11] Gawain's friends, having ridden "till nightfall" in an immense and shadowy forest,"[12] fell asleep immediately. The wood Guinebal entered was actually called "The Perilous Forest,"[13] not only because of the dangers within but also for the brave deeds that may be accomplished there. The twelfth-century novel *The Invisible Lady* had a tragic ending in which distant cries heard in the forest were coming from "a poor soul … lost somewhere without a shred of hope that he will be found."[14]

The sea joined the trio of horrors, illustrated with fantastical images of suffering: downpours of rocks or fire, islands that divert sailing ships with their deposits of magnetic iron and terrifying monsters with jaws of bronze. These reported threats were so convincing that, in the twelfth century, the rules of Oleron established a "compensation scheme" in maritime law: "If a seaman is injured serving on a sailing ship, he must be treated and his wounds bound up at the expense of the shipowner."[15]

Which travelers?

Knights errant, merchants, and powerful men such as princes or bishops all faced risky journeys whose harshness was always recognized and emphasized. The actual experience was as terrible as it was banal. Travel was important and was becoming more and more necessary and yet "exhausting." First of all, profit seeking lured merchants and agents to faraway places and distant fairs: Champagne, but also Lyon, Cologne, Augsburg, Mainz, Venice, Mantua, Milan, Naples, Brindisi."[16] The mural Ambrogio Lorenzetti painted in 1339 in the "Sala dei Nove" in the Palazzo Pubblico in Siena, *The Allegory of Good and Bad Government*, included flattering views of lively cities, crowds thronging the streets, and merchants walking beside pack animals laden with goods.[17] The sight was simultaneously bustling and calm. The caption, however, addressed the scenes' danger indirectly: "May every free man walk without fear."[18] Travelers certainly sensed the dark side of journeys. Gilles Li Muisis poetically protested those threats in the thirteenth century: "Merchants travel across countries and regions / By sea and by land goods are threatened / Always in danger / Rarely safe."[19]

In May 1344, the scribes of the duke of Burgundy used dry bureaucratic language to record the toll taken by accidents and diseases during his trip to the Papal City. Illnesses and especially deaths were the ultimate symbol of the scores of difficulties they encountered; between May and October 1344, fifty-four members of the entourage fell ill (and were left behind), as well as almost a third of the "outriders," four of whom died, in an expedition of approximately 170 people.[20] A letter that King Charles VI sent to the king of Castile in 1387 underlined this concern indirectly when he cautioned that the "two thousand fighting men" he was sending had to be convoyed as "smoothly and carefully as possible."[21]

The litany that Eustache Deschamps devoted to travel in the fifteenth century illustrated this again, although the writer balanced his long list of inconveniences with the admonition that one must venture into the world in order to appreciate it:

> Those who don't leave home,
> To travel through different lands,
> Don't feel the agonizing pain,
> Of those afflicted,
> By evils, doubts, dangers,
> Of seas, rivers, and routes,
> Hearing languages they don't understand,
> The bodily suffering and exertion,
> But one knows not how much one had missed,
> By never venturing out.[22]

Religious proscriptions also illustrated attitudes toward travel when they advised moderation. Medieval archbishop Raoul de Bourges issued a decree "protecting" his priests from excessively long journeys. This allowed priests who "live six or seven miles from the city" to form groups of ten and send one as their representative on Holy Thursday. He would receive the vials containing the holy water used in baptisms as well as the holy oils used to anoint catechumens [persons taking religious instruction before baptism] and the ill."[23] Bishops' visits too were fairly uncommon; they were always solemn occasions but still "infrequent"[24] before the eleventh and twelfth centuries.

Pilgrimages were so numerous, diverse and variable that they were recognized as the "most common reason for travel."[25] They were a way "to walk in Christ's footsteps"[26] within a religious universe whose "savior," himself an itinerant preacher, was still the "archetypal traveler."[27] The special status of pilgrims' travels was clear, inverting the ordinary meaning of fatigue so that it was no longer a torment imposed on travelers but a desired outcome. Fatigue was no longer an unanticipated byproduct but a providential one whose "greatness" was acknowledged once the final destination was reached. Pilgrims with their staffs, beggars' bags and bare feet represented not only the medieval image of the redemption that came from visiting holy places and seeking out sacred relics but also the atonement earned through the rigors of the journey. Fatigue was integral to redemption: "Every medieval pilgrimage is to some extent an act of penance because of the difficulties of the journey (extreme physical exertion and exposure to danger)."[28] Alphonse Dupront put it concisely: "The trial by distance makes the pilgrim."[29] Travelers in the Middle East crossing the Sinai desert to reach Christ's tomb dramatically illustrated both the pilgrims' pain and their expiation; the experience was, after all, torment culminating in enlightenment: "We climbed with great difficulty, after much exertion, up to the peak, encountering paths so arduous in such a state of decrepitude that is hard to believe. Oh weary flesh! What pain and exhaustion you endure to achieve divine grace."[30]

Some even paid others to "exhaust" themselves in a paradoxical calculation of pain and atonement. Guy of Dampierre, who became the count of Flanders in 1251 and passed away in 1305, included in his will "the sum of eight thousand pounds to the person who, in the event the count cannot fulfill his vow, will make a pilgrimage to the Holy Land in his place."[31] This was a considerable amount to promise when, by comparison, Guy's chaplain was allotted "enough hay to feed two horses every day, sixteen pounds for his linen, and twenty pounds as an annual pension."[32] This "pilgrimage barter" was an example of the practice of "indulgences" (financial compensation for forgiveness of sins) that had been authorized in the canonical decree of 993. The hefty sum offered in the count's will also revealed how arduous the journey was expected to be.[33]

The feet, the first symptom

The fatigues voluntarily endured in the middle years of the Middle Ages had specific characteristics. Images of pain were represented by particular stigmata, revealing the kinds of exhaustion the sufferers experienced. Our gaze was focused on one part of the body, concentrating on the wear and tear of walkers and their wounded feet. Such injuries had a practical basis, since "in the Middle Ages specialized footwear for traveling long distances on foot did not exist."[34] Shoes were usually made of one piece of leather[35] and didn't protect walkers navigating difficult terrain or going for days and weeks at a time. But such injuries also ennobled the journey by adding yet another pain to the inventory of projected suffering. This was why some people voluntarily walked barefoot. In the twelfth century, Saint William de Verceil "became famous for walking unshod to Compostela at the age of fifteen."[36] Scenes of atonement or processions in such difficult conditions became more common and were depicted on the capitals of columns in churches. In the twelfth and thirteenth centuries we read about more pilgrims walking barefoot.[37] Karin Ueltschi called this "a popular scourge," citing Percival's acts of penance as an example.[38] The order issued by Saint Louis (Louis IX of France) after the conquest of Damietta in 1249 also attested to this, requiring that "corpses of men and animals, and other filth, be removed" from the city before a procession through the town, "all barefoot, of noblemen and commoners, very devoutly."[39] Accepting this kind of suffering lent a person grandeur and was also a precise, clear-cut route to salvation.

Walking barefoot was a penitent act, surely, and another was humbly giving solace to others by washing their feet as an act of contrition. Every Saturday Saint Louis "would wash the feet of the poor secretly."[40] Isabelle, the daughter of the king of Hungary, attained sainthood in 1230 by serving the poorest of the poor:

> And when the poor came to Vespers to rest, she noticed those who were badly shod; these are the ones whose feet she washed; and the next morning she

> gave them shoes to fit their feet; because she always kept a supply of large and small sized shoes to give those who needed them; she personally helped to put them on. And then she would transport them and accompany them until they were safely en route.[41]

Feet, therefore, were a symbolic locus of pain, of fatigue and of an era.

4

"Redemptive" Fatigue

Another side to redemptive fatigue included a number of different actions and challenges undertaken voluntarily, solely for the purpose of atonement. The Church set the parameters, and a range of judiciously selected acts calibrated the intensity of the suffering. For clergy especially the quest for salvation was at the core of physical acts of penance. In the Middle Ages mysticism was accompanied by ever more exquisite suffering.

The "penalty" journey

Some pilgrimages were not simply a personal matter. They were so exhausting and actually symbolic that an authority imposed them as a penalty and used them to substitute for other punishments. Thus, a pilgrimage became a question of social rather than individual salvation. The action metamorphosed into a public sentencing calculated to fit the offense. The itinerary and the destination resembled an actual "punishment" more closely since the expiation was codified and the length of the journey depended on the seriousness of the misdeed. A priest sketched out the route, "blessing the penitent, giving him a hat, beggar's bag and staff, and providing him with a safe conduct or letter of transit ...; fulfilling the pilgrimage means the offense is discharged."[1] In this way the journey was "jurisdictional," because it is a sentence determined by judges or by the Church, and concerned an offense serious enough to be in the realm of the criminal. In 1387 a letter pardoned Jean Bigot of Saint-Maurice-des-Noues, who was guilty of homicide, "on the condition that he go to Notre-Dame du Puy and have one hundred masses said for the salvation of the deceased's soul."[2] Forgiveness was extended in 1393 to two residents in the Azay-le-Brûlé parish, who were accessories to the murder of a looter and the robbery of a woman, "on the condition that one goes to Dame du Puy and the other to Santiago de Compostela."[3] These penalties acknowledged the perils and exertions of travels "associated with dangers and fatigues one can hardly imagine nowadays,"[4] said Victor Derode in 1848.

But these judgments had limitations. The sanctions penalized but also "abandoned" the defendants to their fate, inflicting "punishments" but also other "losses." Roads became less safe once convicted criminals, troublemakers and other antisocial types were also traveling on them and causing problems. Despite this, in 1433 Gilles Charlier of the Basel Council still associated the pilgrimage with penance for an "expiation of sins."[5] But reality did take hold, however; such travel was faulted for providing "an opportunity for scandal more than an occasion for sanctity."[6] Instances of criticism became less frequent as the tradition died out in the fourteenth and fifteenth centuries; flagellation and hair shirts replaced it. Even though it was a short-lived phenomenon, the pilgrimage as penalty was still significant, since it embodied a significant point of view: it was a type of fatigue that was identified in the Middle Ages primarily with taking risks by crossing the sea or traveling long distances over land.

Duty as salvation

Work could also be "oriented," in a specifically religious interpretation that recurred in didactic accounts, inasmuch as *acedia* (laziness, sleepiness) in the Middle Ages was seen as a disturbing symptom. In the monastic realm it was labeled "the soul's enemy,"[7] a sign of boredom, of a "suspicious" disinterest and lack of passion.[8] One had always to strive for self-sacrifice and unswerving dedication, as did the "young ladies" in hospices "single mindedly devoted to serving the wants and needs of the poor,"[9] or the example of Saint Douceline, who founded the Beguine order in Marseille and doubled and tripled her "exhaustion"[10] in caring for her charges. Another saint, Saint Julian, opened a hospice with his wife and exhausted himself trying to "accommodate all the poor."[11] We are in the realm of overwork and fragmented, disconnected tasks whose attributes were hardly described; the weight of the burden mattered more than the specificity of the work, and the amount of time spent meant more than the diversity of its benefits. The ill effects of such overwork were inescapably linked to a particular necessity: never to let up, not even for a minute, in maintaining the spirit of self-sacrifice. The rules of the Hotel-Dieu in Paris revealed a never-ending daily grind: from laundering to making beds, from heating the boilers to drying the linens, from cleaning to bathing, from providing everyday necessities of life to the last rites. All the tasks were "difficult"[12] because they were "never-ending" and any normal sense of time was upended: "day becomes night and night turns into day."[13] We must add to this long list the implicit expectation of self-harm associated with this kind of labor; self-inflicted stigmata, brutal penances, and deliberate injuries were all characteristic of the middle decades of the Middle Ages. For example, Saint Douceline adopted an unforgiving system to interrupt her rest periods in order to "serve" even more. She would loop a rope around her waist and above her bed so that, "when she stirred in bed, the rope tightened and she awakened."[14] Saint Jerome, a hermit living in the desert who aided desperate travelers in need,[15] struck himself over and over to stay awake: "if I was overcome by sleep despite all my resistance, I would hurl my weary bones onto the ground, almost shaking my body apart."[16]

From inflicting pain to immersion in contemplation

When we trace the evolution of Saint Douceline's self-sacrifice throughout her life, we see something else: at the end, contemplation was valued more highly than work, and there was a shift from earthly concerns to heavenly ones. The extreme nature of her labors seems to have influenced this. Douceline engaged less in everyday tasks over the years, instead seeking out "remote places."[17] She constructed a "very secret chapel," where she experienced "extreme exaltation" and sometimes "spends thus an entire day"[18] in an ecstatic state in which she levitated off the ground. Her transformative experience attracted curious visitors and devout followers, and this encouraged her to intensify her "prayerful acts." This underlined the "great tradition" of the medieval Church, which was to celebrate the dignity of a contemplative life over an active one."[19] Certainly, the value system was complicated, and the significance of mystical monks uniting "prayer and manual labor"[20] was undeniable, as demonstrated by the Cistercian order and Bernard of Clairvaux.[21] Physical exhaustion, representing "man's sinful condition,"[22] could not be ignored, but it was a stage on the journey. Prayerful contemplation was meant to overcome it.

That is the lesson drawn from Saint Douceline's life, affirming the belief of her contemporary the mystic Peter John Olivi of Languedoc: "The goal of the active life is to prepare for contemplation."[23] A redemptive fatigue could also serve as a "phase," a preparatory stage on the way to a higher goal. This brings us to another sort of fatigue, the ecstatic state, the "uprooting" of the self that, for lack of a psychological lexicon, contemporary thinking described in physical terms rather than spiritual ones. The internal exhaustion had to be visible; it had to be manifest externally since it could not be explained in psychological terms. Thus, we read about the unusual exhaustion of the great mystics, which could be "witnessed." Saint Douceline "surrenders herself to God with such passion that her body seems to falter under the weight of the great spiritual fervor burning inside her."[24]

In the twelfth century, William of Tyre saw the same signs of religious passion and of overwhelming spiritual aspirations and dedication to prayer in the new king of Jerusalem, Baldwin II: "He was tireless when engaged in prayer, so much so that his hands and knees were covered in callouses because of the number of times he would kneel or prostrate himself."[25] The bodily wear and tear was noted, as well as the ravages of repeated actions, signifying what was essentially a private act and spiritual struggle. Taking many shapes and forms, the redemptive fatigue that was prized in the medieval world was expressed in a wide variety of torments: the pilgrim's long road, the endless drudgery of nuns and monks, the painful ecstasy of the mystic. The peril of fatigue was a persistent symbol of the aspiration for salvation.

5

Ordinary Work and Everyday Workers: A Relative "Silence"?

After the travails of combat, of travel and of "redemption," it is impossible to overlook the fourth "arena" of fatigue in the Middle Ages: ordinary physical labor. Work was, however, rarely discussed or acknowledged. Workers' fatigues were not notable compared with those of travelers, warriors or "saints," which were significant and praiseworthy. Laborers' actions were banal and quotidian, the jarring pains in their bodies going virtually "unnoticed" in the daily grind. The fate of the nobodies, the marginalized people, was to live in obscurity and never attain greatness or salvation.

The triviality of rural life

This non-status can be traced back to that of serfs in the tenth and eleventh centuries who were dragooned into forced labor, toiling "day and night"[1] at an endless number of tasks. Their servitude tied them to countless burdens; they were compelled to do "anything and everything." Their continued survival and the justification for their existence came from "the lack of limits on their duties … that clearly expressed their status as objects."[2] This immediately eliminated fatigue as worthy of attention. One repeated truism is: "Serfs are granted all the misery, all the pain, all the sorrow."[3] An indifference to their fate compounded the elites' ignorance of what they were suffering. In the twelfth century the book *Sirvente*, by Bertrand de Born, even justified this brutality: "We should never pity a nonentity if we see him breaking an arm or leg or if he lacks any necessities."[4] Workers everywhere had no rights and their fate was determined by a higher power; a divine law decreed fatigue was an inescapable part of their lives and thus unworthy of attention, whether it was a permanent condition or a transient one.

Nevertheless, the perspective started changing between the twelfth and thirteenth centuries, when fatigue was indirectly, rather than overtly, noted. At first, scholars in technical fields addressed it in discussions of innovations such as watermills and camshafts that provided an alternative to labor-intensive manual rotation. These mechanical methods of hammering and grinding highlighted the contrast between old and new ways of working and suggested that somehow physical limitations had been "surpassed." Monks in the Clervaux Abbey workshops in the thirteenth century observed:

> The river … alternately lifts and lowers these heavy pestles, these mallets or especially these wooden bases … and thus relieves the brothers of exhausting labor … How many horses would have been worn out, how many men would have exhausted their muscles in tasks that the generous river performs for us; we owe our bread and clothing to her. She joins her efforts to ours.[5]

The increased use of the word "engine" in the Middle Ages is another example, giving concrete form to a perception: one could "maneuver" power and multiply or leverage its force. As the Norman verse chronicle *Roman de Rou* noted: "The engine assists the craftsman."[6] This led to a new category of makers: "engine men" are known for their machines; artisans are "tool men."[7] These machines were simple, certainly, with hands-on interventions that were necessary or even "urgent," but the descriptions of technical innovations suggested a vision of a new world where fatigue would be vanquished.

Rural society was also transformed by the end of serfdom in the twelfth and thirteenth centuries. The economic boom of the time enabled many serfs to purchase their freedom, thereby changing their "never-ending" workday into one with "calculated" parameters. Treatises on agriculture or the economy recommended hiring day laborers and organizing farm work by task for increased efficiencies and higher yields: "People in 1250–1260 are concerned with productivity and technique."[8] This resulted in new ways to categorize tasks and calculate salaries and led to more direct "management."[9] Here too were indirect allusions to overwork, not because laborers' wellbeing was recognized or prioritized but because exhaustion was seen as an obstacle to the effective organization of work. This entirely intuitive evaluation arose from a desire for efficiency. The laborers involved had little status, but their fatigue clearly affected the work itself. In the thirteenth century, Pietro de Crescenzi suggested that employers look first at what laborers "have already done" and what "they do most willingly and with the least amount of fatigue."[10] The goal was to coordinate activities, shorten rest periods and encourage "time limits."[11] Another recommendation reflected the same outlook but focused on measures of space and time: "See how much sowing each man can do in one acre."[12] For the first time fatigue was perceived as a potential limit, which, if breached, meant a man could no longer finish the required task. The same question was posed for a laborer and his wagon, this time combining distance and time spent: "And find out how many acres a plow can cultivate per year and how many leagues horses and oxen travel when they work an acre of land. Some say that one plow is sufficient for nine acres of land and not eight. I will tell you two reasons why."[13]

Different types of terrain and the most effective use of animals were assessed with the same criteria. Horses, for example, were thought to be better adapted for "rocky ground" but were still more costly than oxen.[14] These practical empirical questions were meant to help in planning the work calendar and in calculating the number of farmhands needed, as well as the type of cartage and plowing and the overall costs. The recommendations were approximate, to be sure, but they did give the reader an accounting, even if it was incomplete:

> And you should know that five men can cut and bale up two acres a day of any kind of wheat, more or less. If each man is paid two deniers a day, you should pay five deniers per acre. And if four of the men each get one denier and one obole a day and the fifth man, because he is the baler, gets two deniers, then you should allot four deniers per acre.[15]

The same advice held for the pay rate: "If they need to work for more time than this, you should not pay for it."[16] This accounting enabled us to see that compensation for work was meant to be proportional according to the amount of "effort"; for example, the baler, who had to gather, shape and bind the sheaves, was paid two deniers, while the "simple" harvester got one denier and one obole.[17] At the Carville farm in 1308, plowing the fields, which involved driving the cart and guiding the plow, was paid better than harrowing, where the farmhand simply raked the soil.[18] Guidelines such as these, though imprecise and infrequent, revealed an intention to rank the expenditure of "effort" through differences in compensation.

Nevertheless, the lowly status of the peasant had not changed. As a scorned and despised creature, even his fatigue was sometimes a subject of mockery. The predicament of the peasant of Bailleul in the twelfth-century fable demonstrated this. When he returned home after having "toiled in his fields and crops," his exhaustion gave his wife an excuse to tuck him into bed so that she could go out to meet her lover. No doubt the poor man was tired, but he was also oafish, devalued and, to add insult to injury, deemed "stupid and repulsive."[19]

The iconography of the time, focusing on actions, people and their surroundings, was also "revealing." These quasi-realistic depictions became signs to be deciphered. Fatigue was evident in the handling of tools, in people's faces, in their tasks, in all the unspoken clues of their gestures and postures. For example, using a spade or a flail in threshing or winnowing was considered an exclusively masculine activity and was believed to be incompatible with "weakness." Weakness was seen as feminine and was thus associated with the less strenuous handling of sickles and rakes.[20] For the first time, images tended to make a distinction between laboring women and men and their respective fatigues. The amount of effort was made visible, sometimes with a view of laborers' backs bent over in toil or by the scale of the proportions, as in the *Vieil Rentier* by Audenarde. This illustrated manuscript, created at the end of the thirteenth century, showed several peasants, their noses close to the soil, arms extended, spading the earth.[21] A similar image in the *Psalter of Saint Louis* showed the tortuously bent backs of laborers who were emptying sacks of wheat in a granary.[22] We must point out again that the illustrations of peasants at work are evocative, demonstrating a willingness to depict activities and the fatigue and exertion that accompany them, but there are no commentaries, explanations or tributes here.

A great many jobs were paid by the task and not by the time spent; in this way the calculation of cost acknowledged the "doing" and not its duration. This makes it difficult to know how effort and exhaustion are evaluated. In the fourteenth century, the archbishop of Rouen paid the laborers in his vineyard a lump sum for the work, not for its frequency or range, nor for any additional tasks or any possible ill effects. The laborer Thommas Le Cauchois earned 4 pounds, 16 sous "for digging, planting, pruning, picking thoroughly and correctly, and worked all season a half arpent (approximately half an acre) of vines in the field called 'clos de roy."[23] Robien Cornilbout was paid 48 sous for having tended a smaller area of vines in the same field."[24]

In this case, the men's pay was calculated by the task, not taking into account how long they labored or how hard, in spite of a detailed inventory of their actions. This was similar to the compensation of Jean de Valenciennes and Jokart, two laborers employed at the estate of la Cressonière at the beginning of the fourteenth century. They "harvest wheat, erect fences ... A warden oversees the fields and the harvests."[25] The true exertions of labor would remain "hard to measure"[26] and barely acknowledged.

Artisans and the invention of timekeeping

Cities played an influential role in aligning the cost of labor, as well as in sparking conflicts over it. Urban development became more visible in the twelfth and thirteenth centuries, when the growth of population centers was spurred by the end of invasions, the rise in commercial markets and the freeing of the serfs. Specialized artisanal labor gained recognition, neighborhoods acquired a distinct character, and in general town life became more diverse: "Sleepy villages turn into lively markets."[27] Customs became institutionalized and regulations more common.

Time was among the first measures to be standardized, and this essential step had implications for the understanding of fatigue. The *Livre des métiers* [Book of crafts and trades] (the first written set of regulations for Parisian artisans) demonstrated this when it was first published in 1268: "The apprentices will arrive every workday at dawn, do their required tasks, and end their workday at dusk. Dusk will last until sunset."[28] The workday was thus standardized, from dawn to dusk. The code did contain some nuances, however, with a few regulations even taking fatigue into account. For example, the masters and apprentices making brass wire "have a rest period at dusk,"[29] and "belt makers" could not work at night, since "the workday is long and the job is painstaking."[30] But night work was not unusual and undoubtedly depended on the task, such as the dispensation for textile dyeing: "Dyers can work at night when there is work to be done"[31] and oil pressers "can work both day and night, as often as they wish."[32]

Disputes over duration

Such vagueness and inconsistency had an effect, sparking conflicts by allowing masters more leeway to "lengthen the workday,"[33] especially before the havoc wreaked by the Great Plague of 1348 and whenever there was a surplus of workers. This led to resistance in the form of disputes over the workday itself, with fatigue as an implicit rationale for determining what was acceptable at work and what was not. The apprentice textile workers in Paris (whose tasks included soaking and beating fabric in alkaline solutions) complained in 1277 that "the masters keep them working too late at dusk."[34] A ruling by the Paris provost specified the length of the workday: "apprentices will work until dusk, and their rest period at dusk will last until the sun goes down."[35] A similar dispute occurred in Senlis in 1346; twenty-eight apprentice cloth-makers brought a complaint against four masters who made them work in winter until compline (approximately 7 p.m.). The bailiff (the king's representative in legal matters) issued a "rule that the apprentices will only work up to the last stroke of vespers, and thus before compline."[36] Fatigue was not specifically mentioned in these cases, certainly, but the specter of overwork fueled the protests and the apprentices' resistance. With that in mind, they implicitly evoked fatigue even when it wasn't overtly part of the discussion.

After 1348, the bubonic plague pandemic led to other changes. Because workers were scarcer and thus more valuable, they could be more demanding. Masters decried the increase in unskilled workers, their laziness and sloppiness, while workers "preferred" less rigor and a slower pace. A detailed decree from the Paris provost in 1395 addressed this type of conflict:

> It has come to our attention that laborers in many trades, such as linen weavers, flannel makers, fabric soakers, pavers, masons, carpenters and several other apprentices to masters in Paris, demand and endeavor to get off early

> and work whatever hours suit them, as long as they are paid for a full day as if they had worked the whole day. This is a disservice, insult and injury to so many masters and artisans, to their trade, and also to the public good. From now on, all apprentices and laborers are required to work at these jobs from daybreak to sunset, only stopping for meals at reasonable times.[37]

From then on, a number of scattered local disputes were set off by yet another flash point: competitions or comparisons between trades. In 1390 the weavers in Beauvais challenged the wool spinners' customary later arrival at their workplace, questioning their excuse of suffering more "fatigue" because of the nature of their work. In this way, an issue such as fatigue caused by the demands of a particular job became more salient and even negotiable. However, the Parliament's decision in this dispute was limited to the weavers' complaint; it mandated identical work hours for all.[38]

Starting in the middle of the thirteenth century, this rash of disputes over work hours (conflicts that nevertheless varied depending on local economic and demographic factors) led to the installation of "work chimes" in several European cities: the *campana laboris* in northern Italy, the *cloque des métiers* in Douai, the *weverscloke* in Bruges, the *campana pro operarii* at Windsor Castle.[39] Imperceptibly, regulating work limits by traditional cues from nature or by the sound of church bells marking the hours was disappearing. Work time became more specific, tailored to particular tasks. This evolution eased tensions but did not eliminate them, as an incident in Provins in 1282 demonstrated. There, textile workers rose up against the mayor, who had decided to extend the workday by ringing out day's end later in the evening, and "the mayor was killed, and the bell was destroyed."[40] Edward I, king of England and count of Champagne, had to issue a decree of amnesty to restore social peace. And at Thérouanne in 1367 the dean and clerical advisory council attempted to tamp down labor unrest by assuring "cloth soakers and other manual laborers" that the town would silence "the workers' chimes for now and forever so that the ringing of bells of this sort does not provoke tumult and conflict in our town or our church."[41] Such incidents showed that time and fatigue were inextricably connected even though that fact was still not clearly and explicitly acknowledged.

As the trades became more established, specific strategies to regulate work breaks and rest periods also became more prevalent. These innovations are meant to prevent conflict. At first the authorities turned a blind eye to the problem, as exemplified by a royal decree issued in 1369 at the request of the merchants and manufacturers in Troyes. The decree denied weavers' request for three work breaks: breaks for lunch, dinner and tea. The text coldly urged them to "work all day without stopping, as the masons, carpenters, roofers, winemakers, and other laborers of all kinds do."[42] Nevertheless, from the beginning of the fourteenth century the concept of regular work breaks was recognized, and some were even instituted. In Tournai in 1302 the town aldermen used "chiming bells to mark the lunch break and another for the return to work."[43] The aldermen in Amiens, finding their current system too inconsistent, asked the king to authorize a new bell that will ring "four times a day, in the morning, the evening, and at the start and end of the meal break."[44]

The workday was segmented in this way between rest and labor, with specified intervals, beginnings and ends. This led to other sorts of regimentation, such as when workers' tardiness was penalized in Pistoia in Italy in 1356, or when laborers working for Capecchio were fined 2 sous because they "took too long to return from their lunch."[45] But now gaps and pauses in the flow of work time were recognized, and rest periods, though still very modest, were becoming incorporated into the day, along with strict surveillance.

Clock time

The invention of mechanical clocks in the fifteenth century led to greater precision in timekeeping. Hours were now of equal length; in the past they varied with the seasons. Nature and its vagaries no longer served as the benchmark, but were replaced by hours and their regularity. This resulted in parameters everyone understood and measurable lengths of time, an innovation that was believed to moderate disputes even if they persisted, as in Bourges in 1443:

> The cloth soakers and weavers will arrive at their workplaces at daybreak, at summer time between 4 and 5 a.m., and will have three hours of breaks for

> lunch, dinner, tea, eating and sleeping, when they run errands they must take the shortest route and go quickly, no matter the cost, and if they are absent when the vespers bell rings, they will not be paid for the day.[46]

Thus, limits on work were integrated into the medieval world, regulating the flow of time, the length of the workday, and marking the boundaries of rest and fatigue. Yet, the gradual recognition of time limits and the workday had nothing in common with the period's florid descriptions of exhausted warriors, no relation to the agonized depiction of the suffering of travelers and no distinct life of its own. Acknowledgements of labor's toll were entirely functional and never went beyond the intuitive or the suggestive. Its stresses were glimpsed in regulations and came to the surface in conflicts, setting off "workers' protests," even if, more often than not, the motive was "implicit."[47] In this way, the ravages of fatigue were expressed mutely, tacitly, but at least for the first time they were called out by those experiencing them and protested by some who were trying to rein them in.

Jobs and the invention of strength

One final distinction played a part in the evaluation of labor: the question of how much muscle power was used and for how long. Agriculturalists, as we have seen, distinguished between the "baler," who, gathering the stalks, shaping and tying bales of wheat, was paid 2 deniers, and the "simple" harvester, whose actions were limited to cutting and received 1 denier and 1 obole.[48] "Tasks" were organized hierarchically in towns too, and workers' compensation differed based on an estimate of the exertion required, but the scale was not obvious nor the calculations overt. Many of the urban jobs were assessed with a single criterion: "To determine the salary, you must really judge how much strength is needed."[49] This opened up the possibility of a sliding scale based on three elements: the muscle power expended, the difficulty of the materials, and the type of activity. When the cathedral in Milan was built at end of the fourteenth century, a worker who sawed wood would be paid between 7 and 8 sous and the stonemason, cutting stone, between 9 and 10 sous.[50] In the middle of the fifteenth century, a laborer in Orleans "piling hay" earned a little more than

0.1 of a Tours pound, while a lumberjack cutting oak was paid 0.5 of a Tours pound.[51] The pay depended on the presumed "difficulty" of the materials and to concepts of strength and the effort exerted in particular kinds of work.

In the same vein, Capecchio, who was hired in 1356 to work on the building site of the baptistery in Pistoia, "earns 6 sous a day to remove construction debris" and 8 sous for "cutting marble."[52] Stone work was more costly than other construction jobs. This type of hierarchy, by the way, devalued women's work. Women in the fourteenth century in Milan's workplaces were paid less than 2 sous, while the lowest ranked male laborer, the *laborator*, earned 3.[53] The pay scales here were no more than an employer's estimate of the effort involved and of the physical toll on the worker. Fatigue was relegated to the shadows, implied and suspected rather than overtly acknowledged.

6

Between Occult Power and the Healing Virtues of Refreshments

It is impossible to overlook the defenses people erected and the efforts they made to tolerate physical exertion and recover better from it. The strategies that were recommended are revelatory of a particular culture and a specific era. We can discern the outlines of fatigue in the remedies proposed to combat or eliminate it. It was certainly a struggle, but there were also preventive measures to take. These were so important that they were often described as obvious and commonplace, even though the details of the maladies they treated often remained elusive.

Prescriptions for travelers

First of all, doctors gave reams of advice, but we can find no proof that their patients actually followed it. Their recommendations for people who were going to walk great distances or travel to faraway places had pride of place at the beginning of medical treatises. This reveals how challenging travel was thought to be in the middle centuries of the Middle Ages. Writing in the vernacular in the thirteenth century, Aldebrandin of Siena prioritized the needs of those who want "to travel great distances"[1] by devoting an entire chapter to this in his book *Regimen of the Body*. Not surprisingly, his deceptively simple and abundant "prescriptions" focused on bodily fluids. Among his recommendations to travelers are: to purge or bleed themselves before embarking on a journey in order to purify and dilute their humors; to eat only light meats and drink plain water or water infused with onion, vinegar or sour apples to purify their humors; and not to eat fruits with excessively "raw" flesh, whose excessive acidity will contort their organs or even dissolve them. In addition, he advised travelers to refrain from speaking, since it exhausted their breath, to cover their heads to protect themselves from the sun's rays, to smear their faces with unguent to moderate the effects of heat and cold and, finally, to keep a crystal in their mouths to calm their thirst. All these protective measures were directed at the liquids in the body, even to the extent of preventing the loss of saliva to avoid dehydration.

Restoration

Unlike this focus on travel, physicians gave little advice about the excesses of combat and devoted few pages to the topic in their treatises. Their emphasis on "moderation" was far removed from the stresses of the battlefield and the clash of weapons. Instead of medical studies, chronicles depicting armies and their long marches gave an idea of how combatants dealt with the rigors of the journey. These were necessarily narratives filled with praise and legendary tales of heroism. When attention was paid to the "aftermath" of battles, once again the focus was on humors, but the emphasis was on the need for fighters to rejuvenate themselves by taking in more liquids, as in the scenes of crusaders regaining their strength after women or servants bring them water: "Rolling up their sleeves and taking off their long mantles, the women carry water to the exhausted knights in jars, bowls and golden goblets. Having drunk, the lords regain all their strength. This is the aid they had longed for."[2]

The water satisfied two of the men's urgent needs: slaking their thirst and purifying their bodies. This was such an important theme that the word "refresh" occurred again and again. Durmart and his companions were "washed and refreshed"[3] after their exhausting battles. Before reaching Jerusalem, crusaders expected that a costly and rare water would revive them.[4] In the thirteenth century, the word "refresh" acquired a more "expansive" meaning, and refreshment was equated with respite; the verb "to refresh oneself" came to mean "to rest." The chronicler Robert de Clari used it in his description of the crusaders' journey to Constantinople: "After crossing the sea they came to a citadel, Poles. They entered there and refreshed themselves. They stayed for a while until they all were well refreshed."[5] In the fourteenth century, Jean Froissart deployed the word in its ordinary sense as he described warriors at the Mauvoisin bridge in 1388 "dipping in their basins" and returning to the fray after having "refreshed themselves well."[6] But Froissart also evoked its multiple meanings when writing of two fighters rearming themselves; the Englishman Nicolas Lam and the Frenchman Saint-Py "refresh themselves" with "new double-edged swords"[7] in their single combat at Saint-Ingelberth. The act of drinking water became a metaphor whose meaning was very close to that of "resurrection"; in other words, drinking water was a way to regain strength as well as to quench thirst.

Jewels and talismans

There were other ways to restore what one has lost, and these too were associated with the idea of "purity." One example was the belief that physical contact with precious stones would enhance one's endurance because their crystalline essence would penetrate the body and infuse it with its powers. We see this especially in the knights' worldview. During the conquest of Jerusalem, Baron Thomas de Marne had "a very valuable talisman that protects him from any injury whenever he wears it."[8] In the twelfth-century tale, the Naked Knight "wears a jewel on his breast that gives him strength and speed."[9] He even attached several jewels to his belt to ensure "he will never be vanquished."[10] Precious stones such as pearls or diamonds were especially powerful and enhanced the body's resistance by repelling "external toxins" and impeding the spread of "internal poisons." In addition to gemstones, other occult and supernatural forces may lend men their secret powers. In *The Perilous Cemetery*, Gawain recovered his strength by gazing upon a cross held by a young lady, who urged him: "Do not hesitate to gaze upon it. You will regain your powers; you will be as you were before and recover entirely from your fatigue." Gawain obeyed, and his "courage and endurance"[11] were restored. Light, or sunlight, also had magical powers, so the same young lady told Gawain how to overcome an evil opponent who was believed to "grow weaker as the sunlight dims." Gawain "must never confront him before the hour of none [3 p.m.]."[12] The hero took her advice and was victorious.

We cannot ignore the importance of occult powers and the fatigues believed to be caused by spells and sorcerers' dangerous schemes. Vengeance was thought to be at the root of various ailments; a person may be afflicted by "an evil spirit," suffer a disastrous "sapping of strength," feel "weak in arms and legs," and experience an overwhelming "need to sleep." But these phenomena were due to "the business of sorcery" and had to be countered by amulets and other magical means.[13]

In addition, precious stones had different and more ordinary uses, such as those catalogued in the twelfth century by Hildegard von Bingen in the *Treatise on Stones*. Among the remedies she proposed are: "If a humor causes you fatigue, warm a crystal in the sunlight and place it on the ailing part of the body. This will expel the humor."[14] Placing a sapphire in one's mouth "quiets the pains of rheumatism"; wearing an emerald will ease the heart or stomach; breathing onto an onyx "strengthens all one's senses";[15] a ruby "restores vitality."[16] Gemstones contained enough healing power to alleviate both illness and fatigue, to combat both exhaustion and disability, such that the distinction between sickness and tiredness was eliminated here. Jewels' aura of protection was somewhat imprecise; if they are always worn, they will protect against all dangers. Other, less ostentatious tokens could also serve as generic defenses against evil, such as a bone hung around one's neck. Even the poorest folk might acquire an animal horn or tooth to wear outside or underneath their clothing. Fatigue was one ailment among many, and it remained ill-defined and rarely described, except as a generalized weakness. The images of highly polished bones, tough, sharp teeth and pointed horns were very revealing; they were testaments of a fierce resistance to death. These natural talismans were invulnerable to decay and "injury" and were simultaneously "within" life and "outside" it. As relics of once living creatures, the talismans transported our earthbound bodies beyond the reach of time.

Perfumes and spices

Inevitably, other substances were also believed to infuse our flesh with a purifying essence. This was especially true of spices, whose volatility and aromas were thought to enhance the subtlest, most spiritual aspects of humors. Their efficacy depended on a particular conception of the internal mechanisms of the body. Spices' volatility enabled them to replace the "spirits" one lacked, restoring the "fire" that was the source of actions and emotions. Their "ether" was a balm for nerves, suffusing the organs and offsetting the dehydration of fatigue. Herb gardens contained "healing" plants to combat dehydration. The plants had multiple uses, ranging from treating illnesses to encouraging relaxation, from their utility as remedies to their benefits as restoratives and from banishing illness to welcoming ease. There were no specific commentaries on their effect on work or the strains of daily life, but we did find some evidence in Paris street vendors' calls touting "spice cake for the heart" among other things.[17] Novels provide other examples, as when the exhausted Ogier is revived by adding pepper to his meal: "Coneys [rabbits] sprinkled with ground pepper / and your heart's vigor is restored."[18]

Much of the evidence suggested that herbs and spices did double duty because of their purifying and stimulating properties. Spices were "powerful" and, in addition to the diffusion of their volatile aromas in the air, when ingested, tickled the mouth and stimulated the body, producing shocks, jolts, and intense physical sensations of reinvigoration. In other words, the body's strong reaction to a spice was interpreted as a sign of a renewal of strength. Because spices infused the body with new "vitality," this led to an entirely subjective belief: we could increase our internal "resistance" and therefore should dose ourselves with spices to prepare for moments of duress. This was demonstrated in the account books of King John II of France [known as Jean Le Bon] who was imprisoned in London in the middle of the fourteenth century. Anticipating the privations of Lent, the king's spice merchants recorded double and even triple orders of ginger, cinnamon, cloves, sugar and coriander for the fasting month of February.[19]

Consuming these products from the East may also have had a sexual subtext. Aromatic and piquant spices were almost invariably considered "sensual." Pepper, for one, "is relaxing and warms up frigid nerves"; anise "stimulates urine and arousal";[20] nutmeg "greatly enhances our desire."[21] Lovers adopted these remedies, as did the "lusty" monks in fables, who, before assignations with lady friends, prepare "cooked meats and pâtés seasoned with pepper"[22] to enhance their pleasure. Another example is Yolaine, an unfaithful wife who sent her "heart's love" out to buy "pepper and cumin," which they consumed with amorous gusto before "lying in bed, kissing and caressing."[23]

Social distinctions

The expense and rarity of condiments from the East such as cinnamon, ginger, cloves or nutmeg, suggested that their consumption was not common. A spice was a luxury item whose value seemed to rise in relation to its scarcity and whose cost enhanced its distinction. Peasants had few resources compared to merchants or business owners. A "pound weight" of saffron cost 64 sous at the end of the fourteenth century[24] and a pound of nutmeg 50 sous;[25] each of these cost more than a cow that was sold for 42 sous in the county of Beaubec in 1396.[26] A pound of pepper cost about a dozen sous,[27] almost the same as a well-fattened sheep that was sold for 10 sous 5 deniers in Saint-Martin-la-Corneille around 1400.[28]

There were finer distinctions to be made between apparently "equivalent" remedies. In fact, other more common products were also consumed for their protective value. "Substitutes" such as garlic were recommended. It was less expensive but also had "powerful essences," explained Baptiste Platine in the fifteenth century, calling it "a strong spice for the masses"[29] and a remedy "good for laboring folk"[30] – in other words, accessible to peasants. Nevertheless, it is difficult to assess the popularity of these remedies. Accounts generally were silent on their connection to fatigue, so it is hard to know exactly how the poor folks' remedies were meant to be used. At the end of the thirteenth century, for instance, inventories of Iberian sailing vessels included stocks of "garlic and onions to protect [the crew] from poisonous sea air and putrid water."[31] In the same way, Aldebrandin of Siena[32] recommended garlic and onions to pilgrims and travelers, since these vegetables, like spices, have many uses.

In the Middle Ages, an explicit, multifaceted campaign against the rigors of fatigue developed in the context of battle and of travel, but the effort was less sharply defined in relation to labor and the activities of daily life. The exhaustion of common people was noted less often as well. This is a testament to a particular culture in which certain actions were valued more than others and were therefore more visible.

PART II

THE MODERN WORLD AND THE CHALLENGE OF CATEGORIES

At the end of the sixteenth century, Cesare Ripa's "Iconologia or Moral Emblems," a compilation of allegorical figures intended for painters and other artists, highlighted how symbols of weakness had hardly changed in the modern period. A "very thin woman, barely dressed and with her breast exposed"[1] was categorized as the symbol of "fatigue." She was "thin" because her body's humors were leaking away. She was "barely dressed" because she was boiling over with heat. Activities and humidity have joined forces; her dehydration was the result of "too vigorous exercise or excessively hot weather."[2] The idea of "lost" fluids was central to the image, just as Cardinal Mazarin was believed to exhaust the French people by "sucking their blood even down to the marrow out of their bones."[3]

Fatigue had still not been explored as a generic universal condition that affected all human behavior. However, curiosity about it was growing and the subjects under investigation, many different actions and symptoms, were increasing. New expressions enter the popular lexicon, such as the "expense" associated with war, city life, the court, estates, travel, gambling ... The arena of fatigue was diversifying in step with the "modern" world, and more concentrated attention was directed at all types of behavior. The range of exhaustion was broader, even though at the same time it had also become more fragmented.

7

The Invention of Degrees

New threats of fatigue began to be recognized in the modern world of the sixteenth and seventeenth centuries. Still, the explanations for them remained the same. Some nuances came into play, however, such as identifying stages of fatigue ranging from tolerable to unbearable exhaustion and making a distinction between mere indulgence and excess. The evidence for fatigue became more specific and the differences among types increased in number. All in all, these new approaches opened up additional areas of investigation.

Distinctions in physical conditions

Intellectual curiosity about fatigue was growing. For example, extreme states were described in more detail. One notable difference was the expression "to become exhausted" and the noun "exhaustion." These words have identified a state of being "absolutely enfeebled" since the sixteenth century.[1] They also came to mean being on the brink of death, as illustrated in the mid-seventeenth century by the perilous condition of Léon Bouthillier de Chavigny, who, having fiercely supported Condé during the Fronde uprising, was overwhelmed by battle fatigue, saddened by betrayal, threatened by Mazarin, and weakened by his own self-sacrifices. In particular, he "ate sparingly" for fear of "getting fat" and subsequently passed away abandoned and alone. "For quite a while his mind was uneasy and his body was tested to the limit from the day that he joined the revolt. He heated up and dried out extraordinarily. Also, the way he lived his life was very much to blame."[2]

The exhaustion of galley slaves was a familiar topic too. Forced labor has played a prominent role in incarceration and punishment since the sixteenth century, as Vieilleville's description of an incident in the bay of Villefranche in 1543 demonstrated. The fleet commander D'Anghien ordered a swift departure from the port that was being threatened by the arrival of the Italian admiral Doria. Vieilleville captured a brutal moment when the commander's order for "a swift sudden turn" resulted in such a painful maneuver that several prisoners "passed out"[3] in their places and had to be replaced by others. The damage was so serious that D'Anghien, astonished, decided to offer compensation of "two thousand écu to be divided among the galley slaves on the eleven vessels and five hundred for the sailors."[4] For the first time, the disastrous human toll of the event was so obvious that the victims' pain was acknowledged this way.

Other distinctions came to the fore, such as the supposed differences between men and women. Women, it was believed, were more susceptible to humors; they are bathed in and softened by these fluids and thus are more prone to fatigue than men are. This was a key distinction that affected everything they did, including gestation. A woman pregnant with a boy was less easily fatigued than a woman "carrying" a girl. Female fetuses are "livelier and ruddier, whereas males have more natural warmth that the mothers feel."[5]

However, a significantly new perspective was brought to bear on other questions, such as heretofore unknown feelings. These newly invented concepts applied especially to the elite. The category of "emotions" expanded to incorporate "subtle" symptoms, vague discomforts and diffuse feelings of unease accompanying, from time to time, undefinable pleasures such as the "sweet languor"[6] that Antoine Furetière's character enjoyed at the end of the seventeenth century. Sometimes the feelings are more distinct and defined, such as the shades of discomfort Mme de Maintenon experienced when she left Fontainebleau for Versailles and found she was suffering from a particular sort of languidness: "I am feeling weary ever since I left Fontainebleau. I was able to rest more there and that affects my health."[7] This unusual word, "languor," surfaced in the lexicon of the elite, where it connoted a generalized weariness that was overpowering but hard to identify. Esprit Fléchier valiantly tried to express this in his description of the dauphine in the years before her death in 1600, but he was unable to settle on a precise diagnosis: "A languor that at first seemed more bothersome than dangerous, a malady that was all the more painful for not being understood and not sufficiently acknowledged … distresses of the mind along with those of the body, and the natural store of energy drained away by the effort expended in maintaining it."[8]

Some more specific and familiar complaints may be associated with these new disorders, such as the insomnia that plagued Guez de Balzac, leaving him with "a languid soul and broken body."[9] Mme de Maintenon suffered from "worries" and was overextended, causing her to feel "prostrated with swelling" and "massacred by the life one leads here [at Versailles]."[10] Even an excess of tears wreaked damage on Mme de Montmorency: "Her ceaseless crying dehydrated her brain so greatly that her nerves shrank, her spine became terribly crooked, and her lungs short of breath."[11]

Other words came into fashion to name these new degrees of fatigue, and they were added to the lexicon: "vapors," "discomfort," "drowsiness." In the middle of the seventeenth century Guez de Balzac experienced this, claiming: "Even though I almost never sleep, I am always drowsy."[12] In particular, the word "inconvenience" appeared frequently in works of literature, in dictionaries and in novels, where it was modified according to a sliding scale of intensity: "It's a great inconvenience to live at the edge of town"; it's a minor "inconvenience"[13] to refrain from one action or another. For the first time, a new recognition of nuances and degrees came to the fore, even though it was subjective or even imprecise.

A gradation of effort

A new scale of effort was developed alongside the contemporary gradation of "feelings," spurring comparisons between people's physical abilities and their potential.

Since the sixteenth century, military leaders have identified what qualities to look for in the most successful recruits, such as an ability to withstand the fatigues inherent in military duty:

> To identify the man most apt for military service, look for these signs: a bright, alert gaze, an erect posture with head held high and torso erect, broad shoulders, long arms, strong fingers, flat stomach, well-developed thighs, slender legs and dry feet. These are the features that usually guarantee overall fitness because a man with this physique will most likely be agile and strong: two absolutely essential qualities in a good soldier. Nevertheless, we must not reject recruits who don't display all of these attributes if they are otherwise willing and capable. We must stress that all new recruits need to be trained

commensurate with their abilities and not make the perfect the enemy of the good.[14]

The treatise *Le Théâtre d'agriculture* [The theater of agriculture] published in 1600 advised farmers to take the fitness of their "farmhands" into account, putting a new emphasis on the most efficient deployment of labor: "Give the strongest workers the most demanding tasks; assign the more intelligent men work that requires more brainpower than brute force."[15] Medieval abbeys had already adopted this distinction in part by assigning certain monks to work with books and others to labor in the fields.[16] Classifications continued to be developed and systematized in an attempt to align the degree of fatigue to each person's store of energy, distinguishing between big, small and medium efforts and intuitively matching the "smallest" with the weakest laborer and the "biggest" with the strongest. In fact, the "ones in the middle" were preferable, since they were at the happy medium between the two extremes. The jobs themselves took on more precise definitions and specialties were recognized. Although some of the judgments were undoubtedly superficial and even hasty, they laid the foundation for standardized categories. For instance, "husky men are good for hard work," such as tending cattle and transporting heavy loads, while "small men" were "better suited" to tend vineyards, "plant trees," "take care of gardens and beehives, or work as shepherds." The "men in the middle" were "almost always capable of performing any task."[17] The emperor Maximillian I issued a decree in 1517 that also attempted to classify work assignments by ability. It categorized laborers in construction and mining by "age, knowledge and physical strength."[18] There were still no specific measures or guidelines, but these examples revealed a general openness to assess workers' stamina and potential before hiring them.

We find a similar point of view in military recruitment. In 1686, Joseph Torrilhon de Prades, a captain in the Piedmont regiment, demonstrated this, challenging his father and objecting to the way he continued to sign up men who were "too weak": "I've written to no avail that we want only tall men but you paid no attention. Out of the eight men you sent only Bayard and L'Éveille have qualified, along with a third man that my valet dredged up. The others are midgets. It would have been better not to do any recruiting. You're only throwing away money."[19] During the reign of Louis XIV, military authorities brought this discussion to another level. Several units of the French Guards[20] required a minimum height: 5 feet 4 inches (1.626 meters). However, there were still exceptions. Vauban advocated for "smaller" men even though "tall" ones were currently in favor: "Vitality, strength and courage are found more frequently in men below average height."[21] More attention was also paid to the physique of potential soldiers in hopes of assessing their strength, endurance and ability to withstand or overcome fatigue. This became problematic when the number of men (and potential recruits) in the population started to fall, leading to the king's decision to forbid "measuring soldiers."[22] Louvois refused to reject recruits "of the right age, strength, and size to serve ably" if the only drawback was "being a few inches shorter than the others."[23] Nevertheless, a man's appearance was still meaningful and idealized to the extent that an exemplary "model" has taken hold since the sixteenth century in which the key factors to be evaluated, mainly intuitively, were energy, heft, arm and leg strength, and, indeed, height.

The method of assessing galley slaves (the forced labor on ships) provided an even more striking example. Smooth navigation was at stake, along with the speed and maneuverability of the vessel, so a detailed system of evaluation was adopted in the seventeenth century, commensurate with the needs of a "modern" fleet. A Huguenot galley slave named Jean Marteilhe, condemned "because of his religion," described the inspection system that began on board the ship: "They make us strip naked to inspect every part of our bodies. They poke and prod us all over, just as they would a steer they were purchasing at a market. After the inspection, they separate us into groups, ranked from strongest to weakest."[24] The "best ones" sat in the first row and set the pace by adjusting either the reach of the oars or the angle. The other ranks took their places, from the "septerol" to the "aposti," their positions depending on their distance from the water and the trajectory of the rowers' movements. Different physical attributes were factored in the equation: age, height, "skin color." In this way, punishments for galley slaves could differ; in 1688 Jean-Baptiste Colbert Seignelay, the minister of the marine, recommended that Huguenots be used on "galley ships bound for Algeria,"[25] where the physical demands were most exhausting.

Ranking social functions

Evaluating fatigue cannot be separated from social factors. Charles Loyseau, focusing on "orders" and "ranks" at the apogee of classical society, indirectly confirmed that the travails of "little people" were of little interest:

> There are jobs that draw more on the body's labor than on the circulation of goods or the quickness of wit, and these are the most miserable. And for that very reason people who have neither profession nor merchandise, who earn a living with the strength of their arms, are called arms folk or mercenaries. Porters, masons' helpers, and other manual laborers are in the lowest rank of the working class because there is no more inferior vocation than not having a vocation.[26]

Most descriptions of daily life passed over manual labor in silence. It was relegated to "invisibility" and was associated with the "base and mechanistic aspects of the Third Estate … the ones excluded from the kingdom's riches."[27] La Fontaine mentioned a woodcutter "groaning with a bent back"[28] but also a shoemaker "singing from morning till night, a joy to see him,[29] or a "mud-spattered stable boy" who was gifted with the wise words "God helps those who help themselves."[30] Claude Fleury ignored the travails of servants governed by inflexible and invasive codes of conduct: "A lackey must follow his master everywhere, and not dare to step away even for a minute."[31] Antoine Furetière mocked the poor man, a "bearded and swarthy" farmhand who had "learned to fast on a diet of water and chestnuts."[32] La Bruyère's description of peasants who, tragically, appeared barely human was exceptional[33] at a time when most commentators barely acknowledged the exhaustion of workers or peasants. Travelers and other social observers in the first half of the century paid little attention to the topic. Joseph du Chesne, the physician of Henri IV, believed that laborers' "extreme exertions" were excellent "exercise for their nerves and muscles."[34] Léon Godefoy, while traveling through Gascony and Béarn in 1646, noticed only the peasants' ruddy complexions, "shameful" for the "populace" of the Armagnac, as they were "so dark as to seem almost black."[35] François de Grenaille, who traveled around Aquitaine in 1643, recorded his appreciation of a "a marvelously fertile land"[36] but failed to acknowledge any effort or pain put into it.

When Sir Francis Bacon compared "ways of life" in his study on natural history, he evaluated the work of everyone from soldiers to clerics and from scribes to laborers, concluding that the farmhand's "rural life" was the humblest but also the healthiest, because "they enjoy unlimited quantities of fresh air; they are always in motion; they abhor laziness; have no cares or worries and mainly subsist on foodstuffs that they gather themselves without having to buy any."[37] There was no mention here of the pain or suffering of laborers, which itself was still rarely acknowledged.

8

Inventing Categories

Although observers were still relatively indifferent to the fatigues of the poorest of the poor, they began noting the range and intensity of fatigue and describing different varieties in other social classes. Life in the modern world was becoming more diverse. Economies were changing along with people's responsibilities and their interactions. The transformations were everywhere: from city life to the royal court, and from trade to the military.

The penalty of fatigue

Far from being overlooked, pain indeed played a role in punishment and repression. The practice of forced labor on galley ships made the connection between criminal sanctions and physical suffering emphatically clear. On January 22, 1513, Louis XII decreed that "all penalties in the duchy of Brittany be corporal punishment."[1] Condemning prisoners to a particular kind of exhaustion was at the heart of this punishment, just as violence was an inescapable daily occurrence on galley ships. In 1564, Charles IX extended this decision to the entire kingdom. It was only in the seventeenth century that distinctions were made between the length of a sentence and the severity of the crime, and between forced labor in the galleys and other punishments. In this way, the suffering in medieval pilgrimages undertaken as an act of penance[2] was revived in a different but equally horrific form. Some witnesses described the punishing labor: "Stand up to pivot the oar behind you, then crouch down to plunge it into the water, fall back onto the bench to propel the oar forward with as much energy as possible."[3] Others described the difficult and unpredictable demands on the men who had to keep up the brutal pace of the "single stroke" and the "double-time stroke," all under the watchful gaze of terrifying "wardens." "The men row for ten, twelve or even twenty hours at a stretch sometimes, with no let-up. At such times the officer who commands the galley crew or other sailors puts a bit of bread soaked in wine in the men's mouths to keep up their strength."[4] But the anecdotes of small mercies on board galley ships did little to counter Marteilhe's harrowing testimony of generalized indifference to the wellbeing and even survival of the convict crews: "If a slave faints and passes out onto his oar (which happens frequently), he is whipped to death and then tossed unceremoniously into the sea."[5] This extreme dehumanization and torture was implied though not explicitly written into the ships' protocols in the seventeenth century. Galley slaves were chained together in threes and attached to positions that they could not leave at any time. They were fed once every two days and slept partly bent over, "in filth, eaten alive by vermin."[6] Writing about occupational injuries in 1700, Bernardino Ramazzini was one of the few dissenting voices, even if his critique of the system was contradictory. He noted that galley slaves were threatened with violence: "a hail of blows." But they had "the advantage" of performing some of their work sitting down. In this position "their stomachs are supported, whereas men who do their work standing are afflicted with distended internal organs."[7] This otherwise well-meaning doctor indulged in a mechanistic fantasy.

The physical toll, no matter how extreme, had to be proportional to the prisoner's "fault." Searing pain and panting breath were meant to be part of the punishment, and the body was the focal point of these corrections. The suffering ought to be – in fact, had to be – visible. A similar conviction underlay the procedures of the General Hospital of Paris, the workhouse for juvenile offenders, "incarcerating boys under the age of twenty-five and girls for the purpose of punishment." It took in young people who were guilty of "mistreating their fathers or mothers" or were "debauched," among other things. Their work assignments were supposed to provoke the most extreme physical exhaustion: "They will be made to work for as long as possible and at the most brutal tasks that their strength and the conditions permit."[8] This extraordinary fatigue was clearly meant to extract the "maximum" in order to subjugate and punish wayward youths.

War

The new categories of fatigue in the modern world reflected experiences associated with a radically transformed way of life. Combat was one of these areas, and military methods changed along with military culture. During the sixteenth century the army became more professionalized. Terms of service were longer and soldiering became a career, a more complex vocation requiring additional training and "education" to deal with long-distance deployments and the challenges of different climates, new terrain and unfamiliar dangers: "The sixteenth century witnesses a significant transformation in the organization of the military in Western Europe … This is when modern concepts of the 'soldier,' 'maneuvers,' and 'discipline' begin to take precedence over those of 'chivalry,' 'status,' and 'honor.'"[9] France now had a standing army with ongoing recruitment. The overriding principle was: "The soldier ends his service only when he is no longer able to perform his duties or if he is no longer needed."[10] The "length of service" became "open-ended."[11] All of this led to a continuous churn of activity affecting military maneuvers and conditions on army bases as well as innovations in methods of warfare, such as those in the construction of earthworks, the delivery of materials, troop transport, and the posting of guards and lookouts. "Preventing the dissipation of troops by keeping them in shape with maneuvers"[12] was at stake. Joseph Sevin de Quincy observed: "We were exhausted in this camp. A day never went by without our being on duty."[13] The soldiers' maneuvers turned into performances. Their staging areas got larger. Their actions were rehearsed over and over as they pantomimed the gestures of combat. The royal court came to observe, as it did at Compiègne in 1660, provoking an unexpected epidemic of exhaustion: "The courtiers were obliged to visit the encampment every day, and it seemed to them that their fatigue outweighed their enjoyment."[14]

More rules and regulations were issued specifying how "the discipline and order His Majesty expects will be upheld by His infantrymen when they are garrisoned in towns or rural areas."[15] In the same way, regulations laid out officers' duties and responsibilities,[16] and training was mandated to ensure "military men's development" in skills such as "marching," "forming columns," and adopting the correct "gait" (the Louvois step).[17] New measures were adopted to "fortify the encampments"[18] and penalize deserters.[19]

A brand-new diagnosis was taking shape, and this condition was not simply the weariness a fighter felt after a battle but, more specifically, "war fatigue" or "army fatigue." Jean de Souvigny used it in 1614 to characterize his uncle's surprise when Jean, at the age of twelve, told him he wanted to join the regiment at Penthièvre: "He asked me if I had enough courage and fortitude to be a soldier and withstand the fatigues of war."[20] The journal *Le Mercure galant* used it too in 1672 to express a visitor's astonishment when he entered a soldier's room and instead found a young lady: "She was very young but quite tall and strapping enough to withstand the fatigues of the army."[21] At the beginning of the seventeenth century, Francis Bacon used the same expression when he mused about "a military lifestyle" that paradoxically could add years to a man's life: "This often happens to those who work hard from a young age. This fosters endurance and, as they grow older, the bitterest fruits of fatigue are transformed into the sweetest ones."[22]

A new awareness of the environment focused attention on soldiers' living conditions, their surroundings, and such necessities of daily life as food, clothing, shelter, rest periods and sleep. These all contributed to a sense of ease or exhaustion unrelated to physical exertion or the strains of battle. In 1552, François de Scépeaux was one of the first to identify filthy uniforms and unsuitable sleeping quarters as reasons for soldiers' weariness, in addition to the rigors of forced marches: "We marched this way for twelve days in extreme deprivation. Only those in the highest ranks, or the wealthiest, slept in beds that were transported along with the regiment. The rest of the troops never even got undressed."[23] Shakespeare's Othello described the same conditions while claiming to overcome them in an attempt to persuade the Venetians: "The tyrant custom, most grave senators, / Hath made the flinty and steel couch of war / My thrice-driven bed of down. I do agonize / A natural and prompt alacrity I find in hardness, and do undertake / These present wars against the Ottomites."[24] Fear of potential fatigue increased in the seventeenth century to the point that Louis-Auguste de Bourbon, the duke of Maine and a son of Louis XIV, "accompanying" the Flanders army in 1689, attributed his weariness to a lack of clean linen, and his having "overcome" this "obstacle" as a great victory. As the young duke explained to his former governess, Mme de Maintenon: "Madame, I had already begun to feel the fatigue of war because I went for three days and three nights without changing my shirt."[25]

A new ethos of tirelessness was pervasive throughout the military. The emphasis was no longer, as in the medieval world, only on endurance in battle. Endurance was now expected whenever a military man confronted all of the obstacles and burdens of life in the field or in the camp. The army officer, more than any other soldier, represented the merits of universal fortitude. In his lengthy profile of Louis-François de Boufflers, Saint-Simon clearly depicted how going to war in the seventeenth century changed perceptions of fatigue of both soldiers and their leaders:

> Accessible at all hours of the day and night, watching out for everyone, careful to prevent others from falling victim to fatigue or avoidable threats as much as possible, he tired himself for everyone, went everywhere and was continually alert, watchful and visible. He slept fully dressed and ready for battle and rarely went to bed more than three times between the opening of the trenches to the beating of the tattoo. It is hard to understand how a man of his age, worn down by war, can keep up such a punishing routine for his body and mind and never lose his composure and his temper. He was reprimanded for taking too many risks; he did so in order to see with his own eyes and supervise everything as he wished; he also did it to set an example and allay his own fears about duties going well and being done correctly.[26]

These were new kinds of fatigue or, more accurately, fatigues that were better recognized and categorized in the context of more and different responsibilities.

As a result, a specific kind of "wear and tear" began to be acknowledged and the fatigue of some occupations taken into account. An injured or ill legionnaire "continues to receive his salary,"[27] and, following the order issued in 1670, former soldiers or sailors were paid 2 ecus a month.[28] The Hôtel Royal des Invalides was inaugurated on October 1, 1674, in Paris. It was intended to house soldiers who had been "injured or crippled fighting for the king."[29] The institution for retired soldiers has a complicated history, clearly, since it was also built to prevent war-damaged veterans from roaming the streets, bridges and town squares.

The city

The city came under scrutiny at this time because life there was also being transformed. The traditional stereotype of the turbulent city and the tranquil countryside was reoriented, taking a different direction from the end of the sixteenth century. A vision of a new kind of fatigue was taking shape. The increasing vitality of urban life, its sensory overload and the emotions that provoked, came to the fore. Cities had grown rapidly and their role had increased significantly. The increasing concentration of commercial, civil and administrative functions in cities had shifted the balance of power, subsuming "the elite of surrounding regions" and the "tax collectors and magistrates of the landed gentry."[30] Shopkeepers, physicians, legislators, attorneys or writers were to be found in droves in cities. Agricultural practices gradually became more standardized and technical, marginalizing the ancient livelihoods of gleaners and smallholders, resulting in an astonishing number of "vagrants filling the streets."[31]

The tumultuous flow of colorful crowds "in constant motion,"[32] the masses of people and things on the streets, hemmed in by the old city walls, produced "an extraordinary crush whose last vestiges can still be seen in the charming remnants of 'old Paris.'"[33] More and more contemporary accounts seized on the presence of crowds, the sense of being overwhelmed and "gasping for air" in a Paris that had become a "towering heap of a city" and "as crowded as a beehive."[34]

Complaints and accusations proliferated in the city, and annoyances and frustrations became ever more acute. Noise was the worst offender, more than any other "inconvenience," because of the din that deafened city dwellers and ruined their sleep. As Boileau satirized it in 1666:

> Everything is conspiring to ruin my sleep,
> And I am complaining about the least of my troubles ...
> But I have hardly turned out the lamp in my room
> When I can no longer shut even one eye."[35]

The dynamism of city life was novel enough to provide material for satire about the noisy nuisances that disrupted rest and led to exhaustion: "Coachmen are so brutal; their voices are so harsh, so horrifying, and the incessant cracking of their whips intensifies the noise to such an extent that it seems like demons are swarming to make Paris a living hell."[36] The "complaint" focused on the disruption of sleep, the cacophony of sounds, the inescapable din. Nicolas Guérard produced a series of etchings at the end of the seventeenth century to illustrate Boileau's satire *L'Embarras de Paris* [The annoyances of Paris]. The scenes of a hectic and chaotic city highlighted the stress caused by sensations of exhaustion and imminent danger. Boileau's narrator pithily describes a city crowded with carriages, animals, performers and pedestrians in this verse: "One hears nothing but a clamor of confused cries, and God thunders in vain to make Himself heard. And I, who should have gone to a certain place, seeing the day decline, and weary of waiting, not knowing what saint's protection to implore – I see myself in danger of being broken on the wheel."[37]

Another "complaint" about modern life focused on a more internalized distress, one that was less visible and had yet to be named, centering on the burden of doing business: the stress of maintaining an office, making decisions and answering all manner of correspondence. The weariness of attorneys, administrators, scribes, merchants and other worthies who were now confronted with waning personal power had been little noticed before, but it was on the rise. Solutions to their problems were becoming ever more complex, and they foresaw no respite from the onslaught. These were symptoms of a world where office work, the clergy, the legal profession, administration, and parliament were becoming more prominent. All of a sudden, long overlooked tensions were now being acknowledged and felt. They were most often expressed in simple words and concepts that framed them physically and morally, as in the message Henri IV sent to Sully in 1591: "All the news I have received from Mantes indicates that you are exhausted and wasting away because of overwork."[38] The same point was raised a few decades later when Saint-Simon described the ailments of Michel Chamillart, worn out by his ministerial duties and tormented by unbalanced humors that were boiling over, drying out and leaking away, causing him as much pain as their possible psychological equivalents might:

> Chamillart, burdened with the double duties of war and finance, had no time either to eat or to sleep … He made do, accepting the situation, but finally broke down: he was tormented with vapors, his eyes dazzled by glaring light, his head aching. Everything went awry, he couldn't tolerate food, and was visibly wasting away. Nonetheless, the wheels had to keep spinning, the work must continue, and he was the only one who could make that happen.[39]

Ezekiel Spanheim also described fatigue in terms of the body when he wrote about Louis XIV and "the fatigue of the position." He noted the sudden onslaught of anxiety afflicting Louis XIV after he ascended to the throne: "An exterior imbued with grandeur and majesty and the constitution of a body able to withstand the fatigues and responsibilities of such a high position."[40] A few decades earlier, Richelieu had likewise framed in corporeal terms his claim of being able to endure administrative "burdens" (as they were newly designated in the seventeenth century). Gilles Ménage described Richelieu's odd secret method of relaxation, entirely physical and even a bit exotic. The minister would "revive" his animal spirits through dynamic movement: "He sometimes didn't have the time to recover from the great fatigue that ministerial duties always elicited. He especially enjoyed strenuous exercise after meals, but he didn't want to be seen doing it … He would amuse himself by traversing the great gallery of the Palais Royal, leaping over the tallest wall and leaping back again."[41]

The threat of exhaustion was not without a certain prestige during this period as a way to demonstrate endurance and "ability." La Bruyère drew an acerbic portrait of a modern character whose supposed "exhaustion" was a badge of honor:

> You are very inconsiderate to sit musing or dozing in your carriage. Rouse yourself and take a book or your papers and begin to read and hardly return the bows of those people who pass you in their carriages, for they will believe you to be very busy and say everywhere that you are hard-working and indefatigable and that you read even in the street or on the high road. You may learn from a pettifogger [low-status lawyer] that you should ever seem to be immersed in business, knit your brows and muse most profoundly about nothing at all, that you should not always have time for eating or drinking ….[42]

In this way, the classic city gave birth to new varieties of fatigue and their opposite: indefatigability.

The court

Significant social changes made the court a locus of a new, specific variety of fatigue due to the centralization of power, the concentration of authority in the state, the disappearance of local fiefdoms, and the waning influence of medieval baronies and their internecine warfare. A new social system arose at this time, with the sovereign at its center and ritual as its foundation. The Valois dynasty at the end of the sixteenth century promulgated an "order" outlining the protocol "the king wishes to be kept in his court."[43] The rules of etiquette made courtiers' ranks explicit and visible, and rituals organized the use of space and time. The system was as complex as it was omnipresent, regimenting everyday life, dictating proper actions and suitable settings, and governing all behavior. Still, a new mindset was needed to recognize fatigue in a condition that before was undoubtedly simply dismissed or ignored.

The expression "court fatigue" became common in the seventeenth century and was used by the courtiers themselves. It was a leitmotif in Mme de Maintenon's writing. For example, she ascribed Mlle de Jarnac's suffering – that is, her swollen legs – to her difficulty in "getting accustomed to court fatigue."[44] She lauded Mme de Montchevreuil, whose lively spirit showed that she "withstands fatigue admirably,"[45] and pitied the maréchale de Rochfort, whose illness betrayed her incapacity to "stand up to fatigue."[46] The marquise herself was so "overwhelmed with cares, visits, preparations for travel,"[47] that she saw herself as a "true martyr"[48] and even dismissed the aviary at Fontainebleau as "fatiguing" because for the last two days it had been "livelier than I've ever heard it."[49] Fatigue was inevitably associated with ceremonies at the court, where positions and facial expressions had to be maintained for insufferably long periods amid an often fruitless search for "something to lean on" to "ease one's weariness."[50] Jean-François Solnon called "standing at attention" the "courtier's awful fate."[51] This posture condemned the cardinal de Coislin to absolute exhaustion: "the poor man, who was quite portly, was bathed in sweat. Sweat poured off him in the antechamber. Dressed in ecclesiastical garb of cape and gown, the cardinal perspired so abundantly that the floor was wet all around him."[52] However, one rule prevailed over all the others: "be diligent,"[53] show that you are "always available,"[54] and, in other words, withstand "discomforts and fatigues."[55] Saint-Simon gave a detailed description of Mme de Montespan's son, the marquis d'Antin, as an example of how courtiers themselves understood this new and specific "court fatigue":

> A strong and healthy body was up to all challenges. And although he slowly became quite heavy, he never shied away from either losing sleep or enduring fatigue. He had a hasty temperament but his good sense kept him gentle and polite and accommodating in his manner; eager to please, he sacrificed everything in the quest for wealth and power … He was the most able and sophisticated courtier of his time and the most unbelievably dedicated. He was relentless: he suffered unheard of fatigue in order to be seen everywhere at all times, with a matchless determination to be present in all places. He made countless efforts, seen by everyone, and always over the top; dispensing attention, demonstrating graciousness, and unleashing a constant stream of flattery, he monitored everything around him with an eagle eye, with an endless font of meanness. Nothing deterred him, nothing stopped him, assumed by people whom he was convinced he would toss away once he was on the verge of actually achieving power. His attentiveness to his mother's children was extreme and his patient attitude toward rejection saw no bounds. He accepted so many insults in his life with an astounding level of pretense.[56]

Subtle, secretive stratagems, superficially petty and yet highly valuable, were used to demarcate privileges and calibrate differences in courtiers' actions that were dictated by convention. Jean-François Solnon gave several examples of this in classic society: "the right to enter the king's residence in a carriage [not on foot] and to have a cushion at Church are privileges at the Louvre palace."[57] Being permitted to sit on a low "stool" and being allowed to remain seated in royal residences was another advantage and a highly prized one. The duchesses who enjoyed this privilege were given the epithet "seated ladies," or simply "stools."[58] Differences in rank were indicated by the type of chair permitted; royal grandchildren could sit on chairs with backs, and princes and princesses of the blood could use armchairs.[59] Quarrels broke out about such seating arrangements, and even innocent mistakes were instantly pointed out. Mme de Sévigné brought this up during an audience with the queen: "Several duchesses arrived, including the young Ventadour, very lovely and pretty. Some minutes went by and no one brought her that divine footstool. I turned to the master of ceremonies and told him, 'Alas! Have one brought to her. Whoever overlooked her is going to pay dearly for it.' He agreed."[60] Another example showed that permission "denied" could nevertheless become permission "granted." This was the case when the queen allowed several ladies to be seated "without any fuss" when protocol would have required them to stand. Princes and dukes in "great numbers" protested against the stools, demanding they be removed "for the sake of the nobility."[61] In this way, "fatigue" clearly indicated one's rank in a hierarchy and reinforced social distinctions. It also revealed new nuances in our perception of fatigue.

The mind

An internal dimension to this thoroughly modern diversification of types of fatigue and their settings reveals a distinctly new attention to the human mind. Fatigue was recognized as having a more profound internal influence, subtly affecting emotions and even producing a sense of weariness in one's "thought processes." Descartes mentioned a "fatigue of the mind"[62] afflicting clerics, monks, literary men and attorneys and, in his attempt to define exclusively mental labor, shifted attention to aspects of behavior that had rarely been discussed. This fatigue was the exhaustion brought on not merely by business responsibilities or the strains of management and judgment but by the exertions of mental labor itself: by calculations, reflections, intense and continuous ratiocination. Earlier, in the fifteenth century, Marsile Ficin and Christine de Pisan had already acknowledged this kind of exhaustion when they described the writer's task and the efforts involved in "understanding." However, they still foregrounded the effects on the body: "When I built the *City of Ladies* … I was tired and wanted to rest; like a weary person who has finished a weighty job, my arms and body were worn out by such long and intense labor."[63] Descartes described a more internalized condition, acknowledging that "we cannot always concentrate on the same thing,"[64] warning of the danger in "spending too much time in study,"[65] and emphasizing how often "vocations taken too seriously weaken the body and weary the mind."[66] Considering the effects of pondering "metaphysical principles," he concluded: "I believe it will be very damaging to our consciousness to think too often and too much about them."[67] Thus, "fatigue of the mind" was identified for the first time; it was defined, localized and specified, even if the description was limited to its name and failed to clarify its substance or particular characteristics. The "internal" symptoms here were understood rather than specified and were suggested rather than defined. Still, they pointed to a "feeling" of weakness, diminished capacity and a loss of mental acuity. The *Dictionnaire universel* of Antoine Furetière in 1690 put it bluntly: "the mind suffers fatigue as much as the body does."[68] In a similar vein, Jean-Baptiste Thiers criticized the game of checkers in his *Treatise on Games* in 1686 as "too serious," since it "tires out the mind as much as a significant business deal does."[69] A reference to fatigue and mental revitalization occurred in the rules governing behavior in monasteries in the classic period too, stipulating that "recreation be pursued to ease the mind,"[70] a consideration that did not exist in medieval times. The rationale was obvious, although it merited a brief explanation: "Human limitations allow neither our minds nor our bodies to be always occupied."[71]

This recognition suggested another sort of fatigue that was also overlooked: the feeling of being "fed up with …" or "tired of ….," revealing the emergence of a psychological "terrain" that was as new as it was slow to be recognized. For example, Antonio's sadness and fatigue in *The Merchant of Venice* betrayed an inner weakness or hidden impotence: "In sooth, I know not why I am so sad. / It wearies me; you say it wearies you. / But how I caught it, found it, or came by it, / What stuff 'tis made of, whereof it is born, / I am to learn …"[72] Expressions of exasperation and of being overwhelmed were novel and unusual symptoms at this time, attesting to a newly awakened interest, especially in the seventeenth century, in personal experiences and emotions. "Because of weariness," Louis XIV resigned himself to Mme des Ursins' return to court even if this might result in troubles with the Spanish monarchy: "Weary of the contradictions he felt, concerned about the dangerous upset that this would bring to their negotiations … Tired of the entreaties they were making and the thoughts they were offering."[73] The maréchal de Villeroy felt, as he reached the end of his life, "tired of the horrors of a court where he had cut such a fine figure"[74] and, after he stepped down in favor of his son, suddenly confronted "the nullity of his life with a feeling of revulsion."[75] On a more prosaic level, Joseph Sevin de Quincy described his friend as "a lover who is fed up, tired of communicating with his mistress only through letters."[76] Because they lived too far apart, the man decided to break with her. A satire published in 1622 referred to the exasperation of a woman in labor whose head was "bursting" from the idle chatter "of those standing at the foot of her bed."[77]

The expressions "tired of" and "fed up with" were adopted so widely in the language of the classical period that they became clichés. But these words extended the reach of fatigue from the strictly physical to the mental, from the outer flesh to the inner self, and gave substance to an interiority that was explicitly acknowledged. Its actual mechanism, however, was barely described and remained obscure. Nevertheless, these perceptions highlighted less visible sources of exhaustion, ones that were more internalized than "physical" stresses and that prompted more self-conscious attention to one's feelings and thoughts. Verbs such as "beseech,"[78] "upset" and "tire" are relevant here, acquiring an almost moral connotation. Bussy-Rabutin sent this reprimand to an annoying correspondent: "You ought to tire of playing dirty tricks on people who then retaliate against you."[79] This was certainly an explicitly personal analysis, invoking the influence of a man's conscience, not his "emotion." This new framing of fatigue was significant, but still rudimentary. Physical metaphors were still dominant, such as vapors being compressed or the body overheating.

For the first time, a handful of narratives described a possible convergence of types of fatigue that were believed to be different. Most notably, one's experience of a specific sort of day resulted in an uncontrollable and identical languor despite the varied difficulties one may have had: physical exertion, endless conversation, night watches or journeys. These disparate experiences somehow combined to produce a distinct feeling of lassitude. The princess Palatine realized this when she carefully noted all her activities in one day: "Today I wrote a long letter to my aunt. I paid a visit to the princess de Conti (her staircase has fifty-six steps that are quite high), I walked through the garden to visit Mme la Duchesse, then I received a visit from the queen of England. And now I am dog tired."[80]

At the end of the seventeenth century, observers began to equate mental and physical fatigue, thanks to the acute attention paid to efforts expended and actions performed, as the princess did, even to the extent of counting steep stair steps or recalling random encounters.

9

The Advent of Numbers

The shadow of fatigue was lengthening in step with modernity. It took different shapes and occupied different settings. Above and beyond the role of fatigue in pain and suffering, it seeped into internal spaces, secretly sapping mental vitality in a way that was poorly understood but was now acknowledged. Numbers and measures led to another expansion of its domain. This did not mean that exertion was assessed precisely with a verifiable calculation of its effects, but now times and distances were measured, calibrations were undertaken, the burdens of work were weighed, and fatigue was implicated in all of it. Until this moment, that was hardly a question.

Travel and time

Travel was the first to show the influence of numbers. Conceptions of the world were changing with modernity even if faraway places retained their strangeness. With more routes and crossings, the surface of the earth seemed flattened out. Many countries began to see themselves as homogeneous and interconnected wholes: "In the kingdom, it takes only 25 days on horseback to go from one end to the other, and we can boast of finding everything we need here, without needing anything from our neighbors."[1] Cross-country routes took on even more significance once Sully was appointed "Master of the Roads" in 1599.[2] Travel over longer distances was transformed. Under Louis IX, a series of post stations were established every 4 leagues along France's "Great Roads" to supply travelers with fresh horses "ready to go at a gallop without stopping along the way."[3]

A supervisory body was appointed to oversee the post road system,[4] to ensure that the "departure time" of the mail was recorded and to guarantee it would be "promptly and safely carried."[5] Rural roads became visible, familiar landscapes for travelers, and fragmentation was slowly transformed into unity even if a great many byways were still, as the stewards admitted, "impassable and unusable for transport."[6] A number of steps were taken to improve overland travel. For instance, the royal roads in the classical period had to be "24 feet wide, free of obstructions and well maintained, with no hedges, ditches or trees in the roadway."[7] The regulations forbade "carters and post-chaise drivers from harnessing more than four horses abreast" or transporting "overly heavy loads," to prevent "the paving stones from sinking down from the weight."[8] Quality control was delegated to "local bailiffs."[9] Renaissance painters had already captured the vistas of wide galleries and vast terraces of swaths of tilled land, unencumbered and undivided, receding into the distant horizon.[10]

Nevertheless, fatigues caused by travel had not disappeared, although they now acquired a new meaning as a "common destiny."[11] This was the case for the passengers in the carriages and post-chaises transporting the elite at the end of the sixteenth century, who shared the experience of jolting, bumpy rides. Even though in 1687 the "locals of the neighboring parishes"[12] had spent several months improving the road, Mme de Maintenon still described the court's move to Fontainebleau as an ordeal: "I still have not recovered from the fatigue I endured on the trip here."[13] Marie Mancini had a similar reaction after her trip to the Abbey Notre-Dame du Lys: "I am still not quite recovered from the fatigue and weakness caused by our journey."[14] Without a doubt, these were signs of greater awareness and sensitivity to the physical effects of travel and the anxieties it aroused: the length of the journey is transformed into a lingering feeling of malaise; the bumping of the carriage becomes a jolt, and the disheveled carter a disgrace. A journey was no longer a medieval trek, impeded by barriers and nearly impassable byways and menaced by unknown and uncharted dangers, but the strains of travel were now quantified on more "comfortable" routes that had their own rough edges. In fact, a new field of study now focused on road building. Henri Gautier published the first essay on the topic in 1663, *Traité de la construction des chemins* [A treatise on road construction],[15] which was soon translated into Italian and German. As the title indicates, it was centered on construction methods, building materials, the proper engineering of the roadway, and analyses of terrain, foundations and road surfaces.

At last, challenges could be associated with roads that were gradually becoming better maintained – more nicely "done up,"[16] as Montaigne wrote – just as they could from the increased frequency of horse-powered travel. "Smoother" journeys led to more stringent goals that were more calculated. Intrepid travelers made an effort to cover more territory in less time and to counter their feelings of fatigue with the satisfaction of adding up the miles. For example, Joseph Sevin de Quincy took distance and travel time into account when he observed, "thus in less than ten hours we did thirty miles."[17] In 1652, Jean Hérault de Gourville kept a precise record when "burning through" the post stations to take a message from Paris to Bordeaux, all the while scrupulously recording the locations and distances between the stations, as well as the hours, the days, the nights and the fatigue he battled: "left Saint-Eustache at 10:30 in the evening, arrived at Charenton at midnight, daybreak at Lieusaint, nightfall at Gien. I went so fast that the following day I arrived at Saumur ..."[18] He had to pass through the Auvergne on his return trip for other messages. In total, he covered 130 leagues in seven days. He acknowledged the onset of fatigue and even emphasized it in his account, but associated it with his determination to "get on: I stayed awake despite my weariness so that I arrived in Paris at the Hôtel de Chavigny at 5 in the morning. And I apologized for my fatigue, since I had hardly slept since I left Agen. Then I went on my way."[19] This represented a new kind of indefatigability: the challenge of longer journeys with less time spent in traveling. Louis the Great [Louis XIV] was one such champion in the eyes of his courtiers:

> The king returned to Fontainebleau almost as quickly he went to Nantes. He was indefatigable, and a few days after he arrived he went to Paris on horseback and came back the same day, after having visited the new buildings in Vincennes, at the Louvre and the Tuileries. He did all this in the morning, dined with Monsieur at Saint-Cloud and arrived back at Fontainebleau early.[20]

This unheard-of tirelessness defied both space and time, with travelers pushing through distances and spiking times.

English horse racing, which began at the end of the seventeenth century, is a testament to this mindset. A smooth track, "specially trained" horses, and reliable methods to measure distance and time were necessary for racing. "Owners of vast estates, loyal disciples of movement, the English hunt frequently, going fast, ranging far and wide. They like to bet on who will go the farthest, the fastest."[21] In addition to new riding trails and racetracks, these equestrian sports required a serious investment in horses trained to build up "lung power" and endurance over longer times and distances. The count Gaspard de Chavagnac claimed to have found the secret to success in horse racing by adapting the design of the bit and entering his horses in preparatory time trials.[22] Jacques de Solleysel, on the other hand, presented horse training not as a secret but as a "science," recommending a step-by-step approach in 1652: "You must start out with small doses and increase them little by little; for example, on the first day you can ride for six leagues, on the second day, eight, and after that ten, twelve or even fourteen if necessary."[23] In this particular context, resisting fatigue was an effort that focused as much on the horse as on the rider, if not more, with trainers and owners "breaking" difficult exercises into smaller units and "upgrading" the terrain in various ways. These are factors medieval horsemen tended to overlook.[24]

One more precaution concerned specifically the weight horses carried, especially the horses traversing the post roads. In order to "prevent irreparable damage" and eliminate one cause of exhaustion, a rule about baggage was issued in March 1697[25] permitting only one "case" per rider. On July 3, 1680,[26] a government order limited the capacity of two-wheeled post-chaises to one passenger and 100 pounds of goods. An order on January 15, 1698,[27] specified the maximum distance post horses were permitted to travel. This was 12 or 14 leagues per day, depending on the region. Each of these measures was meant for "the preservation of horses,"[28] but preventing fatigue was also at stake.

The work and the rule

A comparable impulse to measure distance, time and movement was slower to materialize in the context of labor. In fact, some assessments did already exist; for a long time treatises on agriculture had specified how much wheat a harvester could reap or a baler could tie up in a day.[29] But, on the whole, such evaluations were fragmentary or incomplete in a world ruled primarily by hours and days.

Disputes over the workday and potentially "excessive" demands made on workers still seemed rare in the classical world. Jean Nicolas found very few in France between 1661 and 1789, despite having examined 462 conflicts.[30] One image recurred in physicians' observations: toil begins at daybreak and ends at sundown, with "no particular hours specified"; "laborers and artisans … work without a break from morning till night."[31]

The hardships of rural life exposed the dangers of "ceaseless" toil in the modern era even more clearly. Jean Liébault and Charles Estienne used the example of farmhands to illustrate the principle of "continual labor"[32] to their ideal reader, a country gentleman in the sixteenth century. The authors' language was harsh: make sure "folks are not idle and don't waste even one minute of the day without working at a task."[33] To add insult to injury, they offered recipes guaranteed to jolt sleepers awake: waft the "odor of strong vinegar or common rue into the nostrils of the patient … or the smell of old shoes, a mule's hoof or human skin."[34] Whether real or imaginary, the impetus to combat the threat of "those indolent laborers"[35] was the norm here.

Nevertheless, some pushback occurred, and in particular peasants fought against the forced labor that estate owners had long believed their "absolute right," obligating "tenant farmers whenever they wanted."[36] Rules were issued at the end of the fifteenth century, and disputes followed. In 1543 the residents of Chalmazel won a concession from the Paris Parliament, reducing the number of required work parties from twelve to six per year.[37] The rural lords' periodic demands for unpaid labor were still significant, although they could no longer be simply "whenever and wherever, with no limits whatsoever."[38] A "final order" on August 13, 1675,[39] restricted work parties in Chaugy to one per month, although they had previously been held once a week. In the same way, a bailiff in Montbrison ruled on January 9, 1699,[40] that the Chalain estate may require only twelve per year. Peasants in Périgord, Quercy and Gascony rose up in revolt against the "authorities" in 1576 with a revelatory slogan, "We are tired!"[41] This was all evidence of "fatigue," certainly, but the phenomenon was poorly defined. The rural protests were significant because they were generic, prompted by forced labor, the damaging aftermath of wars, catastrophic weather, tithes, the salt tax, land tax and other taxes.

The time constraints imposed on artisans were important but less salient in the historical record. Salaries were a priority. For example, masons in Paris in June 1660 seditiously called for better daily pay: "But they were arrested by royal edict and we believe the danger has passed."[42] Protests erupted sometimes when pay was cut by 1 sou "per day."[43] This was not overlooked when considering the length of the workday "if, like the majority of 'mercantilist' theorists, we need low salaries to force workers to work."[44] Getting a raise might be traded off against limits on work hours, which was a factor in 32 percent of the disputes analyzed by Jean Nicolas.[45]

Modernity, on the other hand, could not fail to lead to more exact calculations. First, these concerned new rules on the amount of labor that was expected, with stricter surveillance and periodic checks of work, even if this was not directly connected to fatigue. During the reign of Louis XIII and Louis XIV, manufacturers began assembling "several workers to work on the same type of task"[46] for the first time. Stringent work rules were enforced by the system of "controllers-visitors-markers" introduced in 1629.[47] Their goal was to increase productivity and to check the quality of the products and not to assess the amount of pain or suffering evinced by the "producers." The 1669 rule on textile manufacturers demonstrated this clearly. The inspector's job was to verify the "length, width and quality of the linen, twill, and other fabrics made of wool and thread."[48] The standard of weaving was "described meticulously,"[49] including the thread count, the patterns, and the smoothness of the fabric. Inspections focused on technical matters. The inspectors, or "gardes jurés,"[50] assessed how well or poorly the standards on quality were respected, so if fatigue was involved in the industry it remained unacknowledged. Pierre Goubert found that weavers' memoirs in Beauvais rarely mentioned their suffering: "What we must emphasize in the experience of wool weavers in Beauvais is neither the length of the workday nor the unsanitary conditions in the workshops. Those conditions were common almost everywhere, and it doesn't seem that the workers protested about it or could even imagine improvements in their lot."[51] So much effort and so much stress on the body resulted in their pain becoming virtually insignificant, their exertions mere shadows, and the wear and tear on their bodies barely visible.

One notable and rare exception, however, occurred in 1666, when a "rest period" was mandated for specific textile workers in Amiens.

These workers, "fullers," had to soften up fabrics soaking in a mixture of urine and water by treading on them. This tedious process released the oils in the wool fibers, making the fabric denser and more flexible. The regulation stipulated that "the fullers' master may process no more than four vats without bringing on different workers, in order to let the fullers rest. Violators will be fined 20 sous."[52] This is an unusual example where, for the first time, fatigue is a factor in regulating the work flow. Nevertheless, it must be emphasized that the inspectors really paid attention only to ensuring the "quality control"[53] of the products.

Work and the dawn of the mechanical era

Observations on "mechanics" emerged very slowly during the sixteenth century, with "theoretical" questions that had been previously neglected. The imagination played a part, as a speculative discussion by Scipion Dupleix in 1623 illustrated. Comparing walking and riding, he attributed the fatigue caused by the latter to the fact that "the body is suspended in the air without support or respite."[54] This thought was informed less by physics than by intuition, surely, since the explanation was far removed from real-life experience and didn't take into account the muscle contractions and momentum involved in walking.

Nevertheless, we see an emerging desire for objectivity in analyses of fatigue's causes and effects. In 1550, Jérôme Cardan was one of the first to try to calculate the difference between locomotion on flat ground and uphill: "Man exerts more effort taking five hundred steps uphill than he does walking four thousand paces on level ground."[55] His calculations seemed precise, using specific numbers to compare the actions, but the rationale for his conclusions was sketchy. Cardan did point out that "on flat ground a person's body is not leaning at all," while on the uphill climb "the body must lean forward with the degree of incline."[56] This concern with "mechanics" was connected to increased attention to limbs, to lassitude and to gait. Moreover, following the lead of Leonardo da Vinci,[57] painters were exploring the differences between various types of exertion, how they affected pivot points and supports, and how actions were depicted in the lines of the body and in the way a subject might bend or grip an object. André Félibien made an important distinction when he advised artists in the middle of the seventeenth century: "When you paint these kinds of actions, the effort has to appear even greater if the limb that is exerting itself in the act of pushing or pulling is farther from the body's center of gravity."[58]

These considerations became more prominent once the mechanical studies of the seventeenth century inaugurated a "science of machines," exploring levers, shafts, planes and power. The old world of "almost approximately" was getting closer to precision.[59] The burgeoning complexity of the earth as compared to the heavens could be calculated and ordered. This was a significant step now that the planets above were no longer the only example of precision. Everyday vectors became subject to geometry. Physical movements were differentiated along a specific axis. Laws could unify places and things. Galileo pointed out that the "fatigue" involved in going down a staircase (and not only going up) was due to the effort of muscles supporting the weight of the body's skeletal structure.[60] A few decades later, Alfonso Borelli defined the body's "center of gravity" and noted, with explanatory measurements, that carrying a load aligned with the center would be less fatiguing than carrying one outside it.[61] In 1680, Daniel Tauvry, using the analogy of levers, posited that holding something with one's arm outstretched was more fatiguing than holding something with a bent arm.[62]

Philippe de La Hire, a member of the Royal Academy of Sciences, assessed the efficiency of winches and cranks, basing his calculations on their circumference or their length. He demonstrated that the input of physical force could be decreased if one adjusted those factors. The economy of effort was the point – in particular, depending on muscle power. The images of gigantic machines suggested that workers could prevent fatigue by using only their bodies as counter-weights to activate cogwheels and pulleys. Huge shafts meant that workers standing up to push them would increase their efficiency. Gears in progressively larger sizes and chains in particular widths would affect the amount of physical force necessary: "The thicker the cable, the smaller the wheel or roller, the more force is needed to move or support the weight."[63] This was the same answer that La Hire gave King James II of England when the latter visited the Paris Observatory in 1690. Thickness or thinness mattered when producing the most "effective force" in capstans.[64] This was a significant conclusion supported by evidence. Hélène Daffos-Diogo saw it as the birth of the science of ergonomics.[65] Thus, the body was mechanized along with life in the modern world; angles and vectors were calculated, theories were developed, and expenditures of effort were ranked hierarchically. Methods for carrying and lifting weights were scrutinized. It is hard to judge the impact of all this on the world of work, even if cranes, hoists and "mechanized" haulage of heavy loads were becoming more common. And in art? Many delicate engravings displayed a kind of abstract geometry rather than a geometry of workshops. People and their arms and legs were erased. Chains and motors stopped at objects that are displaced, rather than on straining muscles. The "human motor" itself was rarely depicted or mentioned; only machines were. Still, a new culture was emerging, one that was more physical, more calculated and more planned than applied. Its influence would soon lead to a major rethinking of assessment.

Work and the beginning of quantified evaluation

A new context was key: the productionist politics of Colbertism, intent on reducing royal expenditures. The projects meant to be "monumental" that were undertaken in the second half of the seventeenth century were also illustrative. One example was the attempt to divert the waters of the Eure River near Maintenon in 1686 to feed the fountains and waterfalls of Versailles by means of a "majestic aqueduct."[66] The ambitious construction involved moving tons of earth, reshaping valleys and securing the foundations of bridges. Louvois' plan, submitted to Vauban for approval, was precise, expressed in numbers and quantities: "We will need to excavate 700,000 to 800,000 square yards of soil. Kindly enclose an estimate of how many troops would be needed to do this excavation over a period of three years, if we begin on April 1 and end on November 15 of each year."[67]

This was quite different from medieval plans, such as Richelieu's request a few decades earlier in 1638, when he asked his generals to proceed with construction projects reinforcing Casal and Pinerolo in Italy without any estimate of the costs: "I would like you to reinforce the fortifications of these places; whatever funds are needed for this will be neither refused nor criticized."[68]

Louvois, on the other hand, also wanted advance notice of the cost of laborers' salaries, asking for an estimate, since the excavators would be "paid by the square yard of soil they remove."[69] This was virtually impossible to predict and would have had to be only an approximation, but the minister intended to analyze everything mathematically: workers' labor and its cost, the length of time the work would take and its final result. This was also meant to prevent cost overruns: strains on the royal budget and wasted effort by laborers. As a result, he insisted on periodic assessments and regular reports "of conditions every fortnight,"[70] covering the number of men employed, the amount of earth moved, and the expenses incurred. Checks and double-checks began. Numbers and reports piled up. Vauban weighed in on them. One detail angered him: the fact that results varied among the work crews and workshops. The results were not uniform and neither were the costs. Even worse, the project in the Eure valley was staggering under its own weight, with discouraging setbacks and an epidemic of disease. The gargantuan project was abandoned in 1688. Saint-Simon saw its premature demise caused by toxic miasmas expelled from the soil, diagnosing "the men perishing from rough work and, even worse, the exhalations of so much disturbed soil."[71] For his part, Vauban saw it as a necessary exercise in crunching numbers and attempting entirely new approaches to rationalize work and the work process. It was an opportunity to institute heretofore untried methods of evaluation combining numbers and observation.

This led to more questions: How to make measures uniform? How to reliably obtain the most favorable results without excessive strain on workers? In 1688, the Alsace workshops provided a locus of experimentation. The workshops were enormous, the challenges were significant and the results were strategically important. For France, the need to reinforce and extend military defenses in the east was highlighted after the sacking of several towns and villages in the Palatinate by French troops in the Nine Years' War. Persistent threats of retaliation by the armies of the Holy Roman Empire clashed with France's expansionist aims and led to an urgent push to reinforce the citadels at Mont Royal, Fort-Louis, Belfort and Phalsbourg. For Vauban, these projects offered the promise of achieving what was left undone at Maintenon: to "establish norms of realistic productivity," to evaluate "the reasonable amount of work a man can accomplish in a day."[72] Knowing that would enable costs to be standardized while allowing laborers to recover from their exertions. The projects in Alsace encouraged this type of planning since they were limited to excavation, earth-moving, and constructing earthworks, as work crews performed the same actions over and over. There was no precedent for the type of mathematical and mechanistic analysis Vauban favored, but he claimed he could get the necessary information by looking at averages and simplifying the accounting, such as coming up with the number of wheelbarrow loads and the amount of earth excavated by a man of "inferior muscle power"[73] who kept at it persistently. The engineer Guy Creuzet de Richerand had collected this data at the building site in Sarrelouis, and Vauban obtained them from the work on Fort Saint-Louis. Such painstaking data collection was unheard of.

Looking at the numbers in total, the future marshal of France concluded that "between 220 and 233 wheelbarrows were needed to transport a cubic fathom of soil [6.13 cubic meters]."[74] To estimate the time necessary for the job, he allotted eleven hours for a man – in other words, one workday – to excavate two cubic fathoms of 'loose soil' and eleven hours to propel the wheelbarrow 30 kilometers on flat ground and 19.5 kilometers uphill (round trip). In this way, he established a norm that served two purposes: to calculate the cost of labor and to assess the results. It hardly mattered that the calculations were petty and the expectations stringent; "likely" results would be calculated in a similar manner. Further refinements to the formulas were also factored in, such as the difficulty or "consistency" of the soil and the depth of the excavations, so that additional workers could be brought on to deal with "impenetrable" ground. Other refinements addressed questions of the effect of rest periods on the work result.[75] For the first time Vauban established uniform criteria for the construction of earthworks and calculated the maximum output achievable without exhausting the workforce: "I find that work can be organized in the following way: Begin, for example, at five in the morning and work until eight. Stop work from eight to nine. Start again from nine to noon. Stop work until two in the afternoon and work until seven in the evening. All told, that makes ten work hours and three hours of rest per day."[76] This proposed timetable was much more significant than previous orders that mandated workers' presence at work sites "from four in the morning until six in the evening, a total of fourteen hours,"[77] with no specified rest periods. Even more important was Vauban's decision to impose different work hours in summer and in winter, reducing the requirement in winter from a ten- to a seven- hour workday. These mandates introduced calculation and precision into a realm where intuition and approximation ruled. It is "pioneering" also in explicitly distinguishing between acceptable and intolerable conditions:

> For the four winter months we can shorten dinner and tea breaks and thereby reduce the workday to seven hours. During that time, I am convinced workers will never accomplish more than the equivalent of a half day's labor in the summer because of the cold and the inclement weather. I insist that we not burden soldiers with anything beyond their assigned duties … If we pressure them more, we will anger them, they'll become susceptible to illness and be unable to work for long periods.[78]

This new approach took into account what is likely and what would be the reasonable, valid limits on work. The dream of one single calculation to determine tasks, the length of the workday and the amount of fatigue this would spare was still an unattainable goal. The approach is limited, focused on one type of project and leaving its applicability to others an open question. It was also an empirical calculus, ignoring many of the variables in particular circumstances, such as the difficulty of the terrain, the work sites' location, the steep hills and jagged depressions. The approach also never defined what was meant by "average exertion." It was indicative of the new interest in quantifying aspects of work, but it also revealed the difficulty of factoring in all the variables that affect work. We see here a "lack" and the impossibility of including all the data. "Blurring" is inevitable when we recognize the impotence of mathematical solutions, despite one's desire to apply them. Vauban disrupted the requirements of precision even while he upheld their continual dependence on the "best guess." These innovations were nevertheless historic. The fortress builder transformed the huge expanses of earthworks into sectors for observation and accounting. Work had never been studied like this before.

10

Diversifying Influences

The world of fatigue was changing along with modernity, including new degrees, new classifications, and the first attempts at using numbers. There were more observations and even more categories. Fatigue changed because of the attention focused on influences, on symptoms, and on possible ill effects. The innovation of "classical" approaches came from their observations of the effects of fatigue and its negative consequences that seemed more important and more serious.

"Painful" adaptation

First of all, the "marks" that fatigue left on the body took on new significance, in particular the effects of exercise and subsequent feelings of exhaustion. Some observations in the seventeenth century, not many but notable, focused on the soreness of one's arms and legs after a period of sustained exertion, and also diffuse sensations of pain and tightness. For the first time commentators associated these symptoms with unaccustomed activity and the "shock" caused by doing something that is not habitual resulting in "pain," discomfort and stiffness. The personal experience of two young Dutchmen in Paris in the middle of the seventeenth century gave an example of this. The two described their visits to riding academies where, as amateur equestrians, their actions resulted in pain and swelling at specific sites:

> We rode three times every day, not counting the practice in the riding ring. This exercise was so demanding at the beginning that we couldn't do anything else until the pain in our thighs had receded; it was so acute at first that we could hardly walk. To console us, an expert explained that it would last for about a fortnight, and that was in fact the case.[1]

The two Dutch visitors' experience didn't prompt any specific scientific studies of these symptoms, which were actually quite vague and weren't investigated systematically, but a new awareness foregrounded symptoms like these in a way they hadn't been previously. In fact, François de Rabutin attributed the death of a number of soldiers in 1551 to excessive exertion after a "long period" of inactivity. The troops were marching between Metz and Lunéville, but their "dissolution in idleness and debauchery" had not prepared them for a march they should have "long been training for."[2] Here we see the beginning of an awareness of the concrete effects of new or unusual activity. The body that wasn't habituated to new or unusual activity was weak and would break down.

The exclusivity of the "pathological"

The effects of all kinds of exhaustion were being explored more generally. Connections were being made and a variety of explanations offered. Nevertheless, the belief that a body was made of fluids persisted in Europe during the "classical" period, as did the idea that fatigue was caused by a loss of humors. But observers' more acute attention, even if it was still entirely subjective, led to different conclusions.

Many different examples illustrated this. For instance, when Queen Jeanne III of Navarre died at the age of forty-four in 1572, her passing was blamed on the efforts she made in "an extraordinary task": the preparations for her son's wedding.[3] Then, the sudden onset of Henri III's earache in 1580 was attributed to various unsavory activities: "He spent entire nights carousing and gallivanting and in other activities that were not conducive to good health."[4] Finally, the duc de Berry's nosebleed in 1698 was said to be brought on by his "overheating" during a partridge hunt.[5] These unexpected ailments were explained by the links to excess and bodily humors. More strict attention was paid at this time to "malfunctions" of humors and their serious and unforeseen consequences, such as "lumbago" among other ailments. Giorgio Baglivi diagnosed it almost symbolically as "a flow of blood seeping into the muscles"[6] after any kind of overexertion. Another danger related to liquids was identified: having a cold drink when one's humors were "disturbed." Countless anecdotes were published of people suffering from "pneumonias" or "coagulating or suddenly thickening blood" because "they thoughtlessly drank cold water after strenuous exercise."[7] The account by Lazare Rivière in 1646 illustrated medical authorities' befuddlement at the diversity of diagnoses of one man, Monsieur Petit, and his ailments, as well as their line of questioning:

> Monsieur Petit, resident of Montpellier, fifty years old, with a bilious temperament, was overwhelmed with business stresses and worries, then exhibited several symptoms of hypochondrial melancholia. He had a tumor under his collarbone on the right about the size of half an egg. It was soft to the touch and the same color as the rest of his skin, which throbbed persistently; it was thought to be an incurable aneurism.[8]

Many other organs were affected. His heart "was greatly irritated by strenuous exercise, by heat, by bathing and sexual intercourse, by intoxication, by drinking strong wine and by quarreling."[9] His lungs were threatened by consumption after bathing, exercise or anger."[10] His brain suffered from "the heat of the sun, excessive exercise, and anything that agitated or heated up the humors."[11] We see an inventory of disparate triggers for illness here: heat, bathing, fatigue, and overindulgence in sexual intercourse.

The travails of workers were rarely mentioned. Although they were generally overlooked, some attention was paid to them, primarily in medical literature. In the middle of the sixteenth century, Georgius Agricola, a doctor in Joachimsthal, Bohemia, and an acute observer of the local mining industry, described the "ailments" and "pains" of miners, who were "tough men, inured to work since childhood."[12] The "maladies" he wrote about were more serious than fatigue: asthma, lung damage, ulcers, eye irritation, drowning, falls, even destructive demons in the deepest mineshafts. Several decades later, François Ranchin delved into the "ailments" and "pains" of post riders, who suffered from some specific occupational pathologies: "raw sores on the buttocks," "burning urine," "hot blood" and "low spirits." Troubles with eyesight were caused, he concluded, by the riders' constant exposure to bumps and jolts on the road, not by eyestrain.[13] At the end of the classical period, Bernardino Ramazzini explored the same topic, occupational hazards, in an impressive comprehensive study.[14] He focused carefully, chose his subjects judiciously and searched for memorable examples of illnesses.

Workers who did their jobs "standing up," such as carpenters, masons, ironworkers or sculptors, were liable to develop "ulcers and varicose veins" due to the pooling of arterial and venous blood."[15] "Miners" suffered from a disruption of their "animal economy" caused by the absorption of "metallic miasmas." Runners, servants whose job, even in the seventeenth century, was to precede the carriages and horses of the nobility, risked damage to the "respiratory organs" after becoming overheated. Gardeners may suffer from "wasting and dropsy"[16] from working in the humid environment of their plants. The ailments were all connected, at least the most visible ones, directly to an occupation and its "particular demands" and less obviously to general feelings of weakness, of a loss of strength, of being overwhelmed. In writing about occupations there seemed to be a willful blindness to categories of fatigue as well as the general conditions of all labor.

The disorders of dehydration

Bodily humors still played an outsized role in these analyses, in particular the effects of dehydration and the loss of fluids. One example is in François Bernier's account of his travels through the Mughal Empire, starting in 1650:

> During the eight or nine days of walking, sweating had leached away all my humors. My body was like a sieve, dry and parched, and I could hardly finish pouring a pint of water into my stomach (at the very least) before I would see it seeping out of my limbs, and even down to my fingertips like a fine mist. I think today alone I drank over ten pints.[17]

This painted an extreme picture of the unstoppable leaking of humors. At the end of the seventeenth century the writer Robert Challe was aboard the vessel *L'Écueil* heading to the "East Indies." He recalls of his fellow passengers that "the heat stops them from taking a breath, breathing burns the entrails,"[18] but "money is spent buying refreshments at the first landfall."[19]

Mme de Sévigné also worried about overheating and the effects of "lost" humors that would result in total collapse. Her concerns signaled the acute sensitivity around this issue, especially among the elite, of whom the marquise was a privileged observer. She wrote about the sun in Provence that turned the room of her daughter, Mme de Grignan, into "an oven,"[20] the games of chess that "harm us as they entertain us,"[21] the hot drinks, the poor food, her posture bent over her writing table that "is killing my chest,"[22] the air in Avignon that "irritates the throat,"[23] the winds blowing across the village of Grignan that "keep me awake"[24] and the ordinary "hustle and bustle every day."[25] Mme de Sévigné decried the situations, actions and positions that she believed were causing dryness and internal dessication, even though there was no objective proof for it and few popular accounts attested to it. Only one of the threats she mentioned referred to liquids and heat. Her unhappy vision was a synthesis combining "burning," "expenditure" and "erasure:" "I feel as if I see you without sleeping, without eating, heating up your blood, consuming yourself from within, hollowing out your eyes and your mind."[26]

"Obscure actions"

Finally, attention was also paid to erotic activity, which was more frequently mentioned in the modern period. "Serious" bodily fatigue was usually believed to lead to impotence. Agrippa d'Aubigné made extraordinary efforts to join his mistress in 1572, and, exhausted and sore after "a trip of twenty-two leagues," he arrived "numb, blind, with absolutely no strength,"[27] to collapse "into the arms" of the lady.

More generally, the aftermath of sexual activity was discussed in this context, with tips for overcoming one's exhaustion after the "exertions" of the night by, for example, ingesting "a broth and two fresh eggs."[28] A number of recommendations, ranging from taking food to taking a rest, from sniffing perfume to sipping a fine wine, from munching on sugared almonds to taking a spoonful of jam, are offered – all with the aim of reviving a "moribund" body.[29] Even though it wasn't described specifically, this sort of fatigue seemed terrifying, nonetheless. Tallement des Réaux described Mme Champré as a vixen driving her husband to the verge of death: "She was beautiful and charming; people said she couldn't keep her hands out of his breeches, so much so that he wouldn't last much longer."[30] The same explanation was given for the death of Louis XII in January 1515. At the age of fifty-two, on October 9, 1514, at Abbeville, he married Mary Tudor, the teenaged sister of King Henry VIII. The downfall appeared unavoidable: "He wanted to be his wife's sweet companion; but couldn't because he wasn't man enough … And the doctors told him that, if he kept on doing it, he would die pursuing his pleasure."[31] Certainly the misogyny that was widely accepted at the time figured in this explanation, but a hard-to-define exhaustion also played a significant role. The "treatises" or "miscellaneous lessons" published by scientists or literary men in the sixteenth century offered numerous examples of such doomed individuals, whose "debauchery and lust" led to the "loss" of "strength and life."[32] Even King Solomon's "love for women" transformed him from a "very wise man" to a "very debauched one."[33] In the animal kingdom, some creatures' short lifespans were due to an "excess of lust." Sparrows, for instance, lived for only one year, according to Scipion Dupleix, but the males had intercourse "over twenty times" a day "with the females."[34] He drew the unavoidable parallel to human behavior, warning that, "for this reason, lusty and salacious men have shorter lives than others."[35]

This also underlay the belief that abstinence enhances one's vigor. Jacques-Auguste de Thou praised the exemplary Count Louis Diacette at the end of the sixteenth century:

> He was over sixty years old when he was killed; but since he had abstained from the usual pleasures of youth from a young age, he was still so hale and hearty that he slept in winter with wide open windows, with no canopy or curtains shielding his bed. He wasn't bothered by the cold, or by drizzling rain or fog, as if God had enabled him to preserve his strength (as he said) for such difficult circumstances.[36]

Associated with sin, bawdiness and debauchery, sexual activity was as much a danger as a pleasure.

11

The Diversification of Remedies

Methods to prevent illness had not changed with the onset of modernity, and the understanding of the body and its functions had not evolved either. Old-fashioned methods were still in fashion. The preferred approach was still to conserve liquids and restore lost humors. Nevertheless, the effects and categories of fatigue as well as their severity kept growing along with observations and personal accounts, prompting recommendations of measures to prevent and recover from fatigue and resulting in an array of remedies. More attention was being paid to subtle warning signs and fleeting feelings of discomfort, and, as a result, new, widely shared defensive strategies were being gradually developed.

Reinventing refreshment

The startling image of overheating was matched by the equally impressive image of refreshment. In the stream of letters offering advice to her daughter, Mme de Sévigné kept coming back to liquids: how to replace them, how to fortify the fluids inside. "My daughter, when someone cares about you, it is not silly to hope that the blood one also is concerned about is calm and refreshed."[1] That's why she advised her daughter to "drink cow's milk; it will refresh you and give you temperate blood."[2] Robert Challe was also eager to fortify himself during his ocean voyage by regularly stocking up on "refreshments at the first landfall."[3] Soldiers were also conscious of this need: they recalled, above all, taking over those enemy citadels that allowed them "to refresh and rid ourselves of accumulated fatigues."[4] The key thing was to restore lost liquids.

Paradoxically, a warm bath was also considered a way to restore oneself. When the pores in the skin opened up in response to the warm temperature, more water seeped into the body to compensate for any fluids lost through exertion. Advocates of thermal baths extolled their advantages: "All sorts of exhaustion are cured in the bath … moisturizing and softening parts of the body that are dry and stiff, replacing and rebalancing the humors. One is convinced that it is beneficial to combat fatigues."[5] The idea was that the bathwater infuses the skin and replaces the fluids that have been lost. The assurances came from a "thermal spa physician"[6] rather than a "city doctor," and thus did not indicate that this practice was common among anyone besides the upper classes at this time. Water was scarce in urban areas, its transport was difficult and its effect was "troubling," invading the body, disturbing it, leaving it "open"[7] and vulnerable to "toxins in the air." We find no mentions of tennis players or hunters relaxing in a bath after their exertions[8] and no bathtubs in the inventory of "doctors' furnishings in the sixteenth and seventeenth centuries."[9] The memoirs of neither Mme de Sévigné nor the princess des Ursins nor the princess Palatine recorded their bathing after a trip. Charles Perrault admitted this "gap" in comparison with the culture of thermal bathing in antiquity but emphasized that, for the moderns, fresh linen played a crucial role. "It is up to us to plunge into a bath, but the cleanness of our linen and the great quantities of it that we have is worth more than all the baths in the world."[10] Thanks to its cleanness or its softness, linen could refresh us by absorbing humors. Laurent Joubert was sure of this when he castigated "old wives' tales": "If you pay attention, you will see that everything is refreshed, revitalized and restored when you change your linen and outer clothing. It stimulates our spirits and enhances our natural warmth."[11] In other words, for the first time, undergarments contributed to the modern world's methods of "restoration."

Multiplying essences

New products associated with water or with clothing, as well as traditional spices believed to refresh the body or hot peppers intended to warm us up, were now discussed. The focus was on "spirits," the most volatile and "subtle" elements of humors, and an ability to stimulate the nerves and promote the physical transformation of internal fluids. Perfumes had this potential, and a vast array of subtle and new essences thought to be "reinforcing" were identified, with "volatile" elements believed to penetrate the nervous system. For example, "perfumed waters" infused with bergamot, marjoram, patchouli, or a "thousand flowers" were recommended, as well as alembic, celebrated since the Middle Ages for its quality of combining water and fire, but now regaining popularity. Benvenuto Cellini's lover Mme d'Étampes used them in the sixteenth century to prevent fatigue and maintain "the clarity of her skin."[12] "Rosemary oil" was recommended by Harlequin in his *Herb Garden* in 1624 because it treated heart palpitations, paralysis, tremors, slack nerves and even poison, even as it was "suitable to keep people hearty, attractive and youthful."[13] There is nothing new here in terms of traditional diagnoses and treatments of illness, but the understanding of humors was subjected to a variety of new approaches, and the cures took on new life with an array of distilled essences.

Wine has been reconsidered too. Theories abound about the "flower" that represented the "intoxicating" element and the liquid that "represents blood."[14] Fermentation techniques were perfected, harvests were improving and the "medicinal" effect of wine was enhanced. The "nectar" coming from sunlight was a metamorphosis of light. Jean de Thou, exhausted during his voyage between Antibes and Monaco in 1589, and suffering from bouts of intense nausea, found that he was completely restored by a "Corsican wine" and had "enough strength and energy to go with Gaspard de Schomberg to visit the city of Genoa."[15] More discoveries about wine followed. The sparkle and clarity of champagne suggested a combination of purity and delicacy, and the tapered shape and look of champagne flutes, mingling gold and silver tones, transformed the "pearls rising to the surface" into a promise of absolute perfection. Saint-Simon believed that Duchesne, physician to the king's daughters, had a long life because "he ate a salad every night and drank nothing but Champagne."[16]

Brandy took a turn in the spotlight now that its alcohol content rose, thanks to the distilling technology that had become more common. Martin Lister confirmed this when he visited Paris in 1698: "We can thank the years-long wars for this. Noblemen and lords who suffered so much from these endless campaigns turned to these liqueurs to help them withstand the fatigues of weather and night watches. Once they came back to Paris, they added it to their cellars."[17] Robert Challe also attested to its utility on board the ship sailing to the East Indies, recalling that it was given to sailors "after a tough job": "Brandy for securing the mizzen mast."[18] Many were relying on brandy's restorative powers, undoubtedly, but sometimes the situations were so banal that they are not worth describing.

From tobacco to coffee

In the sixteenth century, plants from the New World, just as those acquired through travels to the East, were thought to have similar curative powers. The use of dried tobacco leaves, following indigenous practices, is a prime example. Light and fragrant tobacco smoke stimulated the body, keeping it energized and in balance. Travelers from distant lands claimed that the filaments of burned tobacco infused one's nerves, endowing them with fiery energy. The Native Americans who inhaled tobacco smoke "through little tubes" could travel long distances, bear heavy loads and even seem to experience a sort of ecstasy: "They inhale tobacco smoke, seem to pass out, then wake up feeling reinvigorated after their rest, with their powers fully restored."[19] European observers predicted that tobacco would have the same effect of enhancing strength and endurance. Le Royer de Prade described the king's soldiers following this regimen: "tolerating the fatigues of war without eating or drinking and only taking a half ounce of tobacco in twenty-four hours."[20] Tobacco was a multi-purpose remedy, especially useful against maladies such as "congestion in the head, gout, rheumatism, viscous humors and mucus ..."[21] Pierre Pomet, a Parisian spice merchant at the end of the seventeenth century, kept adding more miracle tobacco cures to each new edition of his *General History of Drugs*.[22]

Tobacco had even more uses, and this in turn spurred recognition of other ailments, such as new kinds of fatigue specific to modern life. Tobacco helped us remain vigilant and mentally alert. It "pacifies the brain," claims La Garenne.[23] It "clarifies our thinking," adds Corneille Bontekoe.[24] More generally, it absorbed the excess from overflowing and agitated fluids. Brienne suggested as much when he described Boileau's life and his vibrant health at the age of eighty: "He used tobacco all the time, day and night, chewing it to dry up superfluous humors. This kept him in such a hale and hearty state, one that few people could hope for at his age."[25] Tobacco augmented the mind's clarity, lengthened one's attention span, increased mental agility, and sustained one's engagement in business, administration or legal affairs.

It was perfectly attuned to combat the malady the seventeenth century called "mental fatigue."[26]

Other exotic seeds and leaves that were dried, burned or roasted follow a similar trajectory; coffee, tea and chocolate were quickly adopted in Western Europe in the classical period. Thévenot was one of the first to write about the beneficial effects of coffee that he observed during his travels in Arabia in the middle of the seventeenth century: "When our French traders have a lot of letters to write and they want to stay awake all night, they drink one or two cups of coffee."[27] This particular advantage was key; the stimulating plants from distant lands underlined the dominance of the new realm of fatigues in modern life, ever present in the suffering imposed by city life, the demands of life at court, in the legal system, in trade, and in offices. Nicolas de Blégny alluded to this when he asks for substances that will "soothe scattered minds, unblock our obstructed nerves, enhance our memories, steady our judgments, and give us strength and happiness."[28]

The evolution of coffee culture was notable in this context. Soliman Aga first brought it to Paris in 1669. He himself was an accomplished con man who claimed to be an ambassador of Mehmed IV, sultan of the Ottoman Empire. The "stimulating" properties of coffee were quickly recognized, and drinking coffee to wake up came close to being a ritual. At the end of the seventeenth century, Saint-Simon described the "coffee services" at Mme de Maintenon's residence where groups of guests would gather around a small round table topped by a tray of these new drinks: "We stood near several cabarets [tables] of tea and coffee and served ourselves."[29] And an entirely new establishment was created in London and Paris after 1670. The "coffee house," a home for casual meetings and lively conversations, used the Ethiopian bean for two purposes: enjoyment and stimulation.

An emblem of social and cultural change, the "coffee house," with its fumes of roasting beans and dissolving sugar, differed from taverns and cabarets selling alcohol. The interior, decorated with mirrors and polished wood, hosted merchants, writers and other members of the middle class: "One sees intelligent people who come to relieve their minds of the stresses of the office," notes Louis de Mailly.[30] The prices determined the clientele. In Paris, the Procope sold a cup of coffee for 2.5 sous in 1672,[31] when a laborer earned between 3 and 6 sous a day.[32]

The effect of the brew was associated less with the shock of a spice or the intoxication of wine and was tied more to mental acuity, a clear mind and an agile brain. Like tobacco, which was meant to relieve fatigue, coffee consumption was supposed to break up the "clouds" of internal fogginess. Its effect was physical and "cerebral" at the same time, enhancing endurance and mental dynamism. Jules Michelet[33] found it to be an almost historic phenomenon: the black beverage versus the red liquor; "alertness" countering "inebriation." Even the English Puritans[34] saw it that way:

> When the sweet Poison of the Treacherous Grape
> Had Acted on the World, a General Rape …
> COFFEE arrives, that Grave and Wholesome Liquor
> That heals the Stomack, makes the Genius quicker …
> And cheers the spirits without making us mad.

This was a cultural sea change in which the values of reason and order took on added significance and stimulation brought new "territories" into play. In other words, rationalism was on the rise, and, with the onset of modernity, it seized on its fatigues as well its remedies.

Making existence more tolerable: a popular response

There was a less visible innovation that was little described or commented on, but it was notable because it was more explicitly material: the "surreptitious" attempts to reduce women's burdens by raising the age of marriage, and decreasing the number of births and the strains of nursing and raising children by reducing "fertility." These were changes that affected ordinary people and everyday lives. This cultural change affected the poorest of the poor despite their lack of a voice. It affected people's bodies. Even a few years' delay in marriage was influential, since that affected reproduction, limiting investments over the long term and even profound suffering. We see this in England in the sixteenth century, and it spread to Central and Northern Europe a century later. The awareness came slowly, but it had significant consequences. It took several years before it became "the key to the prior demographic system."[35] The median age of marriage rose from less than twenty to over twenty-four in one century for the women in the Paris region;[36] from 19.1 to 23.4 between the years 1578–99 and 1655–70 for women in Athis;[37] and from 18.9 to 22.3 between 1560–9 and 1610–19 for women in Bourg-en-Bresse.[38] Cities, in fact, had later marriage ages than rural areas, since awareness was more acute and limitations were less tolerated in urban settings. Women in Saint-Malo and Lyon around 1700 married at twenty-seven or later.[39] Delay in marriage could reach almost eight years, depending on the area over the century. The "natality of the rich and powerful," who still enjoyed financial stability and domestic help, was still "greater than that of the poor."[40] This was the first "Malthusian revolution"[41] and was a widespread but little articulated response to fatigue. There was no victory over illness or death in this new definition of marriage age; there was a reduction, however minimal, of the usual trials and tribulations of daily life. At end of the day, this behavioral change was an unheard-of strike against "life's burdens" and fatigues.

We can see no new image of the body in this step toward modernity and no new discoveries transforming our understanding of fatigue. Yet, it had been diversified. Curiosity about it had increased. The "tolerable" old ways had become less "tolerated." A "normality" had been displaced. This was clearly a cultural shift, even if the landmarks and the explanations had not changed.

12

Poverty and "Exhaustion"

A range of fatigues was identified in the sixteenth and seventeenth centuries along with a variety of remedies. A number of new vulnerabilities, rarely discussed in the past, were looming on the horizon of classical Europe that affected the poorest of the poor and were rooted in rural areas, the "deserts" that afflicted a level of society that was usually ignored. An impression of "widespread" deprivation and of generalized impoverishment is evident and, although the image was not specific, it pointed to heretofore unacknowledged distress. This new face of poverty emerged only at the end of the seventeenth century, when the deprivation that had long been hidden, and even despised, started coming to light.

Destitution

This new consciousness had a particular context: a vision by leaders such as Colbert and Louvois of enhanced national productivity and wealth, based on the efficiency of labor and the potential of the land and the people who worked it.[1] As a result, a new realm of disability came to the fore, one that was above and beyond the "subtle" fatigues acknowledged by classical era elites or the more "common" ones that people had partly rejected or overlooked. It was associated with less visible threats: poverty, anemia, food shortages. All these obstacles to profitability reflected a group weakness or almost collective "fatigue." We should not assume that the social value of low-status people was rising at the end of the seventeenth century, or that more attention was being paid to the miserable conditions of workers. In fact, the change in focus can be traced to images of extreme poverty, of "intrinsic" helplessness, and a belief that this was an endemic condition caused by the vagaries of geography and the climate, the ravages of war, or even the false expectations affecting daily life and productivity. At the end of the century

La Bruyère presented a tragic and dehumanizing vision of the misery of peasant life: "wild animals, the males and the females, roving the countryside, black, mottled, sun-burned, tied to the soil that they delve and scrape with unshakable stubbornness."[2] Particular circumstances, such as the food shortages at the end of the century, colored this abysmal image. Local administrators and lords of the manor described the horrors they witnessed, and some accounts were even backed up by numbers. In Limoges in 1692: "the vast majority are forced to uproot ferns, dry them and grind them up for food. People get so weak that they die from starvation, and the mass deaths may in turn cause an epidemic."[3] In Reims in 1694: "at the present time the city is in a calamitous and miserable state … Everything we've done hasn't prevented the deaths of more than four thousand from weakness and starvation over the last six months."[4] The damage inevitably persisted and multiplied in an economy with little capacity or incentive for stocking reserves of essentials. Among other disasters, the poor harvests of 1693–4 affected the profits of landholders, which damaged the markets and devastated tradesmen and shopkeepers: "directly and indirectly, famine leads to slaughter."[5]

Mass vulnerability

Recognizing and recording these kinds of catastrophes didn't begin at the end of the seventeenth century. Disasters and "climate crises"[6] wreaked havoc in past eras. At the beginning of the seventeenth century, the epic poem "Les Tragiques," by Agrippa d'Aubigné, vividly evoked the desperation of people reduced to eating "grass, carcasses and raw food."[7] Later, however, the view of the subject was transformed and the results were understood differently. It was analyzed more through the lens of economics, leading to a more "comprehensive" vision and condemned by a stricter central authority. Poverty itself seemed to be considered in a different light: "the new element at the end of the seventeenth century appears to be rooted in a realization of mass vulnerability, not the same as the secular consciousness of mass poverty."[8] An unexpected fragility was found at the heart of collective strength, and this development, seen as more tragic, awakened traditional fears of the danger of vagabonds spreading illness and violence. Newer anxieties were added, including the threat of work projects bogged down by exhaustion and enterprises halted for lack of funds. The letters directed to financial comptrollers illustrated this. For example, Rouen's chief steward was "astonished to see the weakness"[9] of port workers in Honfleur impeding the operations; the bishop of Mende reported on "the widespread exhaustion of laborers and the people in general," such that "some farmlands are not being cultivated and serious outbreaks of diseases are occurring."[10] The chief steward of Limoges found that "the population has been so beaten down by the past years' calamities that it is still very short of funds and even of labor."[11]

"Surcharges" of taxes and "weakening"

Vauban's memoir in 1696 was one of the most eloquent on this point. Writing about the election at Vézelay, he evaluated current income and future resources, carefully assessing "revenues" based on "the quality and customs of the inhabitants" while aspiring to "an increase in the population and also in their herds and flocks."[12] One preliminary observation appeared neutral and even conventional, though moralistic: "poorly cultivated fields ... idle and careless inhabitants," some fields almost abandoned, with "weeds and brambles" taking over and rocks and gravel encroaching on the soil. The neglect was attributed to age-old woes, but Vauban's account quickly shifted to an inventory of the current causes and issues. This sort of deprivation "is apparently due to the food they eat, because what we call the lower class eats nothing but bread made of barley and oats ... We should not be surprised if such malnourished people are so lacking in strength."[13] Their clothing was pieced together from "ragged worn cloth," and they went "barefoot all year round,"[14] shod only in clogs, aggravating their poor physical condition. A subterranean fatigue that was never directly identified afflicted these presumably "idle and feckless"[15] people. Every day it held them in a tighter grip.

No one doubted the causes of this poverty. However, the solutions Vauban proposed to eliminate it were usually dismissed out of hand: lowering taxes and correcting the "abuses and mistreatment in the collection of tithes."[16] These reforms would ensure a "genuine respite for the kingdom."[17] Fatigues could be overcome, strength would succeed weakness, and work would win out over despondency. The nation's greatness would increase: "Because when the common people are not so downtrodden, they will marry more fruitfully, they will dress and eat better; their children will be hardier and better behaved; people will manage their own concerns, and in fact will work harder and longer when they see that the bigger share of the profits will be theirs."[18]

Vauban identified a problem of generalized weakness, and his program aimed to restore workers' endurance and vigor, instill these qualities in future generations and ensure healthier, longer lives. For him, population equalled prosperity: "One of the most certain indices of a country's wealth is the great number of its people, just as the loss of population is a clear signal of the opposite."[19]

PART III

THE ENLIGHTENMENT AND THE CHALLENGE OF THE PERCEPTIBLE

The seventeenth century extended the reach of possible fatigues as well as proposing new remedies for them. There were more and different causes of fatigues and preventive measures had been reinvented. The landscape of languor had become more extensive and had even been redefined. Nevertheless, the concept of humors and their loss persisted, without their substance being clarified. The work of measurement and counting, despite its novelty, was at present incomplete and even random; it still was far from precise.

The depth of knowledge was different in the eighteenth century. The perspective had shifted, and the language had as well, even to the extent of encompassing "feelings." The "sensitive" Enlightenment man, the person who had lost touch with the Good Book and gained faith in himself, had to redefine himself in light of this new autonomy. For him, languor was transformed into a more intimate and more pressing phenomenon. It was the acute perception of the obstacles to initiatives, to freedoms, and also of the anxieties feeding back into each person's "feelings." This resulted in that uniquely new effort, a more individualized quest for affirmation, and thus a "modern," even "psychological" attempt to overcome fatigue in a deliberately "unreligious" manner. Fatigue became a challenge, and one had to travel the world, climb the highest mountain, and discover the unknown in order to fulfill the quest of feeling and understand it.

Just as the image of the human body had changed under the new lens of individualism, greater attention was paid to nerves and to stimuli;

flesh and its vitality attained new significance and were subject to new scrutiny, including the body's weak points, flaws and disabilities. This outlook was tempered also by pragmatism and a closer attention to methods as well as their drawbacks, to the intrinsic value of applied technology, of manufacturing and artisanal production. This led inevitably to an emphasis on efficiency and even "progress" in a world where opportunities and perfectibility were flourishing.

13

Feelings at Stake

Growing convictions about individual autonomy play a major role here, putting an "internal" limit on principles of action, reviving our sense of danger and of curiosity. More sources of weakness were acknowledged, pointing to the possible personalization of fatigue. In a crucial cultural shift, people's inner lives were more complex, with the individual at center stage, scrutinizing the self. Fatigue was considered primarily an ordinary "discomfort," an ill-defined disorder, but it soon became a challenge that affected our endeavors and the way we lived and conducted our lives. As a result, it was now more of a force in personal accounts and in literature.

"To listen to oneself living"

Of elites in particular, one essential aspect of liberation[1] was the affirmation of a "taste for a free life."[2] Past authorities were viewed with suspicion, and vulnerabilities were also being reassessed. Perceptions of weakness were gradually changing, and fragility was being humanized by making it more personal and individual. Weakness no longer signified our fallen sinful nature or the unbridgeable gulf between the world and the heavens that condemned us to "impotence" for neglecting the obvious.[3] It flowed between one person and the next, became more visible, reflecting on the individual, integral to his identity, present in his thoughts and affecting his perceptions. Because a person was limited to his self alone, he needed to understand himself as an object of "nature," become familiar with his states of mind and body, prioritize his own experiences, and analyze himself based on that evidence and not on an "elsewhere" that was acting on him.

The present was more vital and pressing, and the risk of failure was more acute. A phrase that crystallized that perception came to the forefront during the Enlightenment: the "sense of being"[4] that was a fundamental experience. In 1786, Victor de Sèze, a physician of the

Montpellier school and a future member of the Convention, defined it in his book on feelings as the "sense" that was "the basis for all the others"[5] and the core of "our self."[6] This concept shifted the conversation from the very Cartesian "I think, therefore I am"[7] to the very empirical "I feel, thus I exist."[8] This change of focus was essential. The person felt "his body constantly reminding him of its presence,"[9] as life meant hearing the "haunting melody"[10] of being. A key innovation was: "we love hearing ourselves live."[11] This changed the status of fatigue itself. It was no longer a simple accident originating outside the self or a many-faceted condition associated with particular places, circumstances, or even divine intervention. Instead, it could be part of one's personal existence and an inevitable companion in everyday life. Mme du Deffand recalled herself "wasting away" and confronting unavoidable obstacles in her daily round: "I got weaker and weaker; even the slightest exertion seemed impossible. I got up very late every day."[12] Julie de Lespinasse expressed her exasperation in her doomed relationship with Jacques-Antoine de Guibert: "I felt overwhelmed, with diminished spirits."[13] Mme d'Épinay acknowledged an inexplicable feeling of loss: "Day after day I felt my strength slipping away."[14] Sometimes, fatigue took hold without warning, coloring everyday actions and changing them into distressing ones, disrupting decisions and impeding actions. It became so commonplace that Marguerite Staal de Launay could begin a trivial anecdote in the 1730s with the phrase "One evening, I was more tired than usual ...."[15] This casual remark highlighted a point, and also women's voices, that had been neglected before.

The "story" of fatigue

New kinds of narratives reflected this attentiveness to fatigue in which suffering developed gradually, and, although people kept up their social activities, stages of fatigue were ever present, associated with a languor that was virtually a part of life. In particular, interactions at court generated these types of stories. The account of Baroness Oberkirch demonstrated this when she visited Versailles three times in the 1780s in the retinue of the "count and countess du Nord." Her memoir captured the general feeling of malaise: "This life at court was tiring me a lot; it was exhausting."[16] But the causes of her fatigue were more concerning and more persistent than the usual "court fatigue."[17] She recalled having to entertain "multiple visitors,"[18] "go to bed late," and "get up early,"[19] and all the while was not granted the "honor of sitting on a stool."[20] She also had to "dress"[21] and "get undressed"[22] in hoop skirts that are "incredibly heavy."[23] The visits "required by protocol" were always "painful and exhausting,"[24] such as the "great debauchery of a party at night"[25] or the walks at Chantilly "lasting till late" that could make her "awfully fatigued."[26] There were also "very tiring drives" between Versailles, Paris, the opera house ... The interminable dinners combined "fatigue and pleasure."[27] The memoir revealed more about the feelings and even the thinking of the baroness on their return to Versailles on June 8, 1780. She noted the supper, dancing and contra-dance, the massing of a "curious crowd" and the "prolonged" festivities. The group left the chateau only at 4 a.m., when the baroness admitted she was "really tired,"[28] comparing, with a certain envy, the faces of the "calm and placid" peasants they passed on the road at daybreak to the sight of the "weary faces"[29] of the courtiers reclining in their carriages. The distinction she drew between peasants and nobles was telling; her consciousness of a "caste" was tied to her blindness regarding the fatigues of the poor.

André Grétry, a prolific composer of comic operas at the end of the seventeenth century, also connected his awful feelings of exhaustion to an endless loop of aural cause and physical effect. His symptoms first appeared after he heard "a tune was sung too loudly"[30] in his youth. The same thing happened over and over for the next twenty-five years. After each of his productions, he suffered from bloody sputum, extreme anxiety and an overwhelming need for rest. He consulted doctors in Rome, Liège, Geneva and Paris, made many attempts to moderate his symptoms, and took the advice of Théodore Tronchin, a contributor to the *Encyclopédie* and physician to Voltaire and the duc d'Orleans. No matter what he did, the results remained the same: "After my last attack I lay on my back for forty-eight hours without moving or speaking. All told, it took me a week to regain my strength."[31] Especially among the elite, a distinctive concept was taking shape specifically about fatigue, and this perception brought ever more acute attention to bodily sensations.

Similar accounts were offered by soldiers and sailors (specifically, the ones who were literate) describing fatigue for the first time as a "condition" – in other words, a long-lasting state. For example, George Anson, an officer on the English vessel the *Centurion*, one of the ships chartered by the navy in 1740 to sail "around the world" challenging Spanish dominance, recalled an episode that lasted nineteen days. It began when the ship broke free of its moorings on September 22, 1742, "seized by an awful gust of wind"[32] during a typhoon when it was anchored off Tinian in the Mariana Islands, north of Guam, in the middle of the Pacific. It returned to its anchorage after long days of horrific "aimless" drifting. The first words of the chapter captured the seamen's strains: "Fatigues and suffering on board ship."[33] The difficulties cascaded: the need to continually pump out the water pouring in through the open gun ports; "three wasted hours" trying to raise the yardarm; then "the rigging gave way," leaving the men so exhausted that they abandoned it, "putting their own lives at risk."[34] For "twelve hours" on September 26, "a day of the cruelest fatigue," they battled "with all [their] might"[35] to pull up the dangling anchor. Finally, the yardarm was raised, and, with "such an enfeebled crew," they "could do no more" at the breaking point of "terrible fatigue"[36] when, on October 11, they caught sight of Tinian Island. All these incidents were scrupulously recorded, with dates and times noted, even though they did not represent any progress in their itinerary or success in reaching their goal. It was an interlude in the vast ocean voyage.

The originality of this account is due to a change in consciousness in which fatigue is understood as a personal phenomenon, a specific experience at a particular time, worth recording in a "daily logbook," in distinct episodes like a serialized novel. This lengthy account revealed, as its conclusion did, a "terrible fatigue."[37] We still find no acknowledgement here of psychological problems and their complexity, of dreams, illusions, breakdowns, or loss of the self of the kind endlessly examined in our modern life. Nevertheless, this presented a new, critical attentiveness to what a person felt.

Comforts and inconveniences

Less noteworthy but also visible was a new insistence, especially by elites, on discomfort. These could be transitory or permanent "states," such as feeling ill at ease, tired, or faint. However, the "condition" might simply be an annoyance that had previously been overlooked. James

Beresford inventoried them in a comprehensively detailed book that had a resounding success at the beginning of the next century. For instance, Beresford described the torments of insomnia that left a person with "eyes burning, head spinning," teeth chattering, arms and legs feeling leaden and numb."[38] On the other hand, too much sleep led to weak, flabby muscles and profound depression.[39] Other threats were not ignored. One might suffer from cramps or spasms[40] after sitting in an uncomfortable armchair or lying in a bed that is too short or too narrow. Spending hours in a room with a smoky fireplace[41] may lead to shortness of breath and feelings of suffocation. Speaking could result in "a dry mouth,"[42] and long evenings of socializing with unfamiliar guests made it hard to "confess one's fatigue."[43] This long list of "tribulations"[44] demonstrated how ailments were being re-evaluated and perceptions altered.

The letters Napoleon sent to Marie-Louise revealed a similar preoccupation, faithfully recording the state of imperial fatigue: "My dear, I arrived at Breskens yesterday evening, rather tired."[45] "My dear, I have reached Posen,[46] a little tired from all the dust." "My sweet, I am very tired."[47] "My dear, it is eleven o'clock at night and I am really tired."[48] "My dear, I seized Bautzen … It has been a good day. I am a little tired."[49] His condition was important enough to be mentioned in every letter and his feelings of weariness deemed more "valuable" than they were before, revealing that one's feelings were worth reporting in order to reassure, upset or simply communicate to another.

"Feelings" were also crucial in private spaces among the elite; the words "convenience" or "comfort" were emblematic of that significance. The recurrent phrase "the ability to live without fatigue"[50] emphasized its newly acquired status, and the search for such comfort led to new methods, equipment and techniques. In 1752 the architect Jacques-François Blondel claimed he was "absolutely mad about" his fatigue-banishing approach, even though his "predecessors were lax and neglected"[51] designs for domestic comfort. The home was reinvented, with new types of furnishings, proportions, and surfaces, focusing on arrangements that decreased the distance between objects and limited wasted movements inside a room or from one room to another. "Chests" were redesigned in different shapes, "circular" ones, "half-moon" shapes, "ellipsoids," "servers" and "side tables" in order to create cosy and convenient groupings and cut down on the need to move from one place to another.[52] Fireplace design became more sophisticated to prevent the accumulation of indoor smoke.[53] In 1765 an inventor advertised a device that would "keep fires from smoking."[54] Other innovations in home furnishings incorporated levers and springs to "animate" them with hidden mechanisms to raise, lower and incline them so their shapes and uses were endlessly varied. Ladies' "sewing tables" were embellished with shelves and drawers to hold different skeins of wool, thread, needles, pins and scissors. "Folding tables" were cleverly engineered to open into a desk, complete with metal-trimmed drawers and compartments.[55] "Secretary desks" unfolded into surfaces for writing and "painting."[56] "Dressing tables" had multiple tiers, drawers on the front and sides, and tops that slid back, exposing mirrors and inner compartments.[57] An ideal of "efficiency" led to the reimagining of everyday actions for the most affluent. English inventions were considered the most "advanced," and travelers exclaimed over the progress of the "mechanical arts" in England, where everything was "more convenient, simpler and better made."[58]

From aches to fainting fits

Medical practice reflected these same concerns. The emphasis on sensitivity influenced descriptive methods and decisively opened up and diversified perspectives that were introduced during the classic era.[59] The Enlightenment in turn focused on symptoms, on conditions and their names, and on causes and effects in an attempt to fine tune "nosology," the study of pathologies. This was a significant change: reworking the traditional nomenclature that identified an illness by its location, such as "ailments of the head, chest, stomach, legs,"[60] in order to explore the differences in the incidence and progression of a disease according to an "etiological method."[61]

"Aching" was now considered the first stage of fatigue and had a specific name and description. William Buchan's *Domestic Medicine, or A Treatise on the Prevention and Cure of Diseases by Regimen and Simple Medicines*, originally published in 1774, gave a standard definition: "dull pains in the limbs, in the back, in the kidneys, in the stomach … feverish feeling in the head, in the guts … agitation all over the body due to some kind of excess."[62] Certainly, this phenomenon wasn't first discovered at the end of the seventeenth century. Some writers had described it a century earlier,[63] and thus the general concept already existed, but now it had a name, a definition and an explanation. It was due to "clogged muscles, swollen blood vessels, lack of nervous fluid."[64] This condition had been neglected before. "No one discussed it," claims William Buchan;[65] it was cloaked in silence, adds Joseph Lieutaud[66] around the same time. Each examined the extent of the "malady" characterized by indistinct pains, vague impressions and hidden repercussions that highlighted the existence of an internal space that was traditionally neglected.[67] Other, similar phenomena began to be acknowledged by "classifying" doctors, who investigated symptoms and their severity. For example, in 1770, the *Dictionnaire portatif de santé* [Portable dictionary of health] included "aching" and also "weakness" that involved a "loss of strength so severe as to impede functioning,"[68] "exhaustion" in which a weakened patient "can barely survive,"[69] and "failure" in which "the vital forces are extinguished."[70] In addition, "faintness" suddenly "terminates all animal and vital forces and functions."[71] These descriptions were approximate, undoubtedly, conventional and even empirical, but they clearly revealed increased attention to these factors. More distinctions appeared in 1743 in the *Dictionnaire de Trévoux*, which noted not only the loss of humors but also that of patience and of ideas.[72] François Boissier de Sauvages' *Nosologie méthodique* in 1770–1 reached the outer limits of categorization, listing seventeen forms of exhaustion, eight varieties of languor, several types of "inflammation," and several kinds of "failure" and of "numbness," all of which fell under the grand classification of "weaknesses."[73] The numbers multiplied in a dizzying manner, all meant to identify and differentiate fatigues due to pathologies from other causes, since it was thought to be "important for a doctor"[74] to recognize every aspect connected with exertion, expenditure and excess. For this reason, the "nosologist" explained: "Exhaustion differs from malignant fever and general paralysis because of each one's symptoms, but we have not clarified this sufficiently before; we must not confuse exhaustion with languor, since languor is a discomfort that is complicated by exhaustion."[75]

One's feelings were a priority in elite culture, in particular the multiple forms and nuances of a "loss of energy" and its influence on all aspects of life. Buffon explained his precautions: "I seldom write because I don't want to tire my eyes, which have become progressively weaker during this year."[76] Beaumarchais wrote about this more subtly and perceptively: "Why is it that a melody that charmed me when played on the clavier is liable to annoy me and then fatigue me in the cathedral chapel?"[77] The prince de Ligne discovered that fatigue even entered his dreams: "I spend part of my nights on horseback, I, who ride so seldom, … I'm climbing a mountain as tall as a wall …"[78]

Nerves: From a Stimulus to a Whirlwind

Changes in understanding "sensitivity" were crucial and had profound resonances, especially among the elite, who view "sensitivity" differently. In a novella by the poet and dramatist Baculard d'Arnaud, Volsan confessed: "I was born sensitive; that is the source of my misfortune and my despair."[1] In Prévost's novel *Manon Lescaut*, des Grieux observed: "nobler people … have more than five senses" and are subject to "ideas and feelings beyond the bounds of nature."[2] One of Dr Samuel Tissot's patients told him in 1789: "I had, as we say, a very delicate sensory apparatus and overly sensitive nerves."[3] More attention was paid to internal tensions and the effects of stimulation with possibly fatal results: a breakdown, exhaustion, the blunting of reflexes. This in turn led to exploring other causes, other explanations and other approaches; new triggers, more vulnerabilities, and greater amounts of anxiety and dissatisfaction were found. Fatigue was experienced differently because it was explained differently.

Stimulations and currents

A new "physical" universe emerged that prioritized the "impressionable" and the excitable. The body was understood to house a cacophony of impulses and reactions, ranging from dynamism to tension, from enthusiasm to irritation. It was seen as an extension of a person's consciousness, expressing its highs, lows and agitations. This new perspective displaced our perspective on our internal selves as well as our perception of the outer envelope of flesh. The conception of a living being had changed. Fatigue was diversified and acquired new facets. Humors were no longer the accepted benchmark, so, instead of measuring their volume and tracing their dispersion, science was concerned with currents, their effects and their valence. The loss of fluids and the shrinking of the body-as-container was no longer a central concern. The focus was now on flesh and how it might lose or maintain its substance. Images that expressed the body's functioning were changed to adapt to other reference points and feelings. Diderot asserted: "Fiber [in the body] is like the line in mathematics"; it was "the basis for the whole machine."[4] In the 1720s, George Cheyne observed: "Some people have overly sensitive fibers, so flexible and prone to vibration, that they tremble violently at the slightest movement."[5] Potential vulnerabilities were being reassessed in relation to parts of the body, especially their firmness and resilience, and their degree of strength or weakness was based on the condition of their nerves and connective tissue. Experiments were also undertaken to test tensions and irritations. In 1778 Daniel Delaroche stimulated a frog's heart, causing "violent" contractions. After that, he found that "fatigue" rendered it "quickly impervious to any additional stimulation."[6] He concluded that exertion and the fatigue that followed it tended to "reduce the circulation of nervous fluids."[7] Scientists were starting to categorize exhaustion as a decrease or loss of muscular activity.

A technical innovation influenced this diagnosis: the discovery of electricity, a "newly open field"[8] of inquiry, with Joseph Priestley's claim in 1770 that "electric fluid is actively present everywhere."[9] Since electric fluid was stimulating, it could counteract "faintness and languor" and even "paralysis."[10] Many "experimental scientists" believed they could harness and direct its power. Witnesses claimed they felt "an extraordinary sensation" throughout the "entire body" after receiving "a series of electric jolts."[11] These "shocks" could interact, spread and be "controlled."[12] The Royal Medical Society concluded that, in stormy weather strikes provoked "a kind of weakness in humans and animals."[13] Their explanation of the phenomenon was turned into "proof" that electricity in the atmosphere was drawn out of living creatures and thus what had been the loss of fluid was now the loss of energy. An article in the French *Journal de médecine* confirmed this, citing personal testimony: "I felt that rainy weather made me sluggish."[14] The inverse also seemed true: "electricity speeds up the pulse."[15] "Electric treatments" were in vogue as an antidote for a weak body. In 1780, Pierre Berthelon even revived one of the oldest of old wives' tales in a new guise with the anecdote of a couple who recovered their fertility by attaching their bed to an electrical source.[16]

The attention to electric currents, stimulation, and the nervous system then gave rise to new associations with fatigue, such as feelings of exhaustion caused by excessive stimulation or "nervosity." In Samuel Richardson's novel *Clarissa, or The History of a Young Lady*, after being kidnapped by Lovelace, Clarissa Harlove's distress made her feel faint: "Terribly fatigued and her mind was more exhausted than her body."[17] Or when Manon Lescaut, "exiled" in America, confronted dangers, disappointments and sorrows that were difficult to assuage, she felt "languid and sapped of strength," but with a desperate final effort "got up despite her weakness."[18] Mlle de Lespinasse admitted she "has more feelings than there are words to name them" and "does not want to be cured, but only to find peace."[19] In 1782, Louis-Sébastien Mercier wrote about the "vaporous ones" in the Enlightenment whose "flabby bodies … rob their bodies' fibers of the elasticity necessary for secretions to circulate normally."[20] Thus, a collapse was followed by feelings of "languor" that turned into "torment" when "the person is still alive but his organs are destroyed and his nerves can no longer transmit sensations, which is their primary function."[21] Currents and stimuli formed the basis for these new benchmarks, and the "sluggishness" of weak or blocked reflexes was recognized as a symptom of exhaustion. Physical metaphors were still a mainstay in the discussion of fatigue, but they were not the same ones.

"Extenuating" stimuli

Causes were identified and analyzed differently. Cities were seen as agglomerations of noise and disorder, as they had been previously, but now they were also recognized as spaces for over-excitation and heated emotions boiling over into "giddiness" and sensory exhaustion. Buffon called city life "a spinning whirlpool" that "is dangerous,"[22] a "clamorous whirlpool" that travelers tried to "escape,"[23] and a "fast-moving and clamorous whirlpool." Louis-Sébastien Mercier decried the relentless imperative to keep moving, to hurry, to join in a "race" of "carriages," "porters," "grooms," "litigants" and even "wig-makers."[24] It all resulted in over-stimulated nerves and an onslaught of "fatigue caused by the spectacle of a city in perpetual motion."[25] The need to rush became a frenzied dash and then, inevitably, turned into exhaustion. As Rousseau observed, a busy city was an "anthill."[26] Court life remained, as it was before, a marathon of social obligations and protocols, but now it also inflicted an "over-stimulation of the senses"[27] and threatened "unbearable nervous crises"[28] because of disturbing and seemingly endless encounters with "various combinations of people, dispersing and getting back together,"[29] that taxed one's alertness and sapped vital forces. Memoirs of combat testified to its stressful nature, especially as the exhaustion of physical exertion was amplified by the sudden shocks of explosions, impressions of chaos and feelings of fear. In the middle of the eighteenth century, Ulrich Bräker, a Swiss peasant who was recruited by force into the Austrian army, described himself as being "literally dumbfounded"[30] during the battle of Lovosice in 1756 when he was hemmed in on all sides by fighting men before he managed to escape and hide deep in the forest. In the 1750s Frédéric Hoffman, a physician, was consulted by a "brave colonel" who was suffering from "a serious nervous collapse" and worn out from the "over-stimulation" of his body and mind."[31]

Doctor Samuel Tissot relayed the "disturbing" confessions of "exhausted" masturbators whose downfall came from the highs and lows of their self-stimulation and release. One patient's painful admission brought to light "an ailment in which extraordinary nervous sensitivity and the malaise that engenders is combined with weakness, distress and despair, afflicting [him] over and over again."[32] Tissot also reported a direct reference to nervous collapse: "My nerves are very weak, my hands have no strength and are always trembling. Sweat continually pours off my body."[33] The onanist was the perfect example of a collapse brought on by a "spasm," which itself represented "a complete loss of strength"[34] or "the nerves definitively letting go."[35]

In a medical journal, Frédéric Hoffman faithfully recorded the convulsions, pangs, aches and cramps of a man who "had experienced a lot of fatigue" after "sinning with women." Hoffman's account demonstrated the acute attention given to these types of symptoms and their association with a "nervous affliction."

> After meals [the patient] felt his skin crawl and a burning sensation in his arms and the joints of his fingers; then he felt a strange pain in his left shoulder. He suffered from spasms, painful cramps in his shoulders, his neck, and along the entire length of his spine such that, with every move he made, he heard a cracking sound. The palms of his hands were uncomfortably hot, but

> that feeling stopped as soon as the perspiration started to flow. He felt vague pains in the muscles around the rib cage; he had bowel movements only after an enema or a dose of Hoffman's balsamic pills. Flatulence tormented him, especially at night, and he felt an ache in his abdomen under the diaphragm, though the pain was milder than before. His saliva had a bitter odor, and it was hard to determine whether this came from tobacco use, since he was a heavy smoker, making him spit a great deal, or if the odor was caused by poor digestion and a residue of pancreatic bile. His appetite began to improve, and he wasn't too weak to ride his horse or go quite a distance without tiring. His night sweats stopped, he slept normally and his pulse was also normal but, despite this, his body didn't recover. In the morning, his urine was pale, almost lemon yellow, but around 10 in the morning the flow was reduced and had a reddish tinge. After a two-hour rest, there was a great deal of sediment in his urine that resembled red gravel and stuck to the sides of the urinal. Recently, in addition to the pains in his arms and hands, his joints were inflamed and a sharp pain coursed through his thighs, and sometimes, especially at night, his neck was very stiff until sweating loosened it up. He often felt a painful ache in his right eye and right cheek, which were also reddened. He exhibited neither an unusual thirst nor a racking cough, though at times he spit out a salty phlegm. Occasionally he produced pale stool and tended to sweat profusely. When he walks, he becomes short of breath, but sexual intercourse makes him feel better. From time to time, he expels a stiff blob of mucus from his lungs.[36]

This was a lengthy account, but the observations were novel and detailed.

Degeneration

This focus on sensitivity inevitably changed the map of our most common vulnerabilities. It increased the number of weak points and generalized them. In fact, the "modernity" of the Enlightenment is its emphasis on "stimuli" and "volatility." A question posed by the examiners at the medical college of Copenhagen in 1777 illustrated this: "If spasmodic ailments and convulsions have become more frequent in the last ten or twenty years, what treatments are best to cure them?"[37] Samuel Tissot also reported on an increase in "nervous ailments," which led to "languishing," in a "little canton" in the Swiss Alps after the 1760s. He associated this with a transition from active outdoor work to sedentary work indoors: from lumberjacking and porterage to crystal cutting and jewelry making, and from carrying out broad, sweeping movements to delicate, restrained ones. The difference was clear: "for over twenty years this place has the greatest number of ailments caused by languor."[38] Nervous afflictions had overtaken it. Weakness was commonplace. Sensitivity had changed once again.[39]

Scientists and literary men both gave the term "degeneration" a more prominent place in their lexicon during the second half of the eighteenth century. The concept was inspired by Buffon's animal studies, which found certain wild traits were eliminated because of domestication. Buffon concluded deterioration was caused by a lack of "stimulation." For example, the wild ram became a "timid lamb" when it was domesticated, penned in and living a sheltered existence. A domesticated animal was weaker and its body flabbier. Life in the city, its "comforts," crowds and tumult, had "changed our bodies"[40] too, making us deformed and feeble. Cities, General Jacques-Antoine-Hippolyte de Guibert asserted, were creating a "nation of cowards."[41] The "most common complaint nowadays" was a "weak, doddering, oversensitive temperament"[42] that led inexorably to "an actual degeneration of our constitutions."[43] The cause was "fiber that is too soft and thus nerves that are too sensitive."[44] The examples were plentiful. In 1778, Jean-Baptiste Moheau asserted that his enfeebled contemporaries couldn't wear the heavy suits of armor of their ancestors.[45] Ferdinando Galiani claimed that present-day men couldn't replicate the intrepid, historic travels of the "conquerors" in uncharted territories: "See how difficult it is for us to venture into the unknown in foreign lands … compared to how our ancestors fared. See how weak, anxious and dissolute we are."[46] Human frailty was put under the microscope. "It is obvious that the human race is gradually degenerating in Europe."[47] The *Encyclopédie* examined the "bastardization of the races."[48] The Anglo-Irish novelist Laurence Sterne satirized this phenomenon in *A Sentimental Journey*, writing in 1767 about a visit to Paris, where everyone is "extremely little – the face extremely dark – the eyes quick – the nose long – the teeth white – the jaw prominent" and "every third man a pygmy! – some with rickety heads and hump backs."[49] Life is in a terrible recession, with fewer births, rising rates of illness, and "so many miserables … arrested by the hand of Nature in the sixth and seventh years of their growth … like dwarf apple trees … never meant to grow higher."[50] However, there was only one explanation for this deterioration: city life, which was both constricting and stimulating.

Certainly, now that some public health threats had quietly receded during the Enlightenment,[51] a sense of untrammeled progress[52] created its mirror image, the fear of degradation and a more targeted, more anxious focus on its embodiment. People with disabilities, deformed bodies or club feet, whose presence had long been ignored or neglected on city streets and country roads, were looked at differently. They were less accepted. They were a disturbing sight that raised new questions: If our progress stopped? If this degradation took hold permanently? That fueled the impression that disabled people were more numerous and that renewed attention had to be paid to populations that were suddenly deemed more "precious" with the still halting growth of industry and the bourgeoisie's incoherent complaints about the old world's "exhaustion."[53] The debate grew among the elites: should they invest in the future or hold fast to the aristocratic past? This was an oversimplification, but the birth pangs of a new world had abruptly valorized collective forces and suggested a widespread restoration of "nerves." In the second half of the eighteenth century, Charles Vandermonde, the editor in chief of the *Journal de médecine*, asserted: "People are the wealth of the state and that is what is the most neglected."[54] An advocate for "regeneration," he urged: "We need to reshape our organs"[55] the way a baker molded and kneaded bread dough. "Public health"[56] was a newly coined expression, with the connotation that health and wellbeing were the state's responsibility. In 1767 Léopold de Genneté expressed a similar concern when he denounced the unhygienic conditions in hospitals, spreading infectious diseases that might cut short the lives of "curable" patients who were manual laborers, simple workers … so useful and necessary for our country."[57] For the first time the population was recognized as a factor, anonymous and voiceless, but one whose strength in numbers could help the state prosper and remain secure. For this reason, any widespread group fatigue was stigmatized and feared.

15

Speaking of Strength

In the 1760s, the idea that the state was responsible for the health of its people was primarily theoretical. Practical initiatives were rare and sketchily formulated. The state's primary aim was to "govern, control and pressure"[1] and not to help or provide assistance. However, new concerns had arisen around the question of "degeneration," along with new insights into the human body and its sensory apparatus – specifically how it functioned and how it was constituted. Interest continued to grow regarding people's strengths, their vulnerabilities, and the limitations of fatigue and disability.

During the Enlightenment two trends ran in parallel. They were hesitant and halting but nevertheless visible, prioritizing measurements of humans' ability to resist fatigue and also the limitations fatigue imposed on human activity. The trends pointed in opposite directions; one focused on interiority while the other made an equally critical turn toward exteriority. Buffon was one of the first scientists to raise these questions plainly: "Civilized men don't know their own strength. They don't realize how much they have lost from inactivity and how much they could regain with regular vigorous exercise," since now they "live in a society where the mind works harder than the body and manual labor is relegated to its lowest level."[2] This crucial observation showed a more acute understanding of people's physical potential, how it could be enhanced and what the limitations were. At the "lowest level of society," manual laborers' expenditure of energy had not been adequately evaluated, leaving aside Vauban's measurements, which were outdated and too narrowly focused on Alsatian workers.[3]

Enlightenment thinkers focused on progress and its potential for a better future. This question, a "specifically human" one that Rousseau defined as "the ability to improve oneself,"[4] brought about a relatively new emphasis on "more" and "better," on the value of abundance and exceeding one's limits. The intense curiosity about "how far man can go"[5] influenced contemporary views of things and of people.

So, two realms of thought developed that intersected at times but at other points remained isolated and independent. One centered on the fatigue caused by people's actions and the other focused on fatigues that were evaluated by observers. One was felt; the other was examined. Nevertheless, they were two sides of the same coin and a phenomenon whose contours were under constant scrutiny.

Questioning the limits

Observers seized on a new area of investigation, attempting to identify the "maximum" possible effort and thus explore heretofore unknown potentials. These new concerns led to new sources of evidence, new experiments and new proofs. This rekindled curiosity sparked exploratory ventures, trips into the unknown, and encounters with "other" people and lands.[6] Buffon's *De l'homme* [On man], published in the middle of the eighteenth century, demonstrated this. This multi-volume treatise on natural history recorded "racial" differences and described amazing feats of endurance achieved by non-European peoples. For instance, Buffon cited the porters known as the "pickers of Constantinople," who carried unbelievable loads "weighing up to nine hundred pounds";[7] the "runners of Isfahan," equally extreme, covered "thirty-six leagues in fourteen or fifteen hours"; and the Hottentots who were marathon walkers:

> They undertake long trips on foot in the steepest mountainous regions, bushwhacking through landscapes where there are no paths or tracks. These men, people say, can travel a thousand or twelve hundred leagues in less than six weeks or two months. Are there any animals, besides birds, that have stronger muscles in proportion to their size; is there any other creature that can endure such excesses of fatigue?[8]

Humans' limits were at the core of these inquiries to measure and evaluate the phenomena they encountered. Such investigations even extended to people's religious beliefs, with the example of the "natives of Loango" who, it was reported, claimed that the amulets they carried "reduce their fatigue" by making their bodies "lighter."[9]

Jean Désaguliers, an engineer and Huguenot émigré in London, had already attempted such measurements at the beginning of the eighteenth century. His observations focused on the weight a man can carry, the distance he can travel, and the speed and amount of time he can maintain the effort. He carefully noted the activities and numbers: "A porter can carry two hundred pounds and walk at the rate of three miles an hour; a coal-carrier or charcoal-porter can carry two hundred fifty pounds, but then he cannot go far to deliver his load although he does often walk uphill carrying it."[10] These systematic empirical observations were comparable to Vauban's reports on laborers,[11] since they looked at similar activities and loads. Fatigue was not explicitly measured even if the jobs were carefully and minutely assessed. Nevertheless, the definition of what is humanly "bearable" was calculated, using criteria such as the pace of work, the amount of force required and the time spent on the task. The approach adopted would remain influential for a long time, since it weighed several characteristics of the actions and the bodies performing them, from speed to strength and from endurance to agility.

Initiating an inquiry

These questions gradually revealed more ambitious intentions. Exploring sensitivity led to examinations of work and the work environment, but the detailed study of labor also gained momentum through the anxiety sparked by contemporary "degenerations," distortions and "deformations." It was influenced too by the increasing status of "utilitarianism"[12] and of "energy,"[13] represented by the "stereotypical image of the Englishman …, the prototype of the energetic man as depicted by authors from Voltaire to Mme de Staël."[14] The world of work, which had been overlooked for so long, was now acknowledged and accorded a new status. Economists began to view it as a source of wealth, and, along with landholding and commerce, labor was recognized as a social good and collective resource. "It was as if work was something that was an abstract and functional invention."[15] As a reserve supply of energy, it had the potential to change the world and was acknowledged as such in an increasingly realistic, pragmatic manner. This was no longer the world where classic "knowledge" reigned alone. Power was shared with the "how to" of the efficiency-minded empiricists.

Fatigue began to be recognized as a factor in the equation and was studied along with workers' capacity for endurance and the strategies or "tricks of the trade" they adopted to deal with difficulties on the job, even if factory inspectors who held the upper hand still prioritized output over other concerns. "The painful experiences of all these people … never aroused their compassion."[16] However, changes would come, and earlier descriptions of work-related diseases by observers such as Bernardino Ramazzini[17] gained new relevance in contemporary studies of labor. Baroness Oberkirch's overly facile view of the happiness that aristocrats could read in a peasant's face would finally be revisited.[18] At this time, writers, doctors, scientists and Enlightenment thinkers were eager for practical proofs.[19] They were exploring a new territory that encompassed customs, professions and physical injuries in ways that were far removed from Vauban's study of porters and roadworkers.[20] Empiricism was key, without a doubt, but so were rough calculations. The motions workers made were considered in a new light and "broken down into steps, annotated like choreography for a dancer."[21] An "elite" had assumed the still ill-defined role of "engineer" or "labor theorist." These time and motion studies were speculative for the most part, but they were a sign of renewed interest in making and doing. The *Encyclopédie* made the study of the technical "arts" an indispensable route to knowledge: "We must look to artisanal work for the most admirable evidence of human wisdom."[22] The French Royal Academy of Sciences designated the "Description of the Arts and Trades" a primary goal.[23] The *Dictionnaire universel des arts et métiers* [Universal compendium of arts and trades] asserted that to analyze technical arts is to renew and revitalize the culture: "All the articles we have published on technical subjects are merely scratching the surface in comparison with the depth and breadth of the field."[24] Explorations were launched, observations were intersected and conclusions were drawn. The studies were mainly modest in scope because they were coming from theoreticians, not practitioners.

The first time and motion studies concentrated on laborers and a variety of tasks, comparing workers' actions, tools and methods in order to zero in on the ones that were more efficient and less taxing. This hesitant, stumbling beginning changed over time since, unlike previous investigations, it had a "practical" goal. As a result, more studies were being undertaken. For instance, in his treatise *Éléments d'agriculture*

[Factors in agriculture], Duhamel Du Monceau found that using long and heavy scythes (meant for cutting oats) when harvesting wheat resulted in a "posture that is painful for the body."[25] He recommended choosing specific tools for specific tasks. In *L'Art du couvreur* [The roofers' trade], he highlighted dangerous negligence and recommended a more "comfortable posture"[26] for roofers perched on steep roofs with ladders and planks. Hulot studied lathe operators' foot pedals and recommended that the "most efficient"[27] ones, with "lateral beam movement," led to decreased resistance and smoother motions. The *Encyclopédie* included a comparative study of rowing and emphasized that one must refrain from rotating the oar on its axis "to prevent fatigue."[28] Charles Coulomb compared techniques in shoveling and recommended not "raising the implement higher than necessary" for maximum efficiency.[29] Even the steps of soldiers on parade came under increasing scrutiny and were rigorously described and annotated with an eye to saving energy. To be precise, "if soldiers raise their legs higher than is needed, they will waste time and tire themselves unnecessarily," and, "if their feet strike the ground with undue force, this movement will also fatigue them unnecessarily."[30] The French general and military theorist Jacques-Antoine de Guibert, whose essay on tactics was reprinted multiple times at the end of the eighteenth century, saw correct marching technique as evidence of "meticulousness." His views on a topic heretofore ignored or discounted underlined the significance of this turn to techniques, assessments and motion studies. "Using the left foot, the soldier steps forward twelve inches, plants his foot firmly on the ground; his body inclines in a forward motion with the weight entirely on the left foot; the right foot is lightly balanced on the tips of the toes, the heel is raised, and the soldier is ready to take the next step."[31] The general produced a meticulous analysis and also a demanding exercise, but his point was clear. He was convinced that marching this way was "more comfortable and less painful."[32] Without a doubt, a new approach to the most basic movements was underway.

Calculating the "amount of action"

Assessments of time taken on tasks had become more sophisticated, and many more were conducted in the middle of the century. For the first time, a watch was used for discipline and punishment. Observations were repeated in order to verify the results. The calculations were used to regulate work gangs, among other things. "Engineers" passed on their conclusions to estate managers and provincial administrators. No doubt the assessments gave fatigue short shrift, but they did set limits and evaluate possibilities in an attempt to establish norms applicable to many types of labor: porterage, stone-breaking, earth-moving, wagon transport. This led to studies virtually ruled by stopwatch:

> For this inquiry we used the length of the typical league; we measured, watch in hand, the time a wagon would take to travel it. We did it several times, averaged the results and came up with a duration of approximately one hour and thirty minutes. Once we established this, we could use it as a fixed benchmark to evaluate everything else. Thus, we developed a proportional table that an assistant engineer can easily use to calculate all possible distances and all ordinary tasks.[33]

From mid-century, there were more targeted attempts to calculate the most efficient investments of energy by comparing efforts and ranking results. In other words, it was an attempt to analyze work more precisely than had ever been the case. The totally new idea was to categorize differences and similarities in work according to the physical expenditure of energy, to find equivalent amounts of fatigue in different job categories, and thereby to make fatigue a measurable and controllable entity. We would know the "cost" of different jobs, which, when all is said and done, shone a spotlight on efficiency.

In 1753, Daniel Bernoulli, building on the insights of Désaguliers,[34] was the first to suggest mathematical equivalences. He introduced comparisons between "mechanical" ratios, trying to find equivalencies. He posited, for example, that fatigue would vary according to the amount of weight carried and the distance traveled, so that a "lighter" weight could be transported "further" in a fixed ratio and one could calculate how a change in one factor would affect the other. Thus, a reduction in load would have the opposite effect on the distance traveled; it would increase, but the amount of fatigue remained the same. The uniqueness of Bernoulli's work was due to the precision of his calculations and his attempt to "reckon with fatigue."[35] His formula kept it at the same level despite changes in the tasks, so that lifting a weight of "twenty pounds to a height of three feet per second" would be equivalent in the same amount of time to "lifting a weight of sixty pounds to a height of one foot"[36] in a stable, unchanging ratio. This was the origin of the concept of the "work unit"[37] (in this case, sixty pounds lifted up one foot) and its potential equivalencies, and also the principle of fixed, proportional relationships between two actions and the fatigue they entail. The formula had constant factors (the relations of force and motion) and variable ones (weight and distance) in a new mathematical calculation. "From this fact, we can add, subtract or divide work, in short make it the subject of an economic algebra."[38] The distinct advance over Vauban's calculations[39] came from recognizing force as a constant and distance as a variable that were always in a ratio. It furthered the goal of establishing fatigue as a "cost unit," since it entailed identifying fixed physical factors in different types of work and establishing equivalencies of effort in a range of actions with the sole criterion "it must be taken into account."[40] This was a central proposition that touched on both resistance and efficiency. Still, an important distinction remained: the definition of fatigue was limited to "supposition." Physical exertion was poorly understood; the physiology of the mid-eighteenth century did not focus on it, and in 1753 bodily stresses were not yet measured. Bernoulli quantified actions but only "acknowledged" exhaustion. He interpreted it, but mostly evaluated it subjectively. He acknowledged this indirectly: "I find that in a day's work a man with average strength and of average size will be able to lift 172,800 pounds to a height of one foot each day without damage to his wellbeing, and I base this estimate on a good number of observations."[41] The work unit as a "universal value" was introduced here; however, the amount of fatigue was not counted or calculated empirically. Its significance was acknowledged, which is crucial. But we have to point out other "limitations"; Bernoulli was less interested in "the welfare of the people involved than in the cold optimization of mechanical methods,"[42] and he overlooked workers' muscle power as a force to be calculated.

Charles Coulomb, an engineer trained in military matters, pursued this line of thought in the 1780s and added a new idea: the "quantity of action" or the "quantity that is produced by the pressure a person exerts, multiplied by the speed and the time that the action takes."[43]

This definition more explicitly referred to physical "exertion" and even "overuse." More attention was paid to the human "engine" as the century progressed, even if the chief motivation for studying it did not. Nevertheless, this focus was critical in the history of studies of workers' fatigue, even if, like Bernoulli's work,[44] its goal was to determine "how much fatigue a man can endure each day without damage to his animal economy."[45] The intention was simple and easily understood: "to get the most from men's exertions, we must find ways to increase output without increasing fatigue."[46] That, in a nutshell, was the goal of Enlightenment thinkers: to systematize efficiency while respecting the limits of the human body. Their studies resulted in a wave of real-life examples, observations and conclusions, such as the journal kept by Coulomb's friend Jean-Charles Borda during his ascent of Mount Teneriffe in the Cascade range in Washington state. Borda duly noted down the measurements he took and went on to extrapolate from the expedition's expenditure of energy to other situations. He calculated that, if the men who, on average, weigh 70 kilos each, were to climb 2,923 meters in a day, their effort would yield a "quantity equivalent to lifting 204,610 kilos up one meter," or "205 kilos lifted up one kilometer."[47] A different situation leads to another "experiment" exploring the energy spent by men carrying 68 kilos ascending a staircase. The staircase is 12 meters high, with equally spaced risers. When workers climbed it multiple times a day, they insisted that sixty-six trips were the maximum they could tolerate before becoming exhausted. This subjective testimony resulted in a formula to calculate the amount of action factoring in distance, weight and time:

> Let us add the weight of the porter to the 68 kilos he is carrying. We estimate he weighs 70 kilos and thus the amount of action required is to lift 138 kilos up 12 meters. If the porter makes sixty-six trips in a day, to calculate the amount of action we need to multiply these three numbers: 138, 66 and 12. We can approach the same problem another way: 109 kilos lifted up 1 kilometer.[48]

It's impossible to ignore the result here that porters lifting 109 kilos to the height of 1 kilometer in a day's work was less impressive than the climbers on Teneriffe, who, not burdened by loads, were able to lift "205 kilos to the height of 1 kilometer." The conclusion was that climbing while carrying a load required less exertion, but its costs can be measured. The question was extended to: what would be the "maximum" weight to carry without resulting in fatigue, factoring in distance and time? The abstract rule for finding "maxima and minima"[49] was adopted. Its algebraic formula allowed for many possible "variables" and selected as the most "balanced" the one that would allow for the most weight transported in the same amount of time, producing the same amount of fatigue. In other words, this was a happy medium and theoretical "ideal" in which debilitating fatigue was eliminated. Coulomb found that the happy medium was a load weighing 56 kilos, thus 12 kilos less than the one in the original study. We have to add that, besides the results of the calculations, the comparisons relied on the height the men climbed but overlooked the differences that are likely between climbing the side of a volcano and a set of stairs.

Similar calculations were made with hand-operated winches that were used to lift or move loads. Measurements were made of the distances and the weights involved, the number of turns of the crank and the length of time on task. A conclusion was reached: "A crank is better than a roller."[50] But neither the stair-climbing porters nor the winch-crank operators could lift "205 kilos up 1 kilometer," as the unburdened mountaineers had. Another observation concerned the efficiency of using one's body as a counterweight, since it was believed to produce the maximum "amount of action." This experiment involved a man climbing a certain distance without carrying any weight and "then descending while carrying a load approximately equal to his body weight."[51] These calculations sought to compare amounts of fatigue in a more "experimental" manner than Bernoulli had and, in addition, to validate the "use value" of body weight.

In addition to the calculations and the "unique observations"[52] conducted only once and therefore not yielding results based on an average of multiple repeatable attempts, some simply offered personal judgments, a drawback also evident in Bernoulli's studies.[53] Fatigue was assessed subjectively and its measurement was random, based only on the testimony of the men involved. The scientists' gaze was focused on actions and not on the person who performed them, and thus discounted the being that exerted itself or exhausted itself. We learned nothing about the "state" of Borda's fellow mountaineers as they ascended Teneriffe or about the porters repeatedly climbing stairs. The focus was on the mechanical aspects of the activity, not the amount of physical wear and tear. This revealed how hard it was to study the "degradation" of the body. And we must conclude that, in actual fact, all labor, or every "work unit," is produced in extremely diverse and disparate conditions, with many different gestures, and cannot be typified by "the basic experiment of lifting a weight to a certain height."[54]

Certainly modern in intent, Charles Coulomb's studies attempted to determine the minimum amount of fatigue that would result from maximum exertion. His work provided the foundation for mechanical theorists at the beginning of the next century. He sharpened the inquiry and refined the questions to ask. However, his was a promising start rather than a concrete final result.

Calculating the amount of oxygen

In 1777, Antoine-Laurent de Lavoisier's goal was equally ambitious, but he looked for evidence in organic exertion, not in mechanical results. The discovery of oxygen was essential to disrupt the calculations, provide new data and even influence our understanding of the body. Organic "losses" could be measured and studied for the first time in a revolutionary change. Lavoisier studied the consumption of this "vital gas" in different activities, and thus the reality of a physiological "load" was not only acknowledged but targeted and the interior of the human body became a space to be measured.[55] A new invention made this possible: an airtight chamber that captured the inhalations and exhalations of people performing activities could measure the amounts processed by their lungs. These hermetic chambers enabled a new and critical insight: that the absorption of oxygen varied with the amount of effort performed, just as equivalencies existed for many other activities. Lavoisier explained this in a detailed paragraph:

> This type of observation entails comparing the expenditure of effort between activities that seem in no way comparable. One can learn, for example, how much weight is displaced by a young man reciting a speech or a musician playing an instrument. One could even assess the effort involved in a philosopher meditating, an author writing, or a composer composing. These strictly mental efforts have a physical or material component that enables the scientist to compare them to those of a laborer.[56]

For the first time actions were associated with a measurable physiological effort, just as a fire uses up a "quantity" of oxygen for an "amount" of combustion. The body was a furnace whose consumption could be measured. Also, work was understood for the first time as a graduated range of losses, and the expected and final costs could be accounted for. All "additional" exertions required "supplementary" consumption of fuel. Every speed up or ramping up of effort meant a hotter burning fire. This was a critical observation, and, even better, Lavoisier's airtight chamber produced data. This in turn disrupted assessments and their subjects, since it foreshadowed, without actually naming it, the concept of "output" in the comparison of inhalation and exhalation. The efficiency of an activity was associated with the amount of oxygen absorbed and how it was used, so here again we were studying minimal utilization for maximum outcome. The experiments didn't, however, reveal much about individual disparities when the "rate" of fatigue depended on strictly unique circumstances, on fitness, or on physical differences that might affect the intake of oxygen. For this reason, even though the central principle had been developed, it had not been applied in a variety of work conditions.

Nevertheless, the discovery was significant, and several experiments took it further. Joseph Priestley, Lavoisier's competitor, succeeded in isolating the gas in a glass tube, inhaled it and pronounced it "the elixir of life." He predicted that, "in time, this pure air may become a fashionable article in luxury" and described an extraordinary sensation: "the feeling of it in my lungs was not sensibly different from common air, but I fancied that my breast felt peculiarly light and easy for some time afterwards."[57] At the beginning of the 1780s, the *Gazette de santé* [Health news] described new "devices" that would help seriously ill patients breathe. The treatment seemed quite basic but the gas was difficult to control, so its use was limited. There was little progress for the rest of the century, just as the studies on labor and its toll on the body had stalled. The time had not yet come for a vision that connected heat and the mechanisms of the body, locating energy in the "combustible" potential of the body and acknowledging the lungs as an indisputably overlooked resource. The time hadn't come when output was analyzed for its complexity as well as its efficiency.

16

Suffering from Fatigue: The Beginning of Compassion

Enlightenment thinkers' interest in actions and methods has had some lasting influence. Their intellectual curiosity and explorations of movements and processes opened up new and different fields of inquiry that even accommodated surprise, astonishment and other emotions. A new focus on industry affected the observers themselves. A mysterious sense of compassion was sparked, elicited not merely by abject poverty[1] but by the new valorization of labor itself, which had traditionally been neglected. Because of this, other aspects of fatigue came to the forefront, not only the internal sensations produced by fatigue, or the cold calculations for preventing and overcoming it, but also the emotional distress of observers who realized how destructive it was. This was a crucial turn for the study of work.

The birth of compassion

Studies that were indifferent became more focused and the travails of workers that had long been discounted more visible. More personal accounts delved into it, creating a surge of interest, and once marginal activities abruptly entered the spotlight. Anonymous people suffering silently were now recognized, gained a voice, and exposed their pain. For example, in 1781 Louis-Sébastien Mercier wrote about the humble porters in *Tableau de Paris* [Panorama of Paris]: "Stooped over, leaning on their walking sticks, they carry loads that would kill a horse."[2] He described the sedan-chair porters, who were "robust mercenaries, streaming with sweat, hunched over their thick shoes studded with iron cleats,"[3] and women burdened with heavy loads, but "we don't see their muscles as we do the men's. These are more hidden but we can imagine the effort, seeing their chest throbbing with painful breaths. Compassion touches your very heart and soul."[4]

At mid-century some writers concerned about inequality also denounced forced labor as "abusive:" "The work gangs on our roads exact the most horrific toll from the laborers who are forced into them. Their daily quota far exceeds their strength and endurance."[5]

These kinds of observations supported arguments in favor of more mechanization of work, even if its advocates were not motivated solely by compassion. Revitalizing the economy, enhancing industrial production and abandoning the dependence on rural sources of wealth were all factors. The Enlightenment was a notable era of inventions, and some "mechanicians" explicitly cited the ways machines would reduce workloads. In 1782, Claude-François Berthelot explained his motivation in designing a "crane that can load and unload ships": "The thought of the dangers to which the poor fellows who must earn their living this way are exposed convinced the Author to incorporate the motor of the milling machine previously described, and add to it pedals to operate all kinds of cranes."[6]

These convictions would not change work culture right away and had little or no effect on workers' lives. But later they would, at the very end of the eighteenth century. By itself, the slow progress of the mechanization of work would not revolutionize most jobs, and the phenomenon attested more to an enhanced recognition of workers' toil in the eighteenth century than to a wholesale upheaval in the conditions of work itself. This new consciousness spoke to a change in outlook and a subtle turn toward sympathy that could be replicated in many contexts. We also saw a renewed interest in childhood and a concern for its "weaknesses" and "fragilities," highlighted in Jean-Jacques Rousseau's *Émile*[7] in 1767, a book that also prompted a reassessment of violence. In 1764, Cesare Beccaria's treatise *Des délits et des peines* [On crimes and punishments] raised questions about the efficacy of torture and the morality of the death penalty.[8] Abbé Guillaume Raynal, in 1770, brought heightened attention to slavery and the human beings "condemned to this frightful state … of endless toil throughout the Americas … working under the lash of a vicious overseer."[9] Clearly, the range of what was acceptable in behavior and customs was being recalibrated and that which was unacceptable or "abhorrent" was redefined. However, this did not mean universal condemnation; there was still room for "indifference." Gabriel Jars, a punctilious inspector of the

European mining industry who investigated labor-saving procedures, found in 1774 that child labor was useful, and even necessary. Children's short stature enabled them to work in the galleries with extremely low ceilings or "partially excavated passageways."[10] Their labor was as unremarkable in the mines as in the tunnels. Their possible suffering was "invisible" too. The genuine concern observers expressed for the plight of some laborers was tainted with what might be termed selective "insensitivity" toward others.

Nonetheless, a new wave of "compassion" was rising along with more vociferous criticism of work gangs, as the estate agents "force the work gangs to perform unpaid labor when the lord of the manor wished."[11] These practices began to be questioned in the second half of the eighteenth century. For example, in 1765 the inhabitants of the Angoumois [the historic county of Angoulême] collectively struggled to put an end to Count Charles-François de Broglie's dominion over more than thirty parishes, which had been awarded by the Seneschal of Angoulême on December 18, 1768. A similar action was partly successful in restricting manorial rights in Alsace, resulting in a decree on December 24, 1783.[12] In 1787 Charles-Alexandre Calonne, the controller-general of finances under Louis XVI, finally reduced internal customs duties and abolished work-gang duty, replacing it with a money benefit, a decision that Count Louis-Philippe de Ségur applauded as "heralding the end of centuries of barbarism."[13]

More workers protested also. Higher pay was the chief demand in the revolts in Lyon in 1786, "kicked off by silk workers and then joined by hatmakers and weavers,"[14] but the workers also condemned silk traders' "despotism" and the "slavery" of their jobs. This echoed the English weavers' ironic protest song from around that same time that denounced low salaries and employers' dirty tactics. Weavers were forced to buy their thread from merchants' silent partners and had to work longer hours to make up their expenses. "It is the cloth merchants' joy" to "exhaust weavers for a miserable salary."[15] Other workers' protests at the Beauvais Manufactory in 1778 focused on the twin goals of "raising salaries and reducing work hours"[16] in a "movement" involving over a thousand workers. A similar demand was made by the "general association" of paper-makers in the Auvergne region in southwestern France in 1780.[17]

Picturing a hard life

A telling detail in the writing of Enlightenment thinkers, elites and scientists in the second half of the century was their evocation of life's difficulties: of physical strains, a reduced lifespan, and the connection between the stresses of work and lives cut short. Diderot was sure of it: "There are many positions in society characterized by excessive fatigue that depletes our energy and shortens our lives."[18] The Royal Society of Medicine reached the same conclusion in 1778 when, in a study of Marseille and its environs, it described the peasants in Provence as "worn out from hard work and overwork … elderly before they reach the age of forty-five and not living much longer."[19] When Buffon compared life in Paris and in the countryside, he found people in the villages were "more tired, more malnourished, and dying a lot earlier than city folk."[20] In 1749 he published comprehensive numerical tables comparing the life expectancy of people in various classes, professions and settings. His approach was novel and rigorous and it showed that, compared to their peers elsewhere, twice as many Parisians lived to age eighty and four times as many reached the age of ninety.[21] At the end of the century, similar studies on the lifespan of miners were published that improved on the seeming indifference of Gabriel Jars's reports in 1774 to miners' quality of life.[22] The threats miners faced were not limited to the toxic substances they inhaled, the miasmas, the drafts, the floods or the possible collapse of tunnel walls or ceilings. They could also be injured working in a cramped space because of the contorted, crouching postures they used when working or going from one site to another: "In many galleries you can only move forward by crawling on hands and knees. In general, you are always crouching or bent over … Since this posture cannot help but do damage to miners' animal economy and shorten their lives, we ought to make all mine ceilings a little higher."[23]

It is notable that workers themselves made similar observations. At the end of the century, Vincent-Marie Vaublanc reported that peasants in Great Saint Bernard Pass in the Alps say that "they don't live long" because of "the frequent fatigue of ascending and descending the mountain."[24] Blacksmiths, though not facing the same working conditions as the mountain folk, also believed that the strains of the new "puddling" metallurgical technique introduced in England in the 1780s shortened their work lives because "stirring the molten pig iron and rolling it to decarbonize it" required such great "muscular exertion" that, "after the age of forty, the workers are no longer able to do it."[25] Duhamel Du Morceau asserted that trimmers had "the most demanding task"[26] in the textile industry. Wielding long and extremely heavy metal scissors to smooth and compress woolen fabrics, they "cannot do the job well after they reach the age of fifty because the task requires strength, manual dexterity and visual acuity."[27]

A concern with lifespan grew throughout the century, as did the recognition that the demands of certain trades may shorten workers' lives.

The division of labor

However, another revolution in thought was needed to disrupt categories of fatigue at the end of the eighteenth century: the concept of the division of labor. Adam Smith first developed the theory in 1776 in *An Inquiry into the Nature and Causes of the Wealth of Nations.* The example he used is still canonical: the textbook case of "the trade of the pin-maker," which Smith divided into "eighteen distinct operations." "One workman … could scarce perhaps with his utmost industry make one pin in a day," whereas "not only the whole work is a peculiar trade, but it is divided into a number of branches of which the greater part are likewise peculiar trades." And if we simplified the actions, assigned specific workers to specific steps and coordinated their activities, we would increase productivity: "I have seen a small manufactory of this kind" where ten workers "could make among them upwards of forty-eight thousand pins in a day."[28] This was an extreme comparison, and the figure he gave wasn't comparable to the production of a single worker. Adam Smith implicitly acknowledged fatigue when he highlighted the "inventions of common workmen" who "naturally turned their thoughts towards finding out easier and readier methods of performing" their jobs. He cited the example of a child laborer who had one task in operating a boiler and found a way to streamline it:

> One of those boys, who loved to play with his companions, observed that by tying a string from the handle of the valve which opened this communication

> to another part of the machine, the valve would open and shut without his assistance and leave him at liberty to divert himself with his play-fellows. One of the greatest improvements that has been made upon this machine since it was first invented was in this manner the discovery of a boy who wanted to save his own labor.[29]

Nevertheless, the originality of Smith's approach was not in reducing fatigue but in eliminating unproductive work time, mechanizing tasks, and intensifying the tempo of production. The flip side of "the economy of effort"[30] was still unacknowledged: suppressing "emotions and reasoning" and declining "intellectual and manual dexterity."[31] An unexpected result was the appearance of an entirely new kind of fatigue that was related not to physical exertion but to the need for constant attentiveness, remaining in one place, and withstanding long periods of monotony. No longer the domains of individual artisans, workshops were transformed into unified and uniform collective spaces that were strictly surveilled. Individual initiative was stifled in favor of universalized norms of behavior and production. This innovation took hold first in England at the end of the century and then spread throughout Europe at the beginning of the next century.

The work task was "becoming narrower," with "strict limitations and boring sameness,"[32] scientifically organized and researched by manufacturers, such that in the 1870s Matthew Boulton in his Soho factory in Birmingham, England, claimed that he could identify the cause of any work stoppage from the sounds of the hammers and wheels.[33] The stress that resulted from this "soulless mechanization"[34] and the daily grind of work still didn't have a name and was barely acknowledged in the treatises of "engineers."[35] Nevertheless, protest movements broke out, and the violence, sabotage of machinery and work stoppages might have also been sparked by the anger of unemployed artisans. Rallies and attacks increased. Josiah Wedgwood, a factory owner in Staffordshire, cited this testimony in 1789: "There were certainly five hundred of them, they told me they had just damaged some machinery, and they intended to do the same throughout the country."[36] In Chorley in 1780 several thousand workers protested with signs and drums, and similar unrest occurred in Yorkshire in 1796. But the repression was brutal. Troops were dispatched, protesters were imprisoned, and the leaders were executed. Threats were also used: protesters would lose their jobs, and women and child laborers would replace them. A law in 1799 was renewed that forbade "worker associations aiming to increase salaries, reduce work hours or any amelioration of working conditions."[37] This was the beginning of many restrictions that Michelet saw as a "malediction weighing on England."[38]

In other words, manufacturing involved another harsh discipline. This was not unusual in the Enlightenment's century of sensitivity: "Philanthropy was fashionable, but for many factory owners it stopped at the factory door. Their compassion for the people of color in the colonies, which cost them little, was the limit of their humanity."[39] A model was invented and built in which the industrial expansion of the nineteenth century would install a regime of exhaustion as specific as it was generalizable.

17

The Fatigue is in Demand: The Challenge Begins

From the lassitude of swooning ladies to the exhaustion of workers, the social range of fatigue was becoming ever more "open" in the eighteenth century. It extended from the euphemistic feelings of the elite to the abject, newly discovered suffering of the marginalized. At the end of the century this included a surge associated with the pace of work in factories and the constant strict surveillance of workers. The shadow cast by fatigue encompassed both extremes in a mixture of sensitivity and harshness.

This recognition among the most fortunate in society and the most advanced thinkers engendered new categories of fatigue in different settings and different types of behavior. This new perspective was associated with the rise of individualism, the desire for autonomy and a new concept of the body and also of time itself. We experienced our physical existence differently, accumulating accomplishments, broadening our horizons and opening new avenues for personal affirmation. For the first time, fatigue was seen as a challenge that we took on voluntarily, and it was sought after, confronted and accepted as an opportunity for self-knowledge and knowledge of the world around us. The concept of fatigue as a "penalty"[1] was outmoded. It had become a "challenge" in our future-oriented thinking.

The challenge of travel

The perceived value of many activities was inverted at this time, enhancing their worth and status. Travel was one of these, although it didn't in principle shed its terrifying aspects. The downside of traveling was regularly noted in letters of the period, such as those of Mme du Deffand, who repeatedly mentioned "the tiring nature of travel."[2] But, for the first time, travel had a "revitalizing" power, restoring our energy and stoking our enthusiasm. Diderot expressed his surprise at this during his long journey to Russia:

> A stroll in the Bois de Boulogne would have tired me more than the eight hundred leagues I've traveled by post carriage over indescribably awful roads. It seems that movement does me a lot of good and a sedentary and industrious life is the root cause of my ailments. In Paris, I would go to bed feeling worn out, and would usually get up feeling even worse. But I haven't felt anything close to that now, even after traveling for forty-eight hours straight, because we have been on the road day and night several times without a break.[3]

The main point was that the bumps and jolts of the journey had restored his vigor. The swaying of the carriage renewed the flexibility of his nerve fibers even though in the past such discomforts were assumed to be an unfailing trigger of exhaustion. "Jostling" in a carriage or astride a horse was previously believed to be tiring[4] because it discharged one's humors, but now it was seen as toning the fibers, stimulating and fortifying them. The feeling was an internal one, of revitalized spirits and a new sense of personal freedom, that buttressed a person's endurance and courage. Moreover, the traditional conception of fatigue as a "loss" (except in the context of religious redemption)[5] was transformed. It now represented a benefit, a profit and a renewal of the self. The travails of a journey were re-envisioned and took on a new positive value: "I have never accomplished more or felt better than when I'm on the road."[6] Dr Jean-Baptiste Pressavin, a Lyon surgeon and future member of the Convention, told an "exemplary" anecdote in 1785. A "swooning lady" from Paris who was overcome by fatigue had to travel to Bordeaux urgently to settle an inheritance. Her departure was so hasty and the trip so unexpected that she was forced to hire any carriage that was available. Her carriage was rickety and the ride was jolting and bumpy, but the lady was amazed to discover when she arrived at her destination that she felt "invigorated." Her fatigue had disappeared. The explanation was familiar: traveling was certainly tiring, but a body that was jostled, shaken and squeezed would also regain "vigor." The movements were revitalizing; sagging muscles became firm and one's depleted strength was restored.[7] This revelation led to new inventions: contraptions intended to banish fatigue by oscillating, pushing and prodding. Thus, we found "mechanical armchairs," "mechanical horses" and "riding stools," mentioned in the *Encyclopédie* or featured in miscellaneous notices and advertisements,[8] devices bristling with gears, levers and toggles dutifully operated by servants, with their users hopefully being re-energized in the comfort of "their own home."[9]

The challenge of time passing

Limits were also being viewed differently; distances and amounts of time became challenges and hurdles to overcome, with an emphasis on personal initiative and intrepid behavior. Scientists were concerned with more than measuring speed and the almost mechanical calculations of travel time between two points, as we saw in the studies of messengers' journeys in the seventeenth century.[10] Instead, the emphasis was on speed itself and the stimulation it provided, and the goal was to accelerate the pace of travel. Again, this was an individual challenge motivated by a conviction that one could confront the "impossible" and achieve the "ultimate" in a quantifiable performance or time trial. The first attempt of this sort in France occurred in 1694, when duc Henri d'Elbeuf bet that his carriage could "make a round trip between Paris and Versailles in under two hours."[11] And he succeeded with seven minutes to spare, demonstrating that time measurements were becoming even more precise. After the mid-eighteenth century, these kinds of exploits became more common and even acquired a sort of royal endorsement. In November 1754, when Lord Poscool attempted to ride from Fontainebleau to Paris in under two hours, the king ordered "the constabulary to remove any obstacles from the route that might impede the rider in any way."[12] In another innovation, Poscool raced with "a watch sewn onto his left sleeve so that he can always know the time."[13] He checked on his progress, transforming time-keeping into an "obsession," and actually arrived with twelve minutes to spare. This performance made the feat into an event worth the name and was described that way by Louis-Sébastien Mercier and Dufort de Cheverny: "People talked about it for the next six months; racing began to catch their attention."[14]

The challenge of overcoming fatigue was indisputably part of these attempts. Highways were upgraded, relays of horses were prepared, and starting and end points were made ready. When the Marquis

Charles-Noël du Saillant wagered on August 6, 1722, that he could "make two round trips between the Porte Saint-Denis and Chantilly Castle, thirty-six leagues in less than six hours," a bed was prepared for him at the destination, a café. Du Saillant rode a total of sixteen horses, arrived twenty-five minutes ahead of his estimated time and then slept for one and half hours at the café – "far too little," in the witnesses' judgment.[15] Edmond-Jean-François Barbier's newspaper emphasized the lessons of this exploit: "This is not a horse race, it's a man's race," reporting that the witnesses following the rider "were out of breath."[16] This was a novel initiative where overcoming fatigue was essential to the wager, as crucial as the exploit itself.

Audiences were treated to a spate of similar exploits after mid-century. The duc de Croÿ favored fast performances and time trials such as skating races on a frozen canal. "I learned that good skaters could make two round trips the length of the canal, which is eight hundred yards, in six minutes." He continued the calculations: "That would make six and a third leagues in an hour."[17] He expressed his surprise at certain feats: "The speed of his race in Flanders, riding in a light horse-drawn carriage, and reaching a speed of five or six leagues an hour, which is amazing."[18] The duke's calculations of units of distance in relation to units of time was a critical innovation. He had invented a constant, and the world of the "almost, approximately"[19] had been left behind. People would think no longer in terms of a time period relative to reaching a certain destination but, rather, of a standardized measure of time spent in traveling a specific distance. Speed was described no longer in random, anecdotal experiences of a specific journey but in a much more abstract way: the intersection of space and time. Speeds could therefore be compared, and stamina too.

The challenge of discoveries

Another way to confront pain and exhaustion voluntarily came to the fore during the Enlightenment. It also involved travel but was different from the jolting bumpy rides already discussed.[20] It was the ocean voyage, characterized by unpredictability and danger. Individuals were no longer taking on the uncertainty of crossing the ocean to travel or vow or make a pilgrimage, risking their lives in gales or hurricanes, as those leaving Europe for the Holy Land had done for so long. Nor were they journeying to conquer other lands or commercialize their riches, like the merchants and captains of empire. Travelers were confronting the same dangers for a more prosaic and more "modern" reason: to learn more about the world, explore the unknown and set foot in remote places. The fact that a demanding journey was freely undertaken enhanced one's stature, and facing up to danger was a means of self-validation. The challenge of these great adventures was different and the goal had changed. One travelled to learn more, confronted difficulties to learn more, and struggled to learn more or simply to live a better life. Suffering thus became more valued and more welcome: "Everything changed with the Enlightenment. The extraordinary effort of the *Encyclopédie* to categorize and systematize the natural and physical sciences gave these voyages an apparently shared goal."[21]

James Cook's second voyage between 1772 and 1775 sought to "make discoveries in the southern hemisphere."[22] Bougainville made a trip around the world between 1766 and 1769, stopping for a time at the islands of the South Pacific.[23] Jean-François de Galaup, comte de Lapérouse, led an expedition to the Pacific, aiming to explore the entire ocean and to "resolve scientific questions that other recent famous expeditions had raised."[24] "Knowledge" was essential to these missions, and a relentless search for it elevated these essentially imperial and commercial ventures. The captains' frank recollections also contained harrowing descriptions of the perils and exhaustion the commanders and crew endured. Yves-Joseph de Kerguelen de Trémarec gave a telling example of this when he recalled his departure for the coast of Greenland:

> In truth, there is some difference between the smiling days of May such as we experience in France and the rigorous weather we had to undergo; and when I compared the comfort of a life on shore with a tolerable competency to the tiresomeness of the sea, especially in bad weather, I wondered why any man enjoying a sufficiency could be induced to trust himself twice to the mercy of the winds and bellows; fortunately for this condition of life, one hour of fair weather obliterates the remembrance of days of danger and toil.

But Kerguelen reminded the reader in the preface that he "always felt for cruizing" [*sic*] and the "order to repair to court upon His Majesty's service … occasioned in me indescribable satisfaction." Like a practical scientist, he put navigational techniques and contemporary maps to the test, concluding:

> The trouble I had navigating while fighting strong currents, riding out frequent storms, sailing amidst ice floes with a compass that wildly oscillated all the time made us constantly question the accuracy of our route. In a word, the obstacles I had to overcome makes me hope that the captain's log, which I have been asked to publish, will be of some use.[25]

During the second half of the eighteenth century a remarkable emphasis was put on this perspective, celebrating the "bold and perilous expeditions" undertaken solely "to learn about the bodies of water that have never been crossed."[26] Anders Sparrman, who occasionally joined James Cook's expeditions but was also an independent explorer, summed up in a few words the dual valorization of a search for knowledge and a voluntary submission to dangers: "It was not at all to enrich myself that I made my collections and enlarged my field of knowledge. It was, as one says, done with the sweat of my brow and at the risk of my life."[27]

The challenge of mountaintops

Another challenge brought new life to the field of exhaustion: climbing mountains. Summiting was an obsession during the Enlightenment, especially because of the particular kind of fatigue produced by mountain climbing and also the opportunity it offered for time trials. Again, the image of expeditions in the mountains has changed, and concerns with weather conditions such as ice and snow, equipment such as climbers' ladders, and actions such as negotiating overhangs and squeezing through narrow passages that had been criticized as pointless and risky were now the center of attention. The search for knowledge, the desire for esthetic satisfaction, and the almost exclusively personal aspect of "testing oneself" were emphasized. To succeed in one's venture by reaching the summit and overcoming the obstacles presented by the terrain was seen as a sort of private victory, especially "among the moneyed leisure classes"[28] who had the time and resources to travel to these remote areas. Contemporary views on ravines and glaciers were changing course. William Windham, an English gentleman-explorer, explained in 1741 why he embarked on his expedition despite many warnings and much criticism: "Our curiosity propelled us and gave us confidence and courage."[29] Recalling the first time he glimpsed the "noble beauty" of Mont Blanc, Théodore Bourrit exclaimed in 1784: "It's amazing that no one yet has tried everything possible to reach the summit."[30] These exploits typified the new culture, with its emphasis on personal decisions, sensory input, and the importance of making contact with the outside world and with things. It also highlighted the receding influence of occult powers and hidden dangers. The new culture of measurement and mathematics played a significant role. Horace-Bénédict de Saussure, one of the first to reach the summit of Mont Blanc, claimed that, in the Alps and the mountainous Jura region, one hour on the road was equal to a climb of 400 meters. Fatigue was included in the calculation, since it was an inescapable element of a successful climb: "Finally, after four hours and a quarter of very difficult climbing, we arrived at the top of the mountain, where we enjoyed a view of the most extraordinary things."[31] Fatigue had become a "reward" and was no longer a sign of personal salvation. Instead, the climbers' exertions produced sensory pleasure and worldly enjoyment: "I couldn't believe my eyes. It was like a dream."[32] It was so significant that even exhaustion could be transformed into wellbeing, in the rather unusual context of "enjoying the sweet sensation of exhaustion."[33] No doubt it was essential to find intrinsic pleasure in physical exertion, which also transformed the effort into an object of study. Saussure plunged into this and included measurements and calculations with his observations: "These hearty men, for whom the seven or eight hours of climbing we had just done was absolutely nothing, had not excavated five or six shovels full of snow before they were convinced that going forward was impossible."[34] His explanation didn't take into account the importance of oxygen to compensate for "shortness of breath," although he focused on the difficulty in breathing: "We understood we had to increase the volume by taking more frequent breaths."[35] He even tried to measure this: "I couldn't take more than fifteen or sixteen steps without taking a deep breath."[36] A very specific fatigue was being studied here in a venture that was previously considered "foolhardy." Now we had a more objective view, based more on data, of something perilous, a place and an activity to be avoided. People were changing their position in the cosmos and suffering, but being conscious of their pain affirmed their existence.

18

The Beginning of Training and the Review of Time

When curiosity has been revitalized, defenses have been too. The concept of endurance was not the same, since our perspective on the human body, on nerves and on tone has changed. Our understanding of endurance was not the same either, since concepts of time, progress and development have changed. These were undoubtedly elite perspectives that incorporated knowledge and the ability to make decisions, but these perspectives definitively and inevitably influenced culture and everyday life. New elements, new habits and new social ambitions were the result.

Tonics

First of all, the belief that nerve fibers and their elasticity played a significant role in our health led to renewed interest in "remedies," even if archaic references to humors had not been completely abandoned in medical and popular thought. There was one overarching rule: strengthen the fibers that were weak and no longer, as in the past, replace liquids that have "evaporated." As we have seen, using electricity as a treatment[1] (even though it was rare and of very limited availability) was a concrete example of this idea. The most popular and commonly used remedies were intended to "firm up" weak points, such as "medicines that will give solids the tone they need to function properly"[2] or those that "fortify the nerves and give tone to the fibers of the skin."[3] The number of astringent and toning potions and lotions on the market kept increasing. Louis Desbois de Rochefort, Corvisart's teacher, recommended "the mint pastilles sold in shops."[4] Joseph Lieutaud, Louis XV's first doctor, prescribed iron therapy, using iron filings "to restore to vessels the elasticity and tone they have lost."[5] In 1760, the scientific journal *Avant-Coureur* recommended "buds of Russian fir trees" to treat "fibers' lack of tone."[6]

The *Encyclopédie* offered a range of options too: bitter orange, "tonic and digestive," English mint, "calming and a boon to the nerves," refined lime scale, "a general tonic for the entire body," an herbal tincture called "eau de carme," incorporating lemon balm and other floral essences, "for palpitations and faintness," and mineral water from the spa town of Balaruc-les-Bains to perk up "the tone of the stomach and intestines."[7] The overarching goal of the various treatments, as the *Dictionnaire portatif de santé* explained in 1760, was to "tighten up all the fibers."[8]

Writers and memoirists had personal favorites too, generally empirical but always toning. The duc de Luynes recommended roses, whose "sap will revitalize one's strength,"[9] while James Boswell, the Scottish barrister, self-described "Hypochondriak" and staunch European traveler, called for "veal bouillon," since it will "restore vigor and calm the nerves."[10] The duc de Croÿ relied on chocolate to keep up his strength on the taxing journey to Arras to report on the parents of the failed assassin Robert-François Damiens, on trial for "regicide."[11]

Also revealing were the references to sexual dysfunction and potential remedies that strengthened fibers and nerves. Casanova's *Memoirs* mentioned "revitalizing elixirs that have marvelous effects."[12] A cup of coffee or a "bowl of punch" was believed to "stimulate"[13] physical prowess, while fine wines and sugared almonds were said to enhance potency. The characters in Sade's novels consumed enormous quantities of such "stimulants," and the words the author chose made clear their connection to nerves. Participants in an orgy were sprayed with "a stimulating lotion scented with jasmine."[14] Special potions would ease "nervous crises" or "convulsions,"[15] whereas "the finest aquavit" would spark vitality for the demands of the night.[16] There were repeated references to "ecstasy powders" to revive the "tired and worn-out buffers"[17] who populated Sade's work. These were certainly tried-and-true remedies, but they were mentioned more frequently at this time and were meant to target specific deficits in the nervous system. This was especially true for the "stimulants" the "English Spy" mentioned in the salacious exposé of the elderly Louis XV in his affair with "Jeanne Bécu" (the countess du Barry): "The king's attachment to [her] was due to prodigious efforts she elicited from him, thanks to an ambergris douche that she used to scent her inner parts every day. One must say that she added to this allure something that decent society hasn't yet tried."[18] No clue was given about the vague "secret" ingredients unknown to decent society; however, the emphasis here was on stimulating the nerves, resulting in a suggestive rather than an explicit "sensual delight."

Using the cold to firm up

Spending time in the great outdoors and in chilly temperatures also tightened our flesh and enhanced our endurance. Mme d'Épinay hoped to achieve this in her trip to Switzerland: "The brisk cold here is strengthening me and is more comfortable than the soggy weather we are having in France."[19] Dominique-Jean Larrey, the chief surgeon of the French army with Napoleon in Egypt, took to swimming in the Nile: "These sessions relax us and fortify our muscles,"[20] unlike bathing in warm water, which in the previous century was thought to be relaxing.[21] Pierre Pomme would submerge patients suffering from "the vapors" in cold water, claiming that the cold would buck them up and "re-establish the elasticity of their solids."[22] Heat, on the other hand, "lengthens the fibers, relaxes them, and causes exhaustion and weakness,"[23] making flesh flabbier and morals looser, and was therefore straightaway "contra-indicated for those with delicate nerves."[24] The new treatments insured the opposite; they were restorative and firming, and had another advantage that Louis-Sébastien Mercier highlighted: signaling opposition to a decadent society and effete aristocracy. He cited the example of a member of the idle rich, a swooning lady who shuttled from "her bathtub to her dressing table and then back to her bath,"[25] her vitality drained by futile actions and humidity.

As a result, cold temperatures took their place in the arsenal of hygienists and educators in the second half of the century, where they were meant to combat the threat of physical deterioration and the social disruption it brings. Exposure to cold ensured long-term "protection," promoted endurance and firmness, and buttressed the body against the onset of fatigue in the future. Jean-Louis de Fourcroy, an enthusiastic disciple of Rousseau and minor functionary in the bailiwick of Clermont, explained that the cold baths his sons had taken since they were only a few months old had greatly increased their wellbeing. The baths had "a toning effect on skin," resulting in an increase in natural body heat and a "protective shield against drafts"[26] for his robust and healthy children. Fourcroy even experimented by comparing the progress of his two boys; when he thought one of his sons was stronger, he was given even more frequent cold-water baths. Mme de Maraise, a colleague of Oberkampf and dedicated reader of Enlightenment medical treatises, espoused a similar regimen. A very active entrepreneur in the merchant class, she carried on a lengthy correspondence where, among the serious queries and responses connected to her decorating business, she decried the "weak and flabby" practices of her contemporaries and described her own approach to raising her children and nephews: "natural" food and cold baths. She was even disappointed that the boys didn't plunge their heads under the water.[27] William Buchan brought such techniques to their ultimate conclusion, describing for the first time an experiment involving immersion in cold water for longer periods of time, proceeding by increments of increased time and decreased temperature as he looked for signs of progress. He didn't attempt to plunge a vulnerable person into a cold stream right away, but instead experimented with water whose temperature was lowered gradually, employing a "less is more" approach to habituate the subjects better. This new conception of progress, applied to a modest experiment, that of bathing, had become an educational method. This was doubly significant: "Even though cold water is very useful for fortifying a weak, flabby temperament, if we try to use it too soon, however, it may have too strong an effect on the exterior of the body, whereas the internal sources of strength will still be too weak, and the subject may suffer grievous consequences."[28]

We see here a new focus on gradual progress and the reinforcement of "internal" forces.

Stages and progressions

The understanding of physical exercise also changed with these new methods of self-revitalization. Now exercise was considered important and rewarding, since it reinforced the strength of the body's fibers that provide endurance. Even religious leaders approved of dancing, whose seductive nature had long been criticized, because it was now a kind of regenerating relaxation. Jean Pontas, an expert in canon law, explained to priests in the middle of the century:

> If you think of dance as a relaxation for the mind and a diversion that prevents someone from suffering from the exhaustion that too demanding work can cause, or as an escape from the tedium of everyday life, we can say that it is exempt from all sin as long as it is performed in circumstances or conditions that would ensure its innocence.[29]

Even more significant, exercise was understood in a different way, gradual steps were introduced, and increases in intensity were factored in. Marshal de Boucicaut's archaic methods,[30] which involved endless repetitions of the same action, had been disrupted. Slowly, the idea of gradual increases of intensity and stages in all kinds of physical activity came to the forefront. The sense of looking to the future allowed for this step-by-step progression. Tomorrow implied a "plus," and the new perspectives on exercise suggested something "better." New studies were underway and conclusions were being formulated. A major change was evident in the time trials of the era in which carriages and horses were viewed differently. A horse had to be ready to properly "get its breath." Before leaving on a long journey, one had to build up to it in short increments: "At first, one makes short trips. So, the first day you travel six leagues. Increase that the second day and, little by little, build up to fourteen leagues a day."[31]A new word, training, appeared in the English lexicon, associated with a gradual increase of activities and their effects. At the end of the eighteenth century, professional boxers were the first examples. In 1789 an article recommended repeated bouts of running and practicing throws that would stop as soon as the boxer "feels tired."[32] Some of the publications about exercises and games at the end of the eighteenth century illustrated the principle of gradual build-up, such as *La Gymnastique de la jeunesse* [Gymnastics for youth], where every "preparatory effort" should be "mild" and the first jumps undertaken should be "very low."[33] Mme de Genlis filled out the picture in the 1780s. When she was a governess for the duc de Chartres' children in 1773, all the physical exercises she recommended were based on numbers. This "systematic" method was representative of a new ideal of "ability." The countess introduced the exercises gradually and carefully, incorporating steps, jumps, weighted jars, dumb-bells and pulleys. She adapted them to create gradations for her students. She paid attention to resistances, stages and achievements. She was looking for signs of regular "improvement."

The exercise of carrying "weighted jars" was representative. The route was laid out precisely: 190 steps on level ground plus forty stairs to climb. In 1788, the twenty-two trips accomplished with some "spillage" convinced her to use "smaller water pots."[34] A few days later she recorded twenty-five trips. Later, an extra weight was added to the container carried by the younger brother, who was born in 1775. A year after that, the elder brother, born in 1773, who was the future Louis-Philippe, could carry containers weighing 56 pounds when earlier he could handle only 40 pounds. The "best" was achieved in the simplest exercises, and this "best" could be improved on still when the action lacked honesty or grace.[35] The results of these programs did not yield significant numbers and were based on only anecdotal evidence, but their significance was associated with the new image of progress as well as a new understanding of fatigue.

At the end of the eighteenth century the French army also adopted progressive exercises. Marching was calibrated, as were drills, rest periods, and the time spent on each. The hygienists in camps and barracks followed one rule: pay attention to "preventable" and "unavoidable" fatigue. These recommendations were typical:

> You can order short marches before the heat of the day and also call a halt from time to time. Such practices, rather than tiring them, will really help keep them sound … It is better to repeat this exercise early and often before the sun makes it too hot than to do it occasionally and for a long time … We must avoid any unnecessary fatigue.[36]

The key was to increase "endurance quietly"[37] and build up strength by confronting tiring activities little by little. The point was to calculate how to make these exercises "most useful for the troops."[38]

With the theme of progress, with measurement and breaking down activities into steps, the Enlightenment thinkers invented a new approach to fatigue and its effects. Their unshakable conclusion was that "Human perfectibility is still limitless."[39]

PART IV

THE NINETEENTH CENTURY AND THE CHALLENGE OF NUMBERS

The nineteenth century gradually revitalized the studies, the categories and the explanations of fatigue, going beyond the inventions of the Enlightenment that disrupted previous ideas and beyond the emphasis on the two factors ("internal" and "external" sensations) that focused on limits in one's activities and one's self-perception. Scientists in the nineteenth century even went beyond the "challenging fatigue" that prompted new investigations. This included calculations intended to measure things systematically: from physical exertions to mental ones, from mechanical principles to the rules of energy, from math calculations to dream logic and ratiocination. The century of "positivism" changed fatigue into a new subject and pursued "evidence" carefully. At this time, we see the increasing affirmation of the individual and the equally salient ambition to measure its "resources" and "deficits."

At the beginning of the century an explicitly significant type of fatigue was recognized. It occurred in professions whose goal, motivated by a desire for equality, was to work for the common good, to transform every weakness into a useful action, and to value efforts in service to all over fealty to traditionally "exploitative" bosses. This was a kind of "ideological" fatigue, both similar to and distant from "redemption fatigue," but it pointed our collective enthusiasm in new directions. Balzac acknowledged this in 1842 in the foreword to *La Comédie humaine* [The human comedy], writing about "the existence of a new moral universe."[1]

Nevertheless, an "unfortunate" fatigue contrasted with this specifically "valued" fatigue. The offspring of an industrial society, it was destructive, wearying bodies, upsetting observers and pushing them to reinvent assessments and evaluations. Closer attention was paid to deprivation and despondency that had festered in the past in isolated rural pockets.[2] The most diverse and stubborn kinds of resistance arose. Research studies advocated for shorter work hours, less exertion, and better control over working conditions. This reduced the level of suffering without eliminating it and sometimes simply shifted it to another context.

More personal initiatives were undertaken at the end of the century to combat potential feelings of weakness. These were improbable and varied strategies, sometimes nothing more than exhortations to "get stronger," "make your own way in life," and increase "your self-confidence." On the other end of the scale, a regimen of "psychic gymnastics" was developed, meant to buttress people's self-confidence. These were all signs of a revitalized culture and an admission that fatigue was ever present, diffuse and threatening. It testified to a belief in willpower that was more anxious and more urgent, if not more convincing.

19

The Steadfast Citizen

Examples of perseverance and even abnegation came to the forefront at the very start of the nineteenth century, when a new way of life was being invented. Its democratic offshoot, the "new citizen," was a generic character who was unfailingly "entrepreneurial," diligent and amenable to "progress." Every project the new citizens attempted was useful and deserved attention; their fatigue, caused by both physical effort and personal willpower, would benefit everyone. The new citizens' world was being formed, and their labor was viewed differently. It had a social legitimacy rather than a religious one and was answerable more to politics than to morality, "now recognized as a foundation of the Republic whose ultimate goal is economic prosperity."[1] The Revolution had cultural effects: every person's responsibility to the community, even if it was physically demanding, was unquestionable and valued.

To serve all of us?

Efficiency was essential and indefatigability was taken for granted. A process was taking shape. Society had changed course and prioritized a collective wellbeing that depended on everyone's participation. Trades and professions reinvented the concept of a fatigue that was worthy and respectable; commitments were shared to enhance social cohesion. Leon Curmer published an illustrated book, *Les Français peints par eux-mêmes: Encyclopédie morale du dix-neuvième siècle* [The French, a group self-portrait], focused on the vagaries of a wide variety of his fellow citizens. Its subtitle, "A moral encyclopedia of the nineteenth century,"[2] was emblematic. The book featured a lawyer, for example, who got up "at 7 a.m., his case files are all in order … by nine he is at the courthouse … he never refuses a case, and no jurisdiction is too minor for him."[3] The doctor got up "at 5 a.m.," by seven "his hospital duties pry him away from his consulting rooms," at eleven he "is still wearing his white coat," and he then spent countless hours in the afternoon meeting his private patients."[4] The pharmacist was a "trustworthy and indefatigable chemist, a voluntary prisoner in his laboratory."[5] Other exemplary characters, concerned with keeping the peace and suppressing violence, were even more praiseworthy. The police captain "would tire out the most inventive lexicographer" with an "enumeration of all his accolades,"[6] and the police officer on the beat endured the "most arduous conditions" as the enforcer of our new and improved laws.[7] The "auditor" could not "sleep at night," so dedicated was he to the pursuit of fraudsters, while he spent his days plotting his "plans of attack."[8] Even humbler tradesmen and women were showered with hyperbolic praise. The herbalist was "busier" than a government minister.[9] The market gardener got up at dawn and had to be on the go "bright and early to find a depot that isn't being swarmed by wagons."[10] The grocer too must "be the first to get up and the last to go to bed."[11] The ragpicker relied on being "as diligent as an ant."[12] The handyman was "always willing and ready."[13] The pious lady thought it was "criminal" to "waste an hour" of her time.[14] And an almost mythic description of the typesetter demonstrated the power of numbers: "A diligent mathematician has found that in one year the typesetter's hand, moving between the type case and the composing stick, makes the equivalent of who knows how many trips around the world."[15]

Apprenticeship took its turn in the spotlight too, since it represented ambition and dogged persistence. In another didactic text with moral lessons, *Les Enfants peints par eux-mêmes* [Children, a group self-portrait], a young carpenter observed: "A board that would have tired me out when I first started working, is no big deal for me now. I know how to use a saw and chisel."[16]

These were idealized images, certainly, and even abstract ones, but the enthusiasm for hard work prepared the ground for an acknowledgement of endemic fatigue, as well as a relentless struggle against it. A whole range of occupations was affected, and specific measures were being taken to combat it. This understanding of fatigue was still purely descriptive and was sketched in terms both dramatic and resigned.

A similar sense of communal solidarity was expressed during the struggles of the Revolution and even during the Empire. For example, in his massive collection of poems *Les Châtiments* [The punishments], Victor Hugo celebrated legendary "useful" and admirable fatigues that were always overcome. In a paean to soldiers, one verse extolled their dogged tenacity: "At sunrise, at sunset, everywhere, in the south, at the poles, / With trusty old rifles hoisted on their shoulders, / Crossing rivers and mountains, with no rest, no sleep, shattered limbs, with no food, / They forged ahead, proud, joyous, sounding trumpets, just like demons."[17]

The hoary "tale" of fatigue[18] took on new resonance as memoirists described their confrontations with extreme hardships and brushes with death while they simultaneously saluted sacrifice and voluntary self-abnegation. The narrative of the retreat from Russia by Napoleon's troops became canonical and was no longer humiliating but, rather, heroic, and not a defeat but a reaffirmation. Sergeant Borgogne's recollections had a symbolic value. He dwelled on the troops' communal fatigue and their sacrifices, which were much more significant because of their "finality." Their struggle was a lesson for everyone. For instance, he lauded the military engineers or sappers at the battle of Berezina, "working at night in water up to their shoulders, sacrificing their lives to save the troops,"[19] as well as the exhausted comrades who supported Bourgogne, "who couldn't walk any further."[20] Some soldiers had given their all, but managed to draw on reserves of strength "to raise their heads and say "strike a blow for the emperor."[21] A new kind of fatigue was at the heart of this narrative. It was not one that was more clearly defined or even more painful because of its context,[22] but it was a kind of fatigue that was more collective, more "uniting," focused on a defined social goal. Bravery and fidelity played roles in it that might inspire non-combatant civilians.

The new citizen and "determination"

This kind of involvement highlighted a series of images: of potential victory, worthwhile sacrifice, and the type of zealous citizen who never gave up and was always seeking progress, wider horizons, and to "shed his skin" (that is, to become a different person). This was a time of even more profound disruptions: the social status or "condition" of each person was no longer accepted as a given or a state that was divinely ordained. Instead, it was an evolving state that could be shaped by ambition and personal initiative. Equality changed everything by justifying social mobility as well as ambition. This was a new vision of a respected member of society, one that was far removed from the classic courtier who bent over backward to imitate the king's every move or to satisfy his every whim.[23] This was also far from the educated man of the Enlightenment who fashioned his own self-worth, authored a narrative of the obstacles he had overcome, or took on challenges to feel more fully alive.[24] The crucial change here was "parity," a type of equivalence heretofore unknown, resulting in equal status for everyone. It was an idea that encouraged striving as much as it elevated a shared ideal, which was that of a "nation." This linked individual engagement to collective efforts and ennobled "useful" struggles or, in other words, recognized a kind of fatigue that elicited gratitude and even admiration.

Competition increased in importance in the culture of persistence and social mobility, highlighting the efforts and struggles of this upward climb. The character "Monsieur Beaudoin," in a little-known collection published in 1840 with the promising title *Vertu et travail* [Virtue and work], typified this phenomenon.[25] A humble employee in a trading company, Beaudoin quickly began to fight his way up the ladder. His travails were described in the florid style of a bad novel: "By the force of his dynamic willpower alone, through his hard work, fatigue and late nights, he manages to rise above the social condition that Heaven ordained for him at birth."[26] His success entailed a specific kind of exhaustion, combining austerity and harshness and connecting his "refusal to rest" to the self-improving studies he undertook "all night long."[27] The outcome was "painful" but predictable: Beaudoin took over the business from his boss, established a new venture, and put his own name on what became a "merchant bank."[28] His resistance to fatigue was a given, but his success was due to both physical and mental sacrifices as he endured physical and mental discomfort. This uplifting tale prescribed an "all out" commitment of one's personal energy as the route to a promising future.

Another example from the same collection, though a more subtle one, focused on a neglected child who achieved dignity and mastered a trade thanks to "relentless work," denying himself "all the little pleasures of life" and "even depriving himself of some of life's necessities."[29] The secret of his success was his stubbornness, and the story's arc traced the many obstacles he faced and the recurrent difficulties he always managed to overcome.

A magazine called *Le Fabricant: journal du maître et de l'ouvrier* [The manufacturer: the magazine of employers and workers] published a number of such success stories in the 1840s; it even had a regular feature profiling these paragons entitled "The Man of the Day,"[30] focusing on inventors, engineers and entrepreneurs, a mixed bag of doers whose only shared trait seemed to be an unshakable drive for progress. We read about Antoine Pauwels, the owner of both a lighting and a steamboat factory, who was able to "overcome all sorts of administrative hurdles" while waging a "long and painful struggle" to establish his plants in Rouen and Paris. The chemist Gustave-Augustin Quesneville wore several hats, as a factory manager, a researcher, an inventor and a writer. The series *Portraits et histoire des hommes utiles* [Portraits and stories of useful men], published during the July Monarchy, developed similar themes. Antoine-Jean Beauvisage's life story was one example among many, representing the triumph of a humble worker who dreamed of "improvements and optimizing performance."[31] He began work as a "dyer," where his future prospects seemed limited. However, his enthusiasm led him to employers who, fortunately, were willing to mentor him. Beauvisage embarked on a serious program of self-improvement, "often interrupting his sleep to take notes,"[32] withstood envious co-workers' sabotage attempts "that never stop,"[33] and finally made an important discovery in which a chemical reaction could "substitute for cochineal dye." A new future beckoned. Nevertheless, overwork resulted in a "very serious inflammation of the stomach," and Beauvisage had to make persistent and "incredible" efforts to pursue the needed medical treatment[34] while he established the factory and business he had longed for. The common theme of these stories was: "hard work is the only solution."[35]

Ambition exacts a price

In this way, continuous striving that might even be obsessive was associated with "social" fatigue and a sort of stubbornness that was signalled more indirectly. It took root in the nooks and crannies of tenacity and was expressed through personal drive and the determination to make use of every minute. It revealed itself and simultaneously erased itself. It intensified at the same time as it faded away. The great characters of Balzac demonstrated this through internal contradictions that were unexpressed but nevertheless significant. For instance, Benassis in *Le Médecin de campagne* [The country doctor] was a conscientious physician, wholly dedicated to transforming his rural commune. He worked ceaselessly, founding more businesses, making more trips, calling for more projects and contributing to their success. At first, the efforts seemed to pay off: the impoverished rural countryside was transformed, roads were improved, connections to other towns were strengthened, commercial exchanges were increased, the city was closer and the markets were diversified. All his activity made it possible, but Benassis didn't dwell on his struggles or the obstacles he overcame. He simply mentioned "incessant" activity[36] and claimed he "exhausted two horses every day."[37] Another example is Desroches in Balzac's *La Maison Nucingen* [The Nucingen firm], one of the character studies in *Scènes de la vie parisienne* [Scenes of Parisian life]. Desroches, having "worked hard from 1818 to 1822," was a symbol of persistence and the "terror of his clerks," who themselves were exhorted constantly: "do not waste time."[38] Like Desroches, the main character of Balzac's novel *Albert Savarus* was indefatigable and suffering. A socially minded and status-conscious citizen, Savarus ran for a position as a deputy from the provinces after an electoral defeat in Paris and toiled ceaselessly at his law practice, building up his case load to gain more prestige, no matter the cost, "getting up every night between 1 and 2 a.m., working until 8 a.m., having breakfast and then getting back to work."[39] Savarus' fatigue, we assume, could be calculated by the number of hours he spent in his office and the rhythm and intensity of his work.

Savarus alluded to fatigue in his progressively more subjective and personal confessions. He was a man who had given his all:

> I've been struggling for ten years now … This battle with men and things in which I devoted all my energy and strength, where I drew on all the resources of my will, has hollowed me out inside, so to speak. Even though I seem healthy and strong, I feel used up. Every day tears a strip off my inner self. With each new effort I feel as if I cannot keep on.[40]

The essence of his fatigue was thus more diffuse, associated with a feeling of limitations and of impotence rather than with the demands of the projects themselves. Fatigue turned into a general malaise with alarming symptoms that had rarely been mentioned before: "My ears are constantly ringing, my hands are clammy with perspiration, my mind is racing and my body is quaking internally, as I play my final card in the game of ambition."[41] This was a crucial example of the discomfort the subject experienced which was seen and felt only by him. His perceptions were undoubtedly linked to a new attentiveness to internal feelings, and even a distinct evolution in self-consciousness. But this evolution was also connected to a new social struggle that was absolutely original, one that the democratic imagination had made possible. Savarus explained this in a letter written to the woman he loved, describing the tiredness he felt dealing with competition and the dog-eat-dog mentality of the time: "What tires and ages me, my angel, is the agony of my wounded ego, the constant annoyances of Parisian life and the battles of competing ambitions."[42]

A new and unusual "temperament" was developing, one not affected by the tough physical demands of the trades[43] but hidden below the surface, expressed in desires more than in actions. It was a method of self-torment: a lassitude born specifically of an anxiety about social climbing and the unexamined drive for social advancement. According to Balzac, this could affect laborers whose only asset was their body: "Then these primates began to stay up late, suffer, work, swear, walk. They are all driven by the desire to earn the gold that fascinates them."[44] Such excessiveness was unheard of until now in Balzac's exploration of its resonance and intensity.

Still, at the beginning of the nineteenth century the domestic servant was the exception among workers. Bound by tradition, identifying with "duty" and mindful of obligations, men and women "in service" did not see themselves as distinct from their masters and could not expect autonomy. They worked in an intimate family setting where hierarchies had been preserved,[45] to such an extent that the ambition of the "valet" was supposed to match that of the "master." Didactic handbooks solemnly invoked the proper attitude and behavior in "servitude": "Every minute of your life must be devoted to the comfort of the people you serve."[46] Popular literature repeated this incessantly: "A servant must be entirely devoted, giving of himself without hesitation or second thoughts."[47]

Nevertheless, with the advent of a democratic society at the beginning of the nineteenth century, the scope of fatigue had become both broader and more visible. It was dispersed among the multiplicity of trades but was also affected by a diffuse and hidden tendency that concerned the use of time. Making use of one's time had been largely rethought and the prescriptions offered were as calculated as they were targeted.

Intensifying the use of time

Making use of time and paying attention to the progression of the hours and the fullness of each moment clearly marked a change in the culture and was a new benchmark. As a result, the outlines of a new kind of fatigue emerged on the horizon, associated with the specific question of how people spent time. This led to a quasi-obligatory survey of different professions. For example, a doctor's workday had clearly demarcated tasks, allotments of time and travel between different locations: the medical office, hospital and consultations with private clients.[48] A lawyer set aside time for appointments and consultations of various kinds, and a journalist began work "around noon" and continued through the evening before attending performances at night and writing up reviews, still busy during the hours when "everyone else is resting."[49] The practice of dedicating certain hours to specific tasks became more common. For instance, the market gardener would "get up before two in the morning," go to the market to sell his wares "until seven in the morning," return home, "lie down for a rest on a pallet," and then quickly get up again to "plant, harvest and water" his crops."[50] The freelance reporter rushed to the Tuileries at seven in the morning, spent an hour or two at the Carrousel watching the messengers coming and going, and then headed to the Stock Exchange "to check on the prices of stocks and shares."[51] Even an ordinary clerk, whose workday wasn't overly demanding, "starting at ten o'clock and ending at four," had to contend eventually with the necessities of marriage, family life and children. These ate up his time, forcing him to seek out other ways to earn money and escape "poverty" in a "thankless seventeen-hour workday."[52]

These descriptions were commonplace yet critically important; activities were divided into steps and work time was apportioned. The concept of a basic work rhythm was not new. For many years, clocks have marked out the time, and so have sounds such as bells and chimes. Monasteries were the first to mark divisions of time in order to put it to better use serving the Lord. The innovation here was the attempt to achieve the ultimate in efficiency with an optimal use of time. It was associated with a widely accepted sense of meticulousness, of recognizing the value in every moment, of making every minute count, and of constantly assuming more responsibilities so that time passing became time profitably spent. This underlined the contrast between the pre-revolutionary kingdom of France [the Ancien Régime], with its static time, frozen in immobility, and the new world of fluid time, where citizens defied rigid limits and strove for progress. As a result, the present was charged with meaning as part of a larger process oriented in a specific direction. For manufacturers, artisans and merchants, punctilious attention to time management was understood as a down payment on the future: "He brings his accounts up to date and never goes to bed without scrupulously planning for the workday tomorrow."[53] Marc-Antoine Jullien gave an example of this in 1808 in his *Essai sur une méthode qui a pour objet de bien régler l'emploi du temps, premier moyen d'être heureux* [Essay on a method to use time fruitfully, the principal means to happiness]. He conveyed the main point in a few well-chosen words: you must know "what time is worth and how to use every minute to your advantage, for your benefit."[54] The essayist urged readers to "exploit" all possibilities, maximize even the tiniest fraction of time, and aim for perfection. Again, this was a real change in culture where making progress was seen as a personal moral challenge. Marc-Antoine Jullien's book was a success and was reissued several times between 1808 and 1830. His recommendations percolated into popular consciousness. As Julien-Joseph Virey exclaimed in 1823, in his *De la puissance vitale* [On our vital powers]: "How many days have been wasted indulging our senses!"[55] Moreover, the prescriptions aligned with pedagogical life lessons. As a book "addressing young people" advised in 1812: "Let's be thrifty with our time. Let's not give away even a minute without getting full value from it. Never let the hours slip through your fingers without building up a reserve, without a profit."[56] In fact, a distinct and novel tension underlay those apparently banal words: an allusion to social advancement, to breaching heretofore impenetrable class barriers with the aid of tenacity, perseverance and also fatigue.

The children of the century, the fatigue of illusion

Ambition was given new life, transformed by time management and the aspiration toward limitless progress, but there was also the ambiguity caused by broken promises, obstacles and unrealistic dreams. At the beginning of the nineteenth century, society was also riven by disappointments, unrealized ideals and distant unattainable solutions. For many, it was an era of "lost illusions"[57] and the particular kinds of fatigue they engendered. Corruption or oppression could thwart hope. Materialism, social divisions and various kinds of deprivation[58] could bring plans to an abrupt halt. "The future seemed to belong to us," but "the power of the new men"[59] turned out to be as exclusive as the privileges of "old men." The poet Alfred Musset wrote melancholically: "There was a time when joyous youth, / Forever fluttered at my mouth, / A merry, singing bird just freed, / Strange martyrdom has since been mine."[60] Balzac repeatedly made this a focus of his novels. Disillusionment almost had a physical presence there and was more painful than the characters' fatigue. In *La Peau de chagrin* [The wild ass's skin], Raphaël de Valentin dosed himself with a "lightly opiated drink" that spurred a "persistent state of sleepiness"[61] after "working day and night without a break," in an effort that was as fruitless as it was overlooked.[62] In the third section of Balzac's *Les Illusions perdues*, "Souffrances de l'inventeur" [The inventor's sufferings], Lucien Chardon felt an overwhelming sense of despair after a "catastrophe" swept away all his hopes when his body and soul were already "battered" by a "long and painful struggle." Convinced that his only option was to commit suicide, he planned to ask his host to "help to lay him out on his bed, all the while asking forgiveness for the inconvenience of his death."[63] Alfred de Vigny bitterly acknowledged a cycle of loss and deprivation: "The reverie that is unproductive makes us weaker."[64] In 1840, the paradox[65] of democratic uplift and downfall is acknowledged in *Les Français peints par eux-mêmes* in the observation: "Many people are wondering: If soldiers can become kings, and a lieutenant in the artillery has become the master of Europe, why can't I be a minister, a general or a deputy?"[66]

The satires published during these years were revealing. In 1838, Honoré Daumier published a series of caricatures, "Les Robert Macaires," showing Macaire practicing a "hundred and one" different professions.

This "phenomenal odyssey" through the world of work got its humor from the obstacles, disputes and "droll" mishaps it presented, much like the encounters with illusions and disappointments of Cervantes' hapless *Don Quixote*. Daumier's *Caricaturana* was an innovative attempt to poke fun at his society's collective ambition, its stubborn drive to succeed, to rise above one's social class, to take risks, to try new things and, come what may, "distinguish oneself from the vulgar mob that is blocking the road to riches."[67] In 1842, Louis Reybaud published a social satire with similar themes of striving and disappointment, *Jérôme Paturot à la recherche d'une position sociale* [Jérôme Paturot seeking a position in society].[68] The humor came from the main character's "descent" down the ladder rather than his "rise," since he had fooled himself into believing he was capable of everything but found he was in fact suited to very little, suffering a "rude, deflating awakening."[69] The crux of both of these satirical works was the tension between the characters' ego-driven, tenacious, painful obsession with social advancement and their disenchantment after exhausting brushes with failure. Their downfall attested to the fact that democratic striving was as new as it was damaging.

A first elitist search for a break

Other creative energies were directed toward, and other defenses were focused on, a "pause." This was a temporary hiatus for elites, at least, to use as a way to combat fatigue. At the turn of the century, "political upheavals" and social struggles were intense, and passions were high and disruptive enough to become the subject of medical students' theses on "nervous ailments"[70] provoked by vaguely identified tensions, tics and discomforts.

First and foremost, writers pointed to cities and their spaces dedicated to relaxation, where troubling thoughts were banished and weary bodies could rest. These were inevitably marketed to a selective clientele seeking peace, quiet and relief from tension. For example, certain bathhouses were socially and culturally identified with this goal: tastefully landscaped and elegantly designed with separate, quiet, well-equipped private rooms. The gentle flow of water promised a sense of tranquility and the silence of the private room offered a respite from the turbulent streets. At the beginning of the nineteenth century, advances in hydraulic engineering with improvements in water pumps and the installation of iron pipes enabled some bathhouses to be built near riverbanks. They were few in number but had a specific purpose, which was not simply to provide a refuge from the noisy crowds and the "vortex" of city streets but also to calm customers' nervous tics, obsessive worries and foul tempers – in a word, to ease tensions. A guidebook described the Tivoli baths in Paris, two blocks from the Seine near the Chaussée d'Antin, offering relief from "nervous ailments, spasms, ringing in the ears and brain fog."[71] The author, who wrote about bathhouses "in the four corners of the world," had high praise for Tivoli's refined pleasures: "refreshing shade and charming walks,"[72] delicate perfumes, scented waters, expertly prepared meals of "fortifying nutrition," with "tonic wine" and "essence of veal bouillon" on the menu.[73] The guidebook also lauded the Vigier baths near Pont-Royal, located on a docked frigate in a romantic setting of sandy, tree-shaded walkways lined with planters filled with orange trees, rose bushes, weeping willows, locust trees, wisteria and lilacs."[74] As a refuge meant to banish all fatigue, it offered a relaxing break for body and soul:

> Your soul will calm down as soon you arrive in this charming byway; you will smile at your recollections of the noisy and tiresome tumult of Paris; its wearying hustle and bustle is already far from your thoughts. Your tired feet, aching from strolling on the paved streets, will meet the verdant lawn with pleasure and the walkways will lead you to the land of repose. The scent of the bushes, the flowering plants, the gentle murmur of the water – everything beckons you to enter deeper and deeper stages of relaxation. The bustle of city life, the clamor dinning in your ears in the midst of the capital city will be transformed into calm, peaceful and delectable sensations here … Everyone and everything around you will add to the new feeling of peace in your soul.[75]

Spa towns were often thought of as social and cultural neighbors to cities and were also seen as refuges, as at Enghien, where "nerves begin to relax, the mind expands, the blood purifies itself"[76] and "nervous ailments" would be cured.[77] At Passy, visitors would forget the tensions "brought on by living in big cities,"[78] and at Mont-Dore visitors would restore their "vital forces."[79]

Thus, travel had a new goal that differed from previous ones. Stendhal was one of the first to see traveling as a strategy to distance oneself from the annoyances of daily life.[80] Jules Janin added a new perspective, suggesting that we should travel not in search of the stimulation and excitement we encountered on the road but for a sense of limitless possibilities and personal freedom. We would be revitalized if we let ourselves go and expected and did nothing. Janin explained that, when "his mind felt stale"[81] and he was fed up with the endless round of duties and responsibilities, he decided to take a trip and have a change of scene: "To let oneself be lulled by the motions of the carriage … To do nothing, hear nothing, decide nothing …."[82] The novelty of his proposal was its change of perspective; it prioritized idleness and isolation. "To live only for oneself, to be alone with one's dreams, thoughts and ideas."[83] This was a new valorization of the self at the dawn of the modern era and an argument for accepting one's internal emptiness and using it as a defense against the toll exacted by ambition, competition and conflict. Jules Janin envisioned, quite simply, taking a vacation as a remedy for the increasing tensions of his age.

20

A World of Numbers: From Mechanics to Energy

At the beginning of the century, shattered dreams, discontent and even society's failures did not thwart economic ambition, confidence in technology and the drive for prosperity. This unshakable belief prioritizing "inventors" and "entrepreneurs" brought our vision of progress into sharper focus and reinforced our determination to develop "the arts and sciences." The ever expanding realm of workshops, machines, motors and other mechanical devices put the focus on material outcomes, natural potential, and methods to re-engineer our actions for utmost efficiency. An unmistakable revitalization spurred by science and technology built on the sometimes halting and disparate advances of the Enlightenment[1] and would now foreground mathematicians and engineers. Institutions created after the Revolution made this clear. The mission of the *Journal de l'École polytechnique* was to "disseminate useful knowledge" and encourage "successful implementation."[2] The École centrale des arts et manufactures was founded in 1829 to foster the development of "empirical knowledge."[3] Ambitious goals such as "bettering the conditions of life for Humanity"[4] focused on maximizing people's productivity while minimizing their exertions. The same concern was adopted by scientific and technical societies. Fatigue was understood as a complement to physical labor. This perspective animated the "Gesellschaft Deutscher Naturforscher und Ärzte" [Society of German natural scientists and physicians] established in Berlin in 1822 and the British Association for the Advancement of Science, founded in London in 1831.[5] Scientists were inevitably focused on work, studying the efforts that are expended and their results, and thus the workshop and worksite received renewed attention and a measure of dignity. Fatigue was being studied in the context of manual labor, physical exertion and the use of muscles and arms. Everything came back to "exertion." Everything had a physical basis.

More generally, at the beginning of the century, the increasing importance of machinery and industrial management techniques highlighted the intersection of the power of mathematics and the logic of the body. Machines became more common, workers had to adapt to them, and human power had to interface with mechanical force. More studies were undertaken on workers' use of their bodies and on increasing the efficiency of their actions. This was the concern of engineers, of course, whose theories promised greater output. Fortunately, lessening the effects of fatigue was also in their purview. Motion studies were now high on the agenda, and power flows and technical operations became the perennial subjects of calculations. Industrialists and their allies expressed a renewed interest in workers' fatigue.

Calculating forces

An entirely new device revolutionized calculations of force. In the 1760s, Buffon had ordered such an instrument from the engineer and inventor Edme Regnier to investigate different kinds of force: not just laborers carrying goods or transporting loads, which was virtually the only activity studied, but also other actions performed at work, such as pushing, pulling, pressing, standing erect, or using one's body as a counterweight. Attention shifted from workers' backs to their arms, legs, torsos and hands. In other words, scientists needed to expand their field of study and critically examine other uses of labor power. After several attempts, at the end of the century Regnier devised something heretofore unseen, a mechanical dynamometer to measure force, consisting of a "double spring that would retain its elasticity despite frequent use,"[6] with a slider to indicate the value of the force expended. Thus, the amount of pressure or resistance could be measured mechanically, enabling new sets of calculations and observations. Regnier published his findings in the *Journal de l'École polytechnique* in 1798, with observations about everyday activities: "the left and right hands" do not exert equal amounts of force; "a blacksmith and a wig-maker" have completely different manual dexterity at a range of one to two; a man and a horse can pull in a range from one to seven; women and men have bodily strength that ranges from two to three.[7] The study did not include specific measurements of fatigue, but assessments such as these were meant to predict or even prevent it by calculating the potential force to be exerted and the efficiencies achieved. The dynamometer began to be used more generally at the beginning of the nineteenth century. For many, it was merely a device that helped to win a bet or impress an audience, so it made its way to fairs and circuses, where it was used by acrobats and strong men to measure the force of their leaps or lifts. Caricaturists such as Daumier and La Bédollière featured it ironically in images of humble "dials" advertised to measure "the strength of your fists."[8] But the dynamometer was also an instrument of scientific investigation used to assess the strength and potential of different parts of the body and to categorize different degrees or intensity of power that had not previously been tested.

Simple observations were made, experiments were repeated, calculations were performed and data began to accumulate. In the 1820s, Adolphe Quetelet used the results to sketch a profile of the "average man," of whom, in this "democratic" society, statistics were intended to reveal "character" and "aptitude." Quetelet studied expenditures of energy in various circumstances and presented his observations; like Regnier, he found differences between occupations. "Masons and carpenters"[9] concentrated force in their arms and hands. Different living conditions affected people's physical capacity, as measured by the dynamometer: "moderate exercise and adequate access to food will help develop physical abilities, but poverty and overwork have the opposite effect."[10] These observations tended to invalidate, or even debunk, long-held beliefs about the connection between size, body weight and strength. Researchers collected new information about resilience and strength.

We must emphasize that fatigue was not a specific factor in these studies, but it was a subtext in the nineteenth-century cult of calculations and in the search for practical improvements and efficiencies at work. Finally, progress based on solid evidence seemed possible. One example was in physical education, where new methods to increase strength and flexibility were introduced, building on the original program devised by Mme Genlis in the previous century.[11] In Berne, Peter Clias adapted gymnastic exercises for use in his school, along with the dynamometer, which he called a "penalty" to be employed on laggard students. His popular treatise described the "renaissance" in 1815 of a frail sixteen-year-old boy who worked out on a variety of machines and gymnastic apparatuses in a program that included stretching, bicep curls and hand grips. Measurements showed that within a few months the boy's strength had doubled.[12] In Paris in 1820, Francisco Amoros adopted a gymnastic program, a dynamometer and a "physiological record card" for each pupil in his school, noting the results of "hand grips," "extensions," "pull-ups," "flips using the left hand," "flips using the right hand," "chest presses," "handstands ..."[13] Earlier methods of relying on a person's appearance to assess their strength, whether for recruits in the military or forced labor in the galley slave ships, were almost entirely abandoned in favor of the power of numbers.

Inventing "applied mechanics"

A new branch of the physical sciences was developed at the beginning of the nineteenth century responding to the plethora of motors and machinery, and workers' increasing reliance on them. Applied or practical mechanics offered a new perspective on the workplace, concentrating on the everyday interactions among bodies, motors, conveyor belts and steel in order to enhance efficiencies and increase profits. In 1822 Gérard-Joseph Christian, the director of the Royal Conservatory of Arts and Trades, defined applied mechanics as "a science whose goal is to learn about and research methods to complement man's strength and abilities and to help him save time in performing work required by his needs and ambitions. We call this science industrial mechanics to distinguish it from pure mechanics, whose purview is quite different."[14]

Far from limiting itself to studying the mechanization of work, applied mechanics also examined the interplay of man and machine. Technical education was introduced to change workers' habits. Charles Dupin studied the results of practical courses in England[15] before adopting them at the Royal Conservatory in 1819, following a decree by Louis XVIII that established free public classes that "apply science to the industrial arts."[16] Similar programs funded by "generous citizens" were started in Lille, Versailles and Strasbourg.[17] In 1829 Claude-Lucien Bergery published his three-volume work on industrial economy and outlined a practical education program for workers in Metz.[18] The lessons were proactive, not prescriptive: "Break from your routine." "Think through all the steps in the work process."[19] And it promised positive results: "You will feel much less fatigued but you will earn much more."[20] In other words, if they adopted this perspective, workers would feel less fatigued but would be productive. Bergery's book addressed many specific circumstances, especially workers' posture and actions: "Standing, using the arms," "Standing, using the legs," "Seated, using the arms," "Seated, using the legs" and "Seated, using arms and legs."[21] Workers had to learn to maintain the optimal posture for their task, such as the "fixed points" of contact when seated with legs parallel and feet firmly planted on the floor.[22] Some "madman authors" of the nineteenth century[23] proposed a slew of methods for "preventing fatigue when sawing, hammering, using a wood plane, carrying loads, forging steel, pushing, pulling …."[24] The tips were often useless, but they are emblematic of the growing trend to theorize about movement and, even more urgently, to recommend methods to make it more efficient.

Illustrations of the time captured views of workers standing, sitting or operating levers; others were shown pushing barrels up inclines. Still others were operating different types of jacks or moving loads by "sliding," "rolling," "pulling" or using "wheels."[25] Some well-known contemporary artists depicted men at work, such as Jean Duplessi-Bertaux, who published an album of etchings in 1822 with scenes of military and urban life that showed the characteristic gestures of blacksmiths, barrel-makers, carpenters and knife-grinders, among others.[26] While calculations and systems proliferated, the studies of force and time zeroed in on ever more specific subjects, as this observation demonstrated: "In general for continuous, uninterrupted work that requires a force of 8 to 10 kilograms and lasts for eight or nine hours, the worker must be standing up and using only his arms; there is almost never a better option."[27]

Coulomb's studies of expenditures of force[28] were revived, but now researchers were focusing not on isolated actions but on repeated ones. The number of calculations grew, as did the number of subjects. More workplaces were studied and more working conditions were inventoried. For example, the output of the forced labor of English prisoners on "penal treadmills" powering grindstones, water pumps or other machinery was measured: "On average, every prisoner must ascend fifty steps per minute, or 3,000 per hour. Each step is 0.2 meters high. The prisoner on the treadmill works continuously for seven hours a day."[29] The excavation techniques of military engineering corpsmen using spades and shovels was studied in 1837. Key factors were the volume of the soil, the angle of the tool and, again, the repetition of the motion. "A man can dig up and deposit in a wheelbarrow approximately 12 to 15 cubic meters of soil a day. When the soil is tossed a distance of 2 meters minimum and 4 meters maximum, or lifted up 1.60 meters or loaded onto a tipcart, we must reduce the number of cubic meters to 10."[30] There were specific parameters for the time allotted to porters and the distances they were to travel: 30 meters for moving wheelbarrow loads and 72 seconds for each round trip.[31] Walking was a perennial favorite for time and motion studies, and one recommended these norms and limits:

> A pedestrian can walk 6 kilometers in an hour at a steady pace on a road, which would equal 100 meters a minute. Each step is approximately 8 decimeters long; thus, a pedestrian takes 125 steps per minute and 7,500 in an hour. He can maintain this pace for eight and a half hours a day and continue doing it for as many days as he wants without damaging his health or diminishing his strength. We conclude from these calculations that the average pedestrian can walk 51 kilometers without affecting or reducing his energy.[32]

As a result, recommendations proliferated, identifying averages, rejecting anomalies and highlighting comparisons. There was a significant drive to collect data and propose standards for agricultural labor; as a result, we learned how much "manure can be unloaded" in a ten-hour workday or how much "wheat can be sown," how many fields can be "mowed," how many turnips can be "transplanted," and how many "sheafs can be loaded onto wagons" and "stored in a barn." Additional calculations were made for work "in distant fields."[33] Nevertheless, "feelings" and "judgment" still trumped empirical data when it came to identifying the toll taken by work, and approximation won out over calculation in this case: "Only experience can determine how much work can be done if one wants to prevent fatigue and to know how much each type of machine, or even a particular machine, can accomplish in a day's work, as well as how many work hours can be spent before fatigue sets in, depending on the task."[34]

Clearly, it was impossible to ignore the "benefits" that "applied mechanics" promised in the 1820s, overshadowing Coulomb's findings on exertion by individuals and the suggestions of Enlightenment thinkers in meticulous but time-consuming description of the trades.[35] Now, every expenditure of effort was studied in an economic context; every recommendation targeted efficiency. Gérard-Joseph Christian gave another example of this in 1822 in his study: "A man will tolerate working for longer periods of time and will suffer less fatigue, all things being equal, if his actions are uniform and steady, at the same pace, with the same amount of effort."[36] He recommended not engaging "all the muscles in the body" simultaneously, to increase force and pressure "by degrees," and to allow for "frequent rest periods to reinvigorate the body."[37] Avoiding unnecessary exertions and enhancing resilience were at the heart of the matter and fatigue was considered only tangentially, more subjectively felt than objectively investigated. An evergreen practical conclusion underlined a "belief" rooted in customs and past practices: "The amount of labor assigned to each living being, the number of tasks and of rest periods, etc., can be determined only by a good amount of experience."[38]

In other words, the field of applied mechanics continued evolving, but physiology remained the realm of estimates rather than calculations.

Inventing energy

Mechanical engineers gradually started to pay more attention to physiology in the second third of the nineteenth century. They were interested in the source of the body's energy (the "motor") and not simply in posture and movement. Researchers began to dig below the surface into areas that Coulomb had overlooked in his studies of observable results, such as Lavoisier's work on combustion and respiration.[39] Lavoisier's discoveries had long been neglected because the results were hard to measure with the available instruments and methods, but now the work was being reappraised, critically evaluated and extended. Everyone agreed that "breathing is the most essential animal function."[40] It produced warmth and provided "fuel" to muscles, for work and for all kinds of physical exertion. In 1843 Gabriel Andral and Jules Gavarret used valves and tubes to study inhalation and exhalation and compared different people's intake of oxygen and release of carbon dioxide. The two scientists recorded their experimental subjects' breathing rates and the composition of their inhalations and exhalations. They concluded that "the amount of carbon dioxide that is exhaled by the lungs varies with the individual, and is greater in people who are more robust and have more extensive muscles."[41] They also found that, "after the age of fifty," the production of carbon dioxide decreases and continues falling "as one ages."[42] The "fittest specimens" were able to burn the oxygen they took in and put it to use efficiently. In 1849 Victor Regnault and Jules Reiset compared respiration in animals, noting the differences by species, weight, age and activity level, and came to a similar conclusion.[43] In the 1850s Gustave Hirn continued this line of experiments, but focused on work; inhaled air was studied for its mechanical and "productive" aspects. Concentrating on differences that he suspected were significant, he compared his own respiration to that of a hardy young girl in an attempt to quantify a person's capacity to "burn" oxygen. Fatigue was measured by the subjects' state of breathlessness as well as by the gases they exhaled.

> In a resting state, I inhaled approximately eighteen times a minute, and the girl took at most twelve breaths. I took in more than one liter of air with each inhalation, but she only took in half of that. Her lungs' capacity to absorb oxygen is much greater than mine. Thus, in one hour, the 350 liters of air that passed through her lungs had greater amounts of carbon dioxide than, proportionally, the 700 liters that moved through mine.[44]

Hirn extended the comparative study to mountain climbing, with himself as a subject. During the ascent, he found he used "four times more oxygen" than he did at rest; much of the oxygen was not being consumed because of his exertions, but because his body was burning a lot of calories, making unnecessary movements, and suffering from overactive reflexes and muscle cramps. The girl's performance was the exact opposite. She generated little excess heat and efficiently powered up the mountain. These observations led to a new distinction between an "efficient" use of oxygen that was turned into energy and an inefficient one, where wasted resources leaked out in perspiration and body heat and impeded one's actions. The efficiently used oxygen was absorbed by the lungs and was broken down "positively." The inefficiently combusted oxygen trickled out from the body, converted into an artificial "ferment." The difference lay in the "heat that is lost" and the "heat that is generated."[45] The latter usefully revved up the "motor," while the former uselessly activated the brakes. Here, Hirn extended Lavoisier's observations beyond discrete measurements of oxygen consumption and exertion. The two types of oxygen used here differed in both function and outcome: "People differ most in the quantity of useless excess heat they generate."[46] Other scientists, such as Sadi Carnot and James Joule, soon confirmed this distinction and developed new theories, and in the 1820s and 1830s applied these principles to steam engines, powered by the mechanical equivalent of heat. These machines "every day right before our eyes present the spectacle of work generated by heat."[47] The most efficient engines reduced the loss of steam that might otherwise escape from pipes, through friction or from leaking out of hatches that were not completely sealed, because they maximized the conversion of heat into energy. Inspired by these advances to compare the work of steam engines with the "human motor," in 1858 Gustave Hirn experimented with a clumsy apparatus that he called a "hermetic alcove," constructed from well-sealed pine planks and furnished with a "bladed wheel and an escalator," where the temperature, respiration and gases produced by a subject working the moving stairs were monitored.[48] He found that increased consumption of oxygen could be temporary, and "work output" was reduced when breathing was labored, actions of the muscles were disordered, and perspiration increased. However, fatigue increased with excessive body heat, panting breath and feelings of overexertion. Hirn saw a parallel between human distress and machines malfunctioning: "A person who is out of breath and sweaty when climbing a mountain is acting just like those clumsy engine-tenders who overheat their furnaces and then have to release steam, which is plainly a loss and a waste. On the other hand, an experienced tender stokes the fire only to the extent necessary to get the output he wants."[49]

The theoretical framework about effort had changed decisively and was a sign of a major, if not complete, revolution in thought. Fatigue was not caused by weakened bodily fibers resulting in slack limbs and limp nerves, as in the eighteenth century,[50] but was due to a dysfunction in respiration and the exchange of gases in the lungs leading, at one extreme, to excessive heat and, at the other, to an inability to modulate temperatures. There was too much agitation at one extreme and too little combustion at the other, and, in the end, no amount of effort could overcome one's lack of energy. Scientific observers had shifted their attention to new subjects. The body's losses were different in kind and in location. Fatigue was caused by the scarcity of a specific element, fire, and tensions and contractions, even pains, accompanied it. Scientific explanations had changed. The scientists' focus was elsewhere. A very concrete and material force was driving this: "If the nineteenth century was obsessed with fatigue, it wasn't only a sign of the "genuine" tiredness experienced by people in industrial society. It was also a reflection of the concept of the body as a thermodynamic machine that is able to create and store energy."[51]

This did not mean that all norms and all categories of work corresponded to the ratio obtained by measuring an exchange of gases. Without exception, scientific commentaries emphasized that "every individual differs in the ability of their lungs to absorb oxygen."[52]

The key point, however, was elsewhere, in the shifting image of workers' fatigue, the explanations for it and the methods to prevent it. One had to avoid any waste of "fire" or any unnecessary tension and strive for feeling at ease with one's "furnace" – and even engage in "training" it. This was a well-worn conclusion, similar to the recommendations of applied mechanics regarding workers' actions, their adaptation to new norms, and the drive for efficiency. Yet, this was also somewhat different; the formulas did not call simply for careful posture and coordinated actions but were concerned with methods of taking in oxygen and expelling carbon dioxide, and enabling combustion at its most efficient level.

The scientists' gaze had definitely shifted. A new subject attracted their attention: the chest, which was now seen as the "furnace" and a key component of the "motor." The cavity protected and defined by the ribs had metamorphosed into a site for measurements and calculations. Its potential was studied and its structure was re-evaluated. Hygienists and physiologists considered it the body's "capital." In 1823 Gabriel Andral began his classes in clinical medicine with a review of "illnesses of the chest,"[53] and in 1828 his classes in hygiene studied "respiration and atmospheric air."[54] This was a novel focus, and physicians were taught to assess the size and shape of the thorax as a gauge of a patient's robustness. In the 1840s the Scottish "founder of military medical statistics," Dr Henry Marshall, recommended that recruits be rejected if "the chest circumference is less than 31 inches."[55] To Eugène-Joseph

Woillez, a paltry chest measurement was a warning sign for pleurisy.[56] Louis Laveran proposed a method of triage that distinguished the strong from the weak: a chest circumference of 83 centimeters (33 inches) for the strong, and 77 centimeters (30 inches) for the weak.[57] Numbers and measurements had taken their place alongside physical appearance and attitude in assessing human capacity.

Scientists continued to explore the question of respiration. Some, for example the "professor of natural and herbal medicine" P. Lutterbach, seemed obsessed with it, as were his contemporaries the "literary madmen." Lutterbach published a pamphlet in 1852 cataloguing almost thirty types of breathing.[58] For example, the "undulating" breath will lift one's mood, "rhythmic" breathing will alleviate the fatigue of walking, "progressive" breathing was best for runners, and so on. The methods to "pleasantly enhance one's life" included "staccato" breaths, "well-rounded" breaths, "vacillating" breaths," "floating" breaths, "purgative" breaths, "salivating" breaths, and other techniques such as the "nursing woman's" breath and "isochromatic" breathing. Lutterbach's inventory, presented with a thin veneer of scientific veracity, may be inflated and verging on nonsensical, but it demonstrated the importance of respiration to all sorts of scientists in the mid-nineteenth century.

More original and useful was the invention of the water "spirometer" by John Hutchinson in 1845. This device measured the amount of breath expelled by the lungs, and thus lung capacity.[59] A calibrated bell inverted in water captured the volume of air exhaled by the subject. Hutchinson proposed a new benchmark, "vital capacity," which was the maximum amount of air expelled from the lungs after a maximum inhalation. In this way, a new "capacity" was added to the roster of measurements and an "internal" aptitude was externalized. The most resilient individuals were the ones with the largest capacity because each inhalation yielded the most combustion. With this invention came the conviction that it was possible to get "valuable evidence to measure people's strength and to use in actuarial predictions about their lifespan."[60]

Reinventing nutrition

Gustave Hirn's experiments kept their focus on respiration, oxygen and the role of combustion, while other studies of energy inevitably turned to the role of food, which was the substance consumed and "burned" by the body. Food made an important contribution to combustion and thus to work. As Albrecht Thaër observed in 1830: "The strength, activity and dexterity of man is infinitely varied and depends a great deal on the food he eats and the healthiness of his surroundings. A worker whom I pay 12 groschen per day can sometimes do more than double the work in quantity and quality than another who is paid 6."[61]

On the face of it, this was a banal observation, since poor nutrition or semi-starvation would intuitively be understood as a cause of weakness and exhaustion. In 1844 Michel Lévy echoed a basic public health principle when he asserted that "overwork is signaled by a feeling of fatigue, and this occurs sooner in weak and malnourished people than in those who are neither."[62] The originality of his statement was due to its references to oxygen and "fire," the two elements of organic combustion identified by chemists in the second third of the century: a flammable gas and its medium, the flame and its fuel. Justus von Liebig's down-to-earth metaphor about body chemistry was easily grasped: "Food is for the animal what fuel is for the stove."[63] The treatise he published in 1842 divided food into two categories: "flexible foods" that provided the building blocks for the body's organs and "respiratory foods" that fueled the body's fire.[64] The latter, "fat, starch, sugar, pectin, wine, aquavit and resin" were rich in carbon and calories.[65] His analysis was innovative since, for the first time, it identified an end product of organic combustion, lactic acid, which was detected in the bloodstream after exertion and exercise. In this way, chemistry provided an explanation for the pain and discomfort brought on by fatigue.

"Energy" was regarded as essential to starting up the machine and to keep it running; both were supported by proper nutrition. At the beginning of the nineteenth century, statisticians and geographers identified nutrition as a new benchmark to distinguish between rich and poor regions and thriving versus struggling populations. Stigmatized for their poor nutrition, five departments in the center of France were identified as "the regions where the most chestnuts are consumed; of the 767,000 bushels consumed in France, these five account for 407,500."[66] Balzac's "country doctor" Benassis also used diet as a benchmark in his campaign to modernize the isolated region's backward rural ways. He advocated for drastic changes in local agriculture and consumption, urging villagers to give up "potatoes and dairy products"[67] in favor of red or white meat, whose superior nutritional value would restore their energy and resilience. "I cured peasants of the diseases that are so easy to treat. It was only a matter of revitalizing their energy through sound nutrition."[68] Sir John Sinclair, a Scottish financier and economist and the first president of the Board of Agriculture, advised farmers to feed draft horses the more "energy-packed" hay instead of straw, assuring them that, "with this diet and two servings of grain per day, horses will not only be able to work three-quarters of an acre in a day but you should expect them to be vigorous and healthy for spring sowing."[69]

Nevertheless, in the 1850s experts still relied more on subjective notions than scientific data. Beliefs were stronger than evidence and convictions trumped experimental results. Meat, especially, occupied pride of place in their recommendations for a healthy diet even though, in Lustig's schema, animal flesh was a "flexible" building block and not a "combustible" energy source. Meat was prioritized and credited with nourishing humans' flesh, muscles and even blood, although the connections were not proven. For instance, in 1852 Pierre-Honoré Bérard paid special attention, in his *Rapport sur le régime alimentaire des lycées de Paris*, to the amount of meat in school meals, specifying the quantities per grade level: "for the upper college, 65 grams per pupil and per meal; for the middle college, 55 grams; for the lower college, 45 grams."[70]

Meat was an essential foodstuff for the military too. As the *Instruction du conseil de santé des armées* recommendation, issued on March 5, 1850 stated, it "has utmost importance in the soldier's diet."[71] The key treatises on health and diet in the middle of the century reinforced these convictions: "Meat powerfully restores one's strength without being hard to digest."[72]

The celebration of meat at mid-century was certainly a diversion, but a minor one, as studies of human biology became more in-depth, diversified and comprehensive; scientists moved from recognizing the importance of breath to acknowledging the role of diet and from studying muscles to developing a choreography of movement. Views on fatigue and resiliency had been definitively transformed.

Defining our "constitution"

Scientists began establishing more precise criteria to assess strength and resilience and more objective methods for distinguishing between robust and frail people. Traditional approaches were receding in importance, and observations about a person's outward appearance – a ruddy or pale complexion, an erect posture, or "lively, bright eyes"[73] – were less relevant, as was the hands-on technique of palpating different parts of the body, used to assess the potential of the king's galley slaves. New principles in physiology and energy added a layer of complexity to such measurements, and the understanding of bodily functions turned inward. Data about respiration, nutrition, and the chemistry of combustion had shifted scientists' attention. The word "constitution" gained currency, encompassing a number of physical attributes that were previously hidden from view, aspects that were both more intimate and more interdependent. In the 1820s and 1830s medical dictionaries defined "constitution" as the "intrinsic physical endowment unique to each person's body and the sum total of its functions."[74] Around 1840 hygienists developed a more detailed definition, targeting the body's "degree of physical strength, the regularity or not of its metabolic functions, its power of resistance to disease, its physiologic vitality and its capacity for endurance."[75] In this way, each person's potential was assessed holistically and systematically, but also recognizing that each individual was unique. The diagnosis was more complicated because the physical cues were less obvious: "It is true that people with an athletic constitution are not at all remarkable for the stability or regularity of their health."[76] A muscular build could be deceptive and a person's "energy potential"[77] could not be judged at a glance.

Scientists had to resort to devices and discoveries from the beginning of the century, such as the dynamometer, the spirometer, and their knowledge of the chemistry of respiration and of blood. Hematology was a new science that provided clues to a person's physical resilience or susceptibility: "We know that an increase or decrease in the number of blood cells reveals the weakness or strength of the body's constitution."[78] The use of such specialized instruments and laboratory tests was limited in everyday life, so researchers started to look for realistic and "usable" criteria to assess newly significant aspects of an individual's physical energy, output and "fire power."

Evaluating military recruits had become more systematic; as conscription increased during the first decades of the nineteenth century, so did the recommendations on fitness issued by advisory bodies. A recurrent term in their guidelines over the years was "constitution," to be categorized as "poor," "weak," "deficient" or "strong." They also called attention to "perfectly developed limbs that move freely and show no deformity, firm flesh, well-defined musculature that is neither over-developed nor bulging but is only visible to a moderate degree."[79] All in all, the recommendations pointed the inspectors toward "harmony" among different parts of the body, except for the chest, whose development was prioritized; it ought to be "rugged, large, shapely, flexible, resonant, and able to expand and contract effortlessly."[80] This criterion, of course, highlighted the importance of respiration when unrestricted breathing and a voluminous chest were considered essential characteristics of a sound constitution. For example, a report delivered to the prefect of the Department of the Nord on the class of recruits of 1840 underlined this: "[I am] convinced that their general constitution must be carefully examined. I think that the capacity of the thorax and the quality of their diet count for much more than any minor deformities, according to the council's recommendations."[81] The checklist for military doctors included phrases such as "poor constitution," "sallow complexion," "bad chest," "curvature of the spine" and "hunchback." Extreme thinness and sunken breastbones were considered warning signs about the recruit's energy potential and figured in a third of the declarations of unfitness for service issued in the department in 1841 (1,188 of 3,851 total rejections),[82] since these characteristics were thought to diminish a soldier's resistance to "war fatigue."[83] Here, one's outward appearance once again affected the diagnosis, but in a totally different way.

These criteria were popularized in other settings. The average citizen's build and posture were looked at differently. New distinctions were drawn, and attitudes toward the body were changing. Our lungs were recognized as our first line of defense. For instance, grape pickers with "broad chests" were thought to be better suited to endure work under grueling, smelly conditions. Their chest circumference was a sign of superior "vigor."[84] And mountaineers, who were accustomed to steep ascents and restricted oxygen, were bound to have "extraordinarily voluminous chests, dome-shaped and more elongated than usual."[85]

Men's fashions in the Romantic era highlighted the same attributes. The vest, especially, was the "showpiece."[86] Brightly colored and worn conspicuously, it accentuated the wearer's chest, making it so unnaturally prominent that it became a badge of identity: "Show me a man's vest and I will tell you who he is."[87] The same was true of the shoulders, where a helpful tailor would add internal padding to coats and jackets, enhancing the wearer's build. A manual on tailoring highlighted the preferred look, which was slim and "robust" simultaneously: "A man's suit answering to the finest tastes in 1828 must enlarge the chest and the shoulders but have a nipped-in waist and fullness in the trousers for an hourglass silhouette."[88] In 1848, the *Guide pratique du tailleur* [Practical tailoring guide] featured a man's suit with the upper half of the body tightly belted and corseted into a trapezoid shape.[89] At mid-century, two male silhouettes faced off: the bourgeois with his sagging belt and protruding belly and the cinched-waist dandy with a puffed out chest. Jean-Jacques Grandville put it succinctly in 1845 in one of his *Cent Proverbes* in a sketch with the caption "All that glitters is not gold,"[90] in which a young pigeon-chested dandy was proudly escorting a fashionable lady while jeering at a rejected suitor, who was richer, older and fatter, a sad spectacle of bulging stomach and sagging flesh.

21

A Universe under Threat: The Poverty of the Workers

The belief that the volume of our chests revealed our energy potential undoubtedly changed the study of the human body. The composition of our diet also separated the weak from the strong. Scientists' attention turned to subjects that had long been overlooked and stigmatized, such as cramped housing, poor ventilation, dampness, cold, the lack of necessities and the money to pay for them.

At the beginning of the nineteenth century, social scientists confronted a new and unfamiliar world of poverty and deprivation. In England at the end of the eighteenth century,[1] the industrial revolution and the reorganization of work brought astounding new sights of factories equipped with row after row of machines, tiring their workers, hemming in their movements, imposing long hours of toil and draining traditional small workshops of their labor force. This radical change upset old verities and erected new landmarks. A new variety of fatigue was detected, one that was described as "unhappiness," ennui or spleen. It arose when workers were condemned to live a barren life with no future and no hope. This was not the rosy vision of progress promised by industrialization. The mechanization of work created a "surplus labor pool, under-employed and defenseless."[2] Urgent concerns were expressed that we would still recognize today: "Of all the problems confronting us nowadays, nothing is more important than the organization of work and the fate of workers."[3] These apparently new types of fatigue flourished in settings where the uncontrollable impoverishment of workers increased their exhaustion. This led to a new interest in social issues, firing up the press, providing fodder for investigations, prompting topics for exam questions, and rewriting the inventory of threats to society.[4] Attention and anxieties were aroused "in the ruling classes about this social reality that they have created and that threatens them at the same time."[5]

Another innovation came from voices that once were silent and now were speaking: workers with a rudimentary education, a burgeoning political consciousness and membership in a community and a culture. Because of this, the fatigues that had always lived in their flesh and bones were mute no longer.

Constructing a worker's lived experience

Social classes tended to be more inclusive and broader at the start of the nineteenth century, and the "very poor" were a more mixed and heterogeneous category, just as the abolition of pre-revolutionary [Ancien Régime] guilds disrupted the segregated professional associations of artisans and merchants and their semi-monopoly over production and trade. But everyone who had nothing but their labor power to sell – the workers, manual laborers, factory hands, farm hands and road crews – were lumped together into one poorly understood, needy but potentially dangerous entity. Balzac characterized the worker as a man who "moves his feet, hands, tongue, back, his arm, his five fingers to make a living"[6] and someone who "depletes all his strength … striving to earn the gold that fascinates him."[7] The bourgeoisie kept their distance from their poorer neighbors, anxiously ignoring any distinction between "the worker and the pauper, the impoverished and the petty criminal"[8] and seeing them all as members of the "dangerous class."[9] Industrialization gave new life to this deeply rooted prejudice. The development of steam-powered factories and businesses on a grand scale resulted in a concentration of productive activities and enabled mass manufacturing at lower costs. This caused prices to fall, hurt artisans and, paradoxically, deepened social divisions and despair, as the "losers" had to struggle to survive. A slow but pervasive decline was becoming more visible. Traditional weavers exemplified this when, despite their hard work and their fatigue, they could not help but fall into poverty and degradation, having steadily lost ground against the machines in the industry that produced textiles much more cheaply: "This category of workers is certainly the worst off because even if they toil fifteen or sixteen hours a day, and often even more than that, they can barely survive. Because of the competition among manufacturers, these weavers see their earnings shrinking day by day."[10]

Lyon's silk weavers and their small workshops were suffering too, since they could not compete against steam-powered manufacturers located in some French cities and "in Zurich, Berne, Cologne and England."[11] The workshop proprietors described this perilous situation to the Lyon Red Cross in 1832, emphasizing the increasing number of hours their workers and apprentices were "forced" to spend at the looms while earning less from the finished product: "Poverty has become so common that a worker toiling for eighteen hours a day cannot afford the necessities of life."[12] Social scientists struggled to find the right words to encapsulate these vast economic changes. For example, the "proletariat" was "a direct product of the industrial revolution"[13] and a term for men and women working in factories; there was also "a large pool of unskilled labor,"[14] a phrase that equated people with their labor power. An English term, "pauperism,"[15] was adopted in the 1820s to distinguish this condition from poverty or destitution, since it was "a permanent state of penury,"[16] a downfall "that has become chronic."[17] Nevertheless, the current vocabulary differed little from the all-encompassing image of "the poor" inherited from pre-revolutionary France. But "tragedies" validated the new language. Workers first rose up against the machinery that was supposed to lighten their burdens, accusing it instead of "starving the people."[18] Around 1820, hundreds of workers in Lodève, Saint-Pons and Carcassonne "blocked the entrances to factories to stop the installation of machinery."[19] Actions such as break-ins and the destruction of engines and gears occurred in this quasi-revolutionary atmosphere, where typesetters, weavers and even peasants protesting the first steam-powered threshers felt that their livelihoods were under threat. The silk-weavers' revolt in November 1831 in Lyon was a powerful example and, with its slogan "Live working or die fighting,"[20] was one of the most dramatic. Troops dispatched from Paris violently put down the protest, but, afterward, this conflict reinforced the sense of a pitched battle between "the haves and the have-nots."[21] Especially among the poorest of the poor, it awakened a feeling of a shared identity and struggle: "We noticed more unrest among the people, the working class in particular."[22]

New voices spoke out, coming from people who claimed they "owned nothing,"[23] but they were most likely "seasoned" workers who were literate and thus aware of their compatriots' history of protest and revolt, such as the 1830 uprisings. The elite of the working class started giving first-person accounts of their work and conditions. Raising the wage was one of their key demands, along with reducing the workday and preventing the excessive fatigue that comes from overwork. A tailor named Grignon advocated for his colleagues in 1833:

> We work fourteen to eighteen hours a day in the most painful positions. Our bodies are deformed and broken. Our limbs swell and cramp, becoming stiff and weak. Our health is being destroyed and we only leave the tailoring shop to go to the hospital. How can we have any time left for education? How can we use our intelligence, improve our minds and uplift our spirits? We all agree that education is important, and they try instead to stupefy us with work that occupies all our time, drains our energy and dulls our senses. Even though they preach about the necessity of work, they live a life of leisure and gorge themselves on luxuries.[24]

Denouncing excessive work hours and an overlong workday were not mere complaints. They were also impediments to self-improvement, to achieving more autonomy and the dream of having more independence. Reforming working conditions was associated with "liberty," and "lightening" workers' burdens was understood as leaving more room for culture, so that improving conditions would, it is implied, result in less, more bearable exhaustion. This was an unusual goal, often couched in terms of "equality": "Why does it [parity] apply only to you?" thundered Jean-Louis Ferrien, an apprentice tailor,[25] who railed against the "elites" in an "Épître aux Parisiens" [Epistle to the Parisians] in 1831.

These protests were undoubtedly limited to a narrow fringe of workers, but the phenomenon still signaled a heightened sensitivity to abuses of labor. Workers' leaflets, letters to Parliament, screeds published and circulated cheaply, and testimonies published in newspapers may have been rare, but they all expressed the same demand: "Improve our miserable conditions."[26] They also emphasized a yearning for education that had been overlooked: "If poor people, artisans, farmers, instead of being overwhelmed by fifteen hours of work per day, which is excessive, could dedicate a certain amount of time every day to culture or to learning ... Oh, what a shame!"[27]

These militant statements contesting the length of the workday were new, coming from inside workers' ranks, combining their aspirations with their lived experience of pain. Gabriel Gauny, a "carpenter-philosopher," offered one of the most perceptive accounts of a day at work, its length and the different phases of a job. He explained that, on his way to the workshop, even before he picked up a tool, his "craftsman's intelligence is already engaged."[28] Doing his job "torments his body [and] roils his thoughts with endless worries."[29] The hours dragged on, "eating away at his soul"[30] minute by minute. Gauny framed his experience of time passing as an obsession. His "weary muscles, after the brief respite of sleep, are working desperately,"[31] his "despair at the ten hours ahead,"[32] his anxious wait for the first meal of the day, "where the worker's stomach, famished by the rough demands of the job, wasn't paying attention to sound nutrition but simply needed to be filled by the more or less tainted dishes of a bad cookshop."[33] He expressed his hatred of "the evil clock that chimes the hour."[34] This is a remarkable text; it is also one of the first workingman's accounts in which fatigue combined physical feelings and mental frustration, exhausted muscles and frayed emotions, energy that was expended and desire that was thwarted. Gauny's account revealed a change in working-class culture among the more "educated" workers at the beginning of the nineteenth century. This was a way, once again,[35] to put equal stress on physical and mental fatigue by connecting "tired muscles" to an emotional exhaustion that was less acknowledged and rarely treated. It certainly provided evidence that self-awareness had increased and that this consciousness was integral to every action, either while performing it or afterward. A specifically internal, intimate suffering arose from the conjunction, still nascent, of physical pain and mental distress. But the linking of external and internal would only continue to grow and deepen in the future along with our sense of self.

The unknown body of the "poor"

In addition to the rare testimony of workers who exposed the misery of poverty, observers began to focus more intently on the subject. This was no longer simply a question of workers' feelings and intuitions; it was also a topic of investigation. Pauperism moved people's hearts and destitution was condemned. An "identifiable" image was created. Characteristics of working-class identity were recognizable, and its "excesses" were reflected in signs that are visible on the body. Spindly limbs, shrunken chests, and a distorted or cramped posture were all indications of a particular kind of fatigue, a sort of insurmountable energy deficit. These traits made their way into the catalogues of characters known as "physiologies" and into some contemporary novels. For example, the seamstress La Mayeux in Eugène Sue's *Le Juif errant* [The wandering Jew], published in 1844, was "grossly misshapen," with "an awfully twisted waist, a hunchback, a sunken chest and her head burrowed deep in her shoulders."[36] In 1845 Friedrich Engels lamented that, in the working-class districts of Glasgow, "residents' lungs don't get their full quota of oxygen. This results in physical and mental numbness and a depression in vital activity."[37] A writer for the English *New Monthly Magazine* described weavers in the Spitalfields neighborhood in London as alien creatures with lopsided frames:

> I decided to travel to these unfamiliar southern regions. It was a holiday. If I had just stepped out of a cloud bank, I couldn't be more stunned … The first thing that struck me was the short stature of the people around me. I saw nothing but puny, withered, diseased, deformed little men who were as unlike the Londoners on the other side of town as a four-foot-tall Laplander is to a towering American. Overwork and poverty have beaten them down into premature old age, and a young man of twenty looks at least forty years old ….[38]

Crooked silhouettes, concave chests and a lack of resilience were among the most common traits, and the proliferation of ailments and malformations prompted investigations by a government that saw itself as more accountable for the public's health and wellbeing. In 1835, the Académie des sciences morales et politiques in Paris followed the lead of English researchers in launching a "comprehensive" inquiry by the economist Benoîston de Châteauneuf and the physician Louis-René Villermé, who were two of the founders of the *Annales d'hygiène publique* [Annals of public health]. Their mission was to travel around the country "in order to ascertain as precisely as possible the physical and moral condition of the working class."[39] Villermé's itinerary, criss-crossing urban and rural areas and visiting workshops and factories, yielded a "portrait" of France's regions. It featured a series of depressingly painful observations: "sallow complexion," "emaciation," "lack of strength"[40] among factory hands in Mulhouse; "curvature of the spine"[41] among Lille's child laborers; "malformations" and "weak constitutions"[42] among factory workers in Amiens. He did not find the same dysfunction everywhere, and certainly some regions made out better than others, but in fact his investigation focused on workers' resilience, especially their physical condition and the shape of their bodies. It seemed as if he was impelled to describe, to bear witness and also to explain their circumstances. Without a doubt, malformations and other physical disabilities were not unknown before then, and the equivalent population in pre-revolutionary France was just as fragile. It was impossible to ignore "the limitations of people's diets before 1730"[43] or to overlook the toll of famines, housing insecurity and physical disability. So much evidence came from ordinary daily life and, because of this, was less often studied. The "interpretation of reality" could not tolerate any "contradictions."[44] Nevertheless, the uniqueness of analyses in the 1830s and 1840s was due to the way they associated workers' wellbeing and factory work, and also to the perspective that highlighted the "scarcity" and "lacks," which their investigations inventoried and contextualized. In fact, since they knew nothing about the role played by the bacterium *Vibrio cholerae* in the epidemic, certain writers even saw fatigue as one possible cause of the cholera sweeping through Paris in 1832. Instead, influenced by the attention focused on labor, they blamed "work demands that exceed human capacity" and "overlong work hours."[45]

The many fatigues of industrial labor

Once again, observers took note of many varieties of exhaustion that were named and specified for the first time. Longstanding ailments and activities were categorized more precisely. The science of physiology was now focusing on the body's major systems, and this relied on a new orientation for research. The traditional diagnostic view of the body, scanning each body part separately, from head to toe, was abandoned in favor of an approach studying interconnected systems, from respiration to digestion, and from the muscles to the nervous system.[46]

At first, studies were centered on the ailments of artisans, as Bernandino Ramazzini had catalogued them in 1700, and targeted the body parts most affected by the stresses and strains of each trade[47] before broadening their inquiries to include more generic conditions. Bakers, as Ramazzini explained, inhaled flour dust in the air[48] and would be likely to suffer from asthma and shortness of breath. A century later, in 1835, Émile-Auguste Bégin concluded that bakers' typical actions – "standing," "using their arms and hands" and "sweating excessively" while working – decreased their resistance, so that most of them "died, worn out, at the age of forty or fifty."[49] Ramazzini had found that blacksmiths' and ironmongers' work affected the "membranes of their eyes" because of the "sulfur produced by red-hot metal."[50] Bégin observed that blacksmiths' and ironmongers' injuries were also caused by "powerful contractions of the arm muscles," the force used to strike the anvil repeatedly, the exertions of stoking the fire and the equally stressful activity of grasping tools and materials.[51] Ramazzini warned that stonemasons' health was threatened by their absorbing mineral particles, while Bégin also brought up repeated actions such as striking hard surfaces and working in contorted positions that left them "hunched over at the end of their lives."[52] Fatigue was no longer a silent partner in laborers' daily lives, virtually unnoticed and neglected. It was recognized, and, crucially, its physical effects were studied "holistically" in the ways it molded, shaped and deformed the body. For example, the constantly "bent back of the winemaker"[53] led to a deformed spine, just as the gardener's repeatedly "pressing his right foot on his spade"[54] cramped and contorted the right side of his body. Lumberjacks "continually flexing the muscles of the upper body" suffered countless aches and pains. In 1843, Edouard Ducpetiaux described miners' work as "painful, tiring, and repulsive," since workers in confined spaces "lack the room they need" to dig coal and had to "stretch out on rough uneven terrain, resting their heads on small wooden planks."[55] These studies assessed physical exertion in specific activities, but fatigue was evaluated for the way it permeated and diffused throughout laborers' bodies. Another ideological difference between the beginning of the century and the middle decades was a general decrease in social enthusiasm, a loss of faith in solidarity and, for workers in particular, a belief in the benefits of "happy fatigue." Now, fatigue was more realistically viewed as nothing more than a symptom of degradation and loss. Another change was the specific attention scientists devoted to "overexertion" and its effects on the heart, the lungs and their functions, especially "pathological excesses … associated with tiring activities, jobs that require serious exertion and the mental agitation that unleashes violent palpitations."[56]

These distinctions were reflected in the carceral culture of the 1830s, where the rules required that "all condemned prisoners, no matter their previous social status, be assigned the most painful work, what we call the great fatigue."[57] The prison doctor at the Toulon jail, Hubert Lauvergne, described these harsh measures in 1841. Prisoners operated winches and treadmills, pulled carts, hoisted and carried heavy weights on their shoulders.[58] Physical exertion, stresses and strains were paramount, as well as the kind of exhaustion that a prisoner "has never dreamed of"[59] in tasks that were often described as "meant to provoke terror."[60] At the same time, the promise of "the little fatigue" was dangled in front of well-behaved convicts on the road to rehabilitation. The context had changed; prison labor entailed brute force while factory work relied more on efficiency and adaptation.

Factory work could be re-engineered to channel force in other directions. New, more devious and unexpected methods became more prevalent and more precise. More machines supplemented human labor. Instead of massive feats of strength and overexertion, for example, workers were immobilized, expected to stay for hours at their posts, supervised and surveilled. Instead of feeling out of breath or drained of the last ounce of strength, they suffered from arthritis, faintness or a pervasive sense of listlessness. Exhausted by "immobility," "lengthy periods" of stasis[61] and the heat on the factory floor, they "lacked even the energy to wipe away the sweat pouring off their bodies."[62] "Since the invention and widespread adoption of the steam engine, extremely demanding work has almost entirely disappeared from factories … Immobility – standing or sitting for twelve hours straight and not using one's muscles – could be the explanation for the lack of muscular development, this atrophy of the entire constitution."[63]

A limited range of motion and endlessly repeated "strictly mechanical gestures, tedious and mind-numbing,"[64] could also do damage. Villermé was the first to note both the psychological and physical effects of "a task restricted to a few movements, repeated with overwhelming monotony, in the close confines of a worksite that never varies. I was introduced to some poor fellows whose listless state couldn't be ascribed to any other cause."[65] He came to a surprising conclusion that fit poorly with his searing descriptions of exhausting factory work: "Hypochondria is the only ailment caused by these factories."[66] However, Villermé's diagnosis subtly but clearly alluded to the emotional toll of industrial labor. The tedium was not only physical but also mental.

Other sorts of fatigue were categorized for the first time and associated with working-class culture. Inquiries delved into their environment, home life and sexual promiscuity. Episodes of social isolation, and even the furnishings and temperature in their lodgings, were scrutinized for the stresses they might produce and the effect they might have on workers' fatigue. Working-class neighborhoods and living spaces in particular were investigated, at times prompting feelings of suffocation and acute discomfort in the observers: "You have to walk down alleyways where the air is damp and cold, as in a cellar. You have to have felt your foot slip on the filthy ground and then fear falling into that muck to get some idea of the awful feeling you have when you visit these poor workers."[67]

In the 1830s, Eugène Buret, conducting research in England, paid particular attention to workers' homes, the size of the rooms, the condition of the floor, and the presence or absence of a table, cupboard or bed. He described the shocking condition of a hovel in the Bethnal Green district of London, housing ten people, which was "barely ten feet long and seven feet high."[68] In Manchester he visited a room where a couple and three children lived that was "as bare as the people sheltering there."[69] He described a single room in Scotland "where two married couples lived, with no beds."[70] Villermé found similar conditions among working-class communities in the north and east of France, writing about "miserable lodgings where two families sleep in their separate corners on piles of straw secured by two wooden boards."[71] These types of field investigation were new, but perhaps even more stunning and rare were the personal testimonies of workers, such as this manual laborer in Lyon during the July monarchy:

> I found work on the construction crew of the railroad tunnel at Loyasse and was earning three francs a day. We worked from 6 in the evening to midnight and then from 6 in the morning till 11. The water oozed out from the rocks and soaked us down to our bones. I was foolish enough to buy sturdy clogs and stuffed a pair of slippers inside. At night I would go back to the workers'

> quarters that were two kilometers from the tunnel on the Saint-Just plain. And what lodgings! A freezing cold room where there was never a fire; twelve beds that were just straw mattresses with rough canvas sheets that were only washed twice a year. Still soaking wet, we try to sleep on these stinking pallets, shared with another worker, no less.[72]

Investigations in the 1830s and 1840s recorded other causes of workers' fatigue: a lack of sleep, inadequate clothing, exposure to the cold, the strains of travel, or a tight budget. Studies broadened their focus to include these aspects of daily life. For example, Mayeux noted the costs of necessities such as "bread, a candle, potatoes and dried beans" and concluded that only 91 centimes were left over at the end of the week to pay for "housing, clothing and heating."[73] In 1835, a study of workers' annual expenditures in Nantes found that, after paying for the fuel, lighting and lodging that enabled their "lives of misery," the workers had "only 46 francs to buy salt, butter, cabbages and potatoes"[74] for the year.

Even upper-class investigators were coming around to the idea that workers were worn out, reeling from the onslaught of one fatigue after another, trapped in one dead end after another, unable to recover simply by getting more rest or marshaling their strength. Endemic conditions were sapping workers' endurance and damaging their health, leading to a "decline" and "chronic wasting"[75] that, when it "infected" and "spoiled" future generations, drained physical resources and threatened the entire community. At the end of the eighteenth century, Sir Frederick Morton Eden, in his three-volume study on *The State of the Poor*, lamented that modern capitalism turned peasants into "free hands," reduced to either selling their labor or enduring "the miserable alternative of starving independently." After an innovative statistical survey of England and Wales documenting widespread poverty, he concluded: "The result of this investigation seems to lead to the inevitable conclusion that manufactures and commerce are the true parents of our national Poor. … A new class [is] being thus insensibly created."[76] Subsistence was the borderline; once crossed, it was impossible to keep up one's strength and offset the body's inevitable decline. The frame of reference was still energy, and the subject was a body whose disequilibrium affected its inputs and outputs. A body unable to fuel its motor was condemned to irreversible decline.

The principle of surplus value

The existence of widespread destitution in industrial societies, although previously unrecognized, perhaps inevitably sparked new forms of opposition and criticism also. Pauperism as an identity lent itself to generalized condemnation, frustration and confrontation. It also encouraged the poorest of the poor to see themselves as a group, protesting and fomenting revolt against the elites. At mid-century, the French industrialist and politician Auguste Mimerel obtusely defended his peers: "Laborers don't have a bad lot. Their work hours aren't excessive since they never go beyond thirteen hours ... The person who needs our sympathy is the factory owner whose profits are declining."[77] After the 1848 uprising, Marshal Thomas Robert Bugeaud fumed in a letter to Adolphe Thiers, dated April 7, 1849: "What violent and savage beasts! How in heaven's name did God let mothers give birth to such creatures? Ah, those fellows, not the Russians or the Austrians, are France's true enemies."[78]

As the confrontations became more tense, building up to "class war," the social unrest gave rise to a number of theories of its root causes, highlighting alternately resistance and revenge. Socialist thinkers from Bakunin to Engels, and from Proudhon to Blanqui, focused on proletarians' extreme deprivation. Although his work was sometimes misrepresented and caricatured, at mid-century Karl Marx offered the most comprehensive and insightful interpretation, one in which fatigue was ever present. He saw the market economy and the relationship between employers and workers as the heart of the matter. Workers were "slaves" who sold not only their "labor" but also their "labor power"[79] in a rigged deal benefiting only the vampiric "buyer." No profits would be made if the value of labor power was equivalent only to the "cost of maintaining the worker and his family."[80] The "capitalist" would "lose" money if the only value created by labor went to its own "subsistence." Capitalists needed to extract more value, make a profit, and accelerate that force in the relationship where they had the upper hand. The inevitable result was that workers must be forced to "produce more than the value of their own labor power,"[81] over and above what they needed for subsistence. In other words, workers had to work longer or harder to produce "surplus value."[82] Capital "has only one natural impulse, one single motivation, which is to take the largest possible share of extra work."[83] This dynamic clearly increased levels of fatigue, and workers' exploited labor became a balancing act between the tolerable and the intolerable, the do-able and the "too much," and a longer, harder workday:

> But in its blind unrestrainable passion, its werewolf hunger for surplus labor, capital oversteps not only the moral, but even the merely physical maximum bounds of the working day. It usurps the time required for growth, development and healthy maintenance of fresh air and sunlight. It higgles over a meal time … It reduces the sound sleep needed for the restoration, reparation, refreshment of the bodily powers to just so many hours of torpor as the revival of an organism, absolutely exhausted, renders essential.[84]

Therefore, a fatigue that is intensified, deliberate and excessive is part of the employment contract, a "surplus value" extracted from workers' bodies.

Another necessity, an additional deviation, led to a unique analysis of the fatigue created by the factory, the machinery and the actions that they orchestrate. A clear-cut image: industrial iron passes through living things, energizing the entire workplace in one coordinated wave of movement, flowing from the mechanical pulleys and levers to the humans operating them, uniting the mechanized arms and the human arms. The alienating effect of this image transformed the factory rhythm into an unnatural force that struck "individuals at the very core of their existence."[85] This was a deliberately shocking vison in which fatigue was directly associated with mechanization, its unnatural constraints, and a dynamic that "distorts the workers, making them monstrous creatures by exploiting their manual dexterity and sacrificing an entire world of aptitudes and productive instincts."[86] Fatigue was caused not only by physical exertion but also by a culture in which workers were alienated from themselves, unable to fulfill all the demands of a job "shackled to a corpse, a machine that has an independent existence without them,"[87] as if a "demonic power" was dragging them into "a feverish, dizzying dance with all the machinery."[88]

Another factor contributing to a longer workday concerned the machinery itself. Since it would wear out and its value depreciate with use, owners were motivated to get the most out of it as soon as possible in order to earn the greatest possible profits. Worn-out equipment would be worth less. Thus, "when machinery is first installed in a factory, its use will be the most intense,"[89] and the workday reflected that.

As a result, Marx highlighted the most extreme and shocking examples of workers "who died from overwork," such as twenty-year-old Mary Anne Walkley, who toiled for twenty-six and half hours straight alongside sixty other young women,[90] and the blacksmiths in Marylebone "dying at twenty-seven years of age rather than fifty."[91] It was "a terrible price to pay, not very different from the brutality the Spanish unleashed on the red-skins [*sic*] of the Americas."[92]

Child labor, the face of chronic wasting

Negotiations, protests and ever more critical testimonies heightened the pressure for change. But the contexts and potential solutions kept evolving. The controversy over child labor in the first half of the nineteenth century was a prime example, with its specific references to "premature" fatigue.

First of all, since the dawn of the industrial revolution the streamlining and standardization of factory work, where mechanization lessened the need for brute strength, led to the hiring of very young children, even some younger than five. The rationales for this were quite "run of the mill," relying on excuses such as unfair competition, the special "aptitudes" of child laborers and the exigencies of profit-making:

> Child labor is necessary in factories; the dexterity of their fingers, the rapidity of their movements and the smallness of their stature make it impossible to replace children with adults in all aspects of factory work without incurring a significant financial loss. Children's labor pays for the bread on the family's table, protects them from the evils of idleness and delinquency, instills habits of discipline and order, and teaches them early in life that one has to earn one's keep.[93]

It is true that child labor was not new, but the innovation here was to take children away from the family setting, the home workshop or family enterprise, with its quasi-intimate atmosphere, and bring them to a regimented workspace with standardized tasks and work hours. The "decline of home weaving workshops"[94] accelerated the phenomenon of child factory work, as larger-scale manufacturing of linen, wool and cotton displaced the older trades. Factory owners, too, were eager to lower their costs, and parents were hoping to augment the family income. Michelet dramatically described the origin of this social evil a few decades later: "In the violence of the great duel between England and France, when English manufacturers told Pitt that workers' high salaries made it impossible for them to pay taxes, he replied with the horrific phrase: 'Take the children.'"[95]

Jean de Sismondi was one of the first to recognize the flaw in that solution: children's lower wages led to a reduction in their parents' wages because of an oversupply of labor.[96] Marx pointed out a similar dynamic: "By increasing the potential labor pool, mechanization increases the level of exploitation at the same time."[97]

Now new employment patterns were framed as a generational threat, resulting in a steady "decline" and a slow draining away of vital energy. The symptoms were visible in "pallid, emaciated faces, the signs of premature death."[98] Personal morality too was under attack, as Balzac's fictional "factory girl" showed: "sent to work in a textile factory at the age of seven … corrupted at twelve, a mother at thirteen, she saw herself shackled to profoundly damaged creatures."[99]

The widespread use of child labor itself, the tender ages of the victims and their abusive working conditions sparked protests, marking a turning point in the understanding of particular kinds of fatigue. "Public outrage"[100] first boiled over in England in 1802 and by 1833 had led to nine bills being proposed in Parliament addressing "child protection."[101] Authors and others concerned with public health raised their voices alongside members of Parliament. This was demonstrated by the rising number of social problem and social protest novels published in this century, as works such as George Sand's *La Petite Fadette*[102] and Charles Dickens's *David Copperfield*[103] shone a spotlight on exploitation in families and childhood "misery." Journalists and investigators issued heart-rending reports of actual child laborers standing upright in "tall metal boots" to keep from falling over from fatigue.[104] Even the series of character sketches *Les Français peints par eux-mêmes*, published in 1840, which described itself as "a moral encyclopedia of the nineteenth century," decried the "barbarism" of child labor, calling for legislative action: "We know that a law designed to abolish the detestable employment of children in factories was introduced in the last session."[105]

But opponents of such legislation did not give up easily. In 1840, Théodore Barrois, a physician and politician from Lille, released a *Mémoire sur l'état physique et moral des ouvriers employés dans les filatures et particulièrement sur l'état des enfants* [Report on the moral and physical condition of workers in weaving factories and in particular the condition of children]. It castigated the critics of working conditions as "a small and noisy bunch of bullies."[106] In 1828, the Minister of Commerce Pierre Laurent Barthélemy de Saint-Cricq equated any legislative reforms with willful blindness about the urgent needs of "productivity."[107]

On the other hand, advocates for legislative action stressed the toll taken by exhaustion, using detailed examples. Investigations in England had already interviewed proprietors, factory foremen and child laborers. The straightforward questioning and often frank answers were chilling:

> "Are you tired after your shift at work?"
> "Dead tired, especially in winter … I hardly know how I manage it, but I go back home, stretch out on the floor, overcome with fatigue … I am exhausted and it's very painful to be on my feet for so many hours … Sometimes I don't know how I can stand it; I feel so tired in the morning it's as if I hadn't slept at all."[108]

The talk returned again and again to specific parts of the body. Painfully swollen feet "make me cry," a stitch in the side "never lets up," a headache "keeps me awake at night,"[109] along with "stabbing pains in the shins, back, and groin"[110] at every step. All the evidence pointed to the damage done by the cramped and immobile positions in the factories designed for mass production. Investigators also asked about long work hours, a point even brought up by the plant foremen: "In my factory, I haven't come across a single child who hasn't complained about the length of the workday."[111] And the children protested: "It's too long; we can't stand it."[112] Villermé addressed this very topic in a lecture at a learned society in Paris, the Institut de France, on May 2, 1837:

> To truly understand how long the workday is for the child laborers in these factories, I want to remind you that our rules and customs limit the workday,

> even for convicts, to twelve hours on site and the breaks for mealtimes reduce it to ten hours. But for these workers the day is fifteen or fifteen and half hours long, of which thirteen are spent working.[113]

Workers themselves condemned the rigors of factory work in the 1830s "separating us and our children, having our homes broken up, severing all the connections that link human hearts."[114]

Major decisions were made then about legal working ages and work hours. Their details reveal the gulf between nineteenth-century reality and ours. On August 29, 1833, legislation in England set the minimum for child laborers at nine years of age in "cotton, linen, hemp, silk and oakum spinning which use steam-powered machines or hydraulic pumps" and limited the workday to eight hours, or, at a maximum, nine hours for children younger than eleven.[115] On March 22, 1841, French legislators passed a law mandating a minimum age of eight for children working "in plants, factories and workshops" and an eight-hour workday for all children younger than twelve.[116] In both cases, access to education was the rationale for these limits, and in both England and France medical examinations for child laborers were required.

These were major breakthroughs, despite their obvious drawbacks, and the legislation was "the first example of government intervention in social issues,"[117] even heralded as "the birth certificate of workers' rights."[118] It was the first time laws intervened in a parent's decision to send a child to work to help the family, just as they limited factory owners' quest for the cheapest labor. The laws intruded in domestic affairs and private life and touched on fatigue also by limiting permissible work hours to specific ages. Nevertheless, these advances were "temporary" and even "narrow," since they concerned only manufacturing, or certain types of manufacturing, and left out other exploitative industries, such as mining, cited in an English report in 1840 and again by Villermé in 1843. Children as young as four were hired to do simple, repetitive but vitally important tasks, such as opening and closing ventilation shafts as coal carts traveled along the passageways, in order to prevent "dangerous drafts" that might lead to "terrible accidents."[119] The English called these boys and girls "trappers," and they could be found huddling alone in recesses in the walls, often spending their entire shift in the dark.[120] The reports described older children performing heavy, physically stressful labor: "Their backs are bent under enormous loads … Half-dressed or completely naked, they are harnessed like oxen to heavy carts that roll on little wheels. They pull these carts filled with coal in passages with such low ceilings that they cannot stand upright. They have to crawl through on hands and knees, or, to put it plainly and vulgarly, on all fours."[121]

These laws were temporary, as we noted, passed in the 1830s and 1840s in England and France, and meant to be revised, since their purview certainly seemed incomplete. Nevertheless, at mid-century they foregrounded an important debate about work-related fatigue, work hours and workdays.

The long-lived "obstruction" of work hours

The length of the workday was emblematic of a larger struggle in industrial society, symbolizing workers' potential to reduce their fatigue, put reasonable limits on their duties and, in the process, even wrest some power from manufacturers. This was an enormous task in which changes in social values and perceptions might lead to victories even as most traditions remained entrenched.

In England, "after three decades of intense advocacy and equally obdurate opposition,"[122] a law was passed in 1847 limiting the workday to ten hours. Marx saw the "shorter" workday and the "complete unity" of advocacy as proof that "for the first time …, visibly and in public, the political economy of the bourgeoisie is defeated by the political economy of the working class."[123] Equally important, the law recognized the government's authority, not that of the proprietors, to set work limits and made "modern" businesses liable for citizens' wellbeing.

Progress moved more slowly in France, but what did occur revealed a distinct and gradual change in consciousness. A ten-hour workday was first proposed in 1837 in the *Aide-mémoire des officiers du génie* [Guidelines for the Engineering Corps]: "In our experience, the optimal workday [for laborers] and for horses is ten hours."[124] On April 6, 1848, a young commissioner in the provisional local government named Émile Ollivier mandated a ten-hour workday in the Bouches-du-Rhône.[125] A month earlier, in March, the bloody uprisings in Rouen demanding a shorter workday propelled Frédéric Deschamps, the commissioner in the provisional government, to limit hours in factories.[126] Other protests in Marseille in May and June broke out when it seemed Émile Ollivier's order would be overturned. People built barricades in the streets, 150 workers were arrested and their leaders were convicted at trial.[127] Paris was struck with a "pervasive feeling of malaise."[128] Still, a ten-hour workday was "decreed" early on in the 1848 revolution, demanded by two hundred worker-delegates, and affirmed by Louis Blanc in his statement as a member of the provisional government: "Overly long work hours for manual labor not only ruin workers' health but also prevent them from nurturing their intelligence and strike a blow against human dignity."[129]

However, those mandates, and any compromises, proved impossible to maintain in the climate of persistent antagonism between bosses and workers, or against the steadfast belief in productivity that denied its toll on workers. Even though no agreement on hours was reached, one thing was clear: "Workers' issues are preoccupying the entire world."[130] The debate raged for decades. On September 9, 1848, the Constituent Assembly in Paris rolled back the previous mandates by a vote of 617 to 57, and a maximum workday of twelve hours was set for factories. However, workshops were exempt, and a longer workday continued there. Adding insult to injury, on May 17, 1851, another decree abolished any limitation on the workday, and workers who "are exhausted by overwork bring their proprietors to court and are shocked to learn that workers have no legal protections."[131]

"Reforms" would not occur until the end of the century. Some limits were approved piecemeal in localities, limiting workdays to eight or ten hours, but no national law was promulgated.

22

The World of Output

As labor struggles intensified throughout the century, the "mad rush" for more machinery turning out more products also explained the rise in disputes over working hours. Factory owners' search for efficiency was growing in tandem with workers' pushback, leading to heightened tensions and confrontations.

In 1887 the *Dictionnaire encyclopédique de l'industrie* [Comprehensive dictionary of industry] popularized a term that truly encapsulated the dynamics of the second half of the nineteenth century. "Output" was defined as "the relation between the amount of productive work done by a machine or any kind of device and the amount of energy used by the machine to perform said task."[1] This calculation highlighted the importance both of measurement and of productivity and was at the heart of Julien Turgan's wide-ranging investigation of "major manufacturers" between 1863 and 1884 focused on improvements in efficiencies and cost-cutting. For example, he praised the Dollfus-Mieg textile factory in Mulhouse for reducing the amount of steam power in its operations[2] while increasing its output and also pointed to the Paris Omnibus Company's strategy for streamlining its fleet and increasing its revenues: "The carriages are lighter, so only two horses are needed to pull them. They have more space for passengers and their routes have been extended."[3]

In addition to the concern with maintaining a balance between input and output, the concept of "surplus value" reigned supreme in manufacturing, setting off a perennial search for "the new and improved." As Léon Poincaré asserted in one of the first studies of "occupational hygiene": "Progress in industrial society means producing goods quickly, cheaply and in great quantities."[4] Besides workers' protests, the belief that "more is better" sparked countless studies on alleviating and overcoming fatigue; paradoxically, in this case workers and management shared the same goal.

Muscle power still played an important role at the end of the nineteenth century. Many, many wheelbarrows crossing the bridges over the Seine and transporting materials for construction were pushed by hand. Jules Amar, in the aptly titled *Le Moteur humain* [The human engine], estimated that "hearty men" could handle a 40-kilo load of bricks, but cut this down to 27 to 31 kilos for men in the "second category."[5] Manual labor was synonymous with strength. A worker's body was still the most essential cog in the industrial machine.

Industrial principles

The plight of the miners in Zola's novel *Germinal* illustrated the inevitable and widespread "excesses" of working conditions. Toiling in the Jean Bart mine, the men and women workers tried to excavate the greatest amount of coal possible in the shortest amount of time because they were piece workers, paid by weight:

> Stretched on their sides, they hammered more loudly with the one fixed idea of filling a large number of trams. Every thought disappeared in this rage for gain which was so hard to earn. They no longer felt the water which streamed on them and swelled their limbs, the cramps of forced attitudes, the suffocation of the darkness in which they grew pale, like plants put in a cellar.[6]

Zola dramatized the miners' single overwhelming desire: to keep digging more, to fill more carts and ignore the pain to earn their miserable pay. It was a vicious cycle because, in order to push the excavations faster, further and deeper, the management had scrimped on the wooden supports that kept the underground passages open, leading to an inevitable tragedy. The miners fought to maintain their wages after new safety regulations called for the installation of more wooden beams, slowing down the pace of excavations, but the management balked at paying for their time. The miners' violent strikes were put down by the military; work began again, the tunnels collapsed, and the workers' torments never ended.

The "mad rush" to productivity caused tragedies as well as workers' less dramatic chronic exhaustion. Even the mine manager Hennebeau in *Germinal* was conflicted, "hopeless" in the face of such exploitation, feeling "a little smaller every day, compromised, forced to dream up a master stroke if he wanted to make amends to the shareholders."[7] Deneulin, his competitor, also became ill because of the strike that shut down his mine: "at first he thought he was going to die, blood was rushing to his head, he was choking with apoplexy."[8] Owners emphasized their own type of fatigue, a persistent "battle" that they found more painful, albeit different from their workers' suffering. "Being the head of a large or small industry means dedicating oneself to endless toil, which is in more ways than one much more exhausting than a day of manual labor, which is the subject of such concern nowadays."[9] This managerial stress was regularly associated, with a touch of exaggeration, with such leading large-scale projects as the excavation of the Suez Canal, completed in 1869 after extraordinary rounds of fund-raising and diplomacy conducted by its developer Ferdinand de Lesseps. The "promoter's" exhaustion did not have the same social or personal resonance as that of a worker, even if both were caused by "overwork." "We all know about and remember the terrible trials Mr Ferdinand de Lesseps had to endure when he pursued the construction of the Suez Canal. We also know that it took superhuman efforts on his part to bring this enormous project to a successful conclusion."[10]

Events depicted in Emile Zola's novel *Germinal* were based on actual labor struggles of the time and on reports of violent protests over work hours and pay.[11] The conflict in Mulhouse was one example among many when, a few days before the Franco-Prussian War, a crowd of two hundred to three hundred strikers shut down all economic activity. Assembling in the Masevaux valley, they called for higher wages and shorter workdays. Two infantry squads sent from Belfort put down the workers' occupation, but that very evening war was declared "and had the effect of a cold shower on the strikers. They dispersed and our soldiers hoisted their packs on their shoulders and marched off to slaughter at Soultz-sous-Forêts."[12]

Labor protests occurred at Anzin and Decazeville also. In January 1886, mine workers in Decazeville went on strike, calling for a salary of 5 francs a day for "the underground crew" who drilled the tunnels, put up wooden supports and mined the coal, and wages of 3 francs 75 for other laborers. The two thousand strikers also called for an eight-hour workday "because of the bad air and fires underground." Their demands were met with adamant refusals from the management, and the conflict turned violent. A delegation of workers beat the deputy director Jules Watrin after he refused to make any concessions; he was pushed out of a window, attacked by the crowd, and died of his injuries.[13] A magazine, *Le Socialiste*, captured the atmosphere of seething anger, proclaiming: "Victory – blood has been spilled and, unlike all the previous miners' strikes, this time it's the bosses' blood, capitalist blood."[14]

The endless quest for "a return on investment" raised the stakes, punctuating the second half of the nineteenth century with unrest and violence, yoking the owners' "mad rush" to productivity with workers' revolts and exhaustion.

Physiological principles

The continuing interest in research and studies was undeniable, however. As militant workers' opposition to the ascendancy of "surplus value" in the workplace grew, so did attempts to control and objectivize labor.

Methods to calculate productivity were devised, experimental schemes were put in place, and numbers proliferated, making fatigue a new focus in the applied sciences. This field of study attracted doctors and engineers who were concerned with details and evidence, in this case anchored in physiology, which became a locus for experimentation and observations. This was a major shift in the status of fatigue, now that the phenomenon was being studied with scientific precision and scholarly methods. At the end of the nineteenth century, fatigue was no longer relegated to the purview of industrial mechanics'[15] time and motion studies or the physics of energy[16] or of combustion. Instead, scientists focused on categorizing signs of fatigue and collecting objectifying data. As Anson Rabinbach noted, this was the inception of a "science of fatigue."[17]

The "ergograph" invented by Angelo Mosso in the 1890s typified this change. The device, used to measure the optimum stage of people's muscular performance, was new, even if it built on studies of frog muscle contractions conducted in the previous century.[18] Going beyond the reactions of dissected muscles to electrical stimulation, Mosso's work was more complex, linking heat, work and energy conversion in living human beings, and, amazingly, it concentrated on a single body part, the middle finger. The experimental subject placed an arm and hand inside an apparatus designed to immobilize the wrist with two clamps. The "ergograph" then measured the muscular activity of the subject's finger as it was flexed to raise or lower a weight at an even tempo and the beat of a metronome. The height of the contractions (or the height of the weight that was raised) was represented graphically on a piece of paper as a wave, curving downward when the finger was relaxed. The waves that were recorded measured the subject's muscular strength. They also captured the evolution or "stages" of the exercise and their cost: "progressive fatigue" was the stage associated with repeated flexes of the finger; "definitive fatigue" was indicated when the wave dipped and the movement ceased. "When one is tired, one can no longer raise the weight, no matter how hard one tries."[19] This was a major step forward in technoscientific precision, one of many studies intended to determine the productive capabilities of the body, and the one that measured fatigue graphically for the first time.

Recognizing the innovative aspects of his experiment, Mosso repeated it multiple times in an attempt to conform to modern scientific methods respecting the standardization of procedures. Based on his results, he proposed "the laws of exhaustion,"[20] a term which was truly as original as it was essential. First of all, he posited that every person had a unique capacity for fatigue: "Some subjects' peak exertion declines rapidly; others fall by degrees, and still others keep on at a steady rate after peaking quickly … The ergograph records one of our most intimate and most characteristic abilities: how we experience fatigue and also the constants in this motor-sensory experience."[21] The personal aspect of the study concerned the almost material development of fatigue and how it pervaded our bodies and penetrated muscles and flesh.

After Mosso pointed out individual variations in capacity, he offered more general conclusions about strength and endurance. One was the effect of repetition. Using the ergograph regularly would inevitably build up muscular strength, as the recording device showed. "Professor Aducco," Mosso's colleague, "doubled his score in one month"[22] of regular practice. Another finding was the proportional relationship between the weight used in the exercise and the frequency of lifts: "The subject can better resist fatigue when he lifts a lighter weight more quickly."[23] Speed affected the results and the subject's endurance. Accidental variations affected the results too, such as the time of day, the season, the subject's diet, emotions and illnesses, whether the right or left hand was tested, and the subject's overall physical condition.[24] Clearly, these were variables that affected human performance, but Mosso's work merely hinted at their importance, leaving this field open for future behavioral and psychological investigation.

Finally, the effect of rest and especially the timing of rest periods were recognized as significant factors. Mosso found that, when a subject was "exhausted" as measured by the ergograph, a two-hour break was needed before he could recover his previous level of performance.[25] Mosso also noted that a brief pause before the subject registered complete exhaustion had a protective effect. In other words, work breaks would delay the onset of exhaustion:

> Let us say that thirty contractions will exhaust a muscle. If the subject makes only fifteen contractions, the rest period needed for the muscle to recover can be shorter (a great deal less than two hours) ... If this exercise is repeated for a whole day, performing fifteen contractions followed by a half hour of rest, the subject will produce identical waves every time as long as the weight to be lifted remains the same. We can see that the amount of work produced is much greater if the subject never reaches a state of exhaustion.[26]

Thus, Mosso achieved a classic goal by a more "calculated" method: a formula that would guarantee the most efficient use of labor, performed regularly and consistently without the disruptive effect of fatigue. The route to equitable labor had been signposted.

A final argument brought into question the usual analogy of a laborer and a steam engine: "A locomotive burns a specific amount of coal for each kilogram-meter of work. But for human beings, when our body is tired, even a minimal amount of work will have disastrous effects."[27] The "fuel" was not at all similar in these two cases, and therefore we had to pay particular attention to fatigue and learn how to predict and prevent it.

Advances in the laboratory enabled scientists to study variables that had been suspected but not previously analyzed. The tired person was turned into a guinea pig. Charles Féré experimented with various stimulants to measure their possible effects on ergographic results. The subjects were exposed to colors, sounds and smells during the test at the point when their muscular contractions declined; the purpose was to gauge the recovery of energy. The stimulants varied a great deal, but in fact most acted as physical rather than psychological or emotional triggers: "Ceylan cinnamon extract; valerian in ammonia water; red colored glass; asafetida spice; a sudden interruption."

Féré collected a lot of data and carefully measured it, finding that stimulants would partially restore the rhythm and intensity of the exertion but that overreliance on them resulted in subjects not being able to "work without stimulation."[28] Nuances were carefully noted: "odors are perceived as stimulating before they are apprehended sensorially."[29] Differences between stimulants were pointed out: "Feeling pain coincides with a noticeable decline in exertion."[30] In this way, the environment was assessed in relation to fatigue for the first time, and, inevitably, in an attempt to identify surroundings that would increase or reduce productivity, questions would arise in future investigations about the workplace setting and the potential effects on workers of lighting, colors, sounds or smells.

Without a doubt, these methods may seem abstract, the laboratory experiments may appear artificial, and the ergograph's focus on the movement of one finger may seem irrelevant to broader physiological conclusions. Clearly, work activity is much more complex than the functioning of one muscle; the parameters of fatigue are less rigidly defined and more varied than a decrease in contractions. Nevertheless, Mosso's positivist convictions were so strong, as Marco Saraceno argued, that he "sees physiology itself as a fundamental element of social reform."[31] Mosso called for urgent action:

> This is not a question of political parties or of social activism, but a profound belief, a sacred dedication to a higher morality that motivates us to study how to distribute wealth equitably, without violence and without shedding blood, so that work will be in harmony with the laws that govern humanity, so that the worker will not become a slave, and so that the human race, exhausted by fatigue, will not fatally decline.[32]

Despite its limitations, Mosso's discoveries prompted other research, inspiring other measurements and formulas above and beyond his almost religious faith in the social value of laboratory science. In particular, his work highlighted the significance of individual capacities, the effect of regular, repeated activity, the restorative power of rest, the influence of circumstantial variables,[33] and the quantifiable relation between the pace of work and the expenditure of energy. Because his studies focused on it, they underlined the cultural and social significance of fatigue. Moreover, his findings were respected because they were produced by a scientist. The laboratory and its apparatus were useful for organizing workplaces and work routines. Shattering the silence of past decades on work and fatigue, his conclusions called for more serious and thorough investigations of working conditions in all their complexity, concerning energy, endurance and psychological factors.[34]

The principle of movement

Another series of studies was inspired by these discoveries in the objectivization of labor. Feverishly measuring, calculating and observing, researchers conducted their inquiries outside the laboratory and, instead, focused on ordinary work settings and tasks, going into workshops and factories to record and analyze the complex movements of workers on the job. In particular, they were guided by the conviction that output could be calibrated by time, weight and distance. Frederick Winslow Taylor's work is a well-known example. At the beginning of the twentieth century, the American engineer delved into the concrete "materiality" of manual labor and developed "principles of scientific management." As the title of his book promised, Taylor's "scientific management" system was meant to improve efficiency, especially labor productivity, and Taylor claimed that, by applying scientific methods of evaluation to workers' movements, his principles would "increase return" without adding to "workers' fatigue."[35] Taylor also trained his lens on factory proprietors and managers and proposed empirical methods for decision-making and problem-solving that would make their organizations function more smoothly. He made the grandiose promise that his methods would bring owners and workers "maximum prosperity"[36] while eliminating fatigue and overwork.

Although Taylor came from an affluent Philadelphia family, he dropped out of Harvard to apprentice as a machinist at a factory owned by friends of his parents and then worked his way up through several positions in the steel industry to the post of chief engineer. His well-known system was based on the conviction that every factory job could be broken down precisely into a series of motions if the smallest details and the timing of the operator's movements were taken into account. In order to increase workers' output, managers had to pay attention to both time and motion and then train their employees in the optimal performance that "did not tire workers out." He studied laborers' actions in a variety of jobs handling different equipment: working in pig iron foundries, in masonry, using a shovel, testing ball bearings. A stop watch was his most important tool in each case, calibrated to one-tenth of a second; his method was meant to economize the number of motions as well as their speed. His studies were much more precise and detailed, more measured and calculated than his predecessors' "industrial mechanics" and "applied industrial science";[37] moreover, they were so individualized that they had no use for Coulomb's "kilogram-meters."[38] The goals of each study were the same: efficiency, productivity and speed. The number was king, used to validate any and all changes. As proof of his method's success, involving many hours of observation and experimentation, Taylor claimed that in one workday a man could now transport 47 tons of pig iron from the furnace to the cart 20 meters away, instead of his former limit of 12. In addition, a mason laying bricks could cut down the movements he made from eighteen to five with no increase in fatigue. The best technique for shoveling was investigated in the following way:

> By first selecting two or three first-class shovelers, and paying them extra wages for doing trustworthy work conscientiously, and then gradually varying the shovel load and having all the conditions accompanying the work carefully observed by men who were used to experimenting, it was found that a first-class man would do his biggest day's work with a shovel load of about twenty-one pounds. ... It is of course evident that no shoveler can always take a load of exactly twenty-one pounds on his shovel, but nevertheless although his load may vary three or four pounds one way or the other, either below or above the twenty-one pounds, he will do his biggest day's work when his average for the days is about twenty-one pounds.[39]

One of Taylor's innovations was to train and employ experienced observers[40] to conduct the field studies and to define the performance parameters. He stressed the importance of the men in "the planning department" who had to be both patient and attentive, since the studies might go on for several years with subtle changes in the testing involved:

> One of them for instance ... uses the slide rules ... to guide him in obtaining proper speeds, etc. Another man analyzes the best and quickest motions to be made by the workman in setting the work up in the machine and removing it, etc. Still a third, through the time-study records which have been accumulated, make out a timetable giving the proper speed for doing each element of the work.[41]

This crucial insight would bear fruit in the future in the form of management executives, administrators and "computers" dedicated to developing the optimal use of movements, tools, behaviors and equipment. A management team had one overarching goal: to improve productivity at the lowest possible cost. A new "science" was born, the "modern subdivision of labor" in "scientific management,"[42] with the emphasis on the word "management." Nevertheless, a perspective integrating workers and the workplace was a great leap forward from the studies of pulleys and levers in "industrial mechanics."[43]

There were obvious drawbacks to the method, since the complexities of work resisted such reductionism. Taylor did not identify an acceptable threshold of fatigue specifically but instead left that to his subjects' self-reporting. Nor did he specify the optimal expenditure of energy or investigate individual psychological reactions, as previous studies had. He also passed over in silence "the restorative value of unnecessary motions."[44] Despite the apparent precision of his work, it had a number of gaps. Even some of his contemporaries brought up these shortcomings: "W. Taylor relies on the worker's self-reporting [about fatigue]. This self-reporting has no scientific validity. Not only may the worker mislead the observer, but more seriously, because of the long-term consequences of fatigue, the worker himself may be mistaken."[45]

Another flaw in Taylor's method was the recommendation to "fire or demote" summarily "the most stubborn [workers] who don't want to put in the effort,"[46] without considering the emotional toll on workers and their dependants. Although Taylor highlighted "harmony" as one of the four goals of his management method, his cold-blooded attitude discounted workers' humanity, despite the findings in earlier studies of the ways emotion influenced performance.[47] Under a Taylorist regime, only the most impervious and most determined would stay on the job, and only the most "adaptable" were worthwhile. Critical commentators who were more attuned to human psychology and the psychology of work condemned Taylor's method for turning workers into "cretinized automatons" and, as *La vie ouvrière* [The workers' life] in 1913 put it, making factory hands "identical and unthinking extensions of the machine."[48]

Beginning in 1910, the American industrialist Henry Ford went even further in his Detroit plants with a program that honed every movement down to its essentials and kept factory hands immobilized at their posts on the assembly line: "No man should have to take more than one step ... the man who tightens the bolt doesn't put the nut in place. The man who puts the nut in place doesn't screw it in."[49] The assembly line system promoted "simplification," with "conveyor belts"[50] moving the parts "past the worker,"[51] and fostered higher productivity through the repetitive, restricted, monotonous motions of workers standing side by side, each performing a separate task. The human costs of fatigue were not factored into the program, although increased production and speed-ups were, resulting in remarkable savings. Ford reported that, in October 1913, the workers on the line took "9 hours 54 minutes to make a motorcar," whereas six months later production time was whittled down to "5 hours 56 minutes."[52] But workers' discontent grew along with the ever increasing "success" of the program. They complained that they were losing "the right to think"[53] and protested individually by quitting or refusing to do certain jobs, so that Ford's plants suffered from constant turnover, with some units having to hire three hundred workers a year to fill one hundred positions.[54] The obvious indifference to workers' morale and welfare and the relentless churn of new hires fed the workers' cynicism: "Don't get cocky there. If you mess around, they toss you out the door in a flash, and you'll be replaced just as quick."[55] In 1914 Ford raised salaries and shortened the workday from nine to eight hours, thereby balancing the need to attract a stable workforce with the need to keep his plants running at full strength.

At the beginning of the twentieth century, studies on fatigue were still incomplete and "compartmentalized," with each one adding some new insight that a previous study lacked. But the studies were not comprehensive, since they overlooked the costs of exertion or the complexity of movements and had little to say about the limits of human endurance. Almost all of them passed over in silence the toll on intimacy taken by fatigue. Some critics, however, were beginning to bring this up.[56]

Principles of energy

At the end of the nineteenth century, another shift in perspective in the field of physiology had crucial ripple effects, impacting the studies about labor by Hirn, Taylor, Ford, Mosso and others. It concerned new insights about energy. Engineers and other scientists were taking a second look at human exertion, in particular in the role of nutrition and how it fueled the body. As before, the studies of consumption were couched in the analogy of the "body as machine," but the specific ways our bodies were nourished was being studied more systematically. The roles of heat and food were re-examined. Losses and benefits were recalculated down to the tiniest detail, especially in the case of foodstuffs. Laboratory experiments in 1890 focused on nourishment, consumption, what our bodies lose and how they lose it. At first, these experiments were conducted in the "hermetically sealed chambers" adopted by eighteenth-century scientists, but, instead of Lavoisier's experiments with gas exchanges[57] and Hirn's heat loss studies,[58] now scientists were investigating the body's inputs and outputs (*ingesta et excreta*), the burning of calories and all the byproducts of energy. In other words, these were comprehensive studies of all the substances that fueled the machine. Their research apparatuses were different, as were their subjects and methods that merged chemistry with physics and mechanical analyses with analyses of flow rate. The "calorimeter"[59] constructed in 1898 by Wilbur Atwater and Edward Rosa in Middletown, Connecticut, was the most representative example. This huge apparatus consisted of an air-tight copper box, rubber tubes and a system of absorbers to measure the gaseous exchange and the heat production of the experimental subject[60] (lying on a bed inside the box), as well as the substances ingested and excreted by the subject. The experiments lasted for several days, with careful observations of the subjects as they engaged in activities such as reading, writing, pedaling an ergonomic bicycle, sleeping, and performing other everyday actions. Atwater and Rosa introduced a new principle to studies of human fatigue, or rather of its absence: the fact that "the subject experiences no changes in weight or in temperament."[61] Certainly, their use of body weight was innovative and, as a measurable quantity, made for a useful, repeatable, simple formula.[62] Instead of the inevitably subjective and approximate estimation of "not fatigued" feelings in previous experiments, this one had a numerical solution: the maintenance of body weight, which was more revealing than it might seem.

The "calorimeter" used Hirn's categories but, in addition, accounted for the role of diet in the calculations, especially when measuring the amount of energy spent in sleeping or working. Constantin Miculescu's discovery in 1892[63] was also significant here, establishing the caloric unit as the mechanical equivalent of a force of 425 kilogram-meters. This new standard was incorporated into recommendations about the number of calories needed to make up for the energy expended in activity.

Atwater and Rosa's dietary recommendations were new and extremely detailed: 107 grams of albuminoids [proteins], 64.5 grams of fat, and 407.5 grams of carbohydrates for a total of 2,602 calories for a subject at rest. Albumen was the equivalent of Liebig's "formative nutrients,"[64] which restored and rebuilt cells, and the fats and carbohydrates were the combustible "respiratory nutrients." When subjects were active, in this case pedaling the bicycle, once they had reached the target of 192,000 kilogram-meters, Atwater and Rosa found that they consumed only one additional gram of albuminoids, from 107 to 108, but greatly increased their consumption of other nutritional elements: "a crucial point that shows muscular exertion does not increase the consumption of nitrogen."[65] This was especially revealing because this small amount of cellular deconvolution limited the role traditionally filled by proteins[66] and instead highlighted the importance of carbohydrates burned during exertion. In other words, dietary principles were being reconsidered, and new elements to prevent fatigue were being proposed. Science was moving away from the verities of Balzac's fictional country doctor, who in 1833 emphasized the importance of consuming "white and red meat" instead of grains and sugars as the first line of defense.[67]

Other studies intended to rationalize diet and nutrition were conducted at the beginning of the twentieth century. Pierre Fauvel, for example, found that a man who weighed 67.5 kilos lost no weight for five years even though, "without tiring himself out, he rode his bicycle 100 to 150 kilometers a day" and consumed only 60 to 70 grams of albumin per day.[68] Russell Chittenden studied the diet of different subjects over a period of several months and arrived at similar results: "These subjects gradually reduced their total intake and in particular their consumption of meat; originally carnivores, they became vegetarians. Not only did they not experience any ill effects, they became stronger. Several gained weight and increased their muscle mass."[69]

In 1907, Josefa Ioteyko and Varia Kipiani compared the physical capacity of subjects following different diets. Using the diagnostic tools of the time, they measured strength with a dynamometer, fatigue with an ergograph, and lung power with a spirometer. In fact, they too concluded a vegetarian diet was superior: "Physical capacity increases by 30 percent."[70] Of course, these conclusions were limited by the small number of subjects in the study, but they did reveal a heightened interest in diet, in meat and in food as an energy source. In 1904 Jules Lefèvre, a member of the Académie de médicine, gave a more nuanced report of his own self-experimentation: "At the end of a strenuous mountain trek, between 4.30 and 6.30 p.m., I made my descent from the Pic de Bigorre at Luz. That is more than 20 kilometers of distance and 2,200 meters of incline, the equivalent exerting of 250,000 kilogram-meters in two hours, or 125,000 kilogram-meters per hour in two hours."[71] He explained that he "didn't feel tired" and was "in fine shape," while his companions, despite their "robustness," said they were exhausted, and some even had to drop out. In compelling first-hand testimony, Lefèvre cited his weight and endurance as evidence of his "indefatigability" thanks to the strict diet he had been following for thirteen years: "a balance of rest and exertion, a little "azote," never more than 60 grams of protein in twenty-four hours," but a diet rich in carbohydrates and especially sugars."[72] The qualitative difference in his intake produced a quantitative difference in endurance. This insight also differed from Gustave Hirn's conclusions about "respiratory strength"[73] in the mid-nineteenth century.[74] Lefèvre, a few decades later, focused on the energy produced by burning calories in a notable shift in emphasis; now "fuel" for the motor was key.

Between action and energy

The workers' motions described and dissected by Frederick Taylor and the ergographic waves studied by Angelo Mosso could now be re-examined using measurements of energy. This new synthesis was proposed by Jules Amar, author of *Le Moteur humain*, who noted that "manual labor is one of the most interesting problems of applied mechanics in the natural sciences," and served as the first director of a research laboratory at the Conservatoire national des arts et métiers [National conservatory of arts and trades], focusing on "work-related muscular activity." The studies were wide-ranging, incorporating new disciplines from thermodynamics to biomechanics to nutrition, and infused with a rational, mechanistic perspective. As always, whether investigating calories or time and motion, the goal was to increase productivity and efficiency. The observations were deliberately varied and even disparate at times, since the physical demands of each occupation were different: "walking and carrying loads, using a file, a hammer, a saw, pruning shears, woodworking, polishing glass, shoveling, stenography, giving speeches …"[75] On the other hand, the results had to be practical and applicable as well as scientifically sound.

The studies conducted on using a file formed one of the most detailed examples, but the basic research question was always the same: "determine the maximum productivity per day … with no excess fatigue."[76] The goals of enhancing productivity and preventing overwork, in other words, were set by the "pressures" of the industrial model: steady input but rising output. Amar's laboratory methods were remarkably precise; the weight and length of every file used in the study was measured and recorded, its cutting edge was categorized, and the filings were weighed. Every movement by the subject was gauged by a device that closely resembled Mosso's ergograph: one reel recorded the respiratory pattern; another measured the subject's pulse as Marey's device did.[77] As part of the physiological monitoring, oxygen and carbon dioxide flowed through "a double valve" attached to a mask.[78] The subjects' fatigue could be detected in several different ways: a slower pace or slower frequency of actions; a decline in force as measured by the ergograph; a faster rate of respiration or blood circulation as recorded on the reels; a perceptible increase in the loss of energy, shown by the wave patterns; an overall decline in the functions as tallied up by the various measures; and, finally, the self-reporting of the subjects who described any pain they felt and its location and intensity. All in all, the experimental data incorporated subjectivity and objectivity.

In Amar's laboratory the experiments were repeated and the data was analyzed. Averages were calculated and, at long last, a conclusion was reached: when handling a file, seventy strokes per minute was optimal to ensure the highest return and prevent fatigue.

> Maintaining the recommended pace of seventy strokes per minute requires a one-minute rest period after five minutes of work. In general, the ratio of rest to exertion is one to five. Thus, we see that, after one hour of exertion, a workman's physical condition is quite similar to a resting state: the number of inhalations increases by only 20 or 25 percent and the pulse on average rises by 20 percent. There are no other changes in the physiological functions of the body.[79]

A job could be done in the same way at the same rate for several days without causing a worker to lose weight. Nevertheless, substituting a tool that differed in size, shape or weight would affect the outcome. For example, the technicians found that using a file that was shorter required an average of 150 motions,[80] and the results of their comparisons and substitutions showed that every task had its own "specificity."[81]

The data collected on the file handler in Jules Amar's original experiment demonstrated the importance of energy: in an hour, when the worker was in a resting state, his body used 85.911 calories; during one hour of work, the total expenditure of calories rose to 218.621; using basic math, we find that exertion in this case used 132.710 calories.[82] When at rest, this same man would burn 2,061.864 calories in twenty-four hours, since his body needed energy for hidden functions such as respiration, blood circulation, and the replacement and repair of cells. If the man worked for eight hours (with ninety minutes of rest periods), he would burn 2,990.834 calories.

Experiments with different subjects, such as an apprentice or a less than first-rate worker making "jerky rapid" movements, showed they "experience fatigue sooner" and "exert much more effort"[83] for less output. They might use more than double the number of calories than the most skillful subject did (around 2,000 over their resting state for the lower-skilled, while a first-rate worker used fewer than 1,000), highlighting some of the obstacles to the most efficient performance. Lower-skilled workers were not "assets, either for workers' health or for the success of the industry that employs them."[84]

The differences between the apprentice and the experienced worker showed up first of all in terms of technique and energy use. Then, the contrast recurred in the amount of nourishment necessary, which was a new area of investigation in industrial hygiene. Jules Amar incorporated the most recent findings on metabolism, or "calorie intake and industrial output," by Robert Tigerstedt and the "seven categories of workers' diets" that he proposed at the beginning of the century.[85] The ranking started at the lowest level, which was a diet providing from 2,000 to 2,500 calories, and continued in increments of 500 to the top level: a diet supplying 5,000 calories and above. The first-rate worker in Amar's experiment consumed a second-level ration of 2,500 to 3,000, while the apprentice consumed at the fourth level: 3,500 to 4,000 calories. The first-rate worker consumed 464 grams of carbohydrates and 104 grams of protein and the apprentice 556 grams of carbohydrates and 136 of protein, according to Atwater's calculations.[86] All in all, the first-rate worker burned (and consumed) fewer calories to get better results, whereas the apprentice does the opposite. Here Amar exposed a chain of cause and effect in the field of the physiology of nutrition for the first time, using very detailed descriptions of work tasks, the fatigue they incurred, and the number of work calories needed for muscular activity. He also pointed out differences between "apprentices" and "first-rate workers," gave recommendations for improved output and estimated their cost.

Clearly, the subjects still incurred "energy losses" above and beyond the demands of the muscle power needed for their jobs. Amar himself referred to "nervous combustion" and to the fact that his experiments did not pinpoint the cause of every lost calorie, acknowledging that the effect of various strains, pains and individual disabilities "cannot be ruled out."[87] At the beginning of the century, Armand Imbert, a member of the French Académie des sciences and one of the first researchers into the "physiology of labor," showed that workers' techniques and motions could not all be explained mechanically. Instead, they varied with workers' perceptions of "feelings" of ease or difficulty, work stress or strain, and other subjective impressions of the work environment. Studies of mountain climbers revealed the intuitive and personal reasoning of those involved; some opted for "the most direct route with a steeper incline while others chose a path that was longer but less steep."[88] Their choices were influenced by feelings, vague instincts and "perceived" difficulties. In a more general sense, the field of psychology had grown at the end of the nineteenth century, recognizing possible disorders, individualized symptoms, and antisocial behaviors that had long been overlooked.[89] Jean-Maurice Lahy saw industrial psychology as a "field" whose parameters were still mostly undefined, but he acknowledged the need for more dedicated applied research: "In the workplace, we are convinced that external factors, such as speed-ups and the emotions they provoke, boredom, a regimented pace and mental constraints, are causes that evade laboratory experiments. But they are at the heart of the most serious accidents at work, and among these injuries, in my opinion, we must include mental disorders."[90]

"Mental health," nervous disorders and neurasthenia occupied a significant space in cultural awareness at the turn of the century, yet this did not reach the world of work. A "psychologization" was in progress, although it had not acquired a specific identity. Nevertheless, the recognition of what it did and did not include was becoming clearer. Alfred Binet asserted that it "is not possible to associate the increased effort of schoolchildren in exam time with bread consumption."[91] Mental fatigue had its own distinct boundaries.

23

The World of "Mental Fatigue"

Scientists' systematic collection of facts and statistics did have consequences; since it focused on physiology and mechanics, it reinforced the analogy of humans and machines. At the end of the nineteenth century, thousands of observations disseminated facts that had not previously been part of the discussion: studies of motion, consumption, energy, the pace and duration of work or exercise, and, finally, maintaining body weight. Relevant assessment methods were adopted.

On the other hand, very little attention had been paid to psychology or human emotions. Now, in the modern era, the intimate side of human life was revealed as being necessary too, and in the twentieth century, slowly but surely, our vast mental universe was acknowledged. Angelo Mosso referred to this earlier when he emphasized that a "territory" existed that was almost impossible to measure, one that mechanics and energy specialists could not capture in numbers: "In studying different signs of fatigue, two phenomena especially strike us: the first is the decrease in muscle power, the second is the internal feeling of lassitude ... We have thus a physical fact that we can measure and compare and a psychic fact that eludes our measurements."[1]

The "psychic sign of fatigue" was inevitably noted at the end of the nineteenth century. It was studied more intensively and even defined by scientists, who flocked to workplaces to get a better grasp of everyday conditions: "At first, we perceive fatigue through our senses, as a specific sensation."[2] It could turn into an "alarm signal" that alerted the body to a possibly dangerous condition. It was also a new addition in the study of consciousness and a new mental dimension to fatigue and its effects. A context highlighted the urgency of this recognition that set off a mental revolution, disrupting conventional thinking and social mores in the 1870s and 1880s. This was the perception of a daily life that was now more "exhausting," evidenced by changes in transportation, the proliferation of steam power, the innovations in electricity and telegraphy, and the dissemination of news and advertising. The new environment grated on our senses and at times overwhelmed us. The "jitters" suffered by the aristocrats (or "*noblesse de robe*") of the Ancien Régime or the "hustle and bustle" that plagued merchants of the classical world[3] confronting the press of business or the anxiety of personal concerns had now taken a new direction. This agitation affected a wider public, provoking more generalized and even unexpected pressures that came from our surroundings or our level in society.

Two possible sources of fatigue were identified more precisely and analyzed more effectively: one affected our muscles and another affected our minds. Two methods emerged to describe it: one looked at fatigue from the "outside" and the other from the "inside." Our internal perceptions were becoming more significant, underlining the growing sense of individual autonomy of people who were self-aware, acknowledging their deficits, discomforts and "impossibilities." These two arenas of fatigue – that is, physical and mental exertion – may certainly intersect when one or both might grow and mutate into countless aftereffects. All of this resulted in a more comprehensive view of fatigue that affected every corner and crevice of the body.

This was a crucial shift in perspective, because it would chip away at traditional, strictly corporeal understandings of fatigue attributed to humors, nervous charges or burning energy. A new field of study was developing that would focus on internal functions that were mostly invisible.

A literary revolution

Literature was a new space to be exploited. The old "fatigue story"[4] invented in the eighteenth century presented episodes of exhaustion tied to actions and situations. Now new content that was more directly personal and individual drove the narrative, giving less attention to circumstances than to feelings; less anchored in the senses and more in the imagination, in emotions, beliefs and illusions, and giving a voice to "living" witnesses, as we saw in workers' testimonies in the 1830s.[5]

This was a contrast, but a very contemporary one, to the evidence collected by energy specialists and industrial hygienists. The workers' personal testimonies made it clear that it is impossible to rely solely on physiology to study fatigue. *Ramuntcho*, by Pierre Loti, was among the novels that included dreamy sequences of fatigue. This idyllic pastoral novel published in 1897 centered on a young and romantic Basque smuggler. One scene mingling reality and fantasy foregrounded Ramuntcho's fatigue and his "sensations" when the "young mountaineer" was returning from Spanish territory by boat. At daybreak, Ramuntcho fell into a reverie, his physical fatigue pleasantly yielding to a daydreaming daze:

> with well-being in all his senses. ... He lost, little by little, the consciousness of his physical life. Ramuntcho, after his sleepless night, a sort of torpor, benevolent under the breath of the virgin morning, benumbed his youthful body, leaving his mind in a dream. He knew well such impressions and sensations for the return at the break of dawn, in the security of the bark where one sleeps is the habitual sequel of a smuggler's expedition.[6]

Zola's novel *Germinal* dealt with the internal repercussions of fatigue differently. Catherine Maheu fell victim to a terrifying vertiginous exhaustion at the Jean Bart mine, where the young woman worked in the punishing job of "router," shuttling carts filled with coal. In one dramatic incident the hoisting cables that carried miners and equipment to the surface broke, and the mining crew was trapped underground. Zola described Catherine's frenzied escape, jostling with other workers up a series of ladders. "By the thirty-second ladder, as they were passing a third loading bay, Catherine felt her arms and legs grow stiff."[7] Zola vividly depicted the young woman's mental confusion amid the disturbingly vague feedback from her body: "At first she had sensed a slight prickling of the skin. Now she could no longer feel the wood and metal beneath her hands and feet. Her muscles ached, and the pain, slight at first, was gradually becoming more acute." She began to lose consciousness, and "in her dazed state" was tormented by memories of "Grandpa Bonnemort's" frightening tales of child laborers tumbling off ladders head first into the depths of the mine.

> She had no further consciousness of her movements. When she lifted her eyes, the lamps turned in a spiral. Her blood was flowing; she felt that she was dying; the least breath would have knocked her over ... As she fainted, she dreamed. It seemed to her she was one of the putter-girls of old days and

> that a fragment of coal, fallen from the basket above her, had thrown her to the bottom of the shaft.

The agonizing suspense was dissipated, and the crew's ordeal turned into a minor triumph when Catherine was hoisted onto other miners' shoulders and carried up to the surface, where she "suddenly found herself in the dazzling sunlight" amid the shouts of the waiting crowd. At first, Catherine didn't understand what was happening since she was so convinced of her immanent death."[8] Catherine's hazy, out-of-body experience, like Ramuntcho's, bore little resemblance to the industrial hygienists' reports and observations of fatigues and breakdowns, but the novelists' empathetic and imaginative reconstructions of their characters' worlds enriched the study of work.

Zola's descriptions were path-breaking since for the first time they delved into the most subjective repercussions of fatigue, focusing on private and very intimate pains and fears, evidenced by panic, anxiety, disordered thinking or breakdowns. These terrifying and unquantifiable aftereffects were the absolute opposite of the statistician's bloodless quest for averages and measurements.

Victor Hugo's novel set in Guernsey, *Travailleurs de la mer* [Toilers of the sea] (1866), also probed the unseen side of fatigue and the psychological impact of emotion and shock on human endurance. This poorly understood instinct impelled Gilliat, a sailor, to repair his battered boat piece by piece in a frenzy he barely comprehended, though he desperately wanted revenge against the person who had smashed the hull, the deck and the mast. Gilliat fought off tiredness by ignoring it, his heroic silhouette seeming to reach up into the vast horizon: "Ordinarily physical fatigue is the thread that keeps us earthbound; but the uniqueness of Gilliat's labor keeps him in a sort of idealized and shadowy region. It seemed to him that at times he was hammering away at the clouds."[9] His movements touched the infinite. His fatigue sprang from the "ineffable," and, in the attempt to unleash unsuspected hidden powers, he merged the relentless willpower of the sailor with the implacable fury of the sea. And, by mimicking the sea, he expressed his desire to unite with it. Gilliat exhausted himself in extreme exertion, prompted by a mysterious and incommunicable state of mind, which was nonetheless vividly shared with the reader.

Other subjective impressions were investigated in athletic contexts such as racing. In 1897 a largely physiological study of cyclists' fatigue colorfully described the minute-by-minute perceptions of the participants in a twelve-hour competition. The study recorded their "impressions" and how they changed or even veered into delusions. For example, at hour seven a racer "sees no one but hears a child's voice calling him"; at hour eight he is struck by "an insane thought. He believes he is on another planet where the cycle track is the orbit. His trainer is the sun, the grass is the vault of space." Later he thinks an aerometer has been "grafted to his back."[10] This study brought to light the internal landscape of illusions and exertion and of fantasies and exhaustion. This was new territory for scientists where internal evidence was prioritized, both the kind that was measurable and the kind that was elusive.

The invention of overwork

Another equally significant "mental" discovery was unveiled at the end of the century. This was the heretofore unrecognized feeling of "pressure," which is the emotional equivalent of output in a physical context: a particular kind of agitation triggered by the urban industrial economic environment and a sort of fatigue provoked by surroundings that were too new too soon. This novel source of "distress" was linked to our lived experience of space and time.

Provincial schoolteacher Baptiste Sandre's first-hand account from the 1880s is an example. Historian Mona Ozouf edited and published the diaries of this family of schoolteachers in 1979, in which Sandre recorded his perception of his position in the village hierarchy, his "recognition" as a local authority, his "multiple" responsibilities, his job as the secretary of village government, his organization of "community lectures," his contributions in "property surveys" and "road work," his participation in "studies in the academy," and his "private correspondence," etc. Sandre used a relatively obscure word to describe his reaction to this whirlwind of activity when he confessed to suffering from "overwork,"[11] the feeling of being burdened with ever increasing responsibilities, of taking on many duties in a short period of time, and of "boiling over" from the pressure of expectations, activities and achievements. At first glance, there was nothing surprising about his complaint, since the excessive demands on him sprang from the new, unusual status of a village teacher in the now obligatory public education system. Still, we should not overlook the nuances and unique aspects of his plight. Sandre's diary revealed a new and unusual perception of time, of the need to act quickly and decisively, to deal with urgent matters and with constraints on his actions, and to juggle multiple, disconnected responsibilities. What made his memoir significant was not only the use of the word "overwork" but also the way his diary connected the threads between simultaneous tasks, a lack of down time, and the need for speed. This schoolmaster was actually one of the chief witnesses to a profound cultural transformation in the second half of the nineteenth century.

The word "overwork" actually first appeared in the 1860s and 1870s in the context of racing and the excessive demands on racehorses. For example, it was used to describe the poor judgment of "a jockey who spurs his horse to an overly fast pace in the first half of the race, in relation to the distance it has to cover."[12] Émile Littré expanded the definition in 1870: "imposing excessive fatigue on a draft animal or other by making it go too fast or for too long."[13] On a physiological level, this kind of prolonged exercise could cause lactic acid to build up in the body. The words "too fast" were integral to the definition because they are both directly connected to the ethos of performance and speed records and emblematic of our world of time-keeping and the drive to surpass limits. The popularity of hippodromes and the "wave of construction"[14] at mid-century were prime examples. The Longchamp racecourse in Paris's Bois de Boulogne, designed in 1854 and opened for racing in 1857, attracted gamblers and sports enthusiasts alike; speed was king in the second half of the century. The racing times of thoroughbreds were compared and analyzed. The *Dictionnaire universel d'histoire naturelle* by Charles d'Orbigny praised the "amazing thoroughbreds" who reached a speed of 80 feet per second, "which means a speed of around 9 myriameters [10,000 meters] or 23 leagues per hour."[15] The claim was probably exaggerated, since a speed of 9 myriameters would be 90 kilometers per hour.[16] The illustrated magazine *Almanach du magasin pittoresque* [Almanac of the picturesque shop] compared the Epsom Derby in England to a "national celebration" and the rush of horsemen to a "storm."[17] The ideal racehorse, a muscular, well-proportioned and sleek creature, was so fast and lithe, it seemed to "fly."[18]

This sudden new intoxication with speed appeared in many contexts. At this point in the nineteenth century, speed "is ever-present,"[19] a factor in the shortening of distances, technical improvements, the proliferation of motors, the rapidity of the telegraph, and the ubiquity of the telephone. It offered the promise of a "new material society,"[20] one that transformed time and space and imposed "a faster pace of life"[21] on people who were abruptly and consciously "rushed."[22] The *Dictionnaire encyclopédique de l'industrie* underlined this in 1888 by comparing seventy-two rates of speed in order to better grasp their specific characteristics and their significance. For instance, it compared walking and running, trotting and galloping, travel by train or by tram, wind speed and hurricane speed, a bullet and a cannonball, a sailboat and a destroyer, the speed of light and the speed of sound, and mechanical versus electrical oscillations.[23] The long list of comparisons pointed to the key factor driving this obsession: the inescapable acceleration of daily life.

The concept of "overwork" can be traced back to this belief, and also to more negative perceptions of expediency; the once unquestionable benefits of swiftness were now associated with pervasive, diffuse, vague "excesses." The hygienist Albert Mathieu, a specialist in stomach ailments and a part-time teacher, identified a specific new kind of fatigue that arose in urban environments. Cities had grown substantially in the nineteenth century, and city life was characterized by agitation and mobility: "Social life in big cities, as structured by our civilization, builds up the causes of nervous exhaustion."[24] This was no longer the Enlightenment's "excitation,"[25] congestion, "whirlpool," or "dizzy spell," brought on by the number of social interactions, nor was it a simple "stimulus" prompting us to react to noises or obstacles.[26] Instead, urban social life was plagued by an exponential increase in messages, pulsating in lights and encoded in movements and signs. People were harassed by a glut of news and publicity that led to a "drowning" sensation and quasi-mental indigestion: "Any prolonged or violent sensory stimulation may bring on fatigue."[27] Our impressions of a world out of kilter provoked this fatigue, which was unique in that it was expressed internally. Excess made us feel overwhelmed, and exhaustion was triggered by the blizzard of advertisements, appeals, messages and calls in modern life. Maurice du Seigneur pointed this out during the Paris Universal Exposition in 1889:

> The display of merchandise, the parade, the poster, the pamphlet, the advertisement – in every shape and size, a sandwich board on a man's back, circulating around town in a carriage, called out by a street vendor, lighting the gas lamps, transforming the booths into luminous marionettes, marshaling the rays of electricity, behold the giant modern spring that makes this human anthill rush along, each man walking past, bumping into another, brushing against another, exchanging greetings, cursing, selling, buying, all paying as they must.[28]

Among other things, electricity, both "fairy and servant,"[29] was one source of this urban sensory overload, powering a dazzling panoply of signs, invitations and advertisements. In 1883 the novelist Émile Zola described a young shopgirl in Paris "yielding to seduction … conquered" by the alluring modern shopfront radiating "a furnace-like glow … It shone out like a lighthouse and seemed to be of itself the light and the life of the city."[30] In 1895 Émile Verhaeren captured the vision of Paris's "towers of fire and light" and its resemblance to "a beast exploding with noise."[31] Other circumstances and other facets of modern life reinforced and intensified these perceptions. The contemporary press, in particular, took aim at the monotony of private life and the sedate pace of the opinion journals, spreading the gospel of speed in daily news and updates, and emphasizing shock and surprise in its coverage. The popular and sensational press aimed to bring the whole world to the reader with the least possible delay. This led to pressure on the writers, who had to produce copy "on the shortest of short notices in this business model."[32] The reader was under pressure too to absorb information at a rapid rate: "People who read a lot become accustomed to experiencing a quick series of disconnected feelings, emotions and thoughts, and then they expect to encounter the same situation in real life."[33] So many news items were covered in the most banal and undramatic categories, but, to the reader a few decades later, it suddenly felt like an intolerable rush, a new obligation that destroyed all peace and quiet. Marie de Manacéine, a Russian scholar investigating "modern civilization" in the 1890s, noted a steady increase in the number of newspapers: from 780 in Germany in 1833 to 2,500 in 1855; from 132 in France in 1827 to 1,637 in 1866."[34] Negative aftereffects were inevitable: "vision problems, vertigo, a rapid, disjointed and confusing flow of ideas."[35] Émile Zola also condemned the "intellectual exhaustion" associated with repeated mixing of "countless problems of all kinds"[36] in the firehose spray of news delivery: "It would be better not to absorb all the racket of this century inside our skulls. A man's head nowadays is so overloaded by the shocking load of things that journalism delivers willy-nilly every day."[37]

Many occupations were affected, as were many actions: from professional activities to intellectual ones, from sales techniques to administrative procedures. "We no longer have time to rest; we have to be ready at any moment to pick up our pens to respond. In this busy life, we don't get a minute to rest, we never have an hour off ..."[38] Many of the examples were taken from the United States, underlining the increasing influence of the New World, which since the 1890s had consistently been cited as the "model of modern life": "fifteen people are handling fifteen different deals"[39] in the same building at the same time; a fleet of "three or four buses"[40] passed by the same spot at the same time. In 1899 President Theodore Roosevelt gave a celebrated speech and later published a collection of essays with the title *The Strenuous Life*.[41] A powerful image of the modern captain of industry took hold: he was a man who no longer had a minute to himself, since he worked non-stop, without a break. Now, however, more attention was being paid to the psychological ramifications of this personality type, to obsessions, to fixed ideas, and to unhealthy doses of obstinance and tenacity:

> I work steadily from eight in the morning to ten at night. I barely have time to eat. Most often, I eat standing up, a meal of cold, bland dishes. At ten o'clock I am so tired that I struggle to bring my accounts up to date. At night, thoughts of the business I was conducting during the day come to mind so insistently that I can only manage to get a little rest in the early morning hours. I feel exhausted when I get out of bed and have to down a few little glasses of cognac to give myself the energy to go back to work.[42]

Overwork no longer affected only our senses or would be explained by a loss of nerve. It could cause psychological distress when our minds were invaded by disturbing, recurring unwanted thoughts. Physical as well as mental aftereffects were possible: illness, uncontrollable emotions and internalized suffering. In short, physical and mental distress came together and were exacerbated as the degree of internal pain intensified.

The shoppers at Zola's fictional department store, the "cathedral" of consumerism in *Le Bonheur des dames*, suffered from "exhausting" excitement as they confronted a dizzying array of choices and made nerve-wracking calculations. They were brought to the edge of delirium by the allure of the merchandise and, manipulated by modern merchants, were frustrated by the limits in their household budgets:

> Right at the summit appeared the exploitation of women. Everything depended on that, the capital incessantly renewed, the system of piling up goods, the cheapness which attracts, the marking in plain figures which tranquilizes … it was woman they were continually catching in the snare of their bargains, after bewildering her with their displays. They had awakened new desires in her flesh; they were an immense temptation before which she succumbed fatally, yielding at first to reasonable purchases of useful articles for the household, then tempted by their coquetry, then devoured.[43]

At the end of the day, having "emptied her purse and shattered her nerves,"[44] a shopper could hardly summon up the strength to leave.

The struggle for life

The new concept of the "survival of the fittest" played an important role in these pressures. No doubt, at the end of the century a superficial reading of Charles Darwin's work had popularized this idea. Democratic ideals with their promise of equality reinforced the same message: "Competition is fierce, and very bitter battles are waged in all the professions, liberal, commercial, industrial. Everyone wants to be on top, always on top."[45] This understanding of competition was debatable, however, since Darwin never claimed that "evolutionary adaptation" in the struggle for existence would lead to the triumph of "the fittest,"[46] but the idea was popular enough to become part of conventional wisdom. It served as a conduit for tensions that afflict social circles, expectations and behaviors. It was also deployed to justify a feeling of urgency, a rush to achieve, a kind of adrenalin rush that had not been seen before, intensified by the spread of competitive capitalism: "Any delay, any hesitation, can make him lose in the struggle that engages us all."[47]

The concept of a "struggle for life"[48] also reinforced the legitimacy of the word "overwork." At the end of the nineteenth century, psychiatrists began warning about the threat of nervous exhaustion: "Unfortunately, the way society is organized today, based on cut-throat economic competition, cannot fail to keep a person in a constant state of overactive nervosity, which is an endless source of neurosis and degeneration."[49]

In the second half of the century, ranking had become increasingly important, in terms both of social class and of technical fields, skills and responsibilities. These hierarchies structured the new terrain of competition and rivalry. An example from the Compagnie des chemins de fer du Nord at the end of the century illustrated this with a deluge of narrowly specific job specifications and ranks: fourteen different levels of administrative staff; twenty-eight for track construction and maintenance; forty-three for "equipment and locomotives"; sixty-four for operators.[50] Clearly, "climbing the professional ladder" was a slow and laborious process. Zola's novel *Au bonheur des dames* describes the "categories" that provoked envy and solidarity among the sales clerks:

> In fact, everyone in the department, from the unpaid probationer longing to become a salesman, up to the first salesman who coveted the position of manager, they all had one fixed idea; and that was to dislodge the comrade above them, to ascend another rung of the ladder, swallowing him up if necessary; and this struggle of appetites, this pushing the one against the other, even contributed to the better working of the machine, provoking business and increasing tenfold the success that was astonishing Paris.[51]

The routes that these strivers took in the quest for self-betterment were comparable in some ways to those in the first wave of democratization in the nineteenth century,[52] but they were also more varied, more complex and less "interdependent." They seemed to diverge more from the "common good" to make their own way and ensure their own benefits. This was a new kind of competitiveness, in other words, that was more personal and even "egoistic," a sign of increasing assertiveness in a democratic society that was also riskier. Adrien Proust and Gilbert Ballet studied these tendencies at the end of the nineteenth century in the context of neurasthenia:

> In the past social classes were enclosed by impenetrable barriers, and very few attempted to leave the milieu dictated by happenstance. Today everyone tries to attain a higher level than the one his forebears occupied; competition has increased, clashes between people and conflicting interests have multiplied in every walk of life … Most people place undue stress on their mental faculties by taking on more work than they can tolerate … Battered by relentless agitation, the nervous system will eventually become exhausted.[53]

This created new rifts in society, stigmatizing the "weakest" and prioritizing an ideal of strength, solidity and even virility. Women were considered less resilient, "more liable to this kind of nervous exhaustion,"[54] or described as "creatures with weak, unstable nervous systems" likely to collapse "in the struggle against their competitors."[55] Some "victims" were more susceptible than others. In other words, the preoccupation of a rapidly changing world, overwork, separated the weaklings from the "feckless" and fragile souls from impervious ones.

Finally, these scientific arguments provided a way to resurrect traditional critiques of those who wanted to "rise above their station." For example, the working-class recruits Angelo Mosso studied in the 1890s were "hale and hearty" but faltered during exams, with "huge drops of sweat dripping on their papers."[56] Philippe Tissié reported on a sailor "with less than an elementary education" who aspired to take the qualifying exam for the post of master mariner. However, he was overwhelmed by the difficulties of studying and suffered physically, "losing weight, becoming sallow and debilitated," coughing until he was exhausted and struggling with "the onset of pulmonary congestion" before "dying of consumption in a hospital bed." This "strapping Breton" met a tragic end."[57] In 1895 the acerbic journalist Francisque Sarcey wrote about a "forty-year-old valet" who wanted to learn to read but was martyred by his ambitions, unable to succeed despite his "willpower." Sarcey described their tutoring sessions: "He listened to me with unwavering attention; I saw the veins in his temples swelling and sweat running down his forehead from the effort. Every day, we spent an hour on the lesson. Afterward, the poor fellow was dumbfounded and couldn't stir an inch. He was lost in a fog. One week later, he came down with brain fever."[58]

Overwork undoubtedly threatened a society obsessed with competition and self-improvement. Zola's diagnosis was grim: "We are sick, that is for certain, sickened by progress. Our brains are overdeveloped, and our nerves are overtaking our muscles."[59] At the end of the nineteenth century, many warned of the advent of the "exhausted generation."[60]

Academic overwork

Inevitably, schools were seen as incubators of this malady. The institutionalization of education in France in the nineteenth century was a major achievement, but the proliferation of subjects, curricula, exams and penalties reinforced the image of a presumed "overreach." Its innovations were troubling because they were ambitious, and teaching and learning were disturbing because of their accessibility.

Academic subjects, first of all, were noteworthy in the nineteenth century because of their ever increasing numbers. Easily digestible compendia of knowledge flooded the market, and during the 1820s and 1830s alone publishers issued the *Encyclopédie des gens du monde*,[61] *Encyclopédie moderne*,[62] *Encyclopédie des connaissances utiles*,[63] *Encyclopédie domestique*,[64] *Encyclopédie catholique*,[65] *Petite Encyclopédie des enfants*[66] and *Nouvelle Encyclopédie de la jeunesse*.[67] The books got fatter and the subject matter more diverse. In 1846 the publisher of the *Encyclopédie moderne* touted its size: "almost twice as big as the original edition"[68] of 1823. In 1866 Pierre Larousse assured his readers that "never before have our minds been so stimulated by new discoveries or been introduced to such a comprehensive collection of thought-provoking questions and provocative debates."[69] This publishing bonanza led to blowback from critics, who fretted about the untrammeled acquisition of scientific knowledge by ill-educated masses, while the expansion of education stoked fears of "force-fed" learning. On July 13, 1844, Adolphe Thiers warned in the Chambre des députés: "They want to fill our children's heads with too much knowledge." A few years later Victor Duruy added, unfortunately without much evidence: "Our children have a longer workday than an adult worker does."[70]

Many began sounding the alarm about the number of lessons and their intensity and about educational imperatives that were imposed too soon. In criticizing these "procedures" in 1868, Victor de Laprade was the first to adopt the term "overwork," the verb previously used in the context of horse racing, to describe schoolchildren's plight. Schooling would "stress their minds through overwork and tire out their bodies."[71] A few years later, Jean-Marie Guyau put this into a physiological context when he condemned the pressures of the classroom: "The brain, which is relatively capacious but not well organized in childhood, will not, if forced to function more rapidly and respond to more demands than it should at this age, reach its full potential for growth or resilience later in life."[72]

This anxiety, summed up in the English expression "overpressure in schools,"[73] pervaded Western societies at the end of the nineteenth century and prompted a debate in the House of Lords on July 21, 1883. Surveys and investigations were launched, such as Hertel's study in Denmark in 1885 focusing on 28,114 schoolchildren, which "finds 29 percent of the boys and 41 percent of the girls suffer from anemia, scrofula or nervous ailments."[74] In Germany, Rudolf Finkelnburg concluded that "80 percent" of the young men who "acquired some sort of secondary education are unfit for military service."[75] In France, the physician Jean-Baptiste Fonssagrives predicted future calamities for "the budding philosophers, the ten-year-olds who astound us with their encyclopedic knowledge."[76] The Académie de médecine in Paris scheduled two debates on the subject in 1886 and 1887.

Selective tests and university entrance exams were also targeted, in particular for their high standards. These kinds of competitions were troubling and disappointing in a "democratic, egalitarian country."[77] In 1881 the newspaper *Le Parisien* condemned the testing regime for creating "overheated minds in weakened and exhausted bodies who only manage to stand up thanks to their youth."[78] Eugène Dally criticized the stringent entrance exam for the Saint-Cyr Military Academy, which caused a "decrease in thoracic perimeter" in prospective students because of missed mealtimes and late nights spent in cramming.[79] Georges Dujardin-Beaumetz took aim at the "morbid effects" of the entrance exam for the teacher training institute of the Seine, where five hundred female applicants vied for twenty-five places: "You can see the terrible aftermath of intellectual overload especially when classes start, after the emotions and fatigues of the exams have taken their toll."[80]

In the cultural consensus of the time, such risks were greater for young career women. Dr Robertson claimed it was a cause of maternal mortality.[81] Alphonse de Candolle believed teaching caused mental illness, considering the "proportion of young women dedicated to the teaching profession locked up in lunatic asylums."[82] The earl of Shaftesbury, surveying the state of education in Wales, found that 145 women teachers, compared to thirty-eight male colleagues, "were admitted to asylums" in 1882.[83] A reporter for the *Medical Times* noted that "many prospective women teachers break down in the second or third year of their studies."[84] As always, the reason given was that the female "nervous system" was "much more impressionable."[85]

More generally, vague and disparate diagnoses fitted mental stress into the physiological framework of the time. For example, the flow of blood to the brain, in response to mental exertion, resulted in untreatable migraines; toothaches were caused by "hyperhemia" (excessive blood flow), as were nose bleeds, goiter, meningitis, stroke and conjunctivitis. Maurice de Fleury, a Paris doctor specializing in "mental afflictions," reported an alarming observation: "An eight-year-old boy who was brought in to my office had discovered all by himself that he should stretch out on the floor to clear his anemic head."[86]

Since the existence of certain microbes had been discovered at the end of the century, and a person in a weakened condition was prone to infections, it followed logically that typhoid fever, pleurisy, and all kinds of invasive and serious illnesses would also be associated with mental strain. Nervous exhaustion characterized by weakness and fatigue became a popular topic for psychiatrists at the turn of the century:

> A professional man works late into the night. He spends long hours concentrating on his work. He goes to bed around three or four in the morning. But he cannot sleep. He cannot control the disordered activities of his brain. Not only is he unable to fall asleep, he feels painful chills in his hands and feet, tightness in his head, aches in his limbs, cramps in his stomach. Usually, a night's sleep will restore our strength. But if the episode of mental fatigue recurs, these symptoms will reappear and the patient may fall victim to "cerebrasthenia" – nervous exhaustion of the brain. … This example shows how all kinds of ailments, especially problems with circulation or digestion, can be caused by mental overwork.[87]

This pessimistic and even alarmist scenario revealed the amount of attention paid to physical symptoms, their unexpected appearance and their diversity: "lack of sleep," weakness of all kinds, acute distress, "abnormal sensations of the skin, tingling, numbness."[88] The first stirrings of the modern individual were seen here, in a perception that one is "trapped" in one's body and alienated from any transcendence, limited to sensory knowledge of one's self. This led to repeated attempts to isolate the root cause, to uncover what disturbs and torments us and identify the obstacles we face, all of which amounted to a systematic project to ferret out fatigue in even the most subtle and diverse symptoms. This was a pessimistic acknowledgement of how seriously progress affected us. It reflected feelings that were shared throughout society about the speed and ubiquity of mechanization, the chug and roar of engines and their predominance in our lives at the end of the nineteenth century. This powerful sensory overload ushered in its opposite: a sense of vulnerability, of exhaustion and of a mismatch between people and their environment that was as harmful as it was inevitable. Feelings of overwork and the social and physical ills that stemmed from them were rooted in this inability to evolve along with a rapidly changing world. "Extreme" speed would be inescapable and would transform fatigue into a lifestyle, an inevitable condition of existence, and our fate.

Neurasthenia

"Neurasthenia" was a generic ailment, and a newly coined word too, that neatly summed up all these disorders. It represented the end point of overwork, a weakness at the very heart of the resilience of the nervous system, and an inability to summon the strength needed to act or react. Descriptions of this phenomenon proliferated in the 1880s.[89] In 1894 Virgile Borel described an English colonel who suffered from an "overwhelming physical breakdown," was "unable to concentrate," and found himself in such dire straits that he "wonders if he really exists." His condition was brought on by "too much time spent on too much mental work" and by experiencing "extreme physical exhaustion" and "great sorrow."[90] This became part of conventional wisdom,[91] and, absorbing the worries and fears of a generation, it fueled accusations, unleashed bigotry, and reinforced anxieties about degeneration through "collapse of the nervous system." Diagnoses could be imprecise and even grossly biased. In 1894 Charles Féré wrote in his book on degeneration about "neuropathic families" with scientific authority and overtly racist language: "The pathological history of the Jewish race is particularly illustrative of this phenomenon … According to Henry Meige, the legend of the wandering Jew was simply the popular version of it."[92] Theories of degeneration provided a way to connect the most repulsive and toxic ideas to the concept of weakness.

Neurasthenia made an appearance in contemporary literature too, with deeply disturbing and memorable images that highlighted its significance in turn of the century culture. Joris-Karl Huysmans's portrait of des Esseintes, the dandyish main character and "hyperaesthetic" neurasthenic of *À Rebours* [Against the grain], suffered from overwrought nerves, neuralgia and dyspepsia:

> The excesses of his youthful life, the exaggerated tension of his mind, had strangely aggravated his earliest nervous disorder and had thinned the already impoverished blood of his race. In Paris, he had been compelled to submit to hydrotherapic treatments for his trembling fingers, frightful pains and neuralgic strokes which cut his face in two, drummed maddeningly against his temples, pricked his eyelids agonizingly and induced a nausea which could be dispelled only by lying flat on his back in the dark.[93]

Literary depictions of neurasthenics became subtler and more nuanced as authors evoked the draining of energy and feeling of blankness that their characters experienced, tormented by an affliction that paradoxically mingled exertion and nullity, deficiencies and pain. They lived, convinced that they "no longer existed" even as they exulted in "feeling more alive than the life that is slipping away."[94] Guy de Maupassant described the feeling of vacuousness, compounded by impotence and exhaustion, in a more realistic vein. His character testified to a condition that seemed simultaneously ephemeral and permanent: "The day tires and annoys me. It is brutal and noisy. I get up with difficulty, I get dressed with weariness, I go out with regret, and each step, each movement, each gesture, each word, each thought exhausts me as though I were lifting a crushing burden. But when the sun goes down, a joy swirls about me, a joy overruns my entire body."[95]

Neurasthenia was a malady afflicting the entire society, a "modern trepidation"[96] that was a reaction to the disturbing flood of stimuli making excessive demands on us and our attention spans. Neurasthenia became the defining symptom of an era when symptoms and lifestyles spread throughout the population: "the recipe for our time: anemia and a weak nervous system."[97] It also revealed a new level of anxiety related to sexual pleasure at a time when open discussion and sexualized representations became more commonplace and the reality more unattainable. The novelist Octave Mirbeau described intense and personal "access" to sexual satisfaction as "one of man's most urgent inalienable rights, but above all one of his most elevated, most sacred duties."[98] Neurasthenia and impotence might be rooted in modern sexual anxiety, leading to a vicious cycle of frustration and suffering that was both painful and intimate, as performance anxiety and fears of impotence added to the neurasthenic's psychic burden. In fact, since mid-century, doctors themselves had reflected this gradually increasing openness to (male) sexual fulfillment by condemning old taboos and "continually insisting" on new conventional wisdom: "If you don't engage in sexual intercourse, you are defying nature."[99]

Though by the end of the century it loomed large, in 1869 George Beard[100] was one of the first to diagnose neurasthenia. Using a striking analogy inspired by mechanical inventions of the day, he compared the human body to an electric condenser with a restricted capacity and to a steam boiler whose volume was also limited.[101] Neurasthenia was triggered when "the surplus" of current short-circuited the system, blocking circulation and the flow of energy. The condition could be summed up in two words: "nervous exhaustion."[102] In other words, this was overwork caused by excessive stimulation and overexertion, its severity dependent on individual differences in endurance and vulnerability. Beard saw this ailment, inextricable from the stresses of "modern life," as particularly "American." In fact, he called the syndrome "American nervousness."[103] European experts such as Professor Ludwig Hirt of Breslau agreed and extended the context from its American "source" to all of modernity: "In fact, neurasthenia was invented by modern life, by the compulsion to become rich as quickly as possible; we can see this in the part of the world where people work, live and grow old the fastest, where nervosity is rampant: we are referring to America."[104]

Other psychological factors were cited more and more frequently: "irritability," restless sleep, "psychic asthenia" (abnormal weakness or lassitude), indecisiveness, obsessions, severe fright, lingering anxiety and groundless fears.[105] This more detailed inventory of psychic malaise was now associated intimately with exhaustion and its aftermath. Emotions, perceptions and personal distress came to the forefront in the continuing study of neurasthenia.

A new conception of fatigue had taken hold, one that was more social and also more intimate; "It all starts with how the body feels,"[106] with our physical and even "moral" fitness. At this point the study of fatigue entered a new stage with an internal focus, and researchers associated feelings of helplessness with a variety of negative outcomes, from lacking confidence and being reluctant to act to falling prey to obsessions, illness and even madness. The old "mental fatigue"[107] that afflicted "intellectuals" or courtiers during the reign of Louis XIV had been reimagined. It now afflicted more people, extending its purview from sensitivity to encompass anxieties and fears too. Jules Déjerine and Emmanuel Gaukler's study of "psychoneuroses" in 1911 presented a modern-day example: an accountant abruptly "passed over" for promotion, who obsessed over his "failures," felt helpless and worthless and was in danger of losing his job. "His sleep deteriorates, and is often restless, tormented by nightmares that resurrect his daytime worries." His mental health was in a downward spiral and "all intellectual efforts exhaust him; very soon doing any work at all becomes impossible."[108] No doubt, above and beyond individual cases, we were witnessing a specific kind of collapse for the first time, a kind of vague internal "agitation"[109] characteristic of modernity, a "new illness rooted in new circumstances."[110] Its symptoms included a general feeling of weakness, helplessness, anxiety and despair that recurred in a vicious circle: "Fatigue provokes anxiety, and anxiety increases fatigue."[111] Progress, so abrupt and so rapid, engendered anxiety as well as fears that these advances were vulnerable and could easily be reversed. As Friedrich Nietzsche wrote in 1884: "Disintegration characterizes this time, and thus uncertainty. Nothing stands firmly on its feet or on a hard faith in itself; one lives for tomorrow as the day after tomorrow is dubious."[112]

Indisputably, more attention was being focused on specific psychological symptoms, on breakdowns whose severity had not previously been described. At the beginning of the twentieth century, Pierre Janet called these disorders "psychoasthenias" and published descriptions and observations of these new "very strange and little-known phenomena" that arose during "genuine crises of exhaustion."[113] One 46-year-old female patient reported that "a mantle of fatigue enveloped me," and a male patient protested that he "feels terrible aches and pains" after performing some simple mental calculations.[114] This newly named pathology joined the growing list of personal disorders and instabilities and was acknowledged as an outgrowth of our culture's endemic fatigue.

"Theorizing" mental fatigue

Now that mental fatigue was a focus of concern and performance, it too became the subject of studies and experiments and a field that invited speculation, interpretation, and the use of laboratory equipment and medical instruments. A vague feeling of lassitude was transformed into a mystery to unravel, thanks to its importance for our shared culture and its role in research about the human mind and our innermost psyche. This was not simply an almost literary exploration of sensitivity or a probe into mental "feelings," consciousness and its limits and vulnerabilities.[115] Instead, it was a specific analysis of the potential role that consciousness played, what constituted it and what influence it had; in short, scientists were determined to understand and define it.

One of the earliest effects of this reorientation was to assign more importance to physical sensations and to examine their impact on behavior. In 1888 the physiologist Fernand Lagrange, one of the first to launch a systematic study, found that "feelings of fatigue are intended to alert us to danger."[116] So, biofeedback was not merely a matter of receiving and interpreting subtle and nuanced sensory information but also a defense mechanism that played a role in the body's self-protection. A new understanding of fatigue resulted from this, and it was no longer seen as solely negative, as an obstacle or impediment. Instead, it served a useful function, sounding an alarm or acting as a stabilizer. This explanation took into account the presence of fatigue "in nerve centers as well as in muscles."[117] Investigating the role of sensory information complemented and enriched scientists' views on fatigue, its onset and development.

Another consequence of this reorientation was to focus even more intensely on "mental fatigue," how it was perceived "from the inside" and how it might affect the rest of the body. In the 1880s more and more studies were being published on "the psychology of attention,"[118] on "intellectual fatigue,"[119] and on the "hygiene of the brain and its intellectual functions."[120] Angelo Mosso, the inventor of the ergograph, also used his apparatus to detect the signs of nervous exhaustion. Analyzing the rising and falling lines on the graphs, he commented: "As far as I know, no one has written a comprehensive study of mental fatigue, so I thought it would be useful to collect and classify these observations."[121] A study that was, in other words, patient and painstaking.

More theories were offered about the subjects who feel "exhausted" after reading, performing calculations or any other brainwork. Perceptions were analyzed, the results were quantified and a wide variety of data points were collected. First of all, the focus was on physical indices: the subjects' temperature, blood pressure, heart rate, respiratory rate and volume of exhalations. Bodily functions were at the center of attention because they were undoubtedly "easier" to study. Dynamometers and other mechanical recording and measuring devices registered the numbers, averages were calculated and conclusions were drawn, since the experimenters presumed that these physical indices were significant. Subjects' heart rate increased, their temperature rose, and their respiration sped up as the mental exercises they were performing became more complex. The danger was clear: "overly demanding work can provoke irregular heartbeats or tachycardia" and may even result in a "contraction of the thorax, making the subject more likely to faint."[122] Mental "exertion" affected bodily functions to such an extent that Théodule Ribot identified cogitation as a "motive power,"[123] whose "silence" immobilized the body's movements. This phenomenon was captured in the portrait of a rigid Saint Catherine painted in Siena in the sixteenth century by Antonio Bazzi (known as "il Sodoma").

Nevertheless, because the results varied among individuals, it was difficult to make use of the observations and measurements collected in the experiments or to draw general principles from them. But they did confirm how "mental work cannot be performed without an effect on the body,"[124] and this, in turn, "expands our concept of fatigue … a phenomenon that becomes more complex the more we study it."[125] Personal accounts became more important, and experts were eager to collect and analyze more of them. For example, Angelo Mosso interviewed his own colleagues in order to amass more data based on their personal experiences and private thoughts. He "recorded" their reactions before teaching a class, taking an exam or writing a paper. The traditional idea was that cogitation precipitated a rush of blood to the head, leading to vertigo, headaches, "dizzy spells," unsteadiness, "bloodshot eyes"[126] or wobbly movements,[127] but these observations were not entirely objective. Whatever the ill effects may be, the aftereffects of mental exertion had become more serious and more varied.

Still, emotions and fears muddied these views of exertion, and distress added a subjective tone, a personal note, to studies of fatigue: "I remember the sleepless nights caused by my nervousness about giving a speech or a lecture. I know how much that agitation tormented me. I would feel so tense before the first or last lesson of the course I was teaching. I could sense my skin flushing, hear my voice trembling, or I would have an awful headache."[128]

Mental fatigue was being defined more precisely and was being recognized as more complex now that emotional distress was being given an unexpectedly serious hearing. Several accounts emphasized its significance. Jean-Martin Charcot was one of the first to investigate "trauma" and its aftereffects. He even developed a unique, truly innovative explanatory schema. The "Case Presentations on General Neurology" delivered at the Pitié-Salpêtrière hospital in Paris between the 1860s and the 1880s offered a number of examples of the effects of destructive and disturbing emotions. Overwhelming sensations of fear "make it impossible for sufferers to go to work or practice their trade for periods of months or years."[129] Though the women exhibited no physical symptoms, they experienced lengthy spells of extreme fatigue that were both painful and insidious.

In 1899 Henri Huchard, a cardiologist at the Bichat hospital in Paris, focused on the role that "depressing" personal circumstances played in provoking "serious problems in the circulatory system," where the heart "suffers repercussions from muscular as well as emotional fatigue."[130] For example, an affluent financier, fifty-nine years old and "the mayor of a well-known city," became embroiled in a political dispute and encountered "losses and disappointments," followed by "a disastrous decline in his personal wealth and political ambitions." He was then "felled" by "cardiac arrest" and found to have "a double aortic malformation."[131]

Looking at another aspect of fatigue, in 1897 Philippe Tissié made a detailed analysis of the contents of dreams that were believed to tire out his patients, resulting in restless sleep and unpleasant aftereffects. He related the case of a young cyclist who dreamt he had embarked on a 60-mile race fraught with obstacles, falls, cheating and run-ins with other contestants. Afterward, he felt exhausted and woke up suffering from "a powerful migraine" and "extreme fatigue affecting the lower half of his body."[132] Tissié concluded that this anecdote provided additional proof of the "influence of thoughts" on our experiences of fatigue.

In 1895 Sigmund Freud explored in detail the "deep-rooted" causes of his patients' distress. He described the case of Elisabeth von R., who first felt "fatigue and pain in the legs," followed by feelings of exhaustion that were attributed originally to "a long walk, lasting a half-hour, taken a few days previously."[133] After this superficial explanation, the account delved more deeply into the patient's family history, describing her father's illness, the nursing done by the patient, his daughter, and the painful memories associated with it: the father's "swollen leg" stretched across her "while she changed his bandages," the regrets, ambiguity, feelings of quasi-uselessness, and the expectations of treating "localized" pain. Deeper still, Freud found emotional "pain" tormenting her, connecting her physical discomfort to the young woman's more generalized "despondency." Thus, her fears of becoming "a lonely old spinster" provoked the psychological and physical sensations of "helplessness" that hindered her walking, drained her strength, and gave her the impression of "being unable to move forward."[134] Finally, the analysis unearthed the revelation that these painful walks were taken with her brother-in-law, with whom she was in love; this taboo resulted in psychic and physical pain.

Scientists were identifying the intersections of physical and mental fatigue. At the end of the century, these studies kept growing and diversifying.

24

Resistance and Growth

Now that the concept of fatigue encompassed both mental and physical exertion, strategies to combat it were increasing in number and becoming more diverse. As evidence of its ravages accumulated, the need to withstand fatigue was more generally accepted and less controversial. Reactions converged and multiplied. Early in the twentieth century, activists who advocated for less demanding work schedules won a limited victory when Sunday was mandated as a day of rest for all employees. Research studies on resilience were undertaken in order to improve training and working conditions. Scientists also investigated substances that would restore vigor and techniques for marketing them. A rather simple "psychologization" promoted images of endurance and strength. A new market niche was established, and magazines and newspapers touted hundreds of products to combat fatigue and weakness. The silhouette of a new society was visible on the horizon.

Rethinking work time

The idea that mental and physical fatigue were connected had become more widely accepted at this time, paving the way for a remarkable achievement in the campaign to reduce work hours. The effects of a seven-day work week on physical and mental wellbeing were being acknowledged. Now that expectations about workers' safety included both physical and emotional aspects, work hours and not simply productivity were more likely to be everyone's concern.

However, this highlighted a central paradox of modern society: managers and industrial engineers insisted that fatigue had been steadily diminishing throughout the century but workers claimed the opposite, insisting that work hours had to be cut back. Alfred Picard's paean to decades of "progress" neatly encapsulated the industrialists' perspective. Making a rapid tour through the ages, the director of Paris's

Universal Exposition in 1900 dwelled on the "remarkable" advances in technology and industry since the days Napoleon ruled the empire. Mining was a prime example, with mechanized "ascents and descents in buckets," "improved extraction equipment," "mechanical drills enlarging mineshafts," "porterage on rails rather than workers' backs" and some "human motors replaced by mechanical ones."[1] All of these innovations were meant to reduce workers' fatigue, but they hardly assuaged the profound sense of being shackled, restrained and suffocated by the demands of industry, so all-encompassing and voracious that no technical advance could overcome them. This was undoubtedly an extreme example, but one that was representative of work as a whole. When the acute consciousness of one's exploitation collided with the implacable pace of economic development, workers unleashed a single demand: lighten the load.

Despite all the technical advances, the shared experience of long work hours and the calls for a shorter work week did not lead to any immediate changes in France's Labor Code. Instead, solutions were slow in coming here and elsewhere in Europe. In England the utopian socialist Robert Owen was one of the first "to demand an eight-hour workday," in 1833.[2] On May 26, 1879, the French deputy and former laborer Martin Nadeau proposed legislation mandating a ten-hour workday and a six-day work week, with Sunday as a day of rest. This was rejected by the Chambre des députés at the time, and again in 1881, 1886 and 1896. Finally, on March 30, 1900, the radical Republican Alexandre Millerand took aim specifically at work hours and proposed "an eleven-hour workday, to be reduced to ten after six years."[3] Despite the slow pace of reform, a change in the air was perceptible as workers began organizing in the second half of the nineteenth century; "workers' unions" were first established in 1867, and by 1884 there were five hundred of them.[4] International labor conventions were held and demands were refined and coordinated. The French Workers' Party, established by the socialist Jules Guesde, approved a platform at its convocation in 1880 calling for reforming the labor code, with an eight-hour workday for adults.[5] The International Labor Conference at The Hague on February 28, 1889, considered a variety of proposals, and Guesde, acting as spokesperson for 138 unions, called for a number of reforms, in addition to an eight-hour workday: "Ban child labor for those under fourteen, reduce the workday to six hours for workers under eighteen, mandate one day off each week, and eliminate night work, with a few exceptions in line with modern industrial production."[6] The Berlin conference that brought together fifteen countries' representatives on February 4, 1890, considered these proposals. Neither England nor France signed up, insisting instead on workers' autonomy: "An adult is his own master and works the number of hours he chooses."[7] Industrial hygienists provided convenient scientific cover for this "freedom": "At present, we are unable to find scientific evidence supporting a limit on the number of work hours."[8] Nevertheless, legislative initiatives continued on the path of reform, demonstrating some politicians' tenacity and the strength of public sentiment. In 1874, a law was passed banning child labor for those under the age of twelve. In 1892, another law set the minimum age of employment at thirteen for boys and eighteen for girls while limiting adult women's workday to eleven hours.[9] Advocates developed new rationales for cutting work hours, in tune with the times. In 1890, *La Réforme sociale*, the journal published by sociologist Pierre Guillaume Frédéric le Play, exploited contemporary fears of degeneration: "The law has intervened in almost every country to limit workers' hours. In fact, it is right and necessary in the interests of the race to protect workers and to protect them from their employers."[10]

Another aspect of labor reform was also concerned with time. First of all, advocates focused on the calendar year and called for rest periods that followed the tempo of the months and seasons. For example, in 1853, the road menders in the Seine-et-Oise department stopped working from June to September, as the prefect's order specified.[11] This was surely an exceptional case, but noteworthy nonetheless. In a broader context, the increasing attention paid to workers' "productive years" was significant, as some government actions acknowledged the toll taken by a lifetime of labor, finding that workers engaged in a "long" career "deserve" protection. For instance, on June 9, 1853, pensions were established for "those employed by the State"[12] over the protests of some who foresaw an insurmountable and unlimited burden on the Treasury.[13] The program specified eligibility and employee contributions: thirty years of service; 5 percent of the bureaucrat's annual salary; a minimum retirement age of sixty or, in the case of "physically demanding labor," twenty-five years of service and a retirement age of fifty-five. The distinction between "sedentary" and "active" employment was new and noteworthy. The law identified "active" job categories such as "postmen, porters, forest wardens, customs agents and port and toll inspectors."[14] Later, in 1876, schoolteachers and, in 1898, prison guards were added to the list.

The diversity of occupations in this category underlined the difficulty of assessing the long-term health effects of employment. Here, conveniently, the job itself, rather than the specifics of any activity, its duration and its physical demands, signaled an association with fatigue. Pension schemes were still relatively rare at the end of the century. In 1898 only 4.35 percent of industrial workers were included; the exception were miners, whose enrollment was mandated by law on June 29, 1894.[15] There were some significant outliers, however. The Saint-Gobain company, a manufacturer of mirrors and glass panes, offered a lump sum payment of one-quarter of their final salary to retiring workers aged fifty-five who had accumulated twenty-five years of service.[16] Other businesses enrolled skilled workers (such as blast furnace operators) in some kind of pension coverage. Reaching the age of eligibility was also rare, though, since at the turn of the century the average lifespan was 48.5 years for men and 52.4 for women.

Reforms affecting railroad workers clearly showed an attempt to measure and quantify the toll of active labor. The legislation was passed on July 21, 1909, guaranteeing pension rights after twenty-five years of service and 5 percent employee contributions, with the retirement age set at fifty for operators, fifty-five for station agents and sixty for office staff.[17] This type of institutional hierarchy put in place by some companies in the nineteenth century[18] clearly distinguished between active and sedentary occupations.

Another change was the evolution in working-class culture, encompassing bolder aspirations for a better future, utopian ideals and the drive, for some, to visualize an entirely different world. In 1883 the socialist activist Paul Lafargue was one of those who insisted on "a right to idleness" once the working class "realize that, by overburdening themselves with work, they exhaust their own vitality and that of their descendants."[19] He described the false consciousness that "the workmen, stupefied by the dogma of work, produce without wishing to consume [goods], without troubling themselves whether there be anyone to consume them."[20] He predicted that when the working class "shall have arisen in its giant strength, not to demand the famous "Rights of Man," which are but the rights of capitalist exploitation, not to proclaim the "Right to Work," which is only the "Right to Misery," but to forge an iron law forbidding everyone to work more than three hours a day, will the old earth trembling with bliss feel a new world stir within it."[21] The anarchist newspaper of the 1890s *Père Peinard* [Father Toiler] fiercely denounced "disgusting and toxic jobs" while proposing a different vision: "If society, instead of being a battle of dog against dog, were organized for genuine sociality, with neither bosses nor masters, us good folks could look forward to living a sweet and peaceful life."[22]

Finally, a new regulation addressing women's working conditions was quite limited in scope but nonetheless revealed the growing concern with fatigue. Inspired by English reforms, the French law passed on December 29, 1900, required certain amenities in female-dominated occupations: "Stores, boutiques and other enterprises where merchandise is handled or sold by women must provide a number of seats equal to the number of women employed there."[23] However, the plight of female domestic servants didn't get the same kind of attention or advocacy. For instance, the caricaturist Paul Guillaume evoked the stereotype of the flighty, venal servant in this dialog between a "mistress" and her "maid" published in *L'Illustré national* on November 23, 1902: "Justine, since you're satisfied with your wages, why do you want to leave us?" "Madam never gives me a night off. If I stayed, I'd end up losing all my boyfriends."[24]

The painfully slow pace of official reforms cannot be ignored. The law mandating an eight-hour workday was passed only on April 23, 1919. Bringing a majority of the Chamber of Deputies on board took decades: ninety were in favor in 1896, 115 in 1900.[25] There was one overriding obstacle; your perspective on work and fatigue depended on where you sat: with the workers or with the bosses.

France's Sabbatarian law, the revision of the Labor Code in 1906 mandating one day of rest in the work week, was a key example. The "idea of the English-style work week, with a half-day Saturday and a full day off on Sunday, has been in force across the Channel since the middle of the nineteenth century."[26] In 1896 the Christian Democrats included a proposal for Sunday rest in the platform of their annual conference in Reims.[27] The social reformer Albert de Mun drew up legislation on it at the end of the century.[28] Some rationales were quite practical; mandating a Sunday day off would prevent the ravages of "Holy Monday" and the "drunken spree that follows the close of business at noon on Sundays."[29] Public opinion was leaning in favor of a mandatory day off, though opponents still promoted a rather contradictory idea of freedom, asking: "Aren't we robbing [the worker] of all responsibility when we force him to abstain from work on that day?"[30] In 1902, the independent Socialist deputy Alexandre Zévaès put forward legislation that mandated a day off work for public and private employees "without specifying the day,"[31] to avoid equating leisure time and religious observance, notably at a moment when "Sunday rest" was coming to "represent a desacralization of time."[32] At the beginning of the twentieth century, both labor unions and socialist organizations endorsed the campaign for an English-style shorter work week, arguing that it would benefit families in the long run and ensure workers a much needed rest period.[33] Finally, in 1912, a law was passed mandating the "English work week" for "industries in this country,"[34] and the tendency to associate Sundays with leisure rather than religious observance grew. The rousing song "Marche des travailleurs chrétiens" [Anthem of Christian workers] proclaimed its fidelity to unions and Sunday rest and was later adopted as the rallying cry of France's Confederation of Christian Workers: "Through our one and only Union, / we want to proudly claim our right, with no holding back. / Through our Contract, we want wages / That keep up with the Cost of living. / Let's have an Eight-Hour Day everywhere! / The English work week in Business, in Industry! / And above all Sunday rest for everyone. / Friends, let's fight on to victory![35]

These reforms were unthinkable without a new understanding by lawmakers and regulators that shortening the work week would have positive results, "conserving our national store of energy."[36] The focus shifted from losses of productivity to gains in efficiency.

Inventing training

Paradoxically, at the end of the nineteenth century a new craze, sports, in which energy was expended for pleasure and relaxation, inspired the most sophisticated methods for combating fatigue and maximizing an efficient use of energy. So many new circumstances and economic and social changes made these innovations possible: from people's access to free time, however limited, to a "revolution" in transportation that enabled meetings in "faraway" locations; the erosion of territorial divisions with a tradition of separate competitions;[37] the growth of activities "open to all," characteristic of a democratic society, with entries that are not limited to specific classes or ranks; and the popularity of "championships" with national reach, in a break from the typical village or regional competition. All in all, modern sports achieved a measure of visibility and social prominence that traditional contests had not.[38]

In addition, the objective of competitions had changed in a profound way, influenced by the new industrial culture. Now, numbers were key, ever present in the scoring and ranking of competitors, in record-setting performances and path-breaking feats, in the recognition of champions and trend-setters, whose scores were calculated, evaluated and recorded. Nevertheless, the new sporting culture had a significant effect: the "extreme" became the norm and was an unacknowledged reason to keep pushing the limits. Pierre de Coubertin made this clear when he legitimized "excess" over the traditional values of restraint and "the happy medium": "Sports is a mechanism that manages power, a device in which effort is the main lever and excess is the primary rationale."[39] It followed logically that fatigue was a necessary complement of "limits" where, quite simply, like any cherished companion, it gave pleasure because it was incontrovertibly associated with success:

> Have you admired their tenacity confronting fatigue and how they have a defiant look on their faces when they are in the throes of competition? You must realize that there is a feeling of joy, bittersweet to be sure, that one experiences after overcoming all the initial obstacles. But this feeling is certainly miles above the pleasure one gets from ordinary athletics, recreation, and activities that don't challenge us.[40]

The idea of personal challenges still existed. In preceding decades, it motivated adventurous tourists and mountain climbers to defy risks and fatigue,[41] but now the emphasis was on testing one's own limits and going beyond them.[42] Pierre de Coubertin insisted that "sports not only inure us to fatigue but make us enjoy it."[43] A number of personal accounts testified to this: "I applied myself to this difficult task with a certain amount of unalloyed pride. When I reached the goal, I was exhilarated!"[44] Others transformed athletics into a spectacle, as in Colette's impressionistic reportage of cyclists speeding toward the finish line of the Tour de France in 1912. The daily newspaper *Le Monde* published her first-person account of the racers glimpsed along the final leg of the route: "Yellow and black backs, with red numbers, three creatures with no faces, spines arched, their foreheads touching their knees, topped by a white cap … They disappeared very quickly, silently amid the uproar."[45]

Sports and fatigue now played an important role, and the emphasis on the "best" and the accumulation of statistics to prove it were goals apart from all the others. They underlined the significance of numbers, record-keeping and ranking. This did not mean that "ranking" was unfamiliar. For instance, English horsemen have long understood how to increase the speed and endurance of their steeds.[46] In the eighteenth century, the countess of Genlis charted her students' progress through numbers.[47] A century later, Angelo Mosso used the ergograph to show precisely how muscular strength increased over time.[48] Nevertheless, sports introduced a new perspective. Repetitions that were so minimal that they were barely noticeable could help to build muscle strength. The new phenomenon of organized competition was the impetus; time trials and qualifying events became the norm. They were institutionalized, programmed and scheduled systematically, from one meeting to the next, measured both in space and in time.

A new technique was devised: "training," with its goal of "accomplishing every day and without fatigue an effort that was greater than the day before."[49] Training involved regularly adding a little more time or intensity to an exercise, with the expectation that such limited, calibrated, carefully paced daily increments would add to endurance and strength. Training was meant "to increase resistance to fatigue to the absolute possible limit."[50] In fact, gradually increasing the intensity and duration of a workout enabled athletes to recover more quickly, as their bodies broke down lactic acid accumulating in the muscles. Training that accustomed them to an activity was an innovation with undefined but positive future benefits, optimizing performance and "surpassing the limits of normally [*sic*] impossible feats."[51] Philippe Tissié explicitly referred to modern competitive culture when he explained in his work on the "physiology of fatigue" in 1897: "Training did not exist in France eight years ago. Bicycle racing changed that."[52]

Many new sports programs and measurements were introduced at this time, such as model lessons for training,[53] progress charts[54] and the "step-by-step" fitness method.[55] For instance, the fame of champions such as cross-country runner Jean Bouin sparked interest in the numbers on athletes' progress charts and the minutiae of their training routines.[56] In 1888, Fernand Lagrange published the daily workout routine of a butcher's helper turned competitive rower.[57] In 1905, Raoul Fabens described the "carefully calibrated doses"[58] of a runner's training regimen before a 16-kilometer race. In 1914, the first sports weekly, *La vie au grand air* [Outdoor life] detailed the step-by-step weekly training program of professional soccer players.[59]

Philippe Tissié declared in 1897 that sports training with its "arsenal of methods had become an actual science,"[60] because so many gradations and calculations promised a new approach to studying fatigue and recovery. Diet played a "very important role in training"[61] too, and, based on research in biology at the end of the nineteenth century, such recommendations tended to favor meat and proteins, such as this example prescribing a daily intake of "130 grams of albuminoids, 404 grams of carbohydrates, 84 grams of fats."[62] On the other hand, by the beginning of the twentieth century, "trainers" and physicians repeatedly sparred over the outsized role of albuminoids: "120 grams of albumen, then gradually over twenty years [reduced to] 110, 100, 80 and even 60 and even much less per day."[63] In this way a new perspective on fitness was being created, replete with exercises and scheduling, calculations and expectations, aiming for a goal of unlimited "personal best" performances and higher resistance to fatigue.

We must remember that the new priority assigned to individual achievement also acknowledged people's differences both during the actual competitions and in the stages leading up to them; it was impossible to propose a "one size fits all" formula. The modernization of sports encompassed comparisons, relativism, and a recognition of individual strengths and weaknesses. The first professional trainers emphasized this: "Exercises have to be tailored to each person's core endurance, which varies."[64] As a result, empiricism and trial and error were inevitable in the attempt to map out training regimens and appropriate measurements.

Establishing typologies

Individuality was inevitably valued now more than ever. The organizers of the 1900 Olympic Games enshrined this with obsessively detailed observations of participants' physiques,[65] including their height, weight, circumference, thickness, waists, chests, lung capacity and body fat. These numerous and disparate measurements, barely categorized, did not provide much of a basis for future investigations and remained a blizzard of numbers, classifications and types. In 1910, Félix Régnault proposed three general categories of athletes' physiques, based on spatial dimensions: "longiforme," "latiforme" and "crassiforme," slotting height, weight, girth and posture into an elementary, three-dimensional schema.[66] Claude Sigaud devised a more comprehensive system that included body type and physiological functions: the "respirator," the "muscular," the "digestive" and the "cerebral."[67] Strengths and weaknesses were more defined, so that the bulging abdomen of the "digestive" was contrasted with the capacious chest of the "respirator" and the toned body of the "muscular" with that of the brittle "cerebral." Thus, to the expert eye, "normality" came in several different versions, each validated by numbers, diagrams and photographs, and everyone's potential and tendency could be taken into account. Recommendations and specializations were offered, addressing speed or strength, heavy or light weight, debility or capability. The point was to foreground "a scientific analysis of individuality."[68] In 1912 Léon Mac-Auliffe and Auguste Chaillou's *Morphologie médicale* was a prime example. The illustrations showed a number of different, representative body types, both generic sketches and actual black and white photographs of men and women posing in front of graph paper.[69]

Training and its emphasis on individuality also took hold in the military. "You should not expect all men to endure the same amount of fatigue when they join your regiment because they do not all have an equal capacity for resilience and cannot, without danger of injury, make the same efforts … the trick is to step up the training gradually and intelligently."[70] The execution of this "trick" was left to the officers in charge, who were expected to recognize differences among recruits and make the proper adjustments. But the categories became clearer and military capabilities more defined, just as in sports. These distinctions were important because, starting in 1889, "military service becomes truly universal, even for seminarians."[71] This led to endless discussions about the steps and stages appropriate for training and comparisons of the strategies used by different militaries. Questions of weight, age, height and chest capacity were revisited in order to evaluate and adapt to recruits' strengths and weaknesses.[72] Troops were surveyed and tested with the dynamometer.[73] Patterns in the data were examined with a critical eye to produce reliable cross-checks. At the beginning of the twentieth century, Maurice-Charles-Joseph Pignet, a military physician in the 35th Infantry Regiment, developed a formula to assess recruits based on three main criteria: height, weight and chest circumference. Statistics provided the foundation, and the data was collected on body mass and respiratory capacity. The assessment involved two steps. The first step was to add the recruit's weight and chest circumference together. For example, a recruit weighing 54 kilos, with a 78-centimeter chest circumference, got a score of 132. The second step involved "subtracting that sum (132) from the recruit's height, which is 154 centimeters … The result is 22."[74] As fantastical as this system seemed, it was "validated" by the number of trials undertaken, and, with sufficiently reliable results, it was soon adopted by the army. The main selling point was that it provided a "standardized" yardstick: "The higher the final score, the weaker the constitution."[75] This led to a five-tier system classifying recruits' readiness: "A score less than 10 = very strong constitution. A score from 11 to 15 = strong constitution. From 16 to 20 = good constitution. From 21 to 30 = good constitution (average). Above 35 = very mediocre constitution."[76]

Thus, recruits were ranked based on a statistical measure of resilience. Their capacities as well as their potential were inventoried. For the first time, their readiness was expressed in a simple number. At the very least, Pignet's schema represented an attempt on a nationwide level to predict each soldier's potential for fatigue quantitatively.

Protective chemistry

The ways to transmute hope into reality were equally unique, including requests to "reconstitute" lost vitality and respond positively to patients' recurrent complaints: "Doctor, I'm tired. I can't drag my feet any longer. I have to get some rest."[77] This was evidence, if anything was, of the incurable malaise of the century that was the sensation of weakness. At first, "classic" remedies were proposed, stimulants such as rosemary "to revive and fortify the mind,"[78] the "extremely refreshing" lemon verbena,[79] and vanilla "to perk up brain activity and increase the stock of energy in the body."[80]

In the second half of the nineteenth century, chemical substances produced in laboratories entered the market, though potential side effects and dangers were not yet understood. Cocaine, discovered in 1855 and widely prescribed by physicians after 1880, was a key example.[81] Gustave Geley recommended sipping on a cocaine and wine cocktail "in a small liqueur glass" at each meal, since it "will quickly restore healthy sleep patterns, increase productive capacity and, in particular, eliminate almost completely the painful feelings of exhaustion and helplessness caused by neurasthenia."[82]

Other, equally risky miracles of modern chemistry followed: "strychnine arsenate," "belladonna extract," powdered opium and Nux vomica, in pills or powders.[83] So many so-called regenerative remedies meant to "revitalize" our blood cells or our essential energy were touted at the end of the century: cordials that infused wine with beef bouillon, iron extract, quinine or coca, such as the frequently advertised "vin Mariani," a patent medicine invented by a chemist from Corsica. Some remedies were sold as lozenges with exotic sounding names, such as "Gelsemium sempervirens," "Colombo" and "Quassine Adrian." "Bruel capsules" were marketed as a cure for "all nervous ailments," while others claimed to fortify the blood, such as the powdered supplement "Quevenne iron" and another "that is guaranteed pure beef."[84] There were as many patent remedies as there are varieties of fatigue: Blanchard pills "approved by the medical academy" combated "overwork, anemia, and periods of crisis."[85] The quest for something "to restore vitality" and overcome "energy drain"[86] revealed more about the cultural ethos than any particular formulation of plant or animal extracts. At the end of the nineteenth century, the medical and paramedical professions' enthusiasm embodied not only false promises but also a misguided faith in technology. Many dangerous experiments were undertaken, intending to boost strength and virility or soothe the nerves, relying on the prestige and supposed miraculous power of injections. In 1892, Constantin Paul aimed to "defeat neurasthenia" with a "nervous transfusion"; the treatment consisted of injecting, every four days, 3 or 4 cubic centimeters of "sheep's brain" that had been marinated in "glycerine and filtered through an Arsonval apparatus." The theory was that adding nerve cells would "greatly improve" one's condition.[87] At the beginning of the twentieth century, Dr Collongues treated patients in Vichy with a "dynamoscope" that vibrated at the same frequency as the sufferers' brain cells and bone marrow, in order to strengthen them.[88] Many chemical remedies, physical interventions, scientific rationales and imaginative therapies proffered some variation of the turn of the century promise of renewal and vigor. Even the thermal springs in different spa towns were rated according to their "electrical charge" or "radioactivity"[89] (a property that had been discovered in 1896). People's fears of "nervous collapse"[90] merged with the astounding productivity of technical and scientific innovations around the turn of the century to foster an atmosphere of uncritical belief in humanity's ability to protect itself from the ills of modern life.

Re-evaluating the territory

Physical activity and exercise could build up a run-down body with more accessible and less technical methods. The *Journal of Nervous and Mental Disease* recommended the "bicycle," recently invented in the 1890s, since cyclists' measured pace, varied routes and "continually changing views along the way"[91] would "positively" influence their mood. The living proof was that "neurasthenics who ride a bicycle are cured more quickly than those who do not."[92] Taking long, unhurried walks exercised but did not exhaust the muscles, as the novelist Octave Mirbeau explained in an account of his own "treatment," claiming that a leisurely stroll enabled neurasthenics "to put the brakes on the whirling merry-go-round of their ennui."[93] Marcel Craponne also advised slowing the pace and "building neurasthenics' confidence step by step in their own abilities and energy."[94] Spa towns featured a "treatment on the ground,"[95] mapping out walking paths that challenge patients incrementally, ranging from "a flat route," to "a slight incline," to a "steeper path," to "an uphill climb."[96] Some spa towns specialized in treating neurasthenics, highlighting a specially tailored experience and environment, featuring calm rather than excitement, activity rather than immobility, predictability rather than disorder, and distant vistas over claustrophobic confines. At the beginning of the nineteenth century, some resorts promised "nervous guests" little more than remoteness from their usual social round.[97] Now these retreats were redesigned for a more intentional use of time and space: "to keep the patients busy from morning till night, every hour ... and not leave them face to face with their distress."[98] This program was satirized in 1886 in a one-act comedy "Aux Eaux" [Taking the waters], in which Alfred Guillon played a doctor in a spa town: "Get up at six in the morning, shower with freezing cold water ... as cold as possible. Promenade to la Raillière, gargle ... afterward with Mahoura spring water ... Return to the hotel for lunch: soft-boiled egg, watercress, no wine or spices ... After lunch, walk back to la Raillière ... We have to tire the suckers out."[99]

At thermal spas, the patient's body, more generally, was on the receiving end of specific treatments: massages, baths, showers, compresses, enemas, concoctions, infusions, stretches, releases and all kinds of exercises.[100] The main point was to zero in on bodily "sensations" and to orient those "sensations" toward recovery. We see here the convergence of new trends in psychology at the end of the nineteenth century, prioritizing the body and its sensations. For example, in 1885, in *Les Maladies de la personnalité*, Théodule Ribot called the body the "physical core of the ego's unity."[101] Earlier in the century Henry Maudsley, a professor at University College London, explained the body–mind connection: "The ego is the unity of the organism declaring itself in consciousness. When I touch a certain part of my body, I am conscious of a sensation of touching and of a sensation of being touched, both sensations in my *self*. The organism is the self and consciousness only makes it known."[102] In this way, sensory perceptions became the basis for reassurance and "reconstitution."

This was why physical weakness and lassitude needed to be countered with reinvigorating treatments. At the end of the nineteenth century, Sebastien Kneipp's "water cure" exemplified this, incorporating water, cold, baths with compresses, affusion (pouring liquid on the head) and steam baths. Kneipp's program included activities giving patients a variety of sensory input, such as "walking barefoot," "walking in wet grass" and "walking in freshly fallen snow." In his book he recommended this approach for patients who "have damaged their health through excessive work and fatigue" and those experiencing a "complete breakdown, with body and mind in a pitiful condition."[103] Neurasthenia originated in a particular context. Another one aimed to undo its ill effects.

One central focus was the domestic interior, one's personal "retreat" and the home that promised rest and recuperation. Reinventing the home enabled publicists and designers to bring an entirely fresh vision of "wellbeing" to light and to reinforce the separation between public and private. Advertisements lauding the "inside" compared to the "outside" seemed quite ordinary, but in fact they revealed something essential about this changing perspective at the end of the nineteenth century. "After an exhausting day at work, it is so natural and so good to relax, wearing your housecoat and warm slippers. Let the business and clients fend for themselves! You belong here, surrounded by your loved ones."[104]

The healing environment also encompassed new furniture designs, with rounded silhouettes, plush fabrics and shapes that prioritized ease and comfort: padded armchairs to sink into and lounge chairs for stretching out. Such items were intended not only to support the body in repose but also to better accommodate the human form with ergonomically appropriate armrests and correctly inclined backs and footrests, all constructed of materials that complement the body's natural curves.[105] Following these renewed calls to de-stress, the word "relaxed"[106] appeared for the first time in dictionaries as the nineteenth century drew to a close. It was taken up by novelists such as Joris-Karl Huysmans during the Belle Époque. He described the main character Durtal in *Là-Bas* [The damned] (1891) relaxing beside a cosy fire during a deceptively quiet moment in his researches into Satanism: "Durtal, made drowsy by the warmth and quiet domesticity, let his thoughts wander. He said to himself, 'If I had a place like this, above the roofs of Paris, I would fix it up and make it a real haven of refuge' ... The glowing stove purred. Durtal felt the sudden relaxation of a chilly soul dipped into a warm bath."[107] The concept of relaxation was popularized by Americans as well. Steele MacKaye,[108] a well-known proponent of naturalistic Delsartian acting, advocated "relaxing" as a method for actors to integrate "control, grace and poise" in their physical expression of emotions. This was undoubtedly also supposed to counteract "American nervousness"[109] and intended to dispel "probably cramped"[110] and "anxious-minded and strained" feelings.[111] At the turn of the century the method was disseminated beyond the world of the theater and in 1904 Eustace Miles and

E. F. Benson presented relaxation techniques for everyday life in their handbook *Daily Training*, with tips such as "don't frown, release the jaw muscles, relax the eyes, fingers and toes." Also "walk, talk, write and eat at a leisurely pace" and "don't tense up the body."[112] When people were overwhelmed by sensory input and stress, relaxation techniques offered a way to blunt their impact.

To thrive

Like relaxation, perseverance was seen as an important weapon in the battle against fatigue. Though this pairing may appear contradictory, both tranquility and tenacity were essential elements of self-control. This is why concepts of "awareness" and simple formulas evoking "mind over matter" figured in early writing on psychology, acknowledging the existence of an inner consciousness but claiming that fatigue could be overcome by willpower and weakness conquered by a shift in perspective. Willibald Gebhardt published *L'Attitude qui en impose et comment l'acquérir* [The winning attitude and how to achieve it][113] in 1900. He began developing his "voluntarist" psychology in the 1890s in a series of pamphlets on topics such as gymnastic exercises, self-hypnosis, the laws of success, and techniques to enhance willpower.[114] He repackaged familiar exercises involving breath, movement and posture and imbued them with a new relevance for internal fortitude and confidence: "After a short period of time, breathing exercises will have an extraordinary regenerative effect on our sense of strength and a general feeling of wellbeing, of energy that cannot be imagined by those who are sedentary and perform only intellectual labor. Our self-esteem will rise as our agility and suppleness increase, and so will our self-confidence."[115]

Exercises involving "willpower" became more popular, associating incremental training methods and aspirations for success. "A man can win through willpower by training every day, increasing a little more and gaining little by little more control over himself."[116] Paul-Émile Lévy even used the term "psychic gymnastics."[117] Attentiveness and tenacity were essential to this initiative; stubbornness and single-mindedness would keep it going, transforming "willpower" into work.[118] So many authors called for personal affirmation, nurturing the hope of getting a foothold on the ladder of success. In other words, these were the dominant themes of a society of competition and contests that, in less obvious terms, expressed the converse also: that "weak wills" would become "the defining disease of our time."[119] A whole new genre of pseudo-scientific commentary was born at the beginning of the twentieth century, promising "self-confidence,"[120] and explaining how to "get stronger"[121] and to "make one's way in life."[122] An American proponent of physical culture, Bernarr Macfadden, promised "supreme vitality" through a combination of bodybuilding, nutrition and healthy living. He touted practices such as fasting or a "milk diet," as well as frequent sexual intercourse, to transform his disciples' "weakness into strength,"[123] enabling them the better to withstand disappointments, negativity and unexpected twists and turns in their lives. Willpower would sweep away the fatigue of modern life.

PART V

THE TWENTIETH AND TWENTY-FIRST CENTURIES AND THE CHALLENGE OF PSYCHOLOGY

The nineteenth century explored the biological effects of fatigue as never before: from mechanics to energy, from oxygen to nutrition, from muscular fatigue to mental fatigue. Scientists ventured into the field of psychology and mental health, disseminating concepts of overwork and neurasthenia. The twentieth century inaugurated the "know thyself"[1] era and turned fatigue into a generalized phenomenon that drained us physically and even mentally. It affected the whole person, setting off feelings of anxiety and discomfort. It threatened our potential for self-actualization and undoubtedly turned everyone's life upside down. Studies were launched into many different effects of fatigue, investigating our "inner" resources, our reserves of self-confidence, and psychic balance. Now that scientific fields of inquiry had diversified, even more of the aftereffects of fatigue were being studied; these new discoveries in biochemistry, hormones, "miracle" molecules and new techniques led to the always precarious belief that limits could be ignored.

Material conditions of our lives changed with the century, so that we had relatively fewer physical burdens but felt more pressure on relationships. Information flowed in the same channels as energy, and careers in "communication" were overtaking those in "creation." This might result in new symptoms of fatigue and express itself in different types of tension, triggered by disappointments, impatience, conflicts and "modern anxiety,"[2] which was a state of exhaustion caused in equal measure by overexertion, irritability and impotence.

In fact, it is impossible to disregard the existence of a larger psychic space in contemporary Western societies, with their more individualized economies and more developed democratic systems that are always in danger of fracturing. Everything changed with the explosion of consumerism and demands for security in health and welfare. Everything changed with the growth of services and products. Everything changed with the expansion of individual protections in Western societies and the apparent legitimacy accorded to choices governed by preference and dictated by individuals. The "world of the internet" had already inaugurated a horizontality "dictated" by its infrastructure, and consumers were increasingly convinced that they could express and fulfill their preferences at ever more granular levels.[3] Add to this a democracy foregrounding an ideology of equality, "on equivalences without limits and without ruptures in the social fabric."[4] Add also new working conditions; individual departments and teams had been transformed by the computer revolution, new manufacturing methods and the growth of the service industry. Big manufacturing conglomerates that employed large numbers of workers laboring side by side were subdivided into hundreds of small units, isolated by distance and separated by autonomy and independence: "Everyone feels more isolated or hemmed into small groups, simultaneously more responsible for themselves and subjected to enormous pressures. This is taken to a new level in bargaining agreements, as this type of management structure emphasizes the individuality of the workers' connection with their company."[5]

The results were more profound than they might seem: a rejection of authority, of any assault on identity, and constant alertness to instances of "harassment" (a word invented in the 1980s, which itself is suggestive). More egalitarian societies could confront authoritarianism and dominance and combat dependency and subjection. Fatigue now arose from what seemed like new personal threats, such as obstacles to personal fulfillment or integrity and promises of self-actualization that were always stymied. Frustration increased, and fatigue became more common. The restrictions permeating exercise and work now invaded our daily lives, penetrating every moment, and impeding the fulfillment of our needs that had also changed. Change was inescapable and necessary, but a new dynamic had taken over. Instead of our physical state affecting our mental health, now the psychology of our circumstances affected our physical condition so seriously that it strained, drained and exhausted us.

Never before had fatigue penetrated daily life so deeply that it was impossible to visualize our existence without it.

25

Revealing the Psyche

The First World War, with its mechanized industrial-scale destruction, was an event of extremes, causing countless traumas as serious as they were revealing and incubating kinds of fatigue that were heretofore unknown. Investigations into fatigue were upended; multiple research projects were launched into different causes and more far-reaching inquiries undertaken about its effects. A new arena of experimentation was accessible, and even the workplace was looked at differently. New kinds of fatigue were identified because the phenomenon was being evaluated in a new manner, one that was especially focused on its effect on our whole personality.

Analyses of the context of fatigue were also transformed, starting in the 1930s with technical advances in travel that revolutionized our relation to time and space: the car, the plane, the cargo ship. These new settings inspired a number of investigations into people's behavior, their attention span, and the excesses induced by overly long periods of concentration. It was a unique situation in which fatigue was more psychological than physical, extending its reach from the body ever deeper into the mind, becoming more intrusive and more complex at every stage until it sometimes took a reverse course, and moved from the inside to the outside.

The trenches, crossing the red line

The First World War subjected combatants to inconceivable levels of fatigue. The language used to describe and evaluate the war experience implied that a limit had been surpassed: "crossing the threshold,"[1] "physical and psychic experiences with no precedent in the history of warfare in the West"[2] and the "terrifying sensation of a nightmare."[3] An anomalous "extreme event" was happening, and personal accounts described the ravages inflicted on both body and mind. Never before have scientists given equal weight to what was "felt" and what was "observed" in the realm of fatigue.

Specific elements of life on the battlefield influenced this perception: the misleading and confusing fog of war; the endless treks along the front lines; the jagged, bombed-out landscape, the disappearance of landmarks; the troops slogging "for hours at a time through a maze of trenches."[4] The horrors of this new kind of warfare layered fear onto exhaustion. For example, soldiers on the battlefield regularly had to stoop and crawl to "appear invisible" and not become an easy target in a tactic far different from the military's traditional "shoulder to shoulder"[5] frontal assaults. These actions inevitably resulted in injuries: "knees bleeding, hands scraped raw, elbows smashed."[6] The physical stresses were unpredictable and endless, but such periods of intense effort were interspersed with long intervals of waiting in damp, muddy, torn uniforms, with irregular meals, flooded trenches and the danger of "'trench foot' … that can turn into gangrene, the result of the abominable living conditions endured by the soldiers."[7] The usual signs of the passage of time were scrambled and soldiers suffered from lack of sleep and constant alarms: "The chronic lack of sleep makes combatants feel exhausted. Biological rhythms are disrupted because of the tactical necessity of night-time combat in the trenches, and the impossibility of relying on a normal alternation of periods of sleep and wakefulness aggravate feelings of fatigue."[8]

There were also the stresses and adrenaline rushes of repeated bombardments that soldiers described as "excruciating:" "It's an awful stress … Our legs crumple under us; our hands are trembling … We've lost all our muscles and our flesh."[9] The "nervous" breakdowns in the aftermath are poorly understood but are acknowledged nevertheless, as in the *Larousse médical illustré de guerre* [Larousse illustrated medical dictionary of war], published in 1916, that described "shell shock" from "explosions" that induced "stupor" and even "delirious agitation with hallucinations."[10] Expressing amazement at the sudden changes in their men, officers and military physicians included this phenomenon in their field reports: "In just a few seconds, the subject seems to be in the grip of overwhelming fatigue; he is pale, listless and groggy. He has headaches, cannot speak and seems to be dumbstruck."[11]

The noteworthy aspects here were not only the facts themselves but the analyses of them and their aftereffects. Observers were using a tone that is both precise and extreme, attesting to the experience affecting both bodies and minds in a way that provided a heretofore missing emphasis. Fatigue was invading new territories, was acknowledged as a significant threat and was inspiring more studies: "The war, with its periods of concentrated and prolonged effort, urgently put the problem [of fatigue] front and center, as well as a pressing need to find practical solutions."[12] The troops in the field were affected by the intense strains of combat and the labor force at home by the crushing demands of war production. From now on, it would be impossible to ignore references to psychic distress, giving new life to the somewhat neglected diagnoses of "disturbed nerve centers"[13] and "depression," or, in laypersons' terms, "the blues" or "the void." All in all, the language highlighted a powerful apathy at the heart of this type of exhaustion. Sufferers described a condition both physical and "mental," where body and mind were drained and a frightening sense of depersonalization set in: "We don't even have the presence of mind any more to imagine, to fear whatever is in store for us …."[14] Fighting in the Argonne, André Pézard warned: "The ones who think too much in the midst of this … will lose their lives."[15] Gabriel Chevallier vividly narrated the feeling of being reduced to a brutish existence:

> I live like an animal, an animal that is hungry and then is tired. I have never felt so stupid, so empty-headed, and I understand that the kind of physical exhaustion that doesn't allow people any time to think, that reduces them to a level where they fulfill only the most primitive needs, is a sure-fire way to dominate them. I understand now why slaves submit so easily to their masters, because they lack the strength to revolt and neither the imagination to plan an uprising nor the energy to carry it out. I understand the clever tactics of the oppressors, who deny the people they are exploiting the use of their brains by overwhelming them with exhausting labor. At times, I feel as if I am on the brink of the void, feeling nothing but monotony and lassitude, almost at the point of that animalistic passivity that accepts everything, that subjection that destroys the individual.[16]

These personal accounts were even more significant because they signaled a major cultural shift, acknowledging a psychological imperative that had slowly gained recognition, beginning with the Enlightenment:

the need for self-affirmation and actualization. The most powerful, most debilitating fatigue overwhelmed individuals and denied them agency, so that it was not simply a lack of energy that kept people from acting but another, more essential lack that obliterated their freedom to think and to feel. For the first time, this obstacle to self-preservation was recognized and named. It was psychological in origin, but was more complex than the historic "mental fatigue." The depersonalization described in these accounts differed also from neurasthenia and its anxieties and feelings of inadequacy. Instead, the stresses in the trenches produced a "walled-in" feeling that was difficult to analyze, to understand and to overcome. From this time on, psychology would no longer ignore fatigue in all its variety.

"War fatigue" became exemplary of possibly the ultimate level of fatigue. The numbers of observations of the war wounded and the new discoveries they enabled put scientists on a path to more generalized and comprehensive insights. In particular, they adopted a more anthropological perspective. This is a change in focus that must not be overlooked.

Routes to "globalization"

Much of the research in the post-war period took a new direction, focusing on uncovering new causes of fatigue and identifying ever more specific psychological effects.

Fatigue crept in everywhere, affecting the farthest reaches of the human body and mind. This fundamentally new perspective saw fatigue affecting all aspects of one's personality. Research studies delved ever deeper and their inquiries were wide-ranging, underlining the new attention to the self. Charles Myers emphasized this in the work of the aptly named Industrial Fatigue Research Board established by the British government in 1920: "Muscular fatigue in the factory cannot be isolated, as in the laboratory, from such influences such as skill and intelligence which depend on the proper functioning of the higher levels of the central nervous system. … he [the worker] regulates his output according to his feelings of fatigue present or anticipated – that is, according to the length of the period during which he knows that he has to work."[17]

Such conclusions set off a new series of scientific inquiries. Industrial hygienists made lists of what they called "underlying causes," delving into workers' characteristics, their backgrounds and their idiosyncrasies, examining "the pre-history of the subject," the "state of the nervous system before and during exertion," "working conditions," "the pace, tempo and work shift" and the "dominant tenor of the nervous system."[18] Their studies uncovered many different types of traumas that resulted in "weakness and muscular asthenia."[19] So many potential liabilities made it difficult to come up with a stable definition, since the "phenomenon takes so many different forms that are dissimilar and in particular are dependent on several factors in the context of the activity."[20] This, in turn, encouraged more research into the finer distinctions of the setting and particular circumstances of exertion and fatigue.

Closer scrutiny of the causes also led to a re-evaluation of fatigue's effects. In the 1930s Kurt Goldstein investigated such reactions holistically: "We have even been able to establish that the organism, under the influence of a particular color, acts distinctly differently, even down to its shape."[21] Maurice Boigey confirmed this hypothesis in his studies of athletes, finding that "undergoing a series of grueling competitions" affected the whole body, not just by inducing cramps or sore muscles. The effect was "generalized," with the subjects' arms and legs less steady, their posture and balance less stable, their mental acuity duller.[22] In other words, a kind of simulated amputation took place, with the effects reflecting the leitmotif of the era: "Fatigue penetrates the deepest recesses of the psyche."[23] It affected the whole person, body and mind, with far-reaching consequences that had been previously overlooked.

In 1928 Elliott Smith investigated the behavior of "tired" workers who "no longer think clearly," easily take offense "at injustices … and hostile attitudes," have "hair-trigger tempers," or sink into "depression"[24] such that their physical exhaustion sabotages their emotions. In 1932 Morris Viteles studied "tired businessmen" who turned into "unpleasant domestic tyrants" and disrupted the family circle and its "sense of wellbeing."[25] There were subtle differences, of course, between the dominant and subaltern classes, with the former becoming abusive and tyrannical and the latter suffering the pathologies of the oppressed. The effects were not "artificially induced" in either case, spurring investigators to new studies and analyses. The image of the "fatigued person" was all-encompassing. Suspicions turned into convictions that all kinds of physical stresses had deep-seated effects. Fatigue was an "essential" phenomenon that "penetrated" every aspect of the individual's life. The shift from body to mind continued and inspired a new round of studies. Exertion and its aftereffects had a profound and long-lasting influence on the mind, and actually altered it.

Defining "industrial fatigue"

During the 1920s and 1930s, scientists and academic programs focused even more intensely on work and working conditions. A "certification in industrial medicine" was granted at Harvard Medical School in 1918[26] and, in France, a specialization in "industrial hygiene and occupational medicine" was recognized in 1933.[27] Among the new theoretical perspectives, Charles Myers's work in industrial psychology was notable. He drew a distinction between two kinds of physical labor that caused fatigue: work that relied on activating muscles and work that required holding certain positions. He labeled the former "clonic" activity and the latter "tonic." "Clonic" activity was easily observable, since the workers were using muscle power. "Tonic" demands on workers were subtler and more insidious since they were associated with control, static postures, cramped muscles, and repeated checks on movements, "inhibiting"[28] wasted motions and "undesirable impulses."[29] The end result was tension and distress; the prolonged blockages affected workers' mental health by disrupting the normal "tonus" that provided "stability and equilibrium."[30] Factory work required both order and balance but undermined them at the same time, even when machine power boosted human labor by doing more and more of the heavy lifting. The evolution of work had far-reaching consequences.

Without a doubt, the human toll of factory work is not new. A century earlier, the horrors of child labor were a prime example of it: rigid postures, long work shifts, repeated circumscribed gestures. Child laborers were also assigned to tend machines but rarely acted on their own. The innovative aspect of the work of mid-twentieth-century industrial hygienists was their elevation of psychology in their analyses of behavior. They highlighted connections between mind and body. "Tonus" was the normal state of slight tension in muscle tissue that facilitated its response to stimulation. Artificial constraints on it could set off a damaging chain reaction: intermittent lack of control, dips in intensity, strains and tears in muscles, and the worries and fears stoked by impaired physical capacity. Once again, a disturbance in the body evolved into one in the mind. Explicitly making the connection between "fatigue and psychoneurosis,"[31] Myers warned of "anxious moods, disorderly unreasoned fears"[32] and increased feelings of fatigue. Myers and the other members of the British Industrial Fatigue Research Board identified a specific, work-related syndrome, "industrial fatigue,"[33] in which physical and psychological factors together produced exhaustion and anxiety, discomfort and depression, but where neither exertion nor muscle power necessarily had a primary role. Punishing repetitions and long work hours were the culprits, leading to a slow, steady wearing down of the self in badly paid jobs with little opportunity for rest and recovery. "Residual fatigue" was a newly minted term describing workers caught up in the daily grind: "The restorative powers of rest during the day and at night are not adequate … If workers' energy reserves are not refilled, a backlash will ensue, affecting work both physically and mentally. For all practical purposes, the question of residual fatigue is now the most important topic in mechanization."[34]

Concerns with residual fatigue echoed those of the dangers of the "wasting" that threatened child laborers in the middle of the nineteenth century,[35] although the twentieth-century malaise was more acute and deep-seated. Incorporating psychological factors such as distress, fear[36] and anxiety, "long-lasting fatigue"[37] was a fresh topic for research and remediation.

Adapting times and places

The attention being paid to the distress, exhaustion and pain caused by working conditions opened up new areas of study. Scientists investigated work shifts, workers' positions and the design of work spaces. The work setting had not been ignored in the past and, for a long time, the material conditions of labor had been part of industrial hygiene research. Insalubrious conditions included damp and drafty workplaces, dust and debris, slippery floors and polluted air. Among other work sites, mineshafts had long been recognized as hazardous. Unhealthy conditions and toxic surroundings made workers prone to ailments from pneumonia to pleurisy, from hernias to bloody saliva, from varicose veins to sluggish circulation.[38]

In the interwar period, the worksite was viewed as a potential source of workers' ill health in general and not just specific diseases that in the past were blamed on miasmas, dust, dryness or humidity. This was a significant change that highlighted the importance of fatigue itself, and investigators attempted to draw ever finer distinctions concerning its origins, setting and characteristics. The physical conditions of the workplace were investigated in detail: "heating, lighting, and ventilation definitely affect the worker's comfort, mood and level of fatigue."[39]

More studies were launched, more evidence was collected, beyond the "assembly line" production model championed by Henry Ford in 1910 that was intended more for "speed" than for maintaining the workers' comfort and diminishing their level of fatigue.[40] In 1927, Jean-Maurice Lahy pursued "the influence of lighting on productivity"[41] and, although his concern was with efficiency, at least one light manufacturer, Ilrin, promised that its brand produced "gentle illumination that is not tiring on the eyes."[42] In 1934, Donald Laird studied the effect of noise "on blood pressure and fatigue"[43] and recommended sound-proofing measures such as rubber cladding and padded walls. Air quality affected workers not only when it was tainted with toxic substances. Poorly ventilated worksites and high heat and humidity could also impact levels of fatigue: "The chief cause of fatigue seems to be stagnant air that impedes the heat exchange that normally occurs between a body at work and its surroundings."[44]

Another notable development in contemporary perceptions of the workplace in the 1920s and 1930s was the growth of the "service" industry (office work), where employees' fatigue was related to the poor design of office furniture and machinery. Furniture advertisements and showrooms focused on the same selling points: more comfortable seating; more efficient use of space; designs and devices that would reduce the aches and pains of the sedentary worker. Cleverly constructed tables with multiple drawers and work surfaces were one solution. Adjustable and rolling desk chairs, with variable heights and inclines, were another. Flexibility and convenience were key. Good design eliminated wasted space and unnecessary motions. For instance, the "Moderny" desk promised to "go easy on your gestures and your nerves."[45] The "Chauvin" shelf units would "save on space and time."[46] "Strafor" drawers responded "to the lightest touch."[47] The typewriter with the electric "Le Porin return" should do away with "the number one cause of typists' fatigue."[48] In the mid-1920s the magazine *Mon Bureau* [My office] surveyed the latest innovations in "appliances that cause the least amount of fatigue in the user."[49]

Another change that was equally significant was the attention given to workers' movements in these new job categories, since office equipment was less durable and lighter than most factory machinery, and a new manufacturing niche for such products was growing. Office work spurred a new definition of "work station" and a new sensitivity to "micro-movements,"[50] such as how employees used their hands, changed finger positions, and made other small gestures in a constricted space. Now occupational hygienists shifted their attention from workers operating heavy machinery or transporting heavy loads to the physical demands of desk work or light industry and from calculations of the "quantities" of energy expended to estimating the "amounts" of concentration required. For example, in 1937 Ralph Mosser Barnes "scientifically" evaluated workers' tasks in light industry:[51] "packing cartons," "quality control of glass bottles," "folding envelopes," "assembling door bells," "assembling rubber syringes."

Assessment methods were changing too. Cameras were used to track the subjects' motions and reaction times. A camera attached to the forearm of a worker could record every tiny gesture. This was an important innovation that took the guesswork out of motion analysis, turning the invisible into the visible and intuitive motions into "measured" ones and formalizing the status of micro-movements in scientific inquiry. Other experiments tracked eye movements and hand–eye coordination. The new science re-envisioned the worker's body as a machine with a nervous system. Efficiency experts offered recommendations such as: "We must reduce to an absolute minimum eye movements and the direction of the gaze"[52] and "Rhythm is indispensable to the smooth and automatic completion of a task."[53]

Naturally, fatigue was still a consideration, but the criteria to assess it were sometimes vague and specific warning signs imprecise once the subjects were no longer engaged in physically strenuous activities where muscular tensions and body chemistry could be measured. As Barnes concluded in his comprehensive study of "motion and time": "In general, workers start feeling tired during long work shifts. This is essentially subjective and, consequently, a researcher cannot measure it."[54] The focus on workers' bodies as "machines with nerves" rather than "machines with muscles" prompted a new look at their surroundings[55] in step with the rapid expansion of the field of industrial psychology. In 1950, Camille Simonin highlighted the significance of the work setting for occupational medicine: "We must take into account the changes in the psycho-sensory environment that cause increased susceptibility to fatigue."[56]

Along with concerns with the use of space and the organization of the workplace, scientists in the interwar period delved once again into time, conducting more detailed studies on the connections between productivity and work shifts. Charles Myers found, not surprisingly, that "An improvement in the rate of output almost invariably results from shortening the working day."[57] The eight-hour day was still the most commonly recommended option, even though the director of the Industrial Fatigue Research Board reported that the workers themselves adjusted their pace and output to shifts of varying lengths."[58]

Studies of "work breaks" added a new slant to the overall examination of work time, and scientists in both the United States and Europe began to publish duly calculated results of their experiments. Among others, Edward David Jones pointed out in 1919 that workers' productivity rose as work breaks gradually increased. The figures supporting his argument were very precise. For example, a worker in a machine shop turned out sixteen units an hour with no work break. That increased to eighteen units with a five-minute break every twenty-five minutes, to twenty-two units with a three-minute break every seventeen minutes, and to twenty-five units with a two-minute break every ten minutes.[59] Another study found similar results in the manufacturing of steel rivets: one worker made 600 rivets a day, but, when the tempo was changed to include a two-minute break after every ten rivets, the same worker turned out 1,600 in a day.[60] After conducting inquiries in 1,050 factories, the National Institute of Industrial Psychology in London concluded in 1939 that breaks should be scheduled "after peak production periods,"[61] although others recommended breaks "when the curve begins to drop."[62] Still other experts advocated for several short breaks throughout the day.[63] Though the recommendations differed, all the scientists used data to back up their claims and shared one overriding concern: to maximize productivity. The point was to get the most work possible while ensuring the physical and mental stability of the worker, which, after all, was not easy to define or guarantee.

Because industrial technology and the mechanization of work kept changing, toward mid-century other notable research projects explored the effects of work time in a different context, that of work assignments lasting for extended periods of time. The evolution of motor power in the interwar period created new challenges for workers in the truck or train cab on long-distance transport runs or those in the factory overseeing machine operations. The minutes, hours and days mounted up: "We see how driving a modern bus or tram, while it has become less tiring, is – if I may put it this way – more acrobatic and can only be assigned to men whose mental and psychomotor skills are constantly on the alert."[64]

In 1937, Jean-Maurice Lahy studied worker fatigue in a new type of transport business, long-haul trucking, which surpassed the limit of eight hours per day established in 1919. He focused on the drivers of a 14-ton tractor-trailer making regular delivery runs of over 500 kilometers in a round-trip, shuttling among three French cities.[65] This business model was becoming more common but was nevertheless a locus of anxiety and risk. In this study, the two drivers took turns behind the wheel for trips that lasted thirty-five hours, and they also handled all the pick-ups and drop-offs for the delivery service. They drove at night, slept in the truck cab, and got their meals along the way. Jean-Maurice Lahy's study of these long-haul truckers was unique at the time and involved using a car to follow the men on their route and an examiner to administer tests every three hours and interview the subjects. Lahy concluded that drivers were most tired "between midnight and 5 a.m." and experienced "hypnagogic illusions" in which they "think their eyes are open, watching the road" but "no longer feel their hands on the wheel" or hear the "rumbling of the engine."[66] The interviews included the drivers' accounts of accidents or near-misses, such as "zig-zagging across the road," "the trailer swerving into the opposite lane," and some very serious collisions.

American researchers focused on the sensory deficits of long-distance truckers: slower reaction times, poorer hand–eye coordination, slower speed in solving math problems, more difficulty keeping their balance.[67] These findings influenced the direction of new research into the psychomotor skills of sensory processing, manual dexterity and micro-gestures, mental resilience, and the ability to distinguish between alarms and noise. A new "psycho-technique"[68] was devised to test potential drivers' concentration and their ability to withstand the pressures and challenges of long-distance runs, prioritizing these qualifications over ordinary driving skills.[69]

The researchers' challenge was to identify and define a specific type of exhaustion that had been encountered intermittently in the past in other circumstances: "hallucinations" at night-time, long trips, accidents in cycle races. Motorized transport made the risk more acute, not only because of the increased mortality in traffic accidents but also the disturbing accounts of the drivers' anxiety and troubled psyches. Certainly, these high stakes were recognized as a new and specific threat. Jean-Maurice Lahy strongly recommended a one- or two-day rest period after each long-haul run. His work relied on both the improvement in technical measurements and the enhanced sensitivity to psychological functions of the time.

Piloting an aircraft involved similar stresses, with single pilots on constant alert on long flights. The aviator Henri Mignet, who built and piloted the *Pou-du-ciel* in 1932, recalled his difficulty withstanding the "hallucinations," surprises and challenges, and the long, lonely hours lost in the vastness of the sky: "Your nerves have to hold up. Your life depends on your concentration … No respite, no letting go"; the outcome itself leaves the pilot "tired, apathetic, frozen, virtually indifferent to everything around him.[70] Charles Lindbergh's account of completing the first Atlantic crossing in 1927 depicted these feelings with stark originality. His memoir was structured hour by hour, for a total of thirty-three, thus emphasizing for the reader the "interminable" nature of his flight. It was very detailed, describing disturbing dreams and frightening periods of "torpor" that ached like an "infected wound," sapping his endurance.[71] He emphasized the effects of his lack of sleep: "My eyes are as heavy as rocks and the muscles of my eyelids are pulling downward with an almost irresistible force."[72] He also brought up a curious contradiction: "The efforts you make to stay awake make you even sleepier."[73] His senses became duller, so that even the acrid "smelling salts" he sniffed barely registered.[74] His body, tormented by "persistent aches,"[75] collapsed after he landed safely.

These accounts connected unique kinds of fatigue to advances in technology, to significant changes in daily life, and to increased sensitivity to our surroundings. Scientific investigations delved deeper and more urgently into phenomena that undoubtedly already existed, but these experiments had a new focus. Previous generations acknowledged the toll of night rides on messengers on cross-country routes, for example, and night workers' struggles with somnolence, but these topics had been cursorily studied until now.

The invention of the interpersonal

In the interwar period, researchers took a closer look at work time and fatigue and incorporated more psychological insights in their investigations of productivity. Interpersonal relationships were an area of special interest, and researchers looked into how they were structured, identifying conditions that fostered or impeded them. Elton Mayo conducted the most well-known investigation into the topic at the Hawthorne factory in the Chicago suburbs that produced parts for the Bell Telephone Company.[76]

Mayo's long-term, detailed study focused on five women who assembled telephone relay devices in the "Test Room," with working conditions distinct from the rest of the plant. For instance, the subjects had a shorter work shift, with regular breaks and a mid-morning snack. They were allowed to chat among themselves but were discouraged from competing against their co-workers. Feeling less pressured and having more privileges at work had an effect. The team's output increased slowly over several years. But, more significantly, the women's output decreased when tensions rose among them, when they turned against one member of the team, against their supervisor and even the investigators. Mayo considered these "negative correlations."[77] Even more noteworthy, he found that output fell when workers had family problems but rose after these were resolved. Among other things, marriage problems struck at the heart of team comity.[78] Thus, "objectively" speaking, "interpersonal relations at work and outside it" caused fatigue.[79] Mayo's study mapped a clearly marked path leading from psychological distress to physical discomfort for the first time.

Investigators widened their focus, conducted more interviews, and noted the "problems" cited by employees: salaries, canteens, grimy and dusty surroundings, fatigue, equipment, furniture or supervisors.

The workers had a voice. Their discontent came to light. Words had consequences, and positive reinforcement, praise or gratitude lifted workers' attitudes and their performance. Workers who felt freer to express themselves achieved higher productivity. Another finding was that "the relations between supervisors and staff are more influential in affecting workers' attitudes, satisfaction, team spirit, and efficiency than any other single factor."[80] For this reason, supervisory personnel were urged to adopt a "flexible and compassionate management style" that took into account workers' "social and moral beliefs" in order to foster "a more congenial work environment."[81] All in all, workers' fatigue could be moderated by paying attention to psychological factors and adeptly managing interpersonal relations. Other studies conducted in Europe came to similar conclusions.[82]

In this way, researchers added new criteria to the already established physiological factors that caused fatigue; psychological factors, mental distress and malaise were acknowledged "clinically" and individually, identified in specific, precise observations in the workplace and collected in experiments or interviews. They were not merely dramatized in literature or personal anecdotes, as before.[83] New trouble spots were added to a growing list: staff turnover, complaints, "pessimistic fantasies," "lack of cooperation," feeling overlooked and unappreciated, boredom, apathy, monotony, depression, and all the submerged and "negative" aspects of the "psychological climate."[84]

We should not downplay the limitations of this focus on "affect" and interpersonal relations at work, although they could also be deliberately neglected in favor of efficiency. Even after incorporating the strategies recommended by Elton Mayo,[85] a number of dilemmas remain, as observers note: "Despite their savvy experimentation with management styles, younger bosses are missing something: workers' unconditional acceptance of their efforts."[86] Georges Friedmann astutely pointed out in the 1960s[87] that something else was missing from these formulas: a recognition of the external forces that influenced the work environment, such as the state of the economy, social tensions, feelings of inferiority experienced by the "have nots," and the dissatisfactions that arose from this. Though workers' class consciousness and militancy were on the rise throughout the twentieth century, these social barriers were part of working-class status. The roles of the boss and the worker could not simply be inverted in a company, nor could the differences between the "deciders" and the "workforce" be eliminated. It was equally impossible to eradicate "violence" from work settings once and for all, and this insight was as noteworthy as all the early discoveries of psychological factors on the job.

A workers' depression?

The interwar period was a time of unprecedented attention to the conditions of work and workplaces. Much of the field research centered on its material and even trivial realities. Investigators collected ever more data and personal accounts that revealed, in particular, an inexorable change in attitude; workers were feeling more beaten down than militant and were suffering more psychologically than physically.

Let's turn to a systematic accounting first: "The soul of our time is measured by the power of our machinery."[88] The proof was in the pictures. François Kollar's photos, taken in the years 1931 to 1934 as he criss-crossed the country,[89] caught the attention of contemporary writers and were a quintessential large-scale inquiry, like Villermé's a century earlier,[90] although Kollar focused on visual elements and relentlessly documented changes. Work had changed. Muscle power was now less important: carts were pulled by electrically powered winches in the mines; multi-ton hydraulic presses bent metal; jackhammers took over from pickaxes; steam powered equipment, instead of the brute force of construction crews, hammered support beams into the ground. It's clear that mechanization was supplanting physical labor: "Mechanization takes over from human labor and reduces physical fatigue."[91] The distinct differences captured in the 1930s by the ground-breaking photo essay collection *La France travaille* [France at work] between "Before" and "Now" and "In the Past" and "Today" was summed up in the refrain: "They are putting down … their tools."[92]

Nevertheless, physical fatigue was ever present, as François Kollar's photos showed: ports where "hooded dockers are lugging sacks of sugar";[93] ships where "crews strain to lower the topsail," where "stokers" shovel coal amidst a "tangle of connecting rods and gleaming sheet metal";[94] mines where "speed-ups are the rule" to compete against "the price-cutting of the other coalfields";[95] and trawlers who went out to sea again and again, responding to "the epic of the trade."[96] The illustrations published in the magazine *Floréal: l'hebdomadaire illustré du monde du travail*[97] between 1920 and 1923 attested to this too, with full-page photos of "road crews," "stone masons," "lumberjacks," "carpenters" and "roofers." Some of the men were conspicuously mopping their sweaty foreheads,[98] and all of them were grasping the tools of their trade – shovels, saws or pickaxes – despite the growing dominance of motors and electric power.

Other examples demonstrated how technical advances created new kinds of fatigue, even though these were little noticed at the time. The jackhammer replaced the pickaxe although the effects of its vibrations were rarely discussed; a painter's face mask protected against fumes but was cumbersome; construction workers' safety harnesses enabled them to scale high-rises and dangle from the sides of buildings, though the workers' potential vertigo was not mentioned; the arm punch took the place of the ironmonger's hammer-pestle for trimming. More generally, technical advances and mechanization enabled more worker surveillance and speed-ups, as industrial psychologists acknowledged: "Semi-automatic or fully automatic equipment lessens the strain on muscles. But the speed of operation and intense concentration required will cause nervous fatigue that is sometimes massive."[99]

Even more significant and telling is the growing importance of work "taking over" behavior, resulting in a loss of self that invaded workers' consciousness. The psychological toll appeared to reinforce feelings of alienation, a loss of direction and of the self. This work-related malaise was more specific than neurasthenia and more profound than disturbances in interpersonal relations and emotional tenor. This was surely the most overt change in the interwar years: the realization that something vital had been severed or shorn off. Constant Malva, a miner in the Borinage in the 1930s, confessed he was "depressed, exhausted physically and mentally." "I'm numb with sleepiness, my mouth is dry as a bone, I have no desire for anything."[100] Maurice Alline, a Renault worker, said that "the thought of doing that for our entire lives was depressing."[101] Albert Soulillou commented on a Ford plant worker in 1933: "It is as if his brain had suffered the ill effects of this exhaustion."[102] The workers themselves talked about this condition affecting mind and body, a combination of physical exertion and mental fatigue. Simone

Weil persuasively connected "movements that hurt" with a "deep sense of discouragement."[103] Georges Navel expressed a feeling of extreme desperation: "I was drowning in mine [depression] for a long time. When I stopped struggling, I was at the end of my rope, I wanted to die."[104]

In just a few decades, occupational psychology had come a long way. In the nineteenth century, it was believed that excessive physical suffering led to a breakdown or to deep discontent. Punishing jobs such as pushing loaded carts of coal in the mineshafts (known as "tramming") described by Zola,[105] or the strain on the nerves documented in George Beard's *American Nervousness*,[106] took their toll. Physical stress and distress seeped into our minds and unleashed waves of fatigue. The breakdowns and depressions documented in the 1930s were very different. They were related to emotions and self-worth and sprang from a feeling of degradation or exclusion that came from certain jobs. They also invaded our minds and provoked debilitating bouts of fatigue, even though they might afflict us before any exertion had taken place. Pain overwhelmed us before we had strained a single muscle. This was due to the increasing importance of the psyche, the fruits of a long development of personalization in the Western world.

Some combatants in the First World War used words such as "depression" or "the blues"[107] and clearly expressed their sense of loss. There was nothing scientific about their self-assessment; it was meant to describe a certain kind of fatigue: a condition where fatigue was not connected to the lack of stimulation, excitement or energy, as was the case with earlier symptoms,[108] but to a lack of vision and perspective. Our psychological horizon had expanded. Some of the actions we had to take are seen as unacceptable or degrading: "My God, what have I done to deserve this punishment?"[109] In other words, this was an entirely new emotional torment for workers, always more acute where fatigue was linked to an internal malaise, difficult to pin down but powerful: a feeling of having no future, of being penned in, facing deadening repetition. This was the first time that workers' consciousness underlined so emphatically feelings of incompleteness and fragmentation. It was the first time too that psychology trumped physiology in this context.

Another innovative aspect of the 1930s was the emphasis on the cultural specificity of women's work. Claude Pigi's 1938 novel depicted "Marie Tavernier's fatigue":[110] the nervous strain of office work; answering the telephone; the indifference of spouses; the build-up of chores at home; the Sundays cut short by "housewife's morning duties" and the "family afternoon stroll," even as Marie suffered from "leaden limbs" and "a complete sense of apathy."[111] "Countless" chores piled up; as "a tired wife" and "overworked mother," Marie had one burning desire: "a long rest, far from everyone."[112] Everything changed when she met a young co-worker and quickly began having an affair. Her defiance of conventional morality was explained psychologically: "One needs great joys to forget great fatigues."[113]

Nevertheless, the innovative qualities of this novel were not revolutionary by any means. Even though it revealed a more acute awareness of women's domestic burdens and a greater tolerance for her infidelity, the book did not advocate better working conditions or shorter work hours for working women. Instead, it offered an emotional solution, through interpersonal relations and love. Traditional roles were changing, but not radically. In 1937 a short story in the magazine *Marie Claire* described a lonely working woman who rediscovered the love of her youth: "One day she caught sight of a new employee in the shop where she had worked for years, and, despite the fatigue and defeat etched on his face, she recognized him. It was her former neighbor, the dear boy she yearned for."[114]

Psychology was acknowledged here, no doubt, but it pointed women toward emotional connections rather than substantive actions.

26

From Hormones to Stress

The more specific analyses of trauma after the First World War showed the increasing influence of psychology. The field had become more theoretically oriented, taking into account more personalized questions and acknowledging the complexity of emotional disorders and our most intimate thoughts. The understanding of fatigue had evolved too and was equally complex. The identification of new pathologies was a major step forward, spurred by the biochemical revolution of the 1920s that brought to light many new instances of behavioral dysfunction, such as overwhelming fatigue, mild but persistent fatigue and, in particular, the "organicity" of mental or physical "sluggishness." This sort of dysfunction was often imperceptible and seemed almost normal. However, the discovery of the role played by the endocrine glands reoriented such analyses by pointing to heretofore overlooked factors that regulated bodily functions. This underpinned a more holistic conception of body and mind that saw hormones influencing our "moods" and the body's reactions to external stimuli. In the final analysis, this led to the invention of "stress" and a recognition of its ever present effects. Our vulnerability to fatigue was mapped out differently at this point, guided by the understanding that it was not only due to physical exertion, overwork or sensory overload. Instead, our way of life, the tensions, emotions and demands of the daily grind, made us susceptible to fatigue. For the first time, science recognized that an organism reacts in a "unified," holistic way.

The new attention paid to hormones made it seem as if physiological explanations of human behavior and a mechanistic point of view would prevail. However, this evolution in scientific thought actually assigned more importance to psychological factors. Once we recognized the effect of "stress," we acknowledged that we were psycho-physical beings who transmuted emotions into physical symptoms and physical ailments into mental ones. In the past, scientists rarely explored this reciprocal relationship. Another key point about the discovery of hormones and glandular deficiency was that it offered the hope that a strategically targeted use would eliminate the most debilitating effects of fatigue. This stage of scientific inquiry was a drama that merged triumph and tragedy and had damning, shocking and exciting consequences.

Hormones and temperament

When at the beginning of the twentieth century surgeons began trying an innovative treatment, surgical extirpation, for goiters, a reinterpretation of minor cases of fatigue was an unexpected consequence. First, consider the serious symptoms: "muscle weakness, paresis [the partial paralysis of a muscle] and psychasthenia [lack of vitality in nervous functions]."[1] By surgically removing the thyroid, they abruptly revealed the important role of its hormones in regulating cell metabolism and metabolic rate. Patients without a functioning thyroid suffered from glandular deficiency and exhibited both symptoms of debilitating fatigue and a disinclination for mental and physical work. For some, the absence or insufficiency of the thyroid precipitated a potentially fatal condition requiring medical treatment and long-term therapy; these patients, suffering from "myxoedema" [hypothyroidism], had puffy, distorted faces, pasty skin, poor muscle development and, in the language of the time, "below normal" or "backward" mental abilities. But minor disturbances sometimes still eluded diagnosis, since, if hormone levels were below normal, thyroid functions affected the metabolism of all types of cells and produced a number of different symptoms. Even small fluctuations in hormones affected our wellbeing, as Léopold Lévi wrote, because "of the influence of the thyroid gland upon the nervous system, especially the vegetative system, and upon the humoral conditions … insufficiency of the glandular function is attended by an extremely diverse symptomatology." In books and publications in medical journals, Lévi posited that patients with an "endocrinian" temperament risked having "minor pathologies gradually develop into full-blown cases."[2]

In fact, as the field of endocrinology grew in the 1920s and 1930s, a schema classifying patients according to their "glandular" type was published. Each type had specific "characters" and "traits," and physicians were urged to take note of underlying persistent feelings of fatigue, since "either with or without a disease one can be unwell."[3] This classification enabled doctors to associate personality types with levels of fatigue. In 1929 Léopold Lévi[4] discussed a number of case studies. One young patient was the "amorph" type, "a child who was totally apathetic," but Lévi reported that, after five weeks of treatment with serotonin, the boy was "so energetic that he can't sit still and constantly plays with his fork at the dining table."[5] The "amorph's" opposite number was the "pressure cooker" type, whose excess energy was due to an oversupply of serotonin. This person was constantly on the go, "the first to get up, the last to go to bed," tired out "friends, family and co-workers who can't keep up,"[6] was "unstoppable," living at "breakneck speed," and whose "impatient, adventurous"[7] manner was fueled by an overactive thyroid. Other personality types were "dominators," "authoritarians," "night owls," "sleepyheads," "wishy-washy," "migraine-prone," "cellulite-prone," "worry-warts" and "melancholics."[8] Underlying all the variety was the conviction that there was a link between endocrine gland secretions and a person's resistance to fatigue. In the final analysis, the parade of personality types revealed that even subtle "deviations from a normal temperament are due to the functioning of the endocrine glands."[9] Discoveries of the body's biochemistry, heretofore undetected and little understood, helped to orient the discourse about people who were overflowing with or drained of energy.

Hormones and vitality

Testosterone was quickly identified as a hormone that might be the source of "our vital energy."[10] Just as rapidly, plans were devised to "supplement" weaklings with corrective doses of it. The discovery and the proposed treatments seemed revolutionary, promising to combat fatigue, lassitude and debility. It was a seductive vision, a formula for reinvigorating the weary and lightening the burdens of daily life, before the claims were debunked and the treatments abandoned. In 1889, Charles-Édouard Brown-Séquard, Claude Bernard's successor at the research and teaching institution Collège de France, experimented on himself, to his colleagues' consternation, injecting extracts from dog and guinea pig testicles. He claimed that, at the age of seventy-two, he felt completely rejuvenated.[11] He undoubtedly did feel that way, but his claim had no scientific merit; testosterone cannot be delivered in a water-based solution.

The surgeon Serge Voronoff took a different approach, and, after his experience with bone grafts during the First World War, he began experimenting with grafting parts of animal testicles onto humans. The first operation was performed on June 21, 1920, despite his lack of knowledge of the science of organ rejection or of interspecies barriers to surgical implants. Voronoff explained his preparations in detail. In selecting (involuntary) donor animals, he opted for primates because of their evolutionary proximity to humans. In selecting patients, he factored in their overall state of health, the ease of access to the site of the incision and their estimated rate of recovery. Slices of chimpanzee or baboon testicles were then implanted in the patient's scrotum. Once the implant was completed, and the animal's testosterone began (presumably) trickling into the bloodstream, Voronoff attested to an almost "miraculous" result: "The graft is steadily influencing the patient's muscular strength and mental activity … reinvigoration of physical capacity and a similar boost in intellectual ability."[12] The cases were described, analyzed and generously illustrated with "before and after" photographs. One was Mr E. L., a 74-year-old obese man, hunched over, with drawn features and dull eyes, who underwent an amazing, quick transformation, "losing half his excess pounds," regaining vim and vigor, and testifying that "I am on my feet all day and don't feel tired … I can climb stairs easily."[13] Another patient, a sixty-year-old architect with a "lumbering gait," suffering from "low energy," perked up again, "taking long walks" that used to be impossible.[14] An "apathetic" bureaucrat admitted to feeling "less fatigued" and "overflowing with vigor."[15] In 1923–4, "listless" women patients were treated with ovarian grafts, and, according to their testimony, they too believed they had been revitalized, recovering "their enthusiasm and zest for life," among them Mme C. K., a graft recipient in June 1924.[16]

Still, this method could not succeed in the long term, since the body rejected the grafted foreign matter, despite the surgeon's very strong convictions. This was where the "confirmation bias" of both doctor and patient came in, indirectly demonstrating how psychological factors influenced the fatigue we perceived and reported. Beliefs and attitudes were key, and their effects continued to be studied. However, for a long time the possibility of failure did not deter Voronoff. He established a "monkey farm" on the hillside near Menton to supply him with graft material. He was inducted into the Legion of Honor, the highest French order of merit, and his work was enthusiastically covered by the press. An article in the magazine *L'Illustration* on November 22, 1924, touted the successful "reinvigoration of physical strength and intellectual capacity after graft surgery."[17] Voronoff was consulted by celebrity clients and literary men such as the notorious author Willy (Henry Gauthier-Villars), playwrights Marcel Achard and Jean Richepin, and poet William Butler Yeats.[18] When he attended the International Surgical Convention in 1923, seven hundred of his colleagues welcomed him with applause.[19]

Yet, strong convictions and clever marketing were insufficient to counter the evidence that revitalization through xenotransplantation was a "chimera." Many physicians criticized Voronoff's method, claimed it had no efficacy and disputed its results. A prominent urologist, Kenneth Walker of the Royal Northern Hospital in London, mocked the procedure as "no better than the methods of witches and magicians."[20] The US news weekly *Time* echoed this, casting doubt on the doctor's sensational claims.[21] Blaise Cendrars satirized the fad in his novella *L'Amiral* in 1935 with his creation of a "wheezy old geezer" who, in a Willy-esque play on words, "had himself Voronoffized so that he could sleep with his new wife Felicia at least once." Sadly, she was not "pleased."[22] In the 1930s the surgeries ended. In fact, Voronoff's main selling point for xenotransplantation, prominently featured in the titles of his many books, emphasized the promise of rejuvenation, restoring youth and vigor, and not the power of the "monkey glands" to combat fatigue. The doctor died on September 3, 1951, after the luster of his fame had definitively faded.

The discovery of hormones clearly had an impact on scientific thought in the 1920s in several ways, enabling researchers and practitioners to identify types of temperaments, differentiate among various kinds of fatigue and propose new treatments for it.[23] The discovery of hormones also sparked hopes of restoring patients' vitality. On the other hand, reckless hormone therapies also led to disillusionment and damage. Still, the new and growing understanding of biochemical principles had an incredible influence on medicine in general, and on bio-psychology in particular. It reinforced a new recognition of how our bodies functioned and the importance of nerve centers. It gave new meaning to our search for resilience and strength. As always, new products, treatments and approaches would follow.

From hormones to amphetamines

In the 1920s research into specific hormonal effects led scientists to investigate other biochemical substances, other molecules, other agents and, finally, other dreams of indefatigability. To be sure, this was a mirage, a tantalizing illusion for the most part, but it showed the persistence of one of our most deep-seated desires. The quest was significant because it motivated so many and had very real and sometimes disturbing results.

It began with an unattainable goal: to administer adrenaline orally. Adrenaline is a hormone secreted by the adrenal glands that prepares our muscles for exertion, increasing blood circulation, respiration and carbohydrate metabolism. At first, scientists were trying to synthesize an adrenaline analog to treat breathing difficulties. They conducted research into plants and biosynthetic compounds, and in 1927 amphetamine, a compound that mimicked the effects of adrenaline and could be administered orally, was synthesized by an American chemist and pharmacologist, Gordon Alles.[24] Since it did not break down during digestion, it had high "bioavailability" and was easily absorbed by the body. Though it was originally marketed to treat respiratory problems, administered in pills or inhalers, its "stimulating" properties were soon recognized. It acted on nerve centers, relieved fatigue, quieted anxiety and kept us awake. Tests showed that experimental subjects could stay awake for forty-eight hours and perform tasks with no dips in concentration, stoked by feelings of self-confidence and even euphoria. Interest in this discovery soared, especially for scientists and others concerned with fatigue, since it rekindled hopes that psychotropic substances could overcome human limitations.

An American company registered the patent and in the 1930s put amphetamine on the market under the name "Benzedrine," jump-starting a new chapter in the history of the drug. Benzedrine was widely prescribed. Athletes took it. Military agencies studied it. Intellectuals flocked to it. Psychiatrists recommended it to "lethargic" patients.[25] Well-known people sang its praises or were rumored to use it regularly – for example, the poet W. H. Auden, who supposedly started his day with it.[26] Norbert Wiener, the inventor of cybernetics, was also said to be a committed user.[27] Researchers at the German pharmaceutical company Temmler developed an "improved" synthetic compound, methamphetamine, that was sold under the name "Pervitin" in a massive marketing campaign that assured the public it would "stimulate hearts and minds."[28] The pills were a tonic for the system and a "cure-all"[29] to energize German households.

However, amphetamine had a downside; it dulled sensations of fatigue but did not eliminate them. It "does not increase the amount of exertion, but simply changes our perception of its difficulty."[30] Serious side effects were reported – in particular, heart failure. In 1939, a mountain climber using Pervitin died before reaching the summit,[31] military officers suffered cardiac arrest,[32] and university students in Munich given experimental overdoses fell into comas and were temporarily "Pervitin cadavers."[33] Regular users reported difficulty with language, gaps in concentration and other drawbacks, and the burden of addiction. Leonardo Conti, the head of the public health service in Germany, warned of the "slow, barely perceptible decline in mental and physical abilities, leading to an inevitable breakdown."[34] The "people's drug" was officially classified as a narcotic in Germany in 1941.[35] Norbert Wiener looked back at his stimulant use and admitted "having ignored for too long the drug's effects on my body."[36]

The success of amphetamine peaked in the 1940s: "The enemy … is fatigue. A strange, untouchable opponent that regularly brings soldiers down, knocks them out, forces them into retreat."[37] Pervitin would protect them. The novelist Heinrich Böll recalled depending on the drug as a recruit at the start of the war: "Of course, I was terribly tired … But I had to stay awake. The effects of Pervitin kicked in and helped me beat back my fatigue."[38] The drug manufacturers Temmler turned out close to a million pills per day, "inundating" the Wehrmacht and Luftwaffe, fulfilling their "gigantic orders."[39] General Heinz Guderian lectured the armored troops as they cross the Ardennes forest: "I insist that you give up sleeping for three days and three nights if that is necessary."[40] His famous tactic was underpinned by massive doses of a drug: "The

'Blitzkrieg' was conducted thanks to methamphetamine, or, to put it plainly, built on the foundation of methamphetamine."[41]

The Allied troops also consumed quantities of the stimulant. In the battle of El Alamein in 1942, the men of the 24th Armoured Brigade swallowed "huge doses of Benzedrine that were distributed on the eve of the attack." They broke through the Axis lines but lost 80 percent of their tanks.[42] During the Battle of Britain in 1940–1, the British supply ministry distributed 72 million tablets of Benzedrine to pilots to enhance their alertness during long night vigils, giving the agile RAF an advantage over the Luftwaffe's heavier fighter planes. Military slang acknowledged the co-dependence of man and drug, calling it the "wake-up," the "co-pilot" and the "eye-opener."[43]

Older approaches to unleashing human energy were surpassed by the new biochemical energy boosters. A new world of stimulants came into being. The preferred image of the body's metabolism was no longer a furnace or a steam engine; energy was generated from ever more hidden sources. Advances in biochemistry were going to revolutionize our nerve centers, until they too failed.

From hormones to "stress"

Discoveries in the field of biochemistry, such as our understanding of the role of hormones, enriched our understanding of fatigue during the interwar years. This led to a revolution in thought and pointed us toward new expectations, new sources and new goals. Building on what we learned about the psyche, these discoveries suggested a new, more comprehensive vision of human potential.

The endocrinologist Hans Selye, investigating the function of endocrine glands in the 1920s at the University of Montreal, found that hormonal secretions increased radically when patients underwent a shock, an attack or a trauma. The endocrine system in overdrive caused a physical response. The sources of trauma are diverse, ranging from wounds to chronic illnesses, to conflicts and other emotional disturbances, and the body reacts negatively to the uncontrolled and disordered release of hormones, which Selye originally likened in an article published in *Nature* in 1936 to an "infection" with "noxious agents." He first identified this phenomenon in experiments with rats that he exposed to cold, tested with excessive exercise, dosed with intoxicating drugs or subjected to surgical interventions.[44] The same pattern of behavior emerged: "swelling of the thymus, changes in adrenal glands, loss of muscle tone, and a drop in temperature." The reactions themselves moved through three stages, starting with alarm, proceeding to adaptation or resistance and, if the assaults on the organism continued, finally ending in exhaustion or death.

The word "stress" was used for the first time in this context to refer to the body's reaction to persistent shocks. The term was originally part of the engineering lexicon[45] of materials science at the beginning of the twentieth century. Stress tests measured how cement, steel, rope and other substances withstood various degrees of pressure, strain or temperature and whether they will corrode, crack, shatter, melt or bend.[46] But now the word was adopted by scientists in an entirely different field, biology, to name a syndrome caused by "harmful" substances, pressures, assaults or invasive injuries that may be capable of ending life.

The word is a permanent part of our vocabulary now and is used worldwide to express a unique perspective on the "affected" person as a "whole." It is a "generic" term describing the way the person experiences an injury and reacts to it. The source of fatigue became more generalized, reinforcing the comprehensive view already expressed in certain analyses.[47] Walter Cannon inaugurated a crucial reimagining of the mind–body relationship when he used the phrase "the wisdom of the body" for the first time to express a holistic vision of human behavior.[48] The diversity of potential "stressors," understood as "shocks," increased exponentially, encompassing both physical and psychological damage, bodily injury and emotional distress, tired muscles and weary minds, in a larger sense the vast field of traumas. Exhaustion broke through boundaries and extended its reach, affecting resilience that was damaged and could not be restored. The types of behavior that were vulnerable increased dramatically: jobs that were too demanding and "crazy-making,"[49] "premature aging" provoked by "constant unrelenting stress that drains the life out of us,"[50] amenorrhea caused by repeated emotions,[51] waves of mental distress associated with an inability to adapt to new and unexpected situations – in short, any upset that disturbed our equilibrium.

This completely new term "stress" was all-encompassing and thus more inclusive than its predecessors, increasing the potential causes of exhaustion and centering the individual in the process. "Stress" was a non-specific response syndrome, a reaction to diverse strains and shocks, to whatever disturbed, threatened or destroyed the body.

27

From the "New Man" to Tragedy

The concept of stress was invented to explain quasi-contemporary problems. It identified a more diverse set of traumas and biochemical deficits, foregrounded individual wellbeing and clarified our vulnerabilities to the emotional stressors of modern life. However, at the same time, in the 1920s and 1930s, some were opting for a different approach, relying on strengthening resilience, buttressing individual weak points, rallying the power of the masses and, tragically, privileging the "virile" over the "non-virile." Totalitarian governments turned beliefs into fanaticism, rejected any kind of weakness, and promoted the "new man," an invulnerable being, in a worldview that entirely excluded fatigue.

Certainly, such "totalizing" politics occurred in a context. The worrying growth of individualism brought threats of division and civic conflict, belying the utopian vision of a "nation" that had been imagined as unified, homogeneous and almost divinely ordained. The brutality of the First World War paved the way for equally punitive violence against "undesirables," while those in power had access to "powerful methods of mass mobilization"[1] and organization made possible by advances in technology. The First World War revealed the potential for leading campaigns on a grand scale with heretofore unimaginable reach. This "new tool," as Marcel Gauchet put it, was the "total state," waging a "total war" and "enabling totalitarianism in government."[2]

One phenomenon, less peripheral than it may seem, persisted: fatigue. We have to factor in the need to overcome fatigue or exploit it, the expressions of contempt for "defective" people, and the repeated contrasts drawn between "greatness" and "weakness." Assessing strengths and weaknesses was no longer solely within the purview of technicians and scientists but was fodder for politicians and their policies on a scale we had not seen before. This led to a belief in grandeur buttressed by impunity and domination made possible by atrocities. Inevitable, toxic extremes were the result; supreme resilience was promised to the strong, exceptional degradation guaranteed for the weak. The violence directed at the latter was so extreme that it spawned a new martyrology of fatigue, characterized by a kind of malevolence that we must never forget.

What new man?

Many different circumstances prepared the ground in the 1930s for the rise of collective resentment and its popular fervor: "After the First World War the number of disappointed and desperate people grew rapidly in Germany and Austria when inflation and unemployment compounded social dislocation in the countries on the losing side. A noticeable proportion of citizens in Europe's post-war democracies shared this disillusionment, and they have propelled France's and in Italy's extremist movements since the Second World War."[3]

Revenge, violence and a lust for power haunted the dreams of these societies on the edge. Superiority, strength and exclusion underpinned their beliefs and gave birth to the fantasy of the "new man," an entirely transformed being who was "dynamic, virile, decisive, toughened up by a Spartan upbringing and by the sublimated influence of strict autarchic principles."[4] Even the cover illustration of the first edition of the Bolshevist journal the *Communist International*,[5] published on May 1, 1919, glorified a "new man," with the image of "a muscle-bound man wielding his hammer to shatter the chains encircling the globe."[6] Mussolini too exploited the body worship of the strong man by showing off "his bare torso, powerful, ready for any physical challenge or exercise."[7] The most "enduring" image was that of the idealized German youth disseminated by Nazi propaganda, riddled with references to iron and toughness: "In our eyes, the German boy of the future must be energetic and agile, as fast as a hare, as impermeable as leather and as tough as Krupp's steel. To ensure that our people do not fall into the clutches of the degeneracy of our time, we have to raise a new man."[8]

In a more general sense, these paeans to toughness and strength stigmatized weakness by setting up an opposition between strong men and weaklings, who were depersonalized in the language of the time as "das Schwache."[9] Jacques Doriot summed it up well, referring to the Collaboration where tireless strong men confronted weary weaklings:

> The member of a movement has to demonstrate exceptional qualities of intellectual vigor, moral rectitude, tenacity and even physical resilience. The truth is that the smallest lapse in judgment, the briefest moment of fatigue, the most infinitesimal misunderstanding of the profound rightness and meaning of the movement will sap respect for discipline and the rituals that embody it. If this ignorance of the movement's essential principles becomes entrenched, discipline and respect for the movement will be unbearable for people who are tired.[10]

Certainly, such terms were conveniently vague and easily understood, but the tactics of domination didn't always exploit exhaustion through carefully calculated programs. One example was the shambles of Soviet planning that set impossible or unreachable productivity goals. The point was to be able to blame the local managers or the workers, "so that a new purge could get underway."[11] Fatigue was thus not only an ideological weapon but also a political tool.

"Totalitarian" propaganda and indefatigability

This weapon came into its own definitively during the Soviet era in the 1930s, when productivity was not only monitored through record-keeping but was also encouraged with bonuses that tied wages to output and given a further boost by the demonization of slackers. An exemplary worker lauded by the press in 1935 changed expectations of production norms and physical exertion. Alexei Stakhanov mined 102 tons of coal in five hours and forty-five minutes during the night shift on August 30. The "Hero of Soviet Labor" produced fourteen times his usual daily quota, hewing the coal deposits "with his jackhammer 85 meters below ground,"[12] ignoring the coal dust choking his nose and throat while keeping scrupulously to recommended work guidelines. That night he burst through the production limits in the Donets basin, set a national record and proved to the world that the Soviet "new man" exists. The actual working conditions surrounding this astonishing achievement have never been fully revealed but, in fact, Stakhanov's triumph was a team effort; breaking with the usual work pattern, timber men installed supports in the mineshaft for Stakhanov and other workers ferried the coal to the surface. Nevertheless, his feat was the centerpiece of a huge propaganda campaign, highlighting the prowess of the Soviet worker and providing a model for achievement nationwide. Stakhanov's words of wisdom were duly reported; he stressed the importance of having the proper equipment and attitude: performing "nerve-wracking work, but feeling alert and joyous."[13] He claimed that the non-stop work didn't tire him out: "I didn't feel at all fatigued and was ready to beat the record again, if we had more timber" for supports.[14] For a totalitarian regime, the public relations campaign touting a "shock worker" was a major step forward because it was totally political.

Stakhanov's feat, a shining example of tenacity and perfectionism, set off a "miniaturized cult of personality"[15] of the new Soviet man, and his face appeared on posters and in photographs while his name adorned streets, village squares and even a town in Ukraine. International media took notice, giving the USSR more standing in the competition between the East's "socialist" and the West's "capitalist" economies and bolstering support for the Stalinist regime among workers in other parts of the world. In the US, the news weekly *Time* featured Stakhanov on its cover on December 16, 1935. The word "Stakhanovism" was coined, and workers in all sorts of industries in the USSR vied to break productivity records. In the 1930s, workers could proudly assume the title of "dvukhsotniki," if they produced 200 percent of their daily quota in a single shift, and "tysyachniki" if they hit the 1,000 percent mark.[16] These were ideological goals, we must remember, and had nothing to do with verifiable measures or analysis: "By refusing to formulate questions of worker fatigue scientifically, the Marxist theoreticians during Stalin's rule claimed (and perhaps believed?) to have eliminated fatigue itself."[17]

A more somber Soviet reality existed away from the spotlight, focused on model and "shock workers." Working conditions were deteriorating, workers' standard of living was falling, and inequality was on the rise.[18] And, the speed-ups needed to fulfill or surpass quotas could even "cause equipment to deteriorate more quickly because of the pace of work."[19] In a more general sense, the periods of intensified output, the disdain for teamwork and the impossible production quotas "resulted in a disastrous imbalance in these nascent industries."[20]

The mindset that valued output over labor created an atmosphere that encouraged penalties to detect "saboteurs" and root out slackers who weren't sufficiently loyal. For example, in the construction industry in Hungary in 1950 an entire work unit with several hundred employees "purged its 'enemy elements'" after "a dam collapsed."[21] Stakhanovism enabled this, and the cleverly constructed image celebrating the "new man" and party loyalist made it easier to eliminate the "degenerates" who didn't toe the line.

Yet, there was a difference between the USSR's socialism and Germany's Nazism. The former premised its legitimacy on the indefatigability of its workers and the latter on the strength of its race and bloodline.

Exhaustion and the void

However, in both cases, a "totalitarian" system functioned by eliminating anyone believed to threaten the "unity and group cohesion" that was so desirable for the all-powerful regime. The "elements that are deemed harmful, racially or socially, had to be eliminated sooner or later."[22] The "new man's" opposite number is the weakling, the degenerate or the "dangerous" individual, and the two worlds were irreconcilable. This legitimated extermination as a political strategy and resulted in the building of camps, where the "foreign elements" threatening a regime were banished, hidden from view and even murdered.

The name "camp" does not do justice to the enormity of the exclusionary system, since some victims were killed immediately and not held in concentration or work camps. The detainees transported to Belzec, Chelmno, Sobibor and Treblinka,[23] where no facilities existed for processing, feeding or housing them, met their fate upon arrival. The sole purpose of these sites was to exterminate quickly people judged to be unassimilable and racially inferior.

"Concentration," on the other hand, was intended "as a preventive measure to isolate from society individuals or groups who were deemed suspicious or harmful."[24] No financial motives prompted the forced labor of "detainees." Instead, the goal was humiliation, weakening and suffering in a gradual process of erasure or, in the Soviet case in particular, a vague notion of reforming and re-educating prisoners. The point of the system was to stigmatize them and to cull the herd. The forced labor in the program was pointless and punitive. Hermann Langbein recalled: "We rushed to carry rocks from one spot to another, carefully piled them up, then, still running, carried them back to where they were before."[25] Exhaustion was always "available," intuitive, blind and overpowering.

At the end of the 1930s the goal shifted, however, with the prospect of long-term internments, the country at war, and a shortage of manual labor. The mass detention program changed its objective, and fatigue was transmuted into a final solution, as forced labor served a dual purpose: providing useful work to the Nazi regime and disposing of detainees who might otherwise be murdered by other means. Heinrich Himmler and the Reich minister of justice Otto Georg Thierack decided to send "prisoners in preventive detention" to the camps "to exterminate them through labor" (Vernichtung durch Arbeit). The detainees were Jews, Roma, Russians, Ukrainians and Poles.[26] They would be worked to death. Here we must again complicate the notion of exhaustion. Physical fatigue was "associated" with a number of other factors that exacerbated it: poor hygiene, violent assaults, starvation, exposure to freezing temperatures and disease.[27] Soviet authorities enforced policies in the Gulag system that accelerated prisoners' downward spiral: "Those who performed poorly ate less. This scheme condemned hundreds of thousands to death and disability, and encouraged the Gulag to try new methods to "motivate" the laborers."[28] Another method used by the SS was to deliberately speed up the pace of the forced laborers' work, insisting on higher productivity in a show of dominance and control. Thus, detainees raced to unload supplies and frantically pushed wheelbarrows uphill, all the while suffering a state of semi-starvation that made the absurd work demands even more punitive.[29] The life expectancy of detainees in Auschwitz was only a few months.[30] The turnover in the labor force was blamed on "Jewish incapacity."[31]

Fatigue was so ever-present that, at times, it became the basis of experiments in which the detainees were used as guinea pigs to distinguish between "tolerable" and "intolerable" conditions. A "foot commando" was organized in 1936 at the Sachsenhausen camp north of Berlin, where prisoners were forced to participate in a specific program, "marching for hours without stopping to test the durability of German-manufactured shoes."[32] The experiment was sadistically fine-tuned so that prisoners were sent to march on different surfaces (sand, gravel, stone, clay), carrying different weights, shod in different shoe sizes. Medical experimentation came into the picture with the "pill patrol" in 1944, when prisoners were enrolled in a test of an "energy compound" for the benefit of the German navy. The final report didn't mince words about the torture involved: "Keep the men awake and ready for action by not allowing them to sleep, or permitting very little rest, for four days and nights, as much as is possible with pills A and D. Prioritize formulas B and C."[33]

Fatigue was turned into a political weapon in totalitarian societies. It was also used for tragic human experimentation on marginalized people in an attempt to try every possible method on the bodies of people who had nothing left to lose.

"Leisure" between totalitarianism and democracy

The danger of fatigue, on the other hand, was taken into account in seemingly positive ways for the "nation's" supported and celebrated labor force. A "leisure time" was even organized in Nazi Germany in the 1930s to balance the damage done by long periods of intense labor and to enhance productivity: "Free time and vacations are intended to completely eliminate natural and inevitable fatigue. We must achieve this goal in order to have a stable and productive workforce."[34] This principle was applied to the "new man," while the exact opposite (no rest, punishing labor) was prescribed for detainees; a short break in the work year was a preventive measure to "fortify the nerves"[35] of German workers. This was a Europe-wide phenomenon after the First World War, where a similar recognition of the value of vacations and leisure time was developing throughout the industrialized countries. Workers were calling for it, and at the first International Labor Conference in 1919 the Swedish delegation declared: "A period of complete rest every year is essential to maintain workers' physical and mental health."[36] On July 11, 1925, a law was proposed by a deputy in the French legislature: "Annual vacation time has become necessary to maintain productivity and ensure workers' wellbeing … making them more productive at work."[37] This was an ambitious goal, and the votes fell short, but the proposal was more comprehensive and complex than the "work breaks" that had been considered up to that time.

The promise of leisure fit easily into totalitarian societies such as Nazi Germany and fascist Italy, always quick to direct and control citizens' every move. The movement "Kraft durch Freude" (Strength through

Joy) was a state-operated tourism organization, part of the Labor Front that replaced labor unions in Nazi Germany in 1933. The annual cruises it offered were a cartoonish example of workers' benefits: no choice of destination; strict "timetables accounting for every last minute";[38] recommendations on the proper attire and attitude; a set bedtime;[39] lists of flowers approved for picking; and esthetic choices that reflected the correct ideology, with "folklore prioritized over 'degenerate art.'"[40] Thus, the largest tour operator in the 1930s promised a contradictory vision of "rest and relaxation" for the masses, one of rigidly programmed activities meant to inculcate the values of National Socialism.

Nothing comparable existed in the democratic societies of the time, since neither "leisure" nor "individuality" filled equivalent roles there. What was new was the idea of "having time for oneself," and even this was not fully grasped by some working men and women. For instance, in the 1950s, when Janine Larrue interviewed a metal worker in Toulouse about his view of vacation time in earlier years, he replied: "Free time? I never thought about it."[41] Nevertheless, on June 12, 1936, everything changed for workers when the French Popular Front voted in the forty-hour work week and two weeks of paid vacation. The policy became "symbolic"[42] of larger victories. Some dubbed it "Year I of happiness";[43] others saw it as "a progression to a better, more humane life," more significant than a mere "compensation for fatigue,"[44] while yet others hailed it as a new incarnation of freedom:

> Not to go to the factory, to be able to stay at home, not to have to get up at dawn, to rush to get there on time, to escape the demands of the foreman and the production quotas, to avoid the penalties handed out for the slightest misstep or missed production goal … Now this state of freedom, a legally recognized freedom (because when we're on strike, we're also free), this was the first time freedom existed for us. This time off that didn't cut into our wages was entirely unheard-of, even weird. Everyone welcomed it enthusiastically, no matter how they spent their free time.[45]

Simone Weil noticed the same emotions as she joined "long lines of workers" heading for the Gare de Lyon: "they cried with joy, they sang and said silly things like "Hooray for Life."[46] In 1936, a painting by the Croatian artist Krsto Hegedušić, *L'Aube* [The dawn],[47] captured the same feelings, showing vacationers on bicycles riding towards an endless horizon. Fernand Léger's *Les Loisirs: hommage à Louis David* [Leisure activities: homage to Louis David] (1948–9), was a modern history painting, of beaches and bathing suits, bicycles and runners, doves and flowers; by glorifying popular leisure activities and the paid vacations granted in 1936, Léger's work underlined the cultural valence of these new institutions.[48] These were just a few of the moments that epitomized this long-term process.

28

The Promise of Wellbeing?

Both totalitarian and democratically elected governments exploited political references to fatigue but took radically different, often opposite tacks. Still, the "happy" recognition of the importance of leisure and "free time," along with the growth of individualism and consumerism in democratic countries, prioritized the issue of fatigue once again. Government leaders promised less fatigue and proposed methods to lessen or prevent it, and post-war welfare state programs also claimed to take this direction. Along with limiting the length of the workday, legislation mandating paid vacations and a national social security and retirement system were significant elements of social change. In fact, at the end of the 1950s a new word, "wellbeing," entered the lexicon, signaling a recognition of society's potential to revolutionize daily life, lighten burdens and simplify lifestyles. The concern with wellbeing was the first institutional recognition of an increased attention to psychology. As sociologist Jean Baudrillard asked, exploring "the social logic of consumption" and "wellbeing": "What is this happiness that haunts modern civilization with such ideological force?"[1] We need to assess its historical reach and its contemporary effects.

Concretizing wear and tear

It is impossible to ignore the new administrative and social measures, and even political responses, taken after the Second World War which addressed the toll that work takes on workers. In 1945 in France, the social security administration introduced a "universal" benefit system that was meant to cover everyone in the workforce. "Les jours heureux" [happy days] is the name given to sweeping proposals developed in 1943–4 by groups of partisans in the resistance movement. The CNR (Conseil National de la Résistance), an umbrella organization of right-wing and leftist groups, called for a national social security system, pensions, and even freedom of the press, in a brochure published in the south of France in May 1944. The "happy days" it sketched out represented a new and different vision and a major change in perspective. One of the major planks in their program was a system of employee and employer contributions that would be the foundation for a social insurance system:

> Seen from this angle, social security entails the establishment of a large national organization of obligatory mutual aid that cannot be fully functional unless it covers everyone and all the possible risks they might encounter. The final goal is to have a plan that covers everyone in the country and insures them against all types of insecurity; such a result will be achieved only after long years of persistent efforts, but what is possible for us now is to present the framework for this plan.[2]

The "post-work period," or a person's eligibility for retirement, was scrupulously defined. Sixty years was the "floor," when participants received a retirement income of "20 percent of their annual salary"; additional increments were offered to those who worked up to age sixty-five, since the goal was to "keep as many as possible in the active workforce to win the battle of production."[3] The age cut-off was of limited practicality, it must be said, at a time when life expectancy was 69.2 years for women and 63.4 years for men.[4]

Especially noteworthy was the attention paid to "arduous work that wears out the body prematurely"[5] and the guarantee of financial protections for those workers. Not only did this explicitly acknowledge the long-term effects of fatigue, the proposal also called for designating specifically "painful" work categories in consultation with the CSSS (Conseil supérieur de la sécurité sociale).[6] The recommendation was nuanced, however, addressing not the harm caused by arduous work but simply the parameters of the pension benefit. This demonstrated, if evidence is needed, how hard it was to make distinctions based on age and the toll work takes in the course of an entire life.

Another nuance that was significant was that "premature wear and tear" could be linked to fatigue and to other factors such as the danger of toxic materials or the work environment, so that investigators began collecting under one rubric everything that might shorten or threaten a worker's life. This perspective went far beyond Ramazzini's inventory of pathologies and acknowledged the ill effects of fatigue and other noxious influences, in the end compiling a list of all the factors that compromise "vitality."

Another impressive aspect of the 1945 program was that it recognized "the existence of a number of special cases above and beyond the rights of all."[7] In other words, the social insurance system had to allow for early retirement for workers whose jobs were believed to accelerate "fatigue" or "disability." This type of work had long been categorized under the labor code as exceptional, and now the program extended eligibility to employees of "government industrial enterprises," railroad workers, miners, "active government services," "companies that deliver gas, electric utility workers," etc.[8] This reinforced the principle of balancing "equity" with "equality," but, by according special rights to those who "earned" or "deserved" them, the system was complicated,[9] with endless debates over eligibility criteria and financing. The "wear and tear" of "special cases" was defined by the job category itself rather than by any particular activity. This highlighted the difficulties in pinning down the sources of "damage" and their long-term effects.

The widening gap between the number of active contributors to the system and the number of eligible retirees led in 1953 to a government decision whose intent was obviously restrictive. "Wear and tear" was brought up, discussed and re-evaluated: "After September 1, 1953, staff associated with the special case categories who do not work in jobs that entail a premature physical decline or who do not exhibit specific physical impairment ... may not request early retirement before the age of eligibility or apply for a pension before reaching the age applicable to civil servants."[10]

As a result, in most instances this meant retirement at the age of sixty, instead of fifty-five, for personnel in so-called active jobs,[11] provoking fierce opposition from employees in those sectors, expressed in protests, strikes by government office workers, a three-week strike by railroad workers, and many other numerous acts of resistance. Reversing its policy, the government rolled back the restrictions a few weeks later: "It is understood that the rules will not affect" the retirement criteria for special cases.[12] This confrontation was indicative of how much "attitude trumps substance"[13] and how workers would reject actual evidence or statistics; it also revealed the extent to which "special cases are seen as a key factor in social status,"[14] and even an aspect of their identity.

From then on, adjustments continued to be made to the system. On June 27, 1956, a "road tax" was enacted, apparently the first attempt to deal with potential deficits in national insurance funding,[15] and motorists paid the fee and displayed the license-plate sticker that confirmed their "contribution" to the effort. All in all, we must emphasize that the French regulations in 1945 represented a big step forward. Broad, sweeping "protections" were developed as a response to "wear and tear." The national retirement system acknowledged its existence, identified and sometimes quantified its effects, even if the criteria were subject to inevitable revision, adjustment or conflict.

Inventing ergonomics

These institutional responses prompted others that were meant to augment the original scope and reach of government action. Scientific expertise was urgently needed to identify work-related damage and fatigue, to diagnose these injuries, and even to justify enshrining prevention or compensation in the legal code. The field of occupational medicine, whose direction had long been sporadic and fragmented, took on a new mission after the Second World War. As a specialty with a defined purpose, it pursued two avenues of research regarding "wear and tear," investigating fatigue itself and the pathology of labor. This resulted in closer scrutiny of "injuries" due to "work-related positions and actions, cramps, skeletal deformities, inflammations of the tendons, exostosis [bone spurs] …"[16] This sort of damage was attributed to a more clearly defined fatigue, above and beyond accidents, infections or other diseases.

On July 28, 1942, a law was passed requiring medical attention in workplaces[17] that had two seemingly incompatible goals. On the one hand, it required employers to ensure a designated medical consultant on site to assess risks, contagion and equipment in the workplace and thus protect workers. On the other, the law mandated job counselors to evaluate unemployed workers in order to assess their ability to return to work and appeared designed to nudge or perhaps shove malingerers back into the workforce.[18] Another law, passed on October 11, 1946, and the order that followed on November 26, 1946, were quite different. These increased the number of medical services in the workplace while "ensuring the independence and the authority of the physicians performing these services."[19] The type of medical attention differed, of course, depending on the size of the business and potential exposure to "hazardous work environments" (sewers, slaughterhouses, refrigeration units, various kinds of pollution). Nevertheless, the doctors' role was clearly preventive: "to improve the sanitation and hygiene of work conditions; prevent fatigue and premature wear and tear by coordinating job requirements with psychosensory demands (assessment of the physical capacity of the workforce); bring mental health resources into the workplace."[20] It is worth pointing out that the scientific criteria here had expanded greatly, encompassing "medical, psycho-affective, physiological, sanitary, technical and social"[21] factors.

After the Second World War, ergonomics, a field that has only recently been defined, gained prominence.[22] The Ergonomics Research Society[23] was established in London in 1949, its name derived from the Greek "ergon" (work) and "nomos" (laws) – in other words, this was a term for the study or science of work. These "laws" had not been ignored, of course. In fact, scientists in the seventeenth century had mapped them out.[24] "Industrial engineers" in the nineteenth century had elaborated on them,[25] while their colleagues in the 1920s developed them systematically.[26] The innovation of modern ergonomics was to prioritize workers' wellbeing and comfort over other practical outcomes such as productivity or speed, focusing instead on how workers could protect themselves and prevent injuries. The scope of the program was vast: "the totality of scientific knowledge related to humans that is necessary to design tools, machines and policies that can be utilized with a maximum of comfort, security, and efficiency."[27]

The old science of work and the imperatives of Taylorism to eliminate wasted motion took a new direction. The goal now was to design a "comfortable" approach to work, with the spotlight on the workers themselves, valorizing their perspectives and prioritizing their perceptions and feelings, and even the most banal observations. Posture and movement were among the first topics to be investigated, with "self-preservation" taking priority over "efficiency." Porters in particular were at risk when they carried loads with "their backs hunched over," stressing their "spinal vertebrae,"[28] and risking the injury known as "straight back syndrome," distorting the normal upper thoracic spinal curvature. Other hazards included maintaining a "strongly flexed" posture,[29] making repeated, often futile motions, and straightening up, "holding one's arms stretched out to the front or the side" for long periods.[30] These positions and movements caused excessive cramping. Ergonomics proposed a solution that positioned workers closer to their equipment. When operating machinery, another point to consider was the location of levers "at shoulder height when one is working standing up ... and at elbow height when one works sitting down."[31] The goal was to make the execution "effortless," or even enjoyable. Ergonomics research focused on work stresses, pains and positions that may have been overlooked before, so the proposed solutions targeted rearranging the work space as well as reorienting workers' use of their bodies. Researchers looked into environmental stressors and potential safety issues such as noise, dampness, heat, lighting, vibrations and the quality of floor surfaces. All in all, investigators took "into account a multiplicity of human factors, sensory input, mental attitude, factors associated with mobility, adaptation, and spatial awareness, as well as the effects of the work environment on performance."[32] The diversity of interests was not new, but now they were more systematically addressed and consciously aimed at prevention.

The amount of attention devoted to work performed while seated, in particular, highlighted the increase of sedentary jobs in the 1950s, ones that were not primarily reliant on strength or physical exertion. Once again, this prompted a revival of interest in designing furniture that accommodated a seated person with a limited range of motion, such as a compact work station where everything was within arm's reach, as the new inventory of office chairs illustrated: "swivel chairs," "hanging chairs," "chairs with adjustable levers," "roller chairs," "retractable seats."[33] Another example of ergonomically inspired design was the control panel that was as uncluttered as possible for the vehicle operator or the machinist, so that the switches, buttons or knobs were at eye level and the function of each one was easily identifiable at a glance. In addition, an ergonomic design prioritized equipment operators having easy access from their usual work position, whether sitting, standing, leaning or patrolling.[34]

Intersecting physics models

In addition to ergonomics, it is impossible to ignore the scientific advances in physics models after the Second World War that reintroduced organic data. The holistic understanding of a biological "unit" was deepened, ranked, intersected and redefined as never before, and that had immediate consequences on our understanding of our body's defenses, providing many clues as to how the body functions.

Metabolism was of primary importance, represented by the familiar image of a burning fire and understood as a process fueled by "oxidation and dehydrogenation."[35] What was new, however, was the increasing precision of data related to that energy and the increase in categorization leading to the establishment of quasi-international norms. In 1945 the United Nations' World Food Programme[36] determined statistically that 3,200 calories was the daily nutritional requirement for the "average worker," an assessment that was not very different from recommendations earlier in the century.[37] But this analysis went into detail, explaining that the recommendation was for a 25-year-old man weighing 65 kilos (for a woman, the recommendation would be 500 calories less per day) and was premised on the principle of maintaining a healthy weight. If the subject was heavier, one would adapt the basic calculation by adding 350 calories for each additional 10 kilos of weight or, if the subject was athletic, from 500 to 1,000 additional calories a day. We see that this daily nutritional requirement is different for men and women even though it considered factors such as participation in sports. The recommendations also noted that people who had not eaten for over twenty-four hours had a faster pulse and respiratory rate. In other words, nutrition ensured and stabilized our metabolism. This was not surprising; muscles could not function without being supplied "for a certain amount of time with a certain quantity of energy."[38]

Because it focused on the connection between input and output, this model could be compared to another that had become increasingly influential throughout the twentieth century. The network of chemical signals regulated bodily functions and constantly adjusted them, sending out internal messages and mediating between organs, working together to "energize" the whole. Hormones were an important component. Throughout the decades, more hormones have been detected and more of their roles have been identified, such as the coordination "of organic functions."[39] Hormones that were in balance or out of balance inevitably affected fatigue. Many examples could be found throughout the system: insulin enabled sugar to enter the cells, thyroxin "reinforced respiratory and circulatory functions,"[40] pituitrin aided the "contraction of the smooth muscles."[41] All of these secretions were investigated in the field of physiology. Minerals also played a key role. Iron was essential for oxidation and "combustion"; calcium built the skeleton and was necessary for blood coagulation.[42] Vitamins too were important. These micronutrients maintained the proper functioning of the body's metabolism in minuscule but essential doses: Vitamin C aided the process of oxidation,[43] Vitamin B helped the body rid itself of muscle byproducts[44] and Vitamin E was crucial for nerves, although "we are not sure what to attribute this to."[45] Diets had been transformed.

The list of minimum daily requirements had never been so long, with a number of entries that added a quasi-qualitative note to the simple quantitative recommendations. At the end of the Second World War, the National Research Council released its recommendations for vitamin and mineral intake, along with the still unchanged calorie count of 3,000 for "normal activity" and "4,500 for "vigorous work."[46] The sources of fatigue fluctuated here between nutritional values and nutrient deficiencies. Assessments became more complex, and supervision grew. It was impossible to depend simply on the recommended servings of carbohydrates, proteins and fats that had long been the staple of institutional menus.[47] One had to add vitamins and minerals. Criticism was directed at "the factory commissary" that neglected the "qualitative" elements in its offerings, guilty of provoking "unprecedented levels of fatigue."[48]

Another model, the nervous system, was envisioned operating as a command-and-control center for all the other systems, monitoring and regulating the body's organs and functions. At the beginning of the 1960s, Pierre Bugard studied participants competing in racing sculls and found an increase of "the excretion of 17-ketosteroids in the urine."[49] This hormone is a breakdown product of the adrenal cortex and of androgens but, in Bugard's study, the results were identical for the rowers and the coxswains, even though the latter were not exerting the same amount of effort. This led to the inevitable conclusion that "psychological factors"[50] such as attentiveness and decision-making activated these releases of "force multipliers" into the muscles, even if they were unnecessary, as a response to "stressors." Bernard Metz also observed athletes and workers who consumed "large amounts of high-quality protein"[51] in an attempt to enhance their performance. He investigated whether the protein loading made a difference and found a "psychophysiological" effect[52] rather than a strictly physiological one. The "central nervous system" was the "predominant organ,"[53] and its processes controlled energy production and consumption and regulated body chemistry.

Finally, the critical role of the nervous system was recognized as being equally important in the outbreak of disorders as well as in the maintenance of equilibrium. A number of disorders and dysfunctions occurred when the nervous system's protective mechanisms were overridden or when reactions were excessive, as many sorts of fatigue now demonstrated.

The concept of a "total" object

Another physiological analysis joined the models that already existed: that of exterior determinants, their diversity, and their representation in the system. An extreme diversity of organic reactions was actually intrinsically more unified. The idea of an "organism" had already incorporated this in earlier decades, indicating the desire for a comprehensive vision exemplified by "stress" and the principle of homeostasis.[54] This resulted in a deliberate and measured increase in more varied approaches and a determination to expand the program more than ever before.

The innovation here was to keep counting the growing number of possible "influences," to keep recording all kinds of echoes, the most profound as well as the most obscure ones, and to use studies of the humanities as well as biology as resources to focus on the convergence between the organic and the social in order to reframe fatigue as a "total" object: "This study of human wear and tear in the modern world is conceived in a psychosomatic spirit: it is not intended to trace physiological, biological and psychological mechanisms separately. Instead, it is meant to show how they work together within a unified personality."[55]

In the 1950s, the term "psychosomatic" was adopted widely to recognize the "repercussions of psychism and instinctive reflexes on each other"[56] extending the etiology as it unified it. This referred back inevitably to each person's history and an attempt to refine our understanding of the individual through studies of one's earliest experiences, the deficits, the losses that were unexpected or repeated; the very individualized sense of feeling "defective." In this way, a key point was expressed clearly: "Fatigue is an archaic process that limits humans' ascendancy over the world; very early in childhood, humans have perceived fatigue as a barrier that separates them from what they want to achieve."[57] This was a challenge to the very essence of humanity, certainly familiar, but always intimate and linked to our past. The first definition was quasi-anthropological and identified fatigue as a regular companion, even if an unwelcome one, of everyone's life and experiences. This led to a more explicit reference to the almost "primordial" feeling of impotence: "Thus, it is important to delve into adults' fatigue as a phenomenon of regression, a return to dependency reminiscent of painful infantile experiences."[58]

Renewed cautiousness came to the forefront regarding the possible extent of interpretation: "the organism is a unified whole; that is why fatigue is singular and also complex."[59] Even more explicitly: "This is a question of a holistic perspective that incorporates the whole person in its existential condition."[60] Studies and surveys kept coming and they expanded what the term "stress" meant[61] by looking at the intersecting influences of "responsibilities" and "pressures," while also making endless lists of potential stressors: genetic inheritance; personal history; psychosocial conditions; living conditions; previous history of fatigue; conditions where it occurred; the intensity, the symptoms and distinguishing signs, etc.[62] An example was pilot's fatigue, which was no longer associated only with hormonal changes or the feelings the subject experienced, as Lindbergh's memoir illustrated.[63] It was also linked to recurrent "emotional shocks," to "fears of accidents," to the quest for higher status and the potential obstacles that might entail, to "unfavorable social conditions" and to "family problems."[64] The same data applied to the ordinary motorist or the professional truck driver. Jacques Fessard and Christian David investigated an accident where a driver skidded and was seriously injured after a 600-kilometer journey. The researchers took a cautious approach: Was it the length of the drive? The lack of rest breaks? The need to meet a deadline? Was it the result of anxiety about the driver's promise to meet, with very little time to spare, both his wife and his mistress? There were so many possible answers, and the researchers did not offer a definite conclusion: "A tendency to have accidents, psychosomatic ailments and ergonomics are conditions that are frequently confused and are permanently interconnected."[65] The "driver's fatigue" was lumped in with domestic turmoil, the driver's need to succeed, and the possibility both of overconfidence and of potential "guilt feelings."[66] As Claude Veil explained in 1958 in his study of "exhaustion," the critical moment was "the encounter of an individual and a situation."[67] In other words, we were looking at a person challenged by circumstances. For these reasons, investigators considered the present and the past, the job profile and the task at hand.

Studies focused on other new targets and investigated personal differences, anomalies and unexpected results. One question, among others, recurred: Why would a worker experience a certain kind of fatigue on one day rather than another, when the task performed is the same?[68] Physical feelings such as stiff leg muscles, slower movements and "inertia in the body"[69] were indicators and emphasized the importance of the subject's perceptions. The number of causes of fatigue continued to grow; it could be a change in the setting, noise, heat, smells or dampness; a change in the reception of one's work, either through praise or criticism; unwelcome duties such as reports to write or accounts to turn in; unpleasant interactions; a change in one's mood; or even "attempts at self-reassurance"[70] for all sorts of reasons. Analyses of work were inevitably becoming more complex and incorporated a "holistic" approach,[71] because nothing relevant should be overlooked.

At the end of the 1950s the long-term study of fatigue in French polar expeditions was an innovative and exemplary step.[72] The data collection was intended to be exhaustive and took into account the strains of physical exertion, the changes in altitude and temperature, psychological and emotional factors, participants' motivations, their background and past history, and their personal foibles. The expedition's six-month assignments exacted a physical toll, resulting in weight loss, hormonal disruption, tachycardia, and a tendency to irritability. These symptoms were aggravated by team members' sense of isolation and of feeling cut off from home, as well as the emotional entanglements of promiscuity. Otherwise, an individual's tendency to experience depression or anxiety may be intensified in that setting. The polar expedition was turned into a quasi-symbolic laboratory where the plethora of stressful, monotonous or extreme living and working conditions could trigger exhaustion.

Criticizing piece work

Many more varied approaches to investigating fatigue were adopted in the mid-twentieth century. Industrial engineering studies themselves took into account more interrelated effects. Nevertheless, traditional methods did not just fade away. After the Second World War, cargo transport, lifting and moving heavy loads and various kinds of porterage were still essential. Jobs "where physical exertion is foremost" continued to be very much with us.[73] Nevertheless, change was imminent; this was a change in perceptions and preferences that entailed a generalized disdain, well founded or not, for certain jobs that were seen as too "demanding," leading to less enthusiasm for them. All these changes were clearly visible, both on a technical and a personal level, and underpinned the great waves of worker migration, especially from the global South, to industrialized European countries in the 1960s. The "strain" was displaced culturally and socially. The worker ranks turned over. Fatigues sought a new equilibrium. Félix Mora's quest for migrant labor was one example among many, criss-crossing the Souss region of Morocco and recruiting, "with the help of local political leaders, young men to dig coal."[74] The main sources of guest workers in industrial Europe have long been documented and the ebbs and flows noted. In 1954, 289,000 and, in 1968, 607,000 Spaniards were working in France. In 1954, 20,000 and, in 1975, 759,000 Portuguese were in the French workforce. In fact, in 1975, of all migrants, Portuguese men and women made up the largest tranche of the non-citizen population, at 22 percent. Algerian migrants were the second-largest group then, at 711,000.[75] Migrant workers were less vocal, more malleable, and less likely to reveal publicly the fatigues of their occupations. They were, of course, "a group of insecure, unprotected laborers at the heart of a stable, legally regulated workforce."[76] If they could complain, the list would include a category of "general fatigue" that was rarely studied, including "physical wear and tear," "emotional instability" and "the difficulties of acculturation."[77] The "long-term asthenia" [acute or chronic weakness] diagnosed in the migrant worker population in the 1950s was attributed, however, to "a lack of dynamic integration in their personalities."[78] A number of complex symptoms were explained away as simply "feedback to events in their lives."[79]

A critically important change in work processes during these years came when all sorts of industries adopted the assembly-line model, resulting in "reconfiguring the most diverse and different types of production into piece work."[80] Henry Ford's venerable invention became widespread at mid-century; the goal was to "shrink workers' skills to the bare minimum."[81] Many enterprises took this on. For example, in the Midlands a garment factory broke the process of sewing a jacket into sixty-five separate steps and work stations. In a bottling plant, two workers performed the same repetitive movements for the entire shift: one placed a label on a bottle, then the next worker glued it. A visitor to a cannery in 1948 relayed the "hallucinatory" sight of "a continuous and noisy flow of cans, ferried along a network of rails encircling us and arching over our heads."[82]

Critiques of this system continued to grow. The limited range of motion in regimented assembly-line tasks and the widespread influence of this production process inevitably sparked new analyses of their impact on workers. This was no longer a question of the "tonic" fatigue Charles Myers described in the 1930s[83] or the listlessness provoked by "boredom" and the "monotony" of the task. Instead, more comprehensive investigations of movement were undertaken, delving into workers' perceptions of themselves and their work assignments. This led to the first recognition of a link between "truncated, restricted motions" and feelings of fatigue, as well as the role played by frustration, dissatisfaction and emptiness. These explanations pointed to the psychological implications of piece work: it was impossible for workers to feel pride in their achievements and find meaning in their jobs. Piece work was "tiring" because it stripped away any personal investment and intentionality from the workers engaged in it. It "depersonalized" the workforce more drastically than the phenomenon of workers' depression documented several decades earlier.[84] It affected individuals in their personhood, just as it denied their agency and very existence. Georges Friedmann surveyed the damage at the beginning of the 1960s, giving new meaning to evidence that had already accumulated: feelings of depersonalization, of the incompleteness of the task, and a sense of being an interchangeable cog in the system.[85] Camille Simonin, the vice president of the Council of Occupational Medicine and the Workforce in 1950, even saw this as a regression to "the system of slavery that we supposedly abolished,"[86] resulting in newly diagnosed pathologies: "physiological and nervous damage," aggravated by the impossibility of "working at one's own pace," producing "irritability, jolting fits and starts, tensions."[87] Personal accounts emphasized the feelings of exasperation, fits of anger, emotional volatility that implicated workers' temperament as much as their "nerves," and spates of annoyance as well as tension. A harsh atmosphere that provoked impetuous and even violent reactions underlined the fact that "nervous fatigue must be distinguished from physical fatigue."[88] Marie-France Bied-Charreton recounted her workmate's sudden outburst of "anger": "Fed up with fatigue, afraid she cannot meet her quota, and harassed by the supervisor's humiliating comments … At the end of her rope, she starts screaming and hurling iron and platinum components."[89] Lathe operators, too, acted out their frustrations with the inhuman pace of work: "In just a few days, two lathe operators have had breakdowns. They turned pale and struggled to take a breath."[90] Even more striking, in Flins in the 1970s, Nicolas Dubost recalled that one of his workmates was admitted to the psychiatric hospital in Belleville. Dubost observes drily: "Assembly-line work is harder on the nerves than on our muscles."[91] It eroded one's vital sense of self.

To confirm "prosperity"

There was an unavoidable paradox, however. At a time when many workplaces were committed to piece work and chipping away at the integrity of labor, Western society was rejoicing at the discovery of a new "art of living," in the happier, more "prosperous" state of "wellbeing."[92] The term "wellbeing" itself was associated both with the steady expansion of the consumer market and the economic growth of the post-war era. "Wellbeing" was "a fundamental value of modern times," as Bernard Cazes and Edgar Morin wrote in the journal *Arguments* in March 1961,[93] in their introduction to the first special edition dedicated to this topic. Technical innovations, advances in household amenities such as plumbing, gas and electricity, the availability of credit, and the stability of the cost of living transformed the scope of simple functional imperatives and the system of everyday objects. As Jean Baudrillard observed about home furnishing: "The current trend ... is to meet successive needs by introducing new objects."[94] Europeans quickly adopted American advertising methods of the 1950s and 1960s, lauding the "autopilots" of new household appliances: ovens that are set to specified cooking programs; washers that automatically run through cycles; toasters that "grill" to perfection; blenders that effortlessly juice any number of fruits. Reynolds aluminum foil ensured that the "modern house" functioned with "magical"[95] ease and was, as Republic Steel Kitchens proclaimed, a haven of "charm and efficiency."[96] Modern "housewives" were liberated from drudgery, chatting on the phone, leafing through a magazine, or putting on make-up while keeping an eye on the appliances that did the housework for them. A whole series of inventions[97] did more than simply streamline household labor; they effectively substituted for the human touch, thereby transforming the domestic interior. Still, the image of the woman at home in these advertisements had not changed. She was the lady of the house, tethered to activities that negated her autonomy, even though by mid-century women working outside the home were no longer an anomaly.[98]

The "wellbeing" promised in the 1950s and 1960s not only permeated the home but overflowed to the exterior, seeping into space and time, enlivening our daily commute and relaxing us in our leisure activities. It offered a means to defuse omnipresent and inescapable feelings of fatigue through the continual mechanization of our surroundings, lightening our loads and fostering a culture of escapism. In January 1963, *Paris Match* proclaimed a "new prosperity," exemplified by "a kind of gentle, deep-rooted wellbeing taking hold of the country and banishing – slowly but surely – pockets of sorrow and darkness."[99] The new sleek industrial design hinted at the abolition of stress and strain. The aerodynamic lines of engines and vehicles promised a lift-off in our imaginations. Cigarette lighters that "nestled snugly" in our hands[100] offered an effortless experience; thick plush carpets deadened the sounds of our tread. Advertising slogans and headlines promoted a revolution in the goods we bought: their flexibility was inseparable from their beauty and their power came from their ease of operation. A "lifestyle" that was totally new and accessible to the masses was popularized and standardized even as cultural distinctions were carefully maintained to differentiate "social levels" and settings in everything from the brand of cars to the size of apartments, the choice of entertainment and the type of vacations. Nevertheless, this managed consumer freedom underpinned the dream of equality. Philippe Perrot analyzed it this way: "Witnessing the transition of society from a traditional to a modern one, the call for equality, religious at first, then political, is accompanied by a comparative obsession, a mimetic compulsion – sparking dreams, ambitions, frustrations – absolutely new in its character, intensity and breadth."[101]

Evidence piled up nevertheless, suggesting that many of the new shiny objects, ranging from the refrigerator to the vacuum cleaner, from the record player to the television set, from technical advances in comfort to technical advances in transportation, were all signs of another iteration of the loss of the self. The "new liberty" was even described as "an awful burden to take up, and people have difficulty getting used to it."[102] There was decision fatigue, no doubt, when consumers continually had to make choices, find a direction, and fulfill themselves in a new freedom that Alain Ehrenberg called the "fatigue of being oneself."[103] The novelist Georges Perec, in *Les Choses* [The things], satirically described the findings of "motivation researchers" who concluded that their subjects "possessed, alas, a single passion, the passion for a higher standard of living," in thrall to an endless and demanding drive for "always more."[104]

We cannot overlook how "technical and industrial development were intended constantly to create new needs – in other words, to transform and expand the idea of wellbeing."[105] It is also impossible to ignore how fatigues were still felt, depending on one's position in society; fatigues differed among classes and income levels, of course, but they were always there, permeating our daily lives, even though the forms they took might be distinct and subtle: for some, it was the feeling of a void that could never be filled; for others, a constant striving for something better; for yet others, it was a crushing sense of defeat, and the nagging feeling of not performing up to par. "Prosperity" was not simply plenty, and thus the culture of prosperity reinforced the feeling of incompleteness and of fatigue. The belief that progress was inevitable in the middle of the twentieth century provoked fatigue in a new guise, version 2.0.

In December 1961 the magazine *Réalités* published the results of a survey of young middle-class women. "Their main topics of conversation were fatigue, how to cope, their spouse's health, and domestic concerns."[106] They had moved beyond Balzac's fictional characters' social climbing[107] and the "survival of the fittest" of the end of the nineteenth century,[108] and their responses, though displaying a heretofore unknown degree of individualism, pointed to a group consciousness of a yearning for something vaguely "out there" that the consumer society promised but held just out of reach. One of the respondents' grandmothers explained: "She hasn't got a minute to herself."

This was the case too for the sales assistant interviewed in Chris Marker's documentary *Le Joli Mai* [The lovely month of May] (1963). He said forthrightly that he was always trying to increase his sales to live more and live better, to the extent that, when he finally took a vacation, he was absolutely worn out: "I'm always hustling, always hustling, always hustling." He acknowledges that his wife feels the same way: "And when I get home at night [she says], 'Gosh, I'm tired.' And I tell her: 'You're right. You *are* tired.'"[109]

On the flip side, in 1963 Pierre Doublot, a metal worker in a Renault factory, was profiled in the magazine *L'Express*. His good fortune seemed to be in stark contrast to the frustrations expressed in Marker's film and the magazine *Réalités*. He was, the reporter explained, "the prosperity worker,"[110] and the Doublots were the proud owners of all the modern comforts: up-to-date household appliances, a car, a garage, a television. They enjoyed leisure time and seemed to have banished their worries, taking a seaside vacation every other year; paying off their debts; taking their car for a spin when they pleased. Doublot expressed no specific dissatisfaction with his job, but he had a few gripes. He had a long commute from their apartment in Bondy to the factory in Boulogne, leaving home at 5.30 a.m. and returning at 7.00 p.m. Traffic was heavy when they went out on Sunday drives, and he felt so tired after work that "around 9.00 p.m. he's ready to crash and rushes to his bed." And the reporter noted that, when he was not working, "Pierre Doublot is so tired that he stays in bed all day Saturday and on Sunday afternoon."[111]

At the beginning of the 1960s, the Third International Conference of Psychosomatic Medicine distributed a survey delving into the differences or similarities of occupational fatigues: for students, office staff and skilled factory workers. Some replies stressed the physical aspects and others the mental strain. In general, members of each occupation suffered from fatigue that affected their performance. However, a common factor among all the job categories was the admission that participants felt more fatigued when "they were obliged to do the work."[112] This was understood as a "profound attack on the self, eliciting feelings of devastation"[113] when the task was perceived as "mandatory" or "compulsory." This was a crucial insight because it identified, among all the possible triggers of fatigue, the one that would apparently predominate in the future: a growing sense of the individual, of self-affirmation, and a desire for autonomy. This heightened perception of the self in the twentieth century would have direct consequences on how we live and "endure." There is no doubt that this perception became more acute throughout the decades. We saw the progression of stresses and strains on our most intimate selves, impacted by external pressures and demands. Now more than ever, fatigue was associated with the idea of being "shackled" or "painted into a corner"; we recognized when we were free and when we were "constrained," or when we had a choice or no choice. "When we tire ourselves out playing sports or finish a home improvement project, we feel a good fatigue that re-energizes us because we feel an adrenaline rush."[114]

Individuals had to strive to succeed in the mid-twentieth century when barriers surrounded them and impeded their progress. They were suffering no longer from the impotence of the neurasthenic but from the despair of the person who must comply with unjust orders. This sparked a reaction and a sense of legitimate grievance and was an unforgettable introduction to what our era has boasted about, promised and not delivered.

29

From Burn Out to Identity

The goal of achieving autonomy seemed even more distant. A question that came up frequently in contemporary writing concerned "the exhaustion we are feeling now": Why are so many of our fellow citizens, even the most accomplished and gifted among us, feeling so dissatisfied, so empty?"[1] The response given was also a common refrain, touching on "unreachable goals,"[2] suggested by ever stronger desires for independence. The breakdown would be psychological at first and then become a general malaise.

Nevertheless, beyond general observations, we cannot ignore working conditions that choked off individual initiative, such as the offshoring of jobs; companies relocating without warning; the increase in temporary jobs; the spread of electronic and digital surveillance technologies; and the blizzard of anonymous and impersonal company guidelines issued from on high. Frictions were rising between workers' growing desire for identity and the increasing use of subtle and undetectable methods to negate it. The intersection of the two forces provoked a painful sense of dissonance. A generalized feeling of fatigue was ever present, affecting all aspects of daily life, belying the metaphoric association of the human body and the machine.[3]

This was no doubt a "victory," expanding the reach of the term fatigue itself, applied to all sorts of situations, omnipresent, underlining the feeling of exhaustion that was more potent than ever. The word popped up in the most disparate contexts, accepted with little discussion of its implications: "democratic fatigue";[4] "political fatigue";[5] "parliamentary fatigue";[6] "administrative fatigue";[7] "institutional fatigue"[8] … contemporary lifestyles and working conditions constantly extended its sprawling sphere of influence.

The new phenomenon of "musculoskeletal pain"?

The service economy had grown immensely, with service-oriented businesses employing up to 79 percent of the workforce in France and over 60 percent of the total in advanced industrial economies.[9] Sales, administration, finance, education and personal care dominated the sector, while the share of "heavy industry" shrank and a substantial portion of the workforce was displaced by mechanization and automation. Many new occupational ailments were diagnosed, attributed to "overwork" and fatigue. The symptoms were familiar and easily recognized: pains, "tensions," inflammations, cramps, searing pain in the muscles, in the joints, and in the arms and legs. The term "musculoskeletal disorder" was relatively new and had been in use since the 1980s in France;[10] in English it was also called the "occupational overuse syndrome."[11] The inventory of orthopedic disorders included tendonitis, osteoarthritis, carpal tunnel syndrome, fibromyalgia and bursitis. To localize it by body part, the symptoms took in lumbar and dorsal back pain, neck pain and shoulder pain.[12] The number of patients affected had been steadily rising, from 15,000 in 2000 to 39, 000 in 2010,[13] so that this diagnosis accounted for over 70 percent of all occupational disorders, becoming "a major factor in workplace health and safety."[14] Among the symptoms were "pains and fatigue" that eased up after work or persistent "pains and fatigue" lasting into the evening and disturbing a patient's sleep.[15] It seemed impossible to pin down one single cause. The syndrome was attributed to "repetitive motions, such as assembly line work; strenuous and prolonged exertion, such as lifting and moving heavy objects; bad posture or positions, such as activities that overstress the joints; maintaining a stationary position for a long time; working with heavy machinery, such as a jackhammer; and stress."[16] Nothing completely new was on this list: repetitive motions and exertion were ever present in labor history; vibrations and stress accompanied every decade of the mechanization of work. If the syndrome could be blamed on the demands of "productivity,"[17] it was not an anomaly but a continuation of a trend: evidence of increased sensitivity to the body's vulnerability and greater precision in the diagnosis of orthopedic injuries. In fact, the surge of "musculoskeletal disorders" could, it seemed, be attributed to an increase in sufferers' self-awareness as much as the diagnostic skills of the clinicians. We had progressively developed our abilities to decode the body's warning signals and their degrees of intensity and diversity.

In the workplace, our movements were restricted, and common factors such as sitting for long periods of time, having a limited range of motion, working in a cramped space, carrying awkward or heavy loads, or being subject to speed-ups have all undoubtedly accelerated the development of orthopedic injuries. The psychological triggers of disturbing social situations or feelings of personal discomfort played a part, and our sensitivity to them was aggravated by feelings of frustration. Survey results showed that the number of responses reporting physical discomfort or strain at work doubled between 1984 and 2016. People identified "painful and tiring" work tasks as "having to maintain a position over a long period of time"; "lifting and carrying heavy loads"; and "walking at work for long distances or frequently."[18] Other surveys noted that "a lack of professional recognition" impacted "team spirit."[19] Survey responses also pointed to anxiety over "digital or managerial control" in the workplace. The percentage of participants acknowledging increased psychological pressures between 1984 and 2016 almost doubled, from 17 percent to over 30 percent.[20] All in all, pain and suffering of various kinds increased in tandem with workers' quota of "dissatisfaction."

Studies mapped out the gradual progression of workers' unhappiness. For instance, Marie Grenier-Pezé described the case of a 24-year-old supermarket cashier named Nacéra, who experienced "terrible pain" after lifting a 6-liter pack of bottled water. After that, the pain continued, and the management did little to accommodate her; instead, it cracked down on what was perceived as lax behavior: "If you pal around with the cashier next to you, they make you change places, so you don't waste time chatting."[21] The managers made a point of demanding efficiency: "When you unload a pallet, [the manager] is standing over you, a watch in his hand: 'I'll give you five minutes to finish that,' when he knows that five minutes isn't enough. And since you have to work, you end up accepting this treatment. The supervisor is always on your back."[22]

This personal account highlighted the increased pressure of speed-ups in the pace of work and also the occupational hazards associated with technology in this workplace. In this case, the scanners used by supermarket cashiers could lead to repetitive motion injuries and carpal tunnel syndrome. But only a psychologically taxing climate of persistent tension could explain this phenomenon: "Working in an atmosphere of sudden physical shocks puts the brachial plexus at risk."[23]

Yves Clot studied particular work-related motions in depth, going beyond the observations published in the 1960s about the ill effects of piece work, repetition and worker alienation.[24] He emphasized the lack of mental stimulation and engagement with tasks that were designed to exclude workers' agency and judgment. Such restricted, superficial and fragmented movements pointed to the need to reincorporate workers' decision-making processes. Yves Clot explained in scientific terms: "We believe that musculoskeletal disorder is a pathology of movement and more precisely a pathological development of motions that are underdeveloped. Hypo-stress of restricted activities in the workplace by the subjects."[25] This was a new, more specific and focused approach, emphasizing factors that constrain the individual and interrogate the relationship between ergonomics and psychology in the workplace.[26] The investigation was clearly focused on the active participant, on impediments to motion, on feelings of prohibition, highlighting the impossibility of inhabiting space when work rules enforce a "straight-jacketing of the body and of time."[27] There was a yawning gulf, in other words, and a painful one, between "thinking" and "doing": "The analysis of the gap between biomechanical reality (movements that are actually made) and psychological reality (movements that you know can be made differently but are not permitted) constituted a way of understanding and describing the processes of changing the trajectory of movements and its effect on health."[28]

This conclusion was not new, certainly, but it incorporated both an analysis of external and internal factors. This was a crucial shift in understanding that the passive suffering endured by workers when their movements were restricted and cramped became even more painful because some of their usual or habitual actions were prohibited or plainly unacceptable.

Designing drudgery

In the 2000s another concept, "hardship," crystallized what had been called "premature wear and tear of the body" in the French labor code in 1945,[29] referring to disabilities that resulted from long periods of arduous labor. The use of the term "hardship" was important, since it was directly connected to the difficulty and physicality of "heavy labor." It centered attention on the workers' bodies themselves and the aches and pains that were psychological as well as physical, associated with fatigue as much as injury. The word "hardship" combined the body and mind in a holistic perspective. Workers didn't suffer only physical wear and tear; they were also damaged deeply and personally in their sense of self and their potential. The word "hardship" (in French "pénibilité") had a generic meaning; dictionaries defined "hard work" as "tiring," "exhausting," "fatiguing" and, in a slang register, associated it with feeling "worn out," "knocked out," "knackered" and "slated." The connotations of the words such as "hardship" and "hard" linked them to "pain" and "suffering," to "difficult" or "heavy work," and thus to fatigue.[30] Hard work could wreak lasting damage that was visible and felt, making a person less vital, less powerful and less whole.

In 2003, the word "pénibilité" was used in preliminary studies for the Conseil d'orientation des retraites [Pension Advisory Council] on the reform of the French retirement system,[31] in the context of "examining eligibility criteria for early retirement or differential benefits." On January 31, 2006, the term was more precisely defined in an agreement among researchers, occupational medicine specialists, and public and private employers to study "hardship" resulting from "physical and psychological stresses of specific professional activities that have distinct, long-lasting, permanent effects on employees' health and may impact their life expectancy."[32] The discussions identified "three hardship factors":[33] 1) stringent physical or psychological restrictions (movements, positions, exertion, etc.); 2) an inhospitable environment (hostile workplace, dangerous or hazardous substances); and 3) specific work schedules (night work, split shifts)."[34] We must emphasize the innovations here. When Bernardino Ramazzini published his book on occupational ailments, he ignored fatigue and concentrated on diseases.[35] But these contemporary studies took wellbeing and its absence into account, included fatigue and workers' perceptions of it, and thereby provided a more comprehensive overview of dysfunction and disease.

Gérard Lasfargues was one of the first to analyze "hardship factors" in depth in a detailed report in 2005. He explored 1) the pace of work, in particular the demands of warehouse work, loads and potential effects on different parts of the body, from the neck to the shoulders, from the elbow to the wrist;[36] 2) "exposure to toxic chemicals," their potential effects on health, whether they are cancerous, or otherwise impact the respiratory, dermatologic, digestive or nervous system ...;[37] and 3) work schedules, night work or split shifts and their possible effects on "recovering from physical fatigue and maintaining mental health."[38] A key decision was announced in an official order issued on March 30, 2011, identifying ten categories of "occupational risks to consider in preventing hardship as well as determining eligibility for hardship-related early retirement claims." The categories themselves fell into three groups. The first, "significant physical restrictions," included a) storage and warehouse work involving heavy loads, for example transporting and moving loads, when lifting, putting down, pushing, pulling, carrying or otherwise shifting cargo, requires physical exertion by one or more employees; b) painful positions, defined as those stressing the joints; and c) vibrations from equipment. The second group, "damaging physical setting," involved a) dangerous chemical substances, including dust and vapor; b) working in a compression chamber; c) working in extreme temperatures; and d) noise levels. The third concerned work schedules and the pace of work, taking in a) night work; b) alternating shifts; and c) repetitive motions, with restraints on work pace required by either assembly-line processes or piece work with specific time constraints."[39]

This order outlined specific categories within the three groups. Defining "risk factors" this way was new, and future iterations were even more specific, identifying levels of intensity and determining cut-off points. This enabled employees to establish a "professional prevention account" with certain benefits: earning credits to finance continuing professional development throughout their careers, moving into half-time work without a reduction in salary, or even qualifying for early retirement.[40] Although the benefits were limited and modest, this process opened up the possibility for workers and workplaces to assess and mitigate hardships. By classifying actions and work settings, this system highlighted the increase in scrutiny and identification of work-related injuries.

The categories were surprisingly incomplete, however, despite the addition of so many subgroups. One category of suffering acknowledged in contemporary culture, and even mentioned in the 2006 reports, was left virtually unexamined: that of subjectivity, of "hardship experienced,"[41] of potential "internalized" suffering, of generalized discomfort[42] that may result in life-long maladaptation[43] and long-term disabilities, as the detailed studies of musculoskeletal disorders revealed.[44] In fact, "physical and psychological constraints"[45] discussed in the earliest studies of work-related hardships were pared down to physical constraints in government and institutional inquiries. Clearly, they were concerned only with what could be measured and quantified, and emotional or psychic damage was hard to assess. This gave rise to a paradox; the word "hardship" was validated but the ambiguity and complexity of the fatigues it encompassed were lost. That distinction, however, was crucial: "We cannot assess the cost of only physical and not psychological wear and tear."[46]

Many recent analyses have underlined the importance of other hardships, less visible but present, of our engagement in social networks, initiated by a simple click. There is nothing more psychological, it seems, than this. Antonio Casilli pointed to social media's progressive invasion of our minds and our free time and the collateral damage of anxiety, distress and internal maladjustment it brought: recurrent dissatisfaction; obsession; the influence it has even when the screen is dark. Telework and volunteer activities on the internet typified yet another "hardship": the "arduous duty of being online."[47] There was no doubt that assessing its damage would be difficult, since social media activity complicated the very concept of hardship.

It is unfortunate, however, that one additional restriction was not included in the Labor Code reform of 2018. Four factors were eliminated from the ten that were already established: "painful positions, mechanical vibrations, chemical risks and carrying heavy loads."[48] It is hard to believe that corporate entities would take responsibility for "preventing the entirety of professional risks"[49] and assess all work assignments for degrees of hardship. The Labor Ministry called it "an unrealistic responsibility,"[50] since so many risk factors, from holding static positions to absorbing vibrations, from chemical exposures to heavy loads, are too embedded in our daily work life, too varied to be "validly" measured and too tied to specific conditions. Nevertheless, so many factors related to "a specific regime"[51] were associated with a specific injury or syndrome. This inevitably opened up new discussions and led to renewed and urgent negotiations. Rinse and repeat.

Many personal accounts disseminated their takes on hardship, demonstrating that the phenomenon was widespread and complex. A farm worker talked about pains caused by equipment vibrations: "After a day spent on the tractor, my upper body, my neck hurts, my shoulders hurt." "I feel like I have a stiff neck after a day spending ten or twelve hours on the tractor." And let's not forget tired legs. "If the work weren't hard on us, we wouldn't feel any pain," a foreman observed.[52] Anaïs Dallier, a roofer at Boisbluche Frères in the Orne, worked in a trade only recently open to women. She described a variety of aches and pains: "The young woman is only thirty years old but has been working in construction for almost twelve years. Regarding the occupational hardship quotient, she reports recurrent pain associated with contorting her body into certain positions and doesn't think she will be able to last more than two additional years in this job."[53] A home health aide who suffered from painful joints emphasized that the women who did this job often got the least recognition: "I've had a lot of difficult cases and that's how I dislocated my shoulder."[54] Finally, a Metro driver observed that his arduous work was not appreciated or rewarded as it had been in the past: "We spend seven hours a day driving in a tunnel. When you drive for six hours on the highway, how do you feel at the end? Here, there's no daylight, the noise makes us crazy and we have to be hyper-aware at every station. Not a hardship job, eh?"[55]

These accounts described many different kinds of occupational hardships, and even though they had been officially acknowledged, with more workers testifying to the havoc wreaked on their bodies and minds, hardship still had to be more clearly defined and studied. The feelings it unleashed were deeper, harsher and more acute.

It became impossible to overlook changes that affected the shape of work itself, in particular the immediate environment. We were investigating no longer the effect of restricted movement but the impact of signals, not the narrow range of gestures but the funneling of information. A significant shift occurred in factory work in the last decades of the twentieth century: "Computer-driven automation and software control systems … have been growing since the 1980s."[56] The interface of humans and machines has been permanently changed: the human touch "classically" associated with machinery, physical agility, precision or strength ceded its place to digital networks and an operator's slight pressure on a button, the click on an icon, or the invisible power of command and control. Factory work, in other words, began taking the "route of demanualization,"[57] where the input of commands took the place of physical exertion and workers' attention was exercised more than their muscles. Thierry Pillon and François Vatin, in their *Traité de sociologie du travail* [Treatise on the sociology of work], described this succinctly as a "process of abstraction."[58] Even the workplace lexicon had changed; movement, gesture, energy and motor coordination were disappearing from ergonomic studies[59] in favor of cognition, chrono-biology, code, signal, communication and the human–computer interface.[60]

The toll of work was no longer directly physical; it was mental. The difficulty of a job was judged by the amount of information the operator had to process: "The human brain can make only a limited number of conscious decisions per minute, approximately sixty to eighty."[61] The problems this caused were more psychological than physiological, especially when automated systems performed a variety of operations and processed routine commands and inputs, but could also be programmed to respond to emergencies and chaotic situations that brought together risk, danger and warning signals. This was the case for aircraft, other transport, integrated networks, and the chemical and power industries, for example. The human operators' response became a priority, and their attentiveness, preparation and guidance were essential. Johan Wilhelm Hendrik Kalsbeek's 1971 study of pilots in computer-assisted aircraft revealed that automation alone did not guarantee safety: "We must take into account the effects of distraction, drugs, fatigue, competition and anxiety on pilots' readiness."[62] The barriers between information and reaction were higher and more far-reaching. The fatigue threshold was being shattered. The consciousness of hazards had grown. The supposedly transparent workings of the "cyber-body" had been internalized, psychologized and diversified more than ever before. Psychological pressures revealed ever more acutely the difficulty of accounting for each person's strengths and weaknesses.

From stress to burn out

The role played by mental health in the culture of everyday life and at work has grown for several decades. One of the first books on the subject, *Stress au travail*,[63] published in 1983, was followed by almost seventy others in French with similar titles – and in English almost twice that number.[64] The trend marked a distinct change in direction in industrial engineering, from the concept of "the human motor," which underpinned "the scientific basis of occupational studies,"[65] and their "objective" criteria, assessing everything from movement to diet, from metabolism to scheduling, and from equipment to organizations. These were superseded by studies on the "psychopathology of work,"[66] and more recently by strategies to "banish occupational fatigue,"[67] focused on "personal," "emotional" or "mental" factors rather than "organic" ones. More and more survey results supported this point of view: "Hardship at work is not new, but it has changed: psychological stress is becoming more unbearable than fatigue and physical wear and tear."[68]

New narratives took hold: "the agony of employees who don't measure up," workers who suffer from "restrictions on their time, the pace of work, the lack of training, apprenticeships, expertise and certifications."[69] This all led to a fatigue that devolved into exhaustion. Rejecting "unbearable situations"[70] became more common, along with the recognition in the 1960s of "psychosomatic" distress, which took into account how frustrations, failures and risks deepened feelings of hopelessness but rarely offered explanations or solutions. The word "suffering" itself was revealing, suggesting "internalized" assaults on personal integrity and identity. It also inspired institutional solutions, such as the development of medical or therapeutic services focused specifically on treating "work-related suffering."[71] More cases came to light after the 1980s and 1990s, involving a range of employees, from laborer to supervisor, from secretary to apprentice, from executives to underlings. The lexicon changed too, favoring the use of "employee" or "staff" over "worker" or "laborer," and thereby illustrating how attention had shifted away from the physical.[72] For instance, Mr B. was interviewed at a low point in his career and his health, "morose, hunched over and depressed," a certified lathe operator who had tried and failed at several jobs, as a technician at the town hall and working in the town cemetery. He was demoted several times because he was seen as "incapable" of doing the work, criticized for his slowness and shunned after he "denounced," apparently with good cause, failures in the administration. Mr B.'s self-confidence had evaporated; he constantly felt weak and suffered from high blood pressure that went untreated.[73] Monique was another example. Her job as a human resource officer in a company that processed raw materials for pharmaceuticals became progressively more demanding when her employer was bought out by another firm. She described a blizzard of new and more complex responsibilities, such as handling a new computer system, dealing with unexpected inventories, "toxic" inspection visits, and long-distance business trips. In addition, she felt unappreciated by the new management as she, a single parent, juggled this heavier work load: "Monique gradually began waking up in the middle of weekend nights … going over her to-do list for Monday." Eventually, she was "so exhausted" that hospitalization was being considered.[74]

Several different psychological "mechanisms" were at play in each of the cases, pointing to new pieces of evidence. Each one revealed how neither feeling overwhelmed and overworked nor personal failings formed the only factor. The lack of appreciation had to be factored in because it was a major source of frustration and, in particular, was expressed by the employees themselves, who believed that they needed and deserved recognition and became even more deeply and dangerously fatigued when recognition was withheld. The key was the negativity, the stymieing of individual engagement and potential. The damage was aggravated and feelings of personal affront intensified as twentieth-century workers gradually gained a sense of self that prioritized autonomy, individualization and personal space. Any rejection of autonomy was perceived as a personal attack; resistance, whether overt or covert, was seen as valid and necessary. Christophe Dejours wrote defiantly: "This book is an act of rebellion against all types of condescension and disrespect for subjectivity, whatever they may be."[75]

Clearly, these "breaking points" were different from the examples of excess and overwork that had been recorded and studied since the end of the nineteenth century. The danger came not simply from the increasing work demands that seemed to multiply overnight or the dizzying pace of work. Instead, the threats were inherent in workers' attempts to deal constructively with them. So many obstacles thwarted personal decision-making and made "doing" a dead-end. So many limits to individual agency lined the route to exhaustion. A key shift was that "dependencies" that used to be tolerated were no longer accepted; nor were the conventional or mutually accepted "brakes" on autonomy. "Harassment" was the first sign of this change. This element of interpersonal relations was long overlooked and was given an official presence and legal definition only in the 1990s, defined as "abusive behavior that, through systematically repeated words, actions, behavior and attitudes, is meant to degrade the living and/or working conditions of an individual (the target of the harassment)."[76] Undoubtedly, harassment was an aspect of traditionally dominating behavior that had long been ignored and quietly tolerated, but it was now explicitly and seriously penalized. This surely pointed to the growing influence of psychology and was the next step in the affirmation of individual identity and an additional source of pain when ignored. More profoundly, acknowledging the existence and scope of harassment was not a simple reference to a "want" that was made explicit but the necessary prerequisite of a "want" that was thwarted.

The exposure of these kinds of cases, and their "seriousness," has risen sharply in recent years, along with recognition of the fatigue that accompanies them. For example, in July 2019, "young sales assistants denounced their working conditions," protesting that they "were tormented in clothing boutiques and shoe shops in Maine-et-Loire, subjected to verbal abuse, sexual banter and all kinds of humiliations from their bosses, as well as being overworked for years."[77] Employees in a small business were the targets of "individual harassment" intended to "reinforce the power" of the owners.[78] University instructors stopped work and took "long periods of time off" to protest their isolation and ostracization.[79] The concept of harassment and its legal definition attested to how much had changed in "the way employees view certain work situations."[80]

This concept could then be applied to different situations, not simply the abuse of power but also the impossibility of "self-fulfillment," the barriers to career advancement, the lack of "expected rewards,"[81] and the disappearance of long-term goals and aspirations. In other words, individuals confronted the reality of failing to achieve their potential. More surveys were launched, underlining the magnitude and diversity of these injuries and emphasizing a key point about work in the twentieth century: it was not simply that physical fatigue invaded and occupied our mental space. Psychological fatigue also invaded our bodies so aggressively that it broke us. In fact, "broken spirits" or "breakdowns" are among the most popular metaphors of contemporary fatigue.

What was new about this was a concept that had been completely re-envisioned. It identified the end point: a physical and mental breakdown, chronic prostration, and the most extreme and essential annihilation. In 1980, Herbert Freudenberger was the first to give a description and name to this phenomenon: "occupational exhaustion" or "burn out." He illustrated the definition with an indelible image: a person who "is shattered" like a "blown-out light bulb."[82] He cited several examples of different people with one thing in common: an unbridgeable gulf between "the endless stream of ideas in their minds"[83] and the impossibility of bringing them to fruition, being blocked at the "dead end" of a lifelong ambition, until a moment of abrupt sudden collapse. For instance, "Georges," the "director of a big international company," had to deal with "challenging contracts" and travel to almost twenty different countries on business. He normally exuded "unstoppable energy" and unmatchable enthusiasm, but he abruptly came down to earth in an English pub, feeling lost and hopeless: "He realized that something awful had happened, and he thought that he had either suffered a heart attack or lost his mind."[84] Another example were volunteers who devoted themselves "body and soul" to helping others in need, who were persistent and single-minded but ended up being overwhelmed by their responsibilities and their powerlessness, emotionally battered and feeling like frauds.[85] Freudenberger's description of "burn out" was versatile enough to be recognized by "36 percent of employees in 2017 who say they have already experienced an episode of burn out."[86] Moreover, it was precise enough to capture feelings of personal "impotence": "When a person's self-esteem is damaged, the individual cannot concentrate or focus on work; the mind and sometimes the body slips into a skid and the machinery is out of order. The symptoms are emotional, physical, cognitive, behavioral and motivational."[87]

In 2016, the Académie de médecine reviewed possible causes and zeroed in on assaults on personal integrity such as "work demands, emotional demands, a lack of autonomy, the absence of social support and recognition, clashes of values, and insecurity of work and the job market."[88] Certainly the list contained no new "pressures," but the symptoms were identified and interpreted differently.[89]

More cases and examples came to light, demonstrating that physicians as well as employees were more aware of the problem, so "they discussed it more."[90] The reach of burn out, and the effects it had on our lives, kept expanding and even became commonplace. In fact, the word "stress" was the first choice of 78 percent of employees when they were asked to describe their work.[91]

Management's role

However, beyond individual sensitivity that was on the alert for it, and beyond the longstanding existence of abuses of power understood in a new light, other developments have taken place; changes in the nature of work itself, its organization and its conditions exacerbated the gap between workers' expectations and their job reality. First of all, the expansion of computerization in the workplace and the surveillance, or even oppression, it enabled added to workers' sense of subjection and powerlessness. The "pickers" fulfilling orders in the Amazon warehouse talked about being constantly tethered to digital monitoring, tracking and timing their every move in a way that heightened feelings of anxiety and fatigue: "The algorithms monitor everyone's location at all times, calculate the amount of time each employee takes to perform a task and flags any time spent not working."[92]

The formula captured every movement, from beginning to end, and the surveillance infiltrated everything, even workers' minds, trapped inside a panopticon, pursued by invisible controlling forces, setting off an endless competition with other employees and with oneself, such that workers were on a constantly moving treadmill of ever higher quotas. "The managers can watch their subordinates at a distance, and the platform facilitates competition among co-workers who are encouraged to supervise, discipline and inform on their peers."[93]

In a report about working conditions on the French railway system, a "train driver" said that he felt under constant surveillance, bombarded by signals, threatened by the smallest lapse in judgment, discombobulated by shift work, and generally exhausted as the stresses piled up: "Your personal life, the whole family's life, revolves around the schedule and its challenges. It's that way for your whole career. All the so-called benefits, including early retirement, are just the flip side of this miserable coin."[94]

Studies repeatedly showed that computerization of work "results in a faster pace, increased workload, and more hardship."[95] The "digital slave" generation[96] are independent contractors who work for different "platforms" whose proprietors remain unknown, never seen or heard. They earn their living this way, driven by a desire for autonomy but dependent on wages and working conditions in which they have no input and where the final decisions are taken elsewhere. For instance, the men and women working for Deliveroo, the restaurant delivery service, work over sixty hours a week and say they feel like "prisoners."[97] The "juice team"[98] servicing electric rental scooters work the night shift from 7 p.m. to 8 a.m.[99] "On-demand" interpreters make themselves available by phone, never knowing when a call might come or what resources they will need;[100] they work with no guarantee of benefits or job security.[101] These working conditions are specific to independent contractors and to certain occupations, certainly, but they presage the future of work, where digital applications and their flexibility conceal a terrible dependency under a veneer of freedom.

Sometimes changing job parameters has had unintended and unwanted consequences. One prime example is hospital care, faced with rising costs but subjected to the eternal public obsession of holding down expenses and avoiding increases, or minimizing additions, to government debt. In December 2019, "one out of every two doctors"[102] claimed to be exhausted and blamed hospital managers, who were overly rigid and made poor decisions, especially by cutting back on personnel and trying to fill every bed. One physician observed: "My department has lost staff. The nurses are fed up and are quitting one after another."[103] Another commented that "Doctors talk about patients and treatments; the administration talks deficits and budgets."[104] Power that had long been in the hands of medical staff has been transferred to "the managers" in the "pivot to management"[105] in today's economy, to the extent that patient intake has been restricted to lower the costs of staff salaries more effectively: "Basically, the administrators at the top think in terms of patient flow,"[106] while medical staff are thinking in terms of patient care, which is variable and sometimes very intensive. For hospital staff, the stringent quotas sparked frustration and a sense of professional betrayal.

It is impossible to overlook the priorities and managerial style of multinational corporations, putting profits above all else, and the endless series of mergers, acquisitions and offshoring that result in layoffs, together with anxiety, depression, job loss or insecurity in the workforce.[107] For example, after learning that her employer, Bombardier, was going to be acquired by Alstom, Laetitia, an electrician, suffered waves of anxiety, since the two corporations were planning to eliminate "redundant" positions. "I'm stressed out. I've been a 'temp' since 2004, with seven short-term contracts at Bombardier and two at Alstom. What are they going to do with us?"[108] Her fears are widespread, in fact, since 40 percent of French workers[109] are worried about losing their jobs and their income. As Alain Supiot wrote, about the epidemic of mergers, acquisitions and "right-sizing": "All these innovations have lured businesses into toxic short-term thinking and unleashed pain on their workforce in an onslaught of depression and false promises."[110]

We cannot overlook situations where harassment was part of corporate reshuffling. The accusation in the trial of France Telecom executives in 2019 is a prime example. They were sued over their implementation of the controversial "Next" reorganization plan intended to rescue the "Orange" subsidiary, which involved cutting "22,000 jobs from the total of 120,000, or approximately one of every six employees, and transferring or reassigning 10,000 additional employees."[111] The plan was even more controversial, since the targeted employees had secure contracts. But the executives pressed on because they saw the downsizing as "necessary": "They were obsessed with hitting their numbers."[112] This led to psychological abuse and harassment. As the chief executive said, memorably, on October 20, 2006: "I will get them out one way or another – through the door or out the window."[113] The corporate reorganization kept on course, with no input from the affected sectors; some employees were transferred, others got negative work evaluations and still others were demoted. People were deeply wounded, feeling helpless and humiliated. One employee confessed she felt like a loser: "What really gets me is that my career is at a dead end."[114]

The physician on site, Monique Fraysse-Guiglini, attested to the damage. There was an increase in "anxiety or depressive episodes, sleep disturbances, loss of appetite and addictions," with a 45 percent rise in infirmary visits between 2008 and 2009.[115] A survey administered in

2009 zeroed in on employees' loss of self-esteem when their "pride in being on the France-Telecom team" cratered from a high of 95 percent to a low of 39 percent.[116] "They are playing with our lives,"[117] employees protested, highlighting the damage done to their sense of self. "They make you lose confidence and, on top of that, you blame yourself."[118] A number of suicides occurred among the staff, as asserted at the trial – "one every week." Executives were found guilty and sentenced to prison, the judgment underlining the significance and reality of workplace harassment[119] and the damage inflicted by "stress and pressure."[120] All in all, this illustrates the major shift from physical to mental suffering. Our understanding of injury has changed significantly, as have our personal criteria.

Why are we tired every day?

We now saw a gradual change in management strategies, moving away from the top-down formulas to a new relaxing of strictures. "Encourage a certain amount of individual initiative";[121] "Factor in employees' career goals";[122] "Foster autonomy among colleagues";[123] "Show your appreciation."[124] A number of "leaders" saw the error of their ways and "repented," confessing to being "a bad boss," "oppressive," "lacking empathy" or "being a rage machine" too often.[125] These admissions were revelatory, focused on dominance that is now considered "problematic," and, if they were followed up with constructive action, they attested to the growing desire for individual recognition coming from subordinates, a testament to the suffering they experienced in an overly restrictive work environment. This seemed to show how serious the loss of independence was.

Domination was criticized and rejected here, as was harassment, shifting the balance toward a measure of self-determination for employees. Workplace blogs echoed that notion: "You are your own boss. Anything else is a grotesque and childish fantasy. Only your intelligence and experience count."[126] The roots of fatigue were traced back to specific situations: a power imbalance; an affront to identity. Popular magazines acknowledged the danger: "Because you are naturally kind and generous, you are constantly giving of yourself. But that can leave you exhausted and empty, with nothing left for the precious person you are."[127]

The context was clear even if the details had changed and the message was less superficial than it might appear. The growth of consumer society has spawned a "mystique of freedom and achievement."[128] A number of analyses of the dynamics of psychic affirmation have described how the "hypermodern" person has become the "hypertrophied person"[129] with "no sense of group solidarity,"[130] always the reference point and the center of attention. The self is a daily, quasi-novelistic obsession: "Let's get back to my topic, which is me. It may not be particularly interesting, but it's my topic."[131] A recent publicity campaign by L'Oréal made the point in the text accompanying the images of their line of beauty products: "Because I deserve it!" and "Because you deserve it!"[132] In this way, the value of the object was transferred to the person and the quality of the product was equated to the superiority of the person, based on a belief that was widely shared, if only implicitly: if acquiring the product is worthwhile, it is because I am worth it. Individual qualities superseded those of the consumer goods themselves.

This individual self-affirmation conflicted with managerial styles that were not exclusively based on gentle persuasion and doling out limited freedoms. Again, that led to friction, disappointment and episodes of exhaustion:

> On one side, all-powerful consumers are encouraged to express themselves through their choices, their individuality and uniqueness. On the other side, run-of-the-mill employees are encouraged not to express themselves. [Their] psychological value is so diminished that they are only capable of submission. This leads to a head-on collision between the new "My-Ego" culture of the cyber-consumer and the anonymous culture of the "Everyman."[133]

The more ordinary and usual result of this sort of opposition, as banal as it is expected, revealed the idealized self inevitably confronted by its impossible end point: an identity that was limited, thwarted or dreamed. There have been so many "victims" of the phenomenon, which occurred at all ages and in every social class. To the neglected employee's burn out, we can add those of the child, the adolescent, the student, the researcher, the relative, the entrepreneur, the lover and the athlete. "An unspoken malaise is eating away at athletes,"[134] many of whom complained of being "trained like robots."[135] People feel something is missing; they sense a gap between attempting and achieving, between what they actually "are" and what they "thought." The advice columnist counseled "burnt-out lovers": "You are feeling frustrated; things aren't as you wish they were."[136] Other advisors reassured members of a burnt-out family: "This is the clash between how parents imagined their family life and the reality of it."[137]

This also gave ammunition to people who wanted to regain their freedom in a marriage, for example. Women in a relationship frequently pointed to "mental stress" and the implied subjugation and abuse of power has been borne out by statistics: in 2010, women reported performing 71 percent of household chores and 65 percent of the parenting.[138] The claims centered on fatigue and the overwhelming psychological strain that permeated every aspect of their lives: "It's pernicious because it's always on my mind. It affects my sleep. It's hard to concentrate at work."[139] When Emma, an illustrator and blogger, posted a sketch of a "mental load" on her blog with the ironic slangy caption "Should've asked," she got positive feedback from hundreds of thousands of readers.[140]

The symptoms can be subtle, however. Not every episode of burn out announced itself dramatically, with the victim going down in flames. Some burn outs were low-key, penetrating, anxiety-provoking, periodic and variable. Some people were constantly on the alert, checking their moods, their behavior, their reactions, inventorying physical as well as mental shifts, watching for blips on their mental radar and obstacles in their path. Some protagonists in contemporary literature incarnate this, such as the main character in Michael Delisle's *Palais de la fatigue* [The palace of fatigue], whose apparently ordinary experiences, always frustrating and repeated every day, center on a lack, a gap, an overreliance on someone, whether it is a remote and inaccessible teacher or well-meaning but interfering friends. His constant refrain is "Why can't I live my life my way?"[141] The novelist Michel Houellebecq created a character who cannot recover his inner fortitude, "crushed" by the unbridgeable gulf between his plans and reality and condemned to a "serotonin" that barely sustains him: "His friends from student days, really the only true friends one makes, would never survive his passage into adulthood. You avoid the friends of younger years to avoid being confronted by witnesses to your dashed hopes, to the proof of your own crushing."[142]

Jean Clair evoked more prosaically the minor insults of everyday life and how they turned, also prosaically, into an interminable fatigue: "The odd lassitude that pervades us every night, leaves us knocked out and exhausted for hours on end. What sin condemns us to this prostration every day? What old debt that we never repaid deprives us of our wits, lulls us into slumber, as if we were pricked by the evil fairy?"[143]

This is nothing more that the culmination of what the Enlightenment thinkers had uncovered, the "self" that is more autonomous and constantly reminded of its own limitations.[144] Nowadays that exploration is more systematic and the self is buried deeper, is more complex, to the point that affirming its existence is accompanied by an even more acute sense of inadequacy. *Philosophie Magazine* posed the question that was so "urgent" it was put on the front cover in November 2019: "Why are we so tired?"[145] The replies kept coming. One of the first dealt with overwork, technical demands, speed-ups, the constant innovations of equipment, the spread of digital technology, the trend toward "instant everything" and "hyperconnectivity."[146] It all led to "excess vitality" in contemporary society.[147] But although societies learned to adapt to the demands of their machines, to foster mediation and fluidity, a second reply seemed more to the point: that is, the close confrontation with a hypertrophied self, that being whose new importance condemns it to constant testing of the limits, as well as constant reinvention.[148] Fatigue has become as persistent as it is natural, as real as it is banal, as familiar as it is inconvenient, a silent, unshakable presence in our lives, a penetrating and unfamiliar intruder, a "*fatigo ergo sum*"[149] that clings onto a life perceived as demanding and different. We suffer from the inability to accept any power over us or to accept any restrictions. Also, obviously, "there is fatigue. Though we don't mention it often, it rules almost everyone's lives. It forces us to make certain choices, abandon certain endeavors, and perceive things a certain way."[150] The connection with our innermost selves looms large, along with a persistent feeling of resistance and an internal agitation that is more pressing than ever. Emmanuel Levinas wrote: "boredom, fatigue, before we perceive them consciously, they are rejections of life in general … Lassitude is an impossible rejection of the incontrovertible necessity to exist."[151] This is a major insight about today's intense psychologization that has irrevocably altered the feeling of persistent and repeated tormented existence.

Escaping the limits or acknowledging them?

The number of protests and reactions has kept increasing, meant to overcome feelings of an inner void, and to restore our integrity. When *Philosophie Magazine* asked the burning question: "Why are we so fatigued?" on its cover,[152] another magazine, *Santé*, gave an equally contemporary answer in December 2019 under the rubric "This concerns me": "Let's get rid of fatigue."[153] This early New Year's resolution was intended to free us from an "unbearable" (and apparently new) condition. The magazines' questions and answers revealed that the phenomenon was, simultaneously, a firm belief, a discovery and a pressing issue: a perception of great pressure and a determination to alleviate it. This only proved, however, that our perceptions and our criticisms continue to grow.

Our obsession with pharmaceuticals is persistent and cannot be extirpated. The prescription drug market tripled between 1990 and 2017.[154] This includes both antibiotics and anti-anxiety medications, treatments that ease our pain as well as those that relieve fatigue and other ailments. The dream of stimulants will never die, and now they are developed by chemical processes that are more "technical" and "marketable." This is why we hear about formulas that will reinforce our stamina and "overcome" all obstacles: "The conditions of modern life, the competition and rivalry among applicants for a job and students for a diploma, striving for success, for professional recognition or emotional fulfillment, make it necessary to take revivifying and stimulating tonics."[155]

This is why we read constantly about drug use in sports, the clandestine and frantic attempts to help high-performing athletes avoid fatigue with a magic pill and the determined official testing regimes to detect and prevent these infractions.[156]

Every day we deal with the monotonous fatigues and exhaustion of our lives, but in the most recent decades this has subtly changed. The physical pain and suffering have not been eliminated, but psychological factors have again predominated and been reformulated. That is the goal of "moderation" in all things, including hardship. Many new publications offer advice that targets our minds and our emotions, our choices and our feelings, focusing on "relaxation," "balance" and "self-care." The headlines and the names of these popular magazines give a sense of it: *Breathe: take time for yourself,*[157] *In the moment: because your self cannot wait,*[158] *DNA, the basics: the guide to wellbeing every day,*[159] *Feelings and health: the body, the mind, the world.*[160] Stress is at the heart of these efforts, just as the rejection of mental strains[161] that might endanger male–female equality is central to women's self-affirmation.

Eliminating strain is the first priority, such as the regular "breaks" Cédric Villani proposed in order to take his mind off research that was too taxing: "I let my mind wander. For example, I take a ten-minute break where I relax and forget about everything else. My body relaxes too and this refreshes me down to the cellular level."[162] Anaïs Vanel suggested "escaping," as she did when she left her editorial office in Paris to go surfing around the world, and thereby finding "the source of my fatigue."[163] In addition to "letting go" and "unplugging," a mental reorientation is necessary to focus on our internal spaces, to decode the signals, zero in on tensions, and identify the pain.

We have to be vigilant to "beat fatigue by knowing how to interpret our body's signals."[164] Now a new vision merges a digital information model with the organic one, emphasizing connections, coding, interrelations and paying attention to consciousness and potential messages, or sensitivity and necessary controls – an endless network where "flesh" itself is psychologized through a system of coordination, convergence, and alarm signals. All of this is wrapped up in a single package. Some absolutely trivial recommendations have been published, such as clarifying the "perception of stress" with fourteen questions,[165] "freeing the mind" with "ten steps,"[166] or choosing five ways to "listen to our emotions."[167] Mantras and breathing exercises are also an option, like the ones described in *Sens et santé* [Consciousness and health]: "Start by taking one quiet minute. Breathe in calmness and breathe out stress. Breathe in energy and breathe out fatigue."[168] These are minimal solutions to major problems, of course, and entirely superficial. But at least they respond to a specific need: to restore a holistic sense of oneself by stimulating one's senses and recovering a feeling of wholeness and uniqueness. In other words, the point is to repair the breaches in the self, confronting the insults and assaults of the outside world. "When the world that surrounds us becomes oppressive and frenetic, we can find tranquility and calm by retreating into our internal space."[169]

This is entirely different from the nineteenth century, when restorative advice prioritized action, exercises, and engagement with the outside world.[170] The emphasis has changed and now centers on the self, even in encounters with the outside world. Space is a key word, and recommendations focus on how to make the most of it: "Losing myself in nature. Sitting cross-legged, I let the place, the distance and the silence envelop me. Slow down, thanks to Mother Nature – far from stress, traffic and to-do lists. I am happy!"[171]

This is entirely different from other, relatively new approaches that are not calming and instead are meant to help us perceive our internal space more clearly, test our limits and live more intensely. The point is to recover a sense of self, even through pain and strenuous exertion. A recent issue of *Anthropologie de l'effort* [Anthrophology of exertion] claims: "When we confront our limits, we transform the individual."[172] Many examples of experiences paradoxically show that "tiring" activities enhance our sense of self. "Extreme sports," "extreme mountaineering," "extreme caving" and "extreme sailing" are all exceptional activities that test our limits, from mountain peaks to oceans, from cliffsides to incredible climbs, from unheard-of routes to tricky itineraries. A number of sociologists have identified this trend as a new form of leisure: confronting dangers and fatal risks that require the testing of autonomy, intelligence, bravery and perseverance.[173] Recent examples of extreme adventures include the "Madman's Diagonal" on Reunion Island, the "Sand Marathon" in Morocco, the "Ultra Trail at Mont Blanc" and the "Athens–Sparta non-stop in thirty-five hours."[174] Mike Horn wrote a best-selling book about his endurance test: "succeeding where no one had before: going around the world at the equator."[175] An almost unimaginable event, the "Double Deca Iron Ultra-Triathalon," was held in Mexico in 1998. It included swimming for 76 kilometers, cycling for 3,600 kilometers and running for 844 kilometers.[176]

The adventures are a way to extend what the Enlightenment thinkers had invented[177] but pushed to the extreme, exploits promising self-possession all the way to infinity. Fatigue turns into pleasure and the control of one's senses. There are many different reactions, clearly, to the challenge, but the main point is the same: from the experience of the void to the sensation of fulfillment and from relaxation to sensory overload. The goal is always to regain or restore autonomy.

We must reconsider the fatigue that oppresses our daily lives. It is more trivial, more ordinary and more intensely felt nowadays, because it threatens us more than ever and jeopardizes our sense of self. That is why there are more recommendations, new and unusual ones, to accept and even collaborate with fatigue. It is so pervasive that, instead of fighting it, we adjust to it; we choose flexibility over firmness in order to preserve our identity or even strengthen it. Éric Fiat recommended a particular defense mechanism with consciousness as well as attentiveness, being eternally vigilant, but calm and relaxed:

> In any case, fatigue is so manifold that you cannot beat it like an enemy that infiltrates everywhere … I suggest you leave combat metaphors behind and become the reed in the La Fontaine fable. Some people want to be the sturdy oak. The problem is that, when the wind blows, the oak resists it and is uprooted at the end. Be the reed, and accept fatigue.[178]

This reversal emphasized the role of the internal, its work, its effects and the dynamic relation that is always present in our contemporary Western society, far from a tradition that limits fatigue to our bodies. This is a distinct change, and in the deepest recesses of our minds, where fatigue multiplies and festers, we acknowledge fatigue as a way of life that is always with us. Hence, we have to collaborate with it. Fatigue, the weakness that pervades us, the dissatisfaction we cannot name and the gap that is never filled, has become a way of life today.

AFTERWORD

30

Surprises and "Viral" Dangers

The Covid-19 pandemic that suddenly appeared and rapidly spread at the end of 2019 has disrupted our daily lives and changed behavior on a grand scale: lockdowns in some affected areas, postponements and cancellations of countless activities, restriction of interpersonal actions and the prompting of people to take protective measures. The end of the first wave of the pandemic prolonged hesitations and difficulties. Restarting businesses and social life did not do away with fear and anxiety. A pervasive sense of powerlessness remained. The impact on fatigue seems enormous: new sources of exhaustion; the interpenetration of fear and tiredness; the elimination of familiar gestures; the substitution of other less tactile gestures and more cautious behavior; and clear demarcation of physical spaces between people, the so-called social distancing. The "time before" seems very distant now. It is a vague memory; familiar landmarks have been moved, space and time transformed, and new, unusual and discomfiting behaviors are required. Our sense of physical vulnerability was heightened by the pandemic measures in place.

Which of these changes are relevant to the topic of this book? Has our modern understanding of fatigue been disrupted? Has the way we think about it or the way we represent it lost its relevance? We need to answer so many questions to understand the import of our lives today.

A new factor was certainly the role played by "essential workers" such as the doctors and nurses, who were applauded, thanked, and noticed more than ever before. They seem to have taken the place of the defenders and protectors, the soldiers and knights, of medieval times.[1] Also new were the community-wide protective measures, provoking their own unexpected fatigues, and, as in other periods in history, certain obligatory actions or articles of clothing.[2] New too were the methods of communication we relied on, in our self- or alternately imposed quarantines, to reach out across great distances and show up on multiple networks and screens. But this digital mediation made exchanges more arduous and more ponderous, when modernity had rendered them fluid and easy. There were so many actions, reactions and new modes of communication that the number of obstacles and glitches rose along with them.

Nevertheless, we have to acknowledge the obvious continuities. Fatigue is persistent now, exactly as it was before, connected to the culture of people who are acutely attuned to their feelings, their senses, their experiences and actions. If we recognize the many guises of fatigue, we find that beyond the explicitly physical factors are less visible ones, of "internal" symptoms, emotions and questions linked to that same culture that elevates the psyche to an ever more central role, even if we don't consciously acknowledge it. When we venture into unfamiliar territory and abandon well-established traditions, we incorporate new elements into our fatigue and highlight its diversity and depth. The pandemic has brought to light certain perceptions and feelings without substantively changing our recent understanding of the sources of fatigue and exhaustion.

Covid-19 has overturned many of our customs and habits, making public health threats a daily occurrence and forcing us to experience space and time differently, with a new array of difficulties. Even so, the idea of fatigue has not really changed.

Health-care workers and exhaustion

Health-care workers are foremost in our minds today. This is even more remarkable since the French health-care system is operating under severe budget restraints. Cutbacks and restrictions were protested vigorously when they were put in place. Before the outbreak of the pandemic, "one in every two physicians"[3] practicing in a hospital reported that they were exhausted and decried the lack of supplies and equipment, the shortage of staff and the cutbacks in services. The criticism inevitably resurfaced because of the obvious strains on the system during the pandemic, reigniting "the anger that we had sounded the alarm so long ago, in vain, about the lack of equipment and personnel, [and] no one ever paid attention. Now that Covid-19 is battering the entire country ..."[4] There have even been shortages of protective equipment, affecting medical workers' ability to act, sparking vigilance, fear and insecurity among emergency staff: "On the whole, health-care workers aren't complaining. Except about the supplies. The lack of masks and of single-use gowns is very upsetting. And it is making them angry ... As soon as the health-care teams get the right protective gear, the tension subsides."[5] Health-care services had to be quickly reorganized to deal with the health emergency, with infusions of funding, the hiring of more staff, and the shifting of patients from one severely affected area to others that were less under strain. In the "saturated" regions, "overtime hours exploded, as did lack of sleep"[6] for the staff working around the clock. Community recognition for health-care workers' sacrifices became a nightly ritual at 8 p.m., with people standing at their open windows or on their balconies and applauding.

This experience is clarifying our idea of fatigue, of being worn out and exhausted. In light of recent events, our understanding and feelings about it have shifted. The categories of suffering have expanded, along with the way it is discussed and the people it affects. Physical exertion is certainly still a key factor:

> At 8 p.m. an ambulance full of patients arrives. Impossible to stop working before 2 a.m. We are on auto-pilot, going through the usual routine of dressing and undressing patients, questioning them, examining them, taking oxygen readings and blood samples. We run in every direction, cubicle after cubicle, all fifteen of us on the team, at a minimum ... You can see the fatigue on everyone's face.[7]

The descriptions captured the look, feel and sense of the experience. "Our auto-pilot takes over in routine tasks but, as we walk along the hallways, we are weighed down. Stunned, wandering, a little lost."[8]

Still, it is impossible not to go further than these eye-witness accounts. There is a more intimate network of tensions within fatigue, influenced by attitudes and relationships. These may usually be overlooked, but they have gained more emotional weight and mental affect and therefore directly influence our perceptions of hardship. We feel a sense of urgency to control the disease quickly, with snap decisions piling up, emotions surging in the face of the illness, fear for other people, fear for oneself, one's daily life taken over by the demands of work. These all play a role. Exhaustion compounds the feelings. Uncertainty, and complications take hold over the long term. The role of individuation is new, as is the increasing importance of the views of the people involved. That represents "real life." Difficulties are expressed. Problems are voiced. The newspapers prioritize personal accounts. *Le Monde* publishes "The diary of the lab coats." *Liberation* publishes "The health-care workers' crisis journal." More than ever, the pandemic brings to light what writers in previous decades had implied about fatigue, its personalization and its complexity.

The feeling of holding back and of restrictions on actions intensifies as the pandemic rages on, and fatigue increases as well, permeating everything. First of all, we are dealing with a mysterious disease and an unknown enemy: "We were overwhelmed by intense waves of anguish that we each had to deal with in our own way."[9] There was a sense that failure lurked around every corner; we had to navigate unexpected turns of events, and we felt surges of compassion. Because of this, "stress" is a constant companion: "We were stunned at how quickly patients took a turn for the worse. It's very stressful because this is when we risk losing them. The pressure, we'll pay for it afterward. Health-care workers really risk suffering post-traumatic stress, from any and every job."[10]

Since the 1980s, care work has been used as an example and even as a symbol of how the complexity of psychological factors affected us. The health-care field is the model for professional burn out; staff are clearly vulnerable to personal crises and "breakdowns." In fact, these symptoms were first identified among health-care workers: "Studying members in these professional categories led us to conclude that repeated exposure to pain and to failure are determinants of the syndrome known as professional exhaustion."[11] The experiences of staff caring for Covid-19 patients confirms this, displaying the hundred faces of fatigue in symptoms that are assessed more accurately nowadays. It is associated with pervasive fear, unclear prognoses, feelings of helplessness, and an unwelcome invasion of our mental space. We read descriptions of a punishing atmosphere that permeates daily lives and fills every moment: "The epidemic indirectly contaminates everything … There are no 'days off,'"[12] says a doctor in an emergency department in Paris. "I have no time to rest, even if I'm taking the required 'safety rest' … Real relaxation doesn't exist any longer,"[13] adds a resident physician in Besançon. Sleep itself is disturbed, and elusive: "I could not fall asleep during the night of March 18th. Usually, I can compartmentalize my emotions."[14]

This is a way of life in which everything narrows down, and our struggle, perhaps in vain, against overwhelming odds opens up fissures in our solidly armored identity. This and the extent of care workers' efforts is at the heart of painful feelings of stress and strain. Social and human factors are fundamentally at stake here, dependent on a possible downturn in the epidemic and promises of improvements in the status of hospitals. But the staff were clearly skeptical, as emphasized by the headline in *Le Monde* on June 18, 2020: "Care workers are 'tired and disgusted.'" [15]

The jobs and the days

The pandemic has shone a light on jobs that are essential for the functioning of society: "ten million police officers, cashiers, sanitation workers and those in the food trade are working, despite the public health emergency."[16] We should add workers in transportation, utilities, communication, home health aides, etc., to the list. A cursory analysis can, once again, settle on a simple formula that equates fatigue with physical exertion: more urgent emergencies, more pressing needs, more tasks and more responsibilities. In fact, a change in overtime rules was officially approved in March 2020 to extend the "maximum length of work shifts during the crisis" in "overheated" sectors[17] of the economy (telecommunications, food and agriculture, energy, transportation). The new limit was set at twelve hours per day and sixty hours per week.[18] These numbers are significant, since they reveal how concerned government and economic leaders were about the current crisis. Needless to say, unions protested the obvious conflict between the urgent need for productivity and the equally pressing need for protection: "Along with the risks of the epidemic, we are adding risks of fatigue and exhaustion through longer work hours and shorter rest periods."[19]

In addition to being associated with increased workloads, fatigue showed itself to be more complex and more frequently acknowledged and felt. Some of this can be attributed to fear and how it impacted us physically, even leading to complaints about the "abusive" nature of work obligations. "All the measures that were announced or confirmed on Monday will not immunize them against a feeling that is spreading among staff who have to show up at work during the epidemic: fear. ... 'We have to report for our shift with "a knot in our stomach."'"[20] A cleaner said, "When I get there, I have a stomach ache."[21] Interpersonal conflicts also occurred with clients who themselves were more anxious and on edge: "Fatigue, physical and psychological, is part of the mix. The first few days have been really hard, with such rude and obnoxious customers."[22] A taxi driver explained the difference between episodes of physical fatigue and mental stress: "At night, my fatigue is physical, but on the day shift my colleagues are on edge because the clients are driving them crazy."[23] Status also played a role. Many workers felt that they were getting the worst of the dangers and the risks, the hard work and the strain, without any appreciation or gratitude to lift their spirits. A home-care aide's drudgery was unacknowledged: "We are the lowest class, the one nobody talks about."[24] Another dubbed this type of job "slave work,"[25] where a lack of education or specialized training added to the burdens, a lack of job protections sharpened the anxiety, and the lack of appreciation was the final touch: "It is a very hard job, very intimate and personal, but there's no recognition, especially from medical staff."[26] Such oppression was linked to gender too; jobs performed by women have less status. Women make up 87 percent of the nurses in France and 91 percent of the nurses' aides.[27] A similar dynamic of oppression existed in "logistics staffing" for service providers. "For us, Amazon has overstepped its authority." For employees, the imbalance in power was "like bringing a knife to a gun fight."[28] New York State Attorney General Leticia James warned the company on April 22, 2020, that "the safety precautions in their warehouses are inadequate."[29] The reply was always the same, whatever the situation: "We need special consideration."[30] Helplessness and humiliation reinforced feelings of fatigue and burn out.

In contrast, working remotely, as a concept at least, seemed more amenable. Surveys gave it a 58 percent favorability rating, and respondents cited such benefits as less commuting, more flexibility, a better balance between "personal and professional life," more self-reliance and less supervision, along with greater "delegation of responsibilities."[31] Some of the sources of fatigue would be eliminated, the number of interpersonal encounters reduced, and innovations in teamwork envisaged: "inventing new ways to collaborate with colleagues and live with my partner and children."[32] Moreover, working from home would give one added protection against the pandemic.

But obstacles remained. Fatigue did not simply fade away when the work space was reimagined. Workers' complaints brought that out. Working remotely, like Covid-19, disrupted our usual spaces and schedules. Surveys of those working in this manner highlighted a troubling "permeability" of life and work when work responsibilities intruded on domestic duties and free time: "The employees who cannot finish their assignment within the designated working week have to work nights and weekends."[33] In addition, one's private domestic space became a workplace as the separation between home and work was blurred: "I use the kitchen table as my desk, so we have to eat on the coffee table in the living room, and my meal preparation has become more complicated."[34] Danièle Linhart pointed to an "anxiety-producing ambiance"[35] that disrupted our homes and enabled management to conduct "digital surveillance" through technology, to the extent that "the value and meaning"[36] of work has fundamentally changed. New pains and sources of discomfort arose. "40 percent of respondents report that they felt unfamiliar twinges of pain": backaches, cramps, shortness of breath; 29 percent report feeling "unusual surges of anxiety," with a majority of complaints originating with women who take on most of the household tasks.[37]

Despite changes in the organization of work, our work life is still the site where physical, social and psychological stresses intersect. Our increased sense of individuality is truly at the cutting edge. It is both a warning signal and a springboard for originality.

Restrictions in time and place

Along with the first-hand accounts of medical staff protesting the cutbacks in national health-care funding and workers' and their unions' response to the demanding conditions of essential work in the economy, there was a "security" angle to this public health emergency. Two concerns took precedence for French government public safety agencies: limiting contact between people and restricting travel. The widespread lockdowns and "stay-at-home orders" implemented in several countries have revived some long-forgotten strategies; options to restrict circulation and production deemed surprising and even "politically courageous" have been out of the picture since the raging pandemics of the nineteenth and early twentieth centuries. At the very least, the restrictions expressed the need for a collective response to the emergency and a refusal to accept staggering levels of death and disease.

We need to highlight the implications of these choices in the context of this book: fatigue in the domestic sphere, where overexertion or effort had always existed, and new kinds of exertion, profuse and excessive. All this is new.

An underlying anxiety spread by the virus was the first sign of this. People felt physically vulnerable, their comfort levels decreased, and their sense of calm and centeredness vanished. Calls to help centers testified to this: "There are many anxiety attacks, panic attacks associated with the situation nowadays."[38] An incident that illustrated the excesses of this concerns the *Zaandam*, an ocean liner that was refused port entry as a result of Covid-19 infections on board. The trip degenerated from "a dream to a nightmare."[39] Many magazines reported on the anxieties of their readers and described the "solidity of a world that crumbled beneath our feet and landmarks that we thought were eternal that have disappeared."[40] All of these symptoms promoted a sense of being blocked, of resistance, failure and difficulties in getting things done. This coalesced into the inevitable "hardship."

The major anthropological categories of space and time were also not meeting the moment: the evidence of restrictions and quarantines in the domestic sphere, of fleeting and insecure moments and avenues that are inaccessible or forbidden. We heard constant warnings that "The stay-at-home requirement is perceived as an assault against individual freedom. In addition, people think there is danger outdoors, and this creates a climate of public health insecurity."[41] This space was "closed" on one side and "threatening" on the other. Surveys showed the growing negativity of people affected by "stay-at-home" orders: 21 percent reported problems with self-esteem; 30 percent reported problems of concentration.[42] We often read about the disparity between classes: "One of the first disparities is between homeless or poorly housed people and others."[43] David Le Breton brought up the need for "a room of one's own," citing Virginia Woolf's essay: "For some people who live from hand to mouth, and may sleep five or six to a room in very small apartments, it's hard to find a 'room of one's own' described by Virginia Woolf."[44]

This time, when a number of initiatives and plans tended to disappear into thin air, was characterized by a certain kind of "ennui" and "lassitude" that we tried to dispel in many different ways. People frustrated by the strictures of lockdown turned to loopholes, violations of the restrictions, chance encounters, and complained of "a claustrophobic feeling as soon as the sun goes down. … Some choose to break the law."[45] Feverish excitement contrasted with languor and restlessness with sluggishness. This time was also perceived more subtly as a personal obstacle, a symbol of limits as much as of unexpected fatigue. The writer and director Christophe Honoré saw it as a "poisonous moment": "So, I feel blocked, shackled. I cannot do anything during lockdown; it is a toxic time. And I would go even further. I don't feel like creating anything out of this event. It's just a rotten time that I don't want to connect to my art."[46]

It should come as no surprise that all over the world the pandemic is associated with uncertainty and no clear timeline for an end to the threat: "What lessons should we learn from this? Without a vaccine to protect against infection, the virus will spread all over the planet in the next twelve to eighteen months."[47] Experts' predictions are vague and have mostly erred on the side of caution, since "modeling an epidemic is difficult and the modelers secretly hope to be wrong."[48] This lack of certainty only exacerbated our malaise and exhaustion.

The behavior affected by the ever-present "virus" and the imposition of strict lockdowns is simultaneously psychological, social, physical and cultural. We are fed up with meeting the same people at the same places; the feeling of being trapped is captured in the headline "The Hell at Home."[49] Being confined with other people in close quarters can result in feelings of "stress":

> Family life during Covid-19 is wearing people down, as the survey by IFOP reveals: one out of every two respondents says that they are quarreling more over household chores. 34 percent say they argue more than before about children's spending time online, and 29 percent fight about education and … even food supplies. The emotional levels are goosed by a generous shot of adrenaline: 41 percent say they are feeling intensely stressed more often,

> and that doesn't even take into account the problems of working at home alongside the rest of the family. Feeling the heat?[50]

At times, sharing one's living space is truly unwelcome, as is the case for students who had to return to the family home and the constraints they thought they had left behind: "How can I live with the people that I tried to avoid for the past three years?"[51]

It is impossible to overlook the effect of "mental stress" on women in the current situation,[52] with so many accounts of the unequal division of household labor. The imbalance of women's "traditional" double duty can be exacerbated by the demands of working remotely that compound domestic pressures. Virginie Ballet described the fatigue that plagued many women: "Neither working remotely, nor part time work, nor home schooling seem to have disrupted the old system. It's exactly the opposite. The women have to keep the house running, plan the meals, go shopping, do the dishes, supervise the homework and take care of all the other joys of daily life, until they collapse, exhausted."[53]

The contours of fatigue have certainly changed with the epidemic, but perceptions and images of it from the last few decades have simply been brought into sharper focus by it. In the long view of history, the epidemic is just one episode, but its sudden emergence and persistent hold on our daily lives have revived old, forgotten fears and confirmed in a new and unexpected way that fatigue is our faithful companion, a presence lurking inside each of us.

Notes

Introduction

1 See Cercle Sésame, *2012–2017: ce que veulent les Français* (Paris: Éditions d'Organisation Groupe Eyrolles, 2011), p. 209.
2 See "Syndrome de burn out: c'est quoi?," www.burnout-info.ch/fr/burnout_c_est_quoi.htm.
3 Guy de Maupassant, "Un coq chanta," *Contes de la bécasse* (1883), in Brigitte Monglond (ed.), *Contes et nouvelles* (Paris: Robert Laffont, 1998), vol. 1, p. 499. Also, "I'm so tired that I'm going to bed, my friend," trans. Laurent Porel, "A Cockerel Sang," in *Tales of the Woodcock* (independently pubd, 2019).
4 See Roger Sue, *La Richesse des hommes: vers l'économie quaternaire* (Paris: Odile Jacob, 1997).
5 See Cercle Sésame, *2012–2017*, p. 200.

Part I The Medieval World and the Challenge of Landmarks

1 Aldebrandin of Siena, *Le Régime du corps* (XIII century) (Paris, Honoré Champion, 1911), p. 68.

Chapter 1 A Clear Picture with Cloudy Landmarks

1 *Tristan et Iseult* (XII century) (Paris: Le Livre de Poche, 1998), p. 88. *The Romance of Tristan and Iseult*, retold by J. Bedier, rendered into English by H. Belloc (London: George Allen, 1900).
2 *Commentaire en vers français sur l'école de Salerne* (X–XI centuries) (Paris, 1671), p. 461.
3 Bernard de Gordon, *Fleur de lys en médecine* (XIII century) (Lyon, 1495), f. c IV.
4 Ibid., f. a IV.
5 See *Les Commentaires de Pierre André Matthiole sur les six livres de Dioscoride* (Paris, 1579), p. 720.
6 Barthélémy l'Anglais, *Le Grand Propriétaire de toutes choses* (XIII century) (Paris, 1556), p. 62. Bartholomew the Englishman, *On the Properties of Things*, trans. John Trevisa (1397) (Oxford: Clarendon Press, 1988).
7 Aldebrandin of Siena, *Le Régime du corps* (Paris : Honoré Champion, 1911), p. 23.
8 See Alexandre Koyré, "Du monde de 'l'à peu près' à l'univers de la précision," *Critique*, no. 28 (1948), pp. 806–23; repr. in *Études d'histoire de la pensée philosophique* (Paris: Armand Colin, 1961).
9 See Nicolas de La Mare, *Traité de la police, où l'on trouvera l'histoire de son établissement, les fonctions et les prérogatives de ses magistrats, toutes les lois et tous les règlements qui la concernent* (Paris, 1705–38), vol. III, p. 68.
10 Ibid., p. 71.
11 See above p. 18.
12 *La Quête du Graal* (XIII century), ed. Albert Béguin and Yves Bonnefoy (Paris: Seuil, 1982), p. 94.

13 *Fieràbras* (XIII century), trans. Mary Lafon (Paris, 1857), p. 48.
14 *Durmart le Gallois* (XIII century), in Danielle Régnier-Bohler, ed., *Récits d'amour et de chevalerie, XIIe–XVe siècle* (Paris: Robert Laffont, 2000), p. 620.
15 Aldebrandin of Siena, *Le Régime du corps*, p. 24.
16 Arnaud de Villeneuve (XIII century), *Régimen sanitatis en français* (Paris, 1514).
17 Aldebrandin of Siena, *Le Régime du corps*, p. 31.
18 Barthélémy l'Anglais, *Le Grand Propriétaire de toutes choses*, p. 64.
19 *La Quête du Graal*, p. 94.
20 *Perlesvaus, le haut livre du Graal* (XIII century), in Danielle Régnier-Bohler, ed., *La Légende arthurienne: le Graal et la Table Ronde* (Paris: Robert Laffont, 1989), p. 193.
21 Barthélémy l'Anglais, *Le Grand Propriétaire de toutes choses*, p. 62.
22 *Commentaire en vers français sur l'école de Salerne*, p. 461.
23 Koyré, "Du monde de 'l'à peu près' à l'univers de la précision," p. 319.
24 Ibid.
25 Aldebrandin of Siena, *Le Régime du corps*, p. 24.
26 Ibid.
27 See Catherine König-Pralong, "Aspects de la fatigue dans l'anthropologie médiévale," *Revue de synthèse*, 129/4 (2008), p. 539.
28 Arnaud de Villeneuve, *Régimen sanitatis en français*.
29 Ibid.
30 Ibid.
31 Barthélémy l'Anglais, *Le Grand Propriétaire de toutes choses*, p. 64.

Chapter 2 The Renowned Fatigue of the Warrior

1 See Georges Duby, *Guillaume le Maréchal ou le meilleur chevalier du monde* (Paris: Fayard, 1984); trans. Richard Howard as *William Marshal: The Flower of Chivalry* (New York: Pantheon Books, 1996).
2 *Fieràbras*, trans. Mary Lafon (Paris, 1857), p. 48.
3 Richard le Pèlerin and Graindor de Douai, *La Conquête de Jérusalem* (XII century), in Danielle Régnier-Bohler, ed., *Croisades et pèlerinages: récits, chroniques et voyages en Terre sainte, XIIe–XVIe siècle* (Paris: Robert Laffont, 2009), p. 188.
4 See above p. 18.
5 Richard le Pèlerin and Graindor de Douai, *La Conquête de Jérusalem*, p. 193.
6 Ibid., p. 261.
7 Ibid., p. 193.
8 Richard le Pèlerin and Graindor de Douai, *La Chanson d'Antioche*, in *Croisades et pèlerinages*, pp. 42–3.
9 *L'Âtre périlleux* (XIII century), in Danielle Régnier-Bohler, ed., *La Légende arthurienne: le Graal et la Table Ronde* (Paris: Robert Laffont, 1989), p. 642.
10 "Relation de Marchiennes" (XIII century), quoted by Georges Duby in *Le Dimanche de Bouvines, 27 juillet 1214* (Paris: Gallimard, 1985), p. 79 ; trans. Catherine Tihanyi as *The Legend of Bouvines: War, Religion and Culture in the Middle Ages* (Berkeley: University of California Press, 1990).
11 *Jéhan et Blonde* (XIII century) (Paris: Union latine d'édition, 1971), p. 92.
12 Georges Duby, "Réflexions sur la douleur physique au Moyen Âge," in *Mâle Moyen Âge: de l'amour et autres essais* (Paris: Flammarion, 1990), p. 205; trans. Jane Dunnett as *Love and Marriage in the Middle Ages* (Chicago: University of Chicago Press, 1994).
13 *Le Livre des faits du bon chevalier, messire Jacques de Lalaing* (XV century), in Danielle Régnier-Bohler, ed., *Splendeurs de la cour de Bourgogne: récits et chroniques* (Paris: Robert Laffont, 1995), p. 1311.
14 *La Quête du Graal* (XIII century), ed. Albert Béguin and Yves Bonnefoy (Paris: Seuil,

1982), p. 94. *The Quest of the Holy Grail*, ed. and trans. Pauline M. Matarasso (London: Penguin, 1969).

15 Richard le Pèlerin and Graindor de Douai, *La Conquête de Jérusalem*, p. 251.

16 Ibid., p. 67.

17 *Le Livre des faits du bon chevalier, messire Jacques de Lalaing*, p. 1255.

18 Ibid., p. 1334.

19 Ibid., p. 1343.

20 Jean de Bueil, *Le Jouvencel* (XV century) (Paris, 1887), p. 21.

21 *Le Livre des faits du bon messire Jean Le Meingre dit Boucicault* (XIV century), in Joseph-François Michaud and Jean-Joseph-François Poujoulat, eds, *Nouvelle Collection des mémoires pour servir à l'histoire de France* (Paris, 1836), series I, vol. II, p. 219.

22 See Henri Stein, *Archers d'autrefois, archers d'aujourd'hui* (Paris: Longuet, 1925), p. 66.

23 Ibid., p. 82.

24 Philippe Contamine, "La segmentation féodale, début Xe–milieu XIIe siècle," in André Corvisier, ed., *Histoire militaire de la France*, vol. 1: *Des origines à 1715* (Paris: PUF, 1992), p. 71.

25 Franco Cardini, "Le Guerrier et le chevalier," in Jacques Le Goff, ed., *L'Homme médiéval* (Paris: Seuil, 1989), p. 122; trans. Lydia G. Cochrane as *The Medieval World* (London: Collins & Brown, 1990).

Chapter 3 The "Necessary" Suffering of the Traveler

1 Michel de Certeau, *L'Invention du quotidien*, vol. 1: *Arts de faire* (Paris: Gallimard, [1990] 2007), p. 177. *The Practice of Everyday Life*, trans. Stephen Rendall (Berkeley: University of California Press, 1984).

2 See Bernard Chevalier, "Introduction," in *Espace vécu, mesuré, imaginé: textes réunis en l'honneur de Christiane Deluz, Cahiers de recherches médiévales et humanistes*, no. 3 (1997), p. 8.

3 Alain Roger, *Court Traité du paysage* (Paris: Gallimard, [1997] 2017), p. 68.

4 Jean Pian de Carpin, *Voyage en Tartarie* (XIII century), in Édouard Charton, ed., *Voyageurs anciens et modernes* (Paris, 1861), vol. II, p. 240. Translator's note: The Italian envoy Giovanni da Pian del Carpine is known in English also as John of Pian de Carpini.

5 Jacopo da Verona, *Liber peregrinationis*, 1335.

6 See Emmanuel Le Roy Ladurie, *Montaillou, village occitan de 1294 à 1324* (Paris: Gallimard, 1975), p. 176. *Montaillou: An Occitan Village from 1294 to 1324*, trans. Barbara Bray (New York: Braziller Books, 1978).

7 See Pierre Bouet, *Le Fantastique dans la littérature latine du Moyen Age: la navigation du saint Brendan* (Caen: Centre de publications de l'université de Caen, 1986).

8 Nompar de Caumont de Castelnau, *Voyage d'outremer en Jérusalem* (XV century), in Danielle Régnier-Bohler, ed., *Croisades et pèlerinages* (Paris: Robert Laffont, 2009), p. 1082.

9 See Micheline de Combarieu, "Le nom du monde est forêt," in *Espace vécu, mesuré, imaginé*, pp. 79–90.

10 Roland Bechmann, *Des arbres et des hommes: la forêt au Moyen Âge* (Paris: Flammarion, 1984), p. 340. *Trees and Man: The Forest in the Middle Ages*, trans. Katharyn Dunham (New York: Paragon House, 1990).

11 *Le Livre de Graal* (XII century), ed. Philippe Walter (Paris: Gallimard, 2001), vol. 1, p. 1386. Norris J. Lacy, ed., *Lancelot-Grail: The Old Arthurian Vulgate and Post-Vulgate in Translation* (New York: Garland, 1992). Translator's note: The king is also known as Loth of Lothian.

12 *Le Livre de Graal*, p. 1411.

13 Ibid., p. 1140. Translator's note: Guinebal is also known as Guinebaut.

14 *La Dame invisible* (XII century) (Paris: Union latine d'édition, 1971), p. 118.
15 *Rôles d'Oléron: coutumier maritime du Moyen Âge*, ed. Auguste Pawlowski de Lannoy (Niort: A. Chiron, 1900), article 7. *The Rules of Oleron*, c. 1266, www.admiraltylaw-guide.com/documents/oleron.html, article VII.
16 *La Dame invisible*, p. 106. See also *Voyager au Moyen Âge* (Paris: Réunion des musées nationaux, 2014) [exhibition catalogue, Musée de Cluny].
17 *La Dame invisible*, p. 107.
18 Ibid.
19 Gilles Li Muisis, *Poésies* (XIII–XIV century) (Louvain: Kervyn de Lettenhove, 1882), vol. 1, p. 57. Translator's note: Gilles Li Muisis is also known as Gilles Le Muiset.
20 Henri Dubois, "Un voyage princier au XIVe siècle (1344)," in *Voyages et voyageurs au Moyen Âge*, Actes des Congrès de la SHMESP (Paris: Publications de la Sorbonne, 1996), p. 88.
21 "Guillaume de Naillac et Gaucher de Passac, chevaliers, chambellans du roi, s'engageant, moyennant une somme de cent mille francs, de mener deux mille hommes d'armes que le roi envoie au secours du roi de Castille, contre le duc de Lorraine" [For the sum of 100,000 francs, Guillaume de Naillac et Gaucher de Passac, knights and royal chamberlains, will command the 2,000 soldiers the king is dispatching to support the king of Castile, against the duc de Lorraine], Paris, February 5, 1387, *Choix de pièces inédites relatives au règne de Charles VI*, ed. Louis Douët d'Arcq (Paris, 1863), vol. 1, p. 77.
22 See "Une 'invitation' au voyage en forme de balade par Eustache Deschamps" (XIV century), www.moyenagepassion.com/index.php/2017/08/08/une-invitation-au-voyage-en-forme-de-ballade-par-eustache-deschamps/. Deborah M. Sinnreich-Levi and Ian S. Laurie, *Eustache Deschamps: Selected Poems* (New York: Routledge, 2003).
23 Florian Mazel, *L'Évêque et le territoire: l'invention médiévale de l'espace* (V–XIII centuries) (Paris: Seuil, 2016), p. 113.
24 Ibid.
25 See Chevalier, "Introduction," in *Espace vécu, mesuré, imaginé*, p. 15.
26 Herbert L. Kessler, "Marcher dans les pas du Christ," in *Voyager au Moyen Âge*, p. 16.
27 Ibid.
28 Cyrille Vogel, "Le pèlerinage pénitentiel," *Revue des sciences religieuses*, 38/2 (1964), p. 113.
29 Alphonse Dupront, *Du sacré: croisades et pèlerinages: images et langages* (Paris: Gallimard, 1987), p. 374.
30 See Nicolas de Martoni and Ogier d'Anglure, *Vers Jérusalem: itinéraires croisés au XIVe siècle* (Paris: Les Belles Lettres, 2008), p. 104.
31 See Victor Derode, *Histoire de Lille* (Paris, 1848), vol. 1, p. 259.
32 Ibid., p. 277.
33 See Pierre-Toussaint Durand de Maillane, *Dictionnaire du droit canonique et de pratique bénéficiale* (Paris, 1761), article on "Indulgences."
34 See *Voyager au Moyen Âge*, p. 51.
35 Ibid. See also Jérôme Doucet, *Chaussures d'antan* (Paris: Devambez, 1913), p. 12.
36 Marcel Girault and Pierre-Gilles Girault, *Visages de pèlerins au Moyen Âge* (Paris: Zodiaque, 2001), p. 261. Translator's note: William of Verceil was also known as William of Montevergine.
37 Ibid., p. 24.
38 Karin Ueltschi, *Le Pied qui cloche, ou Le Lignage des boiteux* (Paris: Honoré Champion, 2011), p. 71.
39 *Les Grandes Chroniques de France, selon qu'elles sont conservées en l'église de Saint-Denis en France*, ed. M. Paulin Paris (Paris, 1836), vol. IV, pp. 311–12.
40 Ibid., p. 354.
41 Ibid., p. 247.

Chapter 4 "Redemptive" Fatigue

1 *Les Grandes Chroniques de France, selon qu'elles sont conservées en l'église de Saint-Denis en France*, ed. M. Paulin Paris (Paris, 1836), vol. IV, p. 247. See also Benoît Lambert, "Les pratiques de la pénitence dans l'Église d'Occident," *Garrigues et sentiers*, October 11, 2010.
2 See Jean Verdon, *Voyager au Moyen Âge* (Paris: Perrin, [1998] 2003), p. 260. *Travel in the Middle Ages*, trans. George Holoch (Notre Dame, IN: University of Notre Dame Press, 2003).
3 *Voyager au Moyen Âge*, pp. 260–1. Translator's note: Santiago de Compostela is the location of the shrine of Saint James, a destination on the pilgrimage route the Way of St James.
4 Victor Derode, *Histoire de Lille* (Paris, 1848).
5 Ibid.
6 Cyrille Vogel, "Le pèlerinage pénitentiel," *Revue des sciences religieuses*, 38/2 (1964), p. 121.
7 Siegfried Wenzel, *The Sin of Sloth: Acedia in Medieval Thought and Literature* (Chapel Hill: University of North Carolina Press, 1967), p. 36.
8 See Anson Rabinbach, *Le Moteur humain: l'énergie, la fatigue et les origines de la modernité* (Paris: La Fabrique, [1992] 2004), p. 58. *The Human Motor: Energy, Fatigue and the Origins of Modernity* (Berkeley: University of California Press, 1992). See also Marc Loriol, *Le Temps de la fatigue: la gestion sociale du mal-être au travail* (Paris: Anthropos, 2000), "Les moines et *l'acédie*: naissance de l'individu," p. 22.
9 Jehan Henry, *Livre de la vie active de l'Hôtel-Dieu de Paris* (1483), ed. Marcel Candille, (Paris : S.P.E.I., 1964), p. 29.
10 *Vie de sainte Douceline* (end of XIII century), in Danielle Régnier-Bohler, ed., *Voix de femmes au Moyen Âge: savoir, mystique, poésie, amours, sorcellerie, XIIe–XVe siècle* (Paris: Robert Laffont, 2006), pp. 301, 315, 317.
11 See Jacques de Voragine, "Saint Julien," in *La Légende dorée*, ed. Alain Boureau (Paris: Gallimard, 2004), p. 174.
12 Henry, *Livre de vie active de l'Hôtel-Dieu de Paris*, p. 34.
13 Ibid.
14 *Vie de sainte Douceline*, p. 302.
15 See Jacques le Goff, in *La Civilisation de l'Occident médiéval* (Paris: Arthaud, 1964), p. 118, on hermits "poorly understood, springing up all around the Christian world, pioneers, hidden away in forests where they are mobbed by visitors, located strategically to help travelers to find their way, to ford a river or cross a bridge, uncorrupted by the politics of the organized Church."
16 Voragine, "Saint Jerôme," p. 813.
17 *Vie de sainte Douceline*, p. 319.
18 Ibid., pp. 322–3.
19 François-Xavier Putallaz, "Thomas d'Aquin, Pierre Olivi, figures enseignantes de la vie contemplative," in Christian Trottmann, ed., *Vie active et vie contemplative au Moyen Âge et au seuil de la Renaissance* (Rome: École française de Rome, 2009), p. 372.
20 Le Goff, *La Civilisation de l'Occident médiéval*, p. 118.
21 See Trottmann, *Vie active et vie contemplative au Moyen Âge.*
22 Marc Vial, "La vie mixte, selon Jean Gerson," ibid., p. 392.
23 Putallaz, "Thomas d'Aquin, Pierre Olivi, figures enseignantes de la vie contemplative," p. 372.
24 *Vie de sainte Douceline*, p. 324.
25 Guillaume de Tyr, *Chronique* (XII century), in Danielle Régnier-Bohler, ed., *Croisades et pèlerinages* (Paris: Robert Laffont, 2009), p. 556.

Chapter 5 Ordinary Work and Everyday Workers, a Relative "Silence"?

1 Guy Fourquin, "Le Temps de la croissance," in Georges Duby and Armand Wallon, eds, *Histoire de la France rurale* (Paris: Seuil, 1975), vol. I, p. 545.
2 Georges Duby, *Guerriers et paysans* (1973), in *Féodalités* (Paris: Gallimard, 1996), pp. 31, 34.
3 S. P. Mayaud, *Le Servage dans la Marche* (Paris, 1878), p. 6.
4 See Youri Bessmertny, "Le Paysan vu par le seigneur: la France des XIe et XIIe siècles," in Élisabeth Mornet, ed., *Campagnes médiévales: l'homme et son espace: mélanges offerts à Robert Fossier* (Paris: Publications de la Sorbonne, 1995), p. 609.
5 Anon. (XIII century). See Anselme Dimier, *Les Moines bâtisseurs* (Paris : Fayard, 1964), p. 177.
6 *Roman de Rou* (1160), Part III, quoted in Hélène Vérin, *La Gloire des ingénieurs: l'intelligence technique du XVIe au XVIIIe siècle* (Paris: Albin Michel, 1993), p. 25.
7 Serge Moscovici, *Essai sur l'histoire humaine de la nature* (Paris: Flammarion, 1968), p. 212.
8 Robert Fossier, "Le temps de la faim," in Jean Delumeau and Yves Lequin, eds, *Les malheurs du temps: histoire des fléaux et des calamités en France* (Paris: Larousse, 1987), p. 143.
9 Robert Fossier and Hugues Neveux, "La fin d'une embellie," ibid., p. 167.
10 Pietro de' Crescenzi, *Trattato della agricoltura* (XIII century) (Milan, 1805), p. 50.
11 Ibid., p. 53.
12 *Traité inédit d'économie rurale composé en Angleterre au XIIIe siècle*, with a glossary by Louis Lacour (Paris, 1856), p. 16.
13 Ibid., p. 11.
14 Ibid.
15 Ibid. Quoted in Georges Duby, *L'économie rurale et la vie des campagnes dans l'Occident médiéval* (Paris: Aubier-Flammarion, [1962] 1977), vol. 1, p. 312. Translator's note: A French denier was worth about one penny and an obole half a penny.
16 Ibid.
17 Ibid.
18 See Léopold Delisle, *Études sur la condition de la classe agricole et l'état de l'agriculture en Normandie* (Paris: Honoré Champion, 1903), p. 623.
19 See Marie-Thérèse Lorcin and Danièle Alexandre-Bidon, *Le Quotidien du temps des fabliaux* (Paris: Picard, 2003), p. 173.
20 See Perrine Mane, *Travail à la campagne au Moyen Âge* (Paris: Picard, 2006).
21 *Vieil Rentier d'Audenarde* (XII century), Brussels: Bibliothèque royale, MS 1175, f. 156v.
22 *Psautier de Saint-Louis* (XIII century) Paris: Bibliothèque de France, MS Latin 10525, f. 23v.
23 Léopold Delisle, *Études sur la condition de la classe agricole et l'état de l'agriculture en Normandie*, p. 454.
24 Ibid. Translator's note: The French "livre" or pound was divided into 20 sous, and each sou consisted of 12 deniers.
25 Gérard Sivery, *Structures agraires et vie rurale dans le Hainaut à la fin du Moyen Âge* (Lille: Presses universitaires de Lille, 1977), vol. 1, p. 397.
26 Robert Fossier, *Paysans d'Occident, XIe–XIVe siècle* (Paris: PUF, 1984), p. 115.
27 David S. Landes, *Revolution in Time: Clocks and the Making of the Modern World* (Cambridge, MA: Harvard University Press, 1983).
28 Étienne Boileau, *Règlements sur les arts et métiers de Paris* (XIII century). See Georges-Bernard Depping, *Le Livre des métiers d'Étienne Boileau* (Paris, 1837), p. 399.
29 Ibid., p. 63.
30 Étienne Boileau, "Baudraiers, faiseurs de courroies," in *Le Livre des métiers* (XIII

century), ed. René de Lespinasse and François Bonnardot (Paris: Jean-Cyrille Godefroy, 2005), p. 181.

31 Depping, *Le Livre des métiers d'Étienne Boileau*, p. 112.

32 Ibid., p. 130.

33 Jean-Louis Roch, *Les Métiers au Moyen Âge* (Paris: Jean-Paul Gisserot, 2014), p. 113.

34 Jean-Louis Roch, *Un autre monde de travail: la draperie en Normandie au Moyen Âge* (Rouen: Presses universitaires de Rouen et du Havre, 2013), p. 154.

35 Ibid.

36 Ibid., p. 156.

37 *Ordonnance du prévôt des marchands* (1395). See Henri Hauser, *Ouvriers du temps passé, XVe–XVIe siècle* (Paris, 1927), p. 78.

38 Gerhard Dohrn-van Rossum, *L'Histoire de l'heure: l'horlogerie et l'organisation moderne du temps* (Paris: Éditions de la Maison des sciences de l'homme, 1997), p. 315. *History of the Hour: Clocks and Modern Temporal Orders* (Chicago: University of Chicago Press, 1996).

39 See Dohrn-van Rossum, *L'Histoire de l'heure*, pp. 310–11.

40 Ibid., p. 310.

41 Landes, *Revolution in Time*.

42 See Corine Maitte and Didier Terrier, "Conflits et résistances autour du temps de travail avant l'industrialisation," *Temporalités: revue de sciences sociales et humaines*, no. 16 (2012); http://temporalites.revues.org/2203. See especially "Conflits autour des pauses."

43 Laure Leroux, *Cloches et société médiévale: les sonneries de Tournai au Moyen Âge* (Tournai: Art et Histoire, 2011), p. 82.

44 Dohrn-van Rossum, *L'Histoire de l'heure*, p. 332.

45 Guiliano Pinto, "La rémunération des salariés du bâtiment" (XIII–XV century), in Patrice Beck, Philippe Bernardi and Laurent Feller, eds, *Rémunérer le travail au Moyen Âge* (Paris: Picard, 2014), p. 320.

46 See Mathieu Arnoux, "Relation salariale et temps de travail," *Le Moyen Âge: revue d'histoire et de philologie*, 115/3–4 (2009), p. 574.

47 Ibid., p. 576.

48 See p. 29 above.

49 Pinto, "La rémunération des salariés du bâtiment," p. 316.

50 Ibid., p. 317.

51 See Philippe Mantellier, "Mémoires sur la valeur des principales denrées et marchandises qui se vendaient et se consommaient en la ville d'Orléans," *Mémoires de la société archéologique de l'Orléanais*, V (1862), p. 440. Translator's note: The value of the French pre-Revolutionary unit "livre tournois," or Tours pound, was originally equal to one pound of silver and was divided into smaller denominations of deniers and sous.

52 Pinto, "La rémunération des salariés du bâtiment," p. 316.

53 Philippe Braunstein, *Travail et entreprise au Moyen Âge* (Brussels: de Boeck, 2003), p. 412.

Chapter 6 Between Occult Power and the Healing Virtues of Refreshments

1 Aldebrandin of Siena, "Comment on se doit garder qui cheminer veut," *Le Régime du corps* (Paris: Honoré Champion, 1911), pp. 68–70.

2 Richard le Pèlerin and Graindor de Douai, *La Chanson d'Antioche*, in Danielle Régnier-Bohler, ed., *Croisades et pèlerinages: récits, chroniques et voyages en Terre sainte, XIIe–XVIe siècle* (Paris: Robert Laffont, 2009), p. 48. *The Chanson d'Antioche: An Old French Account of the First Crusade*, trans. Susan B. Edgington and Carol Sweetenham (Farnham: Ashgate, 2011).

3 *Durmart le Gallois*, in Danielle Régnier-Bohler, ed., *Récits d'amour et de chevalerie, XIIe–XVe siècle* (Paris: Robert Laffont, 2000), p. 589.

4 Richard le Pèlerin and Graindor de Douai, *La Conquête de Jérusalem*, in *Croisades et pèlerinages*, p. 97.
5 Robert de Clari, *La Conquête de Constantinople* (1215), in Albert Pauphilet, ed., *Historiens et chroniqueurs du Moyen Âge* (Paris: Gallimard, 1952), p. 15.
6 Jean Froissart, *Chroniques* (XIV century), ibid., p. 511.
7 Ibid., p. 708.
8 Richard le Pèlerin and Graindor de Douai, *La Conquête de Jérusalem*, p. 263.
9 *Le Chevalier nu: contes de l'Allemagne médiévale*, ed. Danielle Buschinger, Jean-Marc Pastré and Wolfgang Spiewok (Paris: Stock, 1988), p. 103.
10 Ibid.
11 Danielle Régnier-Bohler, ed., *L'Âtre périlleux*, in *La Légende arthurienne* (Paris: Robert Laffont, 1989), pp. 628–30. *The Perilous Cemetery*, trans. Nancy B. Black (New York: Garland, 1994).
12 Ibid. p. 633.
13 There are many references to sorcery in medieval texts, such as in the compendium published by Leonard Vairo, *Trois Livres de charmes, sorcelages ou enchantemens* (Paris, 1583), pp. 55–7.
14 Hildegard von Bingen, *Le Livre des subtilités des créatures divines: les plantes, les éléments, les pierres, les métaux* (XII century) (Grenoble: Jérôme Millon, 1988), vol. 1, p. 268.
15 Ibid., p. 241.
16 Ibid., p. 257.
17 Quoted in Camille-Louis Husson, *Histoire des pharmaciens de Lorraine* (Nancy, 1882), p. 5.
18 Léon Gautier, *La Chevalerie* (Paris, 1884), p. 634.
19 "Journal de la dépense du roi Jean le Bon en Angleterre (February 1, 1359 – February 8 1360)," in Louis Douët d'Arcq, ed., *Comptes de l'argenterie des rois de France au XIVe siècle* (Paris, 1851), p. 195.
20 Nicolas de la Chesnaye, *La Nef de santé avec le gouvernail du corps humain et la condamnation des banquets* (XV century) (Paris, 1507).
21 Baptiste Platine, *De l'honnête volupté* (XV century), in *Le Platine en français* (Paris, 1871), p. 176.
22 Quoted by Étienne Barbazan, *Fabliaux et contes des poètes français des XIIe, XIIIe, XIVe et XVe siècles* (1756) (Paris, 1808), vol. IV, p. 182.
23 Quoted by Anatole de Montaiglon, *Receuil général et complet des fabliaux des XIIIe et XIVe siècles* (Paris, 1872–90), vol. V, p. 222.
24 Georges d'Avenel, *Histoire économique de la propriété, des salaires, des denrées et de tous les prix en général, depuis l'an 1200 jusqu'en l'an 1800* (Paris, 1898), vol. IV, p. 500. Translator's note: A medieval pound, or "livre," weighed 489 grams.
25 Ibid., p. 503.
26 Charles de Beaurepaire, *Notes et documents concernant l'état des campagnes de la Haute-Normandie dans les derniers temps du Moyen Âge* (Paris, 1865), p. 353.
27 Ibid., p. 385.
28 Ibid., p. 386.
29 Platine, *De l'honnête volupté*, p. 181.
30 Ibid.
31 See Jean-Jacques Hémardinquer, "Sur les galères de Toscane au XVI siècle," in *Pour une histoire de l'alimentation* (Paris: Armand Colin, 1970), p. 88.
32 See p. 37 above.

Part II The Modern World and the Challenge of Categories

1 Cesare Ripa, *Iconologie, ou, Explication nouvelle de plusieurs images, emblèmes et autres figures hiéroglyphiques des vertus, des vices, des arts, des sciences … et des passions humaines*

(1613) (Paris, 1698), vol. I, p. 123. *Iconologia or Moral Emblems*, ed. Pierce Tempest (London: Benjamin Motte, 1709).

2 Ibid.

3 "Lettre d'un religieux envoyée au prince de Condé," January 18, 1649, *Choix de mazarinades, publié pour la Société de l'histoire de France par C. Moreau* (Paris, 1853), vol. I, p. 94.

Chapter 7 The Invention of Degrees

1 See Alain Rey, *Dictionnaire historique de la langue française* (Paris: Robert, 1994), entry "Épuisement." However, this word does not appear in Antoine Furetière's *Dictionnaire universel* of 1690.

2 Valentin Conrart, *Mémoires*, in Joseph-François Michaud and Jean-Joseph-François Poujoulat, eds, *Nouvelle Collection des mémoires pour servir à l'histoire de France* (Paris, 1836), series III, vol. IV, p. 602.

3 François de Scépeaux de Vieilleville, *Mémoires*, ibid., series I, vol. IX, p. 36.

4 Ibid.

5 Scipion Dupleix, *La Curiosité naturelle rédigée en questions selon l'ordre alphabétique* (Paris, 1623), p. 94.

6 Antoine Furetière, *Dictionnaire universel* (Paris, 1690) entry "Langueur."

7 Mme de Maintenon, letter dated October 23, 1713, in *Lettres inédites de Mme de Maintenon et de Mme la princesse des Ursins* (Paris, 1826), vol. III, p. 4.

8 Esprit Fléchier, *Oraison funèbre de Marie-Anne-Christine de Bavière, dauphine de France* (Paris, 1690), p. 28.

9 Jean-Louis Guez de Balzac, *Lettres familières à M. Chapelain*, August 30, 1639 (Paris, 1659), p. 177.

10 Mme de Maintenon, Lettre à Mme la comtesse de Caylus, May 15, 1705, in Théophile Lavallée, ed., *Correspondance générale de Mme de Maintenon* (Paris, 1867), vol. V, p. 339.

11 Mlle de Montpensier, *Mémoires*, in Michaud and Poujoulat, *Nouvelle Collection des mémoires pour servir à l'histoire de France*, series III, vol. IV, p. 322.

12 Guez de Balzac, *Lettres familières à M. Chapelain*, July 6, 1650, p. 25.

13 Furetière, *Dictionnaire universel*, entry "Incommodité."

14 Raymond de Rouer Fourquevaux, *Discipline militaire de messire Guillaume du Bellay, seigneur de Langey* (Lyon, 1592), p. 18.

15 Olivier de Serres, *Le Théâtre d'agriculture et mésnage des champs* (Paris, 1600), p. 59.

16 See the rule of St Benoît (VI century), in Jean-Pie Lapierre, ed., *Règles des moines* (Paris: Seuil, 1982), p. 113. "As for delicate or sickly monks, assign them a task or a craft that will prevent idleness without overwhelming them with overexertion."

17 Serres, *Le Théâtre d'agriculture et mésnage des champs*, p. 77.

18 Philippe Braunstein, "Le travail minier au Moyen Âge d'après les sources réglementaires," in Jacqueline Hamesse and Colette Muraille-Samaran, eds, *Le Travail au Moyen Âge: une approche interdisciplinaire* (Louvain-la-Neuve: Institut d'études médiévales, 1990), p. 333.

19 Jean Torrilhon de Prades, "Un petit capitaine au Grand Siècle," *Revue historique des armées*, no. 2 (1980), pp. 5–31. See Michèle Virol, ed., *Les Oisivetés de Monsieur de Vauban* (Seyssel: Champ Vallon, 2007), p. 1040, n. 1.

20 Sébastien Le Prestre de Vauban, "Moyens d'améliorer nos troupes et de faire une infanterie perpétuelle et très excellente" (1703), ibid., p. 1040. Translator's note: The French Guards formed an elite unit of the royal army, part of the "military household" of the king.

21 Ibid.

22 Camille Rousset, *Histoire de Louvois et de son administration politique et militaire* (Paris, 1863), vol. III, pp. 296–7.

23 Ibid.
24 Jean Marteilhe, *Mémoires d'un galérien du Roi-Soleil* (1757) (Paris: Mercure de France, 1982), p. 102.
25 Jean-Baptiste Antoine Colbert Seignelay, Letter of April 18, 1688. See Gaston Tournier, *Les Galères de France et les galériens protestants des XVIIe et XVIIIe siècles* (Montpellier: Les Presses du Languedoc, 1984), vol. I, p. 116.
26 Charles Loyseau, *Traité des ordres et simples dignités* (1610), in *Œuvres* (Paris, 1666), p. 52.
27 Pierre Goubert and Daniel Roche, *Les Français et l'Ancien Régime*, vol. I: *La Société et l'État* (Paris: Armand Colin, [1984] 1991), p. 84.
28 Jean de la Fontaine, "La Mort et le Bûcheron," *Fables* (Paris, 1668–94). *The Fables of La Fontaine*, trans. Elizur Wright (Boston: J. W. M. Gibbs, 1882), Book I, no. 16, "Death and the Woodman": "A poor wood-chopper, with his fagot load / Whom weight of years, as well as load, oppress'd, / Sore groaning in his smoky hut to rest, / Trudged wearily along his homeward road …"
29 "Le savetier et le financier," ibid. *The Fables of La Fontaine*, Book VIII, no. 2, "The Cobbler and the Financier": "A cobbler sang from morn till night; / 'Twas sweet and marvellous to hear, / His trills and quavers told the ear / Of more contentment and delight, Enjoy'd by that laborious wight / Than e'er enjoy'd the sages seven, / Or any mortals short of heaven."
30 "Le chartier embourbé," ibid. *The Fables of La Fontaine*, Book VI, no. 18, "The Carter in the Mire": "'Well,' said the voice, 'I'll aid thee now; / Take up thy whip.' 'I have … but, how? / My cart glides on with ease! / I thank thee, Hercules.' / 'Thy team,' rejoin'd the voice, 'has light ado; / So help thyself, and Heaven will help thee too.'"
31 Claude Fleury, *Les Devoirs des maîtres et des domestiques* (Paris, 1688), p. 104.
32 Antoine Furetière, *Le Roman bourgeois* (1666), in Antoine Adam, ed., *Romanciers du XVIIe siècle* (Paris: Gallimard, 1958), p. 1047.
33 See Jean de La Bruyère, *Les Caractères* (1688) (Paris: Garnier, 1954), p. 295. *The "Characters" of Jean de La Bruyère*, trans. Henri Van Laun (London: Nimmo, 1885), no. 128:

> Certain wild animals, male and female, are scattered over the country, dark, livid, and quite tanned by the sun, who are chained, as it were, to the land they are always digging and turning up and down with an unwearied stubbornness; their voice is somewhat articulate, and when they stand erect, they discover a human face, and, indeed, are men. At night they retire to their burrows, where they live on black bread, water, and roots; they spare other men the trouble of sowing, tilling the ground, and reaping for their sustenance, and, therefore, deserve not to be in want of that bread they sow themselves.

34 Joseph du Chesne, *Le Pourtraict de la santé* (Paris, 1618), p. 237.
35 Léon Godefroy, *Voyages en Gascogne, Bigorre et Béarn* (1644–6), in Jean-Marie Goulemot, Paul Lidsky and Didier Masseau, eds, *Le Voyage en France* (Paris: Robert Laffont, 1995), p. 369.
36 See Yves-Marie Bercé, *La Vie quotidienne dans l'Aquitaine du XVIIe siècle* (Paris: Hachette, 1978), p. 25.
37 Francis Bacon, *Histoire de la vie et de la mort* (1627) (Paris, 1637), pp. 184–5. *Historia vitae et mortis: The Historie of Life and Death with Observations Naturall and Experimentall for the Prolonging of Life* (London: Humphrey Mosley, 1638).

Chapter 8 Inventing Categories

1 Jean Kerhervé, "Aux origines du bagne: galères et galériens à Brest, au temps de Louis XII," in Jean-Pierre Leguay, ed., *La Ville médiévale en deçà et au-delà de ses murs* (Rouen: Presses de l'université de Rouen, 2000), p. 243.

2 See above p. 23.
3 Jean-Antoine de Barras de La Penne, *Les Galères en campagne* (early XVIII century), quoted in Paul Masson, *Les Galères de France (1481–1781): Marseille, port de guerre* (Paris: Hachette, 1938), pp. 72–3.
4 Jean Marteilhe, *Mémoires d'un protestant condamné aux galères de France pour cause de religion*, quoted ibid., pp. 73–4.
5 Ibid., p. 74. See also Gaston Tournier, *Les Galères de France et les galériens protestants des XVIIe et XVIIIe siècles* (Montpellier: Les Presses du Languedoc, 1984), pp. 139–49.
6 Louis de Rouvroy de Saint-Simon, *Mémoires complètes et authentiques* (end of XVII–beginning of XVIII century) (Paris, 1829). Barras de La Penne, *Les Galères en campagne*, p. 75.
7 Bernardino Ramazzini, *Traité des maladies des artisans* (1700) (Paris, 1840), p. 157.
8 Regulation of April 20, 1648. See Nicolas de La Mare, *Traité de la police* (Paris, 1705–38), vol. I, p. 528.
9 Claude Gaier, *Armes et combats dans l'univers médiéval* (Brussels: De Boeck-Wesmael, 1995), p. 309.
10 Jean Chagniot, *Guerre et société à l'époque moderne* (Paris: PUF, 2001), p. 116.
11 Ibid.
12 André Corvisier, "Louis XIV, la guerre et la naissance de l'armée moderne," in *Histoire militaire de la France*, vol. 1: *Des origines à 1715* (Paris: PUF, 1992), p. 407.
13 Joseph Sevin de Quincy, *Mémoires du chevalier de Quincy* (end of XVII–beginning of XVIII century) (Paris, 1898–1901), vol. I, p. 99.
14 Saint-Simon, *Mémoires complètes et authentiques*, vol. II, p. 201.
15 De Lamont, *Les Fonctions de tous les officiers d'infanterie, depuis celle du sergent jusqu'à celle du colonel* (La Haye, 1693), p. 105
16 Ibid., pp. 7ff.
17 Ibid., pp. 65ff.
18 Ibid., p. 142.
19 Ibid., p. 120.
20 Jean de Gangnières de Souvigny, *Mémoires 1613–1638* (Paris: H. Laurens, 1906–9), vol. I, p. 11.
21 "Fille soldat," *Mercure galant* (1672), pp. 140–1.
22 Francis Bacon, *Histoire de la vie et de la mort* (1627) (Paris, 1637), p. 185. *Historia vitae et mortis: The Historie of Life and Death with Observations Naturall and Experimentall for the Prolonging of Life* (London: Humphrey Mosley, 1638).
23 François de Scépeaux de Vieilleville, *Mémoires*, in Joseph-François Michaud and Jean-Joseph-François Poujoulat, eds, *Nouvelle Collection des mémoires pour servir à l'histoire de France* (Paris, 1836), series I, vol. IX, p. 143.
24 William Shakespeare, *Othello*, Act I, scene 3.
25 Duc de Maine, letter to Mme de Maintenon, May 1689, in *Correspondance générale de Mme de Maintenon* (Paris: Charpentier, 1865–6), vol. III, p. 176.
26 Saint-Simon, *Mémoires complètes et authentiques*, vol. VI, p. 359.
27 Benjamin Deruelle, "Le Temps des experiences, 1450–1650," in Hervé Drévillon and Olivier Wieviorka, eds, *Histoire militaire de la France* (Paris: Perrin-Ministère des Armées, 2018), vol. I, p. 256.
28 Thierry Tauran, "Les prémisses," in Tauran, ed., *La Sécurité sociale: son histoire à travers les textes*, vol. VII: *Les Régimes spéciaux de sécurité sociale* (Paris: Association pour l'étude de la Sécurité sociale, 2015), p. 29.
29 Elisabeth Belmas, "L'infirmerie royale de l'hôtel des Invalides," in Giorgio Cosmacini and Georges Vigarello, eds, *Il medico di fronte alla morte (secoli XVI–XXI)* (Turin: Fondazione Ariodante Fabretti, 2008), p. 54.

30 Roger Chartier and Hugues Neveux, "La ville dominante et soumise," in Georges Duby, ed., *Histoire de la France urbaine* (Paris: Seuil, 1981), vol. III, p. 34.
31 Letter of Sixte-Quint (1587), quoted by Philippe Erlanger, *Les idées et les moeurs au temps des rois, 1558–1715* (Paris: Flammarion, 1969), p. 63.
32 Chartier and Neveux, "La ville dominante et soumise," vol. III, p. 34.
33 Pierre Goubert and Daniel Roche, *Les Français et l'Ancien Régime*, vol. I: *La Société et l'État* (Paris: Armand Colin, [1984] 1991), p. 152.
34 Giovanni Paulo Marana, *L'Espion dans les cours des princes chrétiens* (Paris, [1684] 1710), vol. V, p. 168.
35 Nicolas Boileau, "Satire VI" (1666), in *Oeuvres complètes*, ed. Françoise Escale (Paris: Gallimard, 1966), pp. 34–6.
36 Charles de Marguetel de Saint-Denis Saint-Évremond, quoted in F. Marcevaux, *Du char antique à l'automobile, les siècles de la locomotion et du transport par voie de terre* (Paris, 1897), p. 229.
37 "Annoyances of Paris," from *The Satires*, in Lionel Strachey et al., *The World's Wit and Humor: An Encyclopedia in 15 Volumes* (New York: Review of Reviews, 1905), vol. X–XI: "Paris." And Nicolas Guérard, *Le Pont Neuf, ou L'Embarras de Paris* (c. 1715), Bibliothèque nationale de France, département des estampes. See also the British Museum #1859,0514.338.233.
38 Maximilien de Béthune Sully, *Mémoires* (1591) (Paris, 1778), vol. II, p. 31.
39 Saint-Simon, *Mémoires complètes et authentiques*, vol. V, pp. 279–80.
40 Ezéchiel Spanheim, *Relation de la cour de France en 1690* (XVII century) (Paris, 1882), p. 1.
41 Saint-Simon, *Mémoires complètes et authentiques*. Gilles Ménage, *Menagiana, ou bons mots, rencontres agréables, pensées judicieuses et observations curieuses* (Amsterdam, 1713), vol. II, pp. 45–6.
42 Jean de La Bruyère, *The "Characters" of Jean de La Bruyère*, trans. Henri Van Laun (London: Nimmo, 1885), no. 6: "Of the Town," p. 168.
43 Edict of Henri III in 1585 regarding "the order that the king wants followed in his court as to the organization of the hours and the way he wants to be respected and served."
44 Mme de Maintenon, letter to M d'Aubigné, Coignac, May 8, 1681, *Correspondance générale de Mme de Maintenon*, vol. II, p. 168.
45 Letter to to M. d'Aubigné, March 2, 1681, ibid., p. 156.
46 Letter to Mme de Brinon, May 19, 1681, ibid., p. 173.
47 Letter to Mme de Brinon, September 17, 1682, ibid., p. 251.
48 Letter to the archbishop of Paris, July 28, 1698, ibid., vol. IV, p. 241.
49 Letter to the duc de Noailles, September 16, 1704, ibid., vol. V, p. 264.
50 Jacques Levron, *Les Courtisans de France* (Paris: Seuil, 1961), p. 57.
51 Jean-François Solnon, *La Cour de France* (Paris: Perrin, [1987] 2014), p. 427.
52 Saint-Simon, *Mémoires complètes et authentiques*, vol. V, p. 21.
53 Eustache de Refuge, *Traité de la cour, ou Instruction des courtisans* (Paris, 1649), p. 189.
54 Baltasar Gracian, *L'Homme de cour* (1647) (Paris: Champ libre, 1972), p. 8.
55 Charles de Marguetel de Saint-Denis Saint-Évremond, Letter of May 2, 1701, in *Oeuvres* (Paris, 1715), vol. V, p. 383.
56 Saint-Simon, *Mémoires complètes et authentiques*, vol. V, pp. 414–16. Translator's note: In the court of Louis XIV, only the king and queen could sit in armchairs. Chairs with backs but no arms were reserved for the closest-ranking relatives, and sitting on a "tabouret" or stool was allowed for certain other members of the royal family or court.
57 Solnon, *La Cour de France*, p. 428.
58 Ibid., p. 427.
59 See Emmanuel Le Roy Ladurie, with Jean-François Fitou, *Saint-Simon ou Le système de la cour* (Paris: Fayard, 1997), p. 49.

60 Mme de Sévigné, letter to Mme de Grignan, April 1, 1771, in *Correspondance*, ed. Roger Duchêne (Paris: Gallimard, 1973) vol. I, p. 205.
61 Saint-Simon, *Mémoires complètes et authentiques*, vol. II, pp. 168–9.
62 René Descartes, letter to Élisabeth, June 1645, in *Oeuvres et lettres*, ed. André Bridoux (Paris: Gallimard, 1953), p. 1190.
63 Christine de Pisan, *Le Livre des trois vertus* (XV century), in Danielle Régnier-Bohler, ed., *Voix de femmes au Moyen Âge: savoir, mystique, poésie, amours, sorcellerie, XIIe–XVe siècle* (Paris: Robert Laffont, 2006), p. 560.
64 Descartes, letter to Élisabeth, September 15, 1645, in *Oeuvres et lettres*, p. 1208.
65 Ibid.
66 Descartes, letter to Élisabeth, June 1645, ibid., p. 1190.
67 Descartes, letter to Élisabeth, June 28, 1643, ibid., p. 1160.
68 Antoine Furetière, *Dictionnaire universel* (Paris, 1690), entry "Fatiguer."
69 Jean-Baptiste Thiers, *Traité des jeux et des divertissements* (Paris, 1686), p. 353.
70 *Règlements des religieuses des Ursulines de la congrégation de Paris* (Paris, 1705), vol. II, p. 31.
71 *Institution des religieuses de l'hôpital de Notre-Dame de Charité, fondé en la ville de Lille* (Tournai, 1696), p. 76.
72 William Shakespeare, *The Merchant of Venice*, Act I, scene I.
73 Saint-Simon, *Mémoires complètes et authentiques*, vol. IV, p. 322.
74 Ibid., vol. VI, p. 84.
75 Ibid., p. 86.
76 Joseph Sevin de Quincy, *Mémoires du chevalier de Quincy*, vol. II, p. 107.
77 *Les Caquets de l'accouchée* (Paris, [1622] 1855), p. 242.
78 See Pierre Richelet, *Dictionnaire français* (Paris, 1680), entry "Fatiguer."
79 Roger de Bussy-Rabutin, *Lettres*, quoted by Pierre Richelet, ibid.
80 Letter from the princess Palatine to her half-sister (end of the XVII century), quoted in Alexandre Maral, *Louis XIV tel qu'ils l'ont vu* (Paris: Omnibus, 2015), pp. 561–2.

Chapter 9 The Advent of Numbers

1 François-Savinien d'Alquié, *Les Délices de la France, avec une description des provinces et des villes du royaume* (Amsterdam, 1670), p. 5.
2 See Éric Alonzo, *L'Architecture de la voie: historie et théories* (Marseille: Parenthèses, 2018), p. 89.
3 See "De l'établissement des postes en France," Nicolas de La Mare, *Traité de la police* (Paris, 1705–38), vol. IV, p. 556. Translator's note: There are many different definitions of a league (lieu); it generally measured approximately 3 miles, the distance a horse or human can walk in an hour.
4 See André Corvisier, *Louvois* (Paris: Fayard, 1983), p. 223.
5 Regulation of January 1629. See de La Mare, *Traité de la police*, vol. IV, p. 564.
6 Yves-Marie de La Bourdonnaye, "Mémoire de la généralité de Rouen en 1697," in Henri de Boulainvilliers, *État de la France* (Paris, [1727] 1752), vol. V, p. 10.
7 "Order for the modification of roads in Normandy," July 18, 1670. See de La Mare, *Traité de la police*, vol. IV, p. 499.
8 Ibid.
9 Ibid. Translator's note: In pre-Revolutionary France, this jurisdiction was a subdivision of a province.
10 See Alain Roger, *Court Traité du paysage* (Paris: Gallimard, [1997] 2017), "L'invention de la fenêtre," p. 83.
11 Sylvie Requemora-Gros, *Voguer vers la modernité: le voyage à travers les genres au XVIIe siècle* (Paris: Presses de l'Université Paris-Sorbonne, 2012), p. 59.

12 Claude Vacant, *Du cantonnier à l'ingénieur: les métiers de la route au fil des siècles* (Paris: Presses de l'École nationale des ponts et chaussées, 2001), p. 36.
13 Mme de Maintenon, letter to Mme des Ursins, September 1, 1714, in *Lettres inédites de Mme de Maintenon et de Mme la princesse des Ursins* (Paris, 1826), vol. III, p. 108.
14 Marie Mancini, *Mémoires* (1676) (Paris: Mercure de France, 1965), p. 101.
15 Henri Gautier, *Traité de la construction des chemins* (Toulouse, 1693). See also Alonzo, *L'Architecture de la voie*, p. 65.
16 Michel de Montaigne, *Journal de voyage en Italie* (XVI century) (Paris: Le Livre de Poche, 1974), p. 136. *The Diary of Montaigne's Journey to Italy in 1580 and 1581*, trans. E. J. Trechmann (London: Hogarth Press, 1929).
17 Joseph Sevin de Quincy, *Mémoires du chevalier de Quincy* (Paris, 1898–1901), vol. II, pp. 140–1.
18 Jean Hérault de Gourville, *Mémoires concernant les affaires auxquelles il a été employé par la cour depuis 1642 jusqu'en 1698* (Paris, 1724), vol. I, p. 56.
19 Ibid., pp. 71–1. Translator's note: The Hotel de Chavigny was a private mansion originally built in 1265. It is now a fire station.
20 François-Timoléon de Choisy, "Est-ce que nous ne ferons pas rendre gorge à tous ces gens-lá?" in Alexandre Maral, *Louis XIV tel qu'ils l'ont vu* (Paris: Omnibus, 2015), p. 255. Translator's note: Monsieur is the king's brother, Philippe the duke of Orleans.
21 Nicole de Blomac, *La Gloire et le jeu, des hommes et des chevaux, 1766–1866* (Paris: Fayard, 1991), p. 19. The observation concerns the seventeenth century.
22 Gaspard de Chavagnac, *Mémoires* (Paris, 1699), p. 235.
23 Jacques de Solleysel, *Le Parfait Maréchal* (Paris, [1654] 1675), p. 141.
24 See above p. 15.
25 "De l'établissement des relais de louage à la journèe," [On establishing post horse rentals by the day]. Order of March 1699. See de La Mare, *Traité de la police*, vol. IV, p. 599.
26 Order of July 3, 1680, ibid., p. 605.
27 Order of January 15, 1698, ibid., p. 599.
28 "Des maîtres de poste, leur établissement, ibid., p. 571.
29 See above p. 29.
30 See Jean Nicolas, *La Rébellion française: mouvements populaires et conscience sociale, 1661–1789* (Paris: Seuil, 2002).
31 Joseph du Chesne, *Le Pourtraict de la santé* (Paris, 1618), p. 335.
32 Charles Estienne and Jean Liébault, *L'Agriculture et maison rustique* (Paris, [1564] 1582), p. 12.
33 Ibid., p. 19.
34 Ibid., p. 23. Translator's note: common rye (*ruta graveolens*) is also known as "fetid rue."
35 Ibid.
36 See Claude Henrys, *Oeuvres* (Paris, 1708), vol. I, p. 303: "Of labor gangs, carters and maneuvers."
37 See Edmé de La Poix de Fréminville, *La Pratique universelle pour la rénovation des terriers et des droits seigneuriaux* (Paris, 1748), vol. II, p. 512.
38 Ibid., p. 517.
39 Ibid., p. 513.
40 Ibid.
41 See Jean-Marc Moriceau, *La Mémoire des croquants: chroniques de la France des campagnes, 1435–1652* (Paris: Tallandier, 2018), p. 288.
42 Guy Patin, letter of June 8, 1660. See Georges Mongrédien, *La Vie quotidienne sous Louis XIV* (Paris: Hachette, 1948), p. 136.
43 Ibid.
44 Corinne Maitte and Didier Terrier, "Conflits et résistances autour du temps de travail

avant l'industrialisation," *Temporalités: revue de sciences sociales et humaines*, no. 16 (2012); http://temporalites.revues.org/2203.
45 See Jean Nicolas, quoted ibid.
46 Antoine Furetière, *Dictionnaire universel* (Paris, 1690), entry "Manufacture."
47 See Michel Vergé-Franceschi, *Colbert: la politique du bon sens* (Paris: Payot, 2003), p. 347.
48 "Règlements et statuts généraux pour les longueurs, largeurs et qualités des draps, serges et autres étoffes de laine et de fil," Paris, August 1668, *in Recueil des règlements généraux et particuliers concernant les manufactures du royaume* (Paris, 1730).
49 Germain Martin, *La Grande Industrie sous le règne de Louis XIV* (Paris: Arthur Rousseau, 1899), p. 164.
50 Ibid. Translator's note: The antiquated title "garde juré" in modern France designates commercial fishery inspectors.
51 Pierre Goubert, *Cent Mille Provinciaux au XVIIe siècle: Beauvais et le Beauvaisis de 1600 à 1730* (Paris: Flammarion, 1968), p. 334.
52 "Statuts et règlements sayeteurs, haulissiers, houpiers, foulons et autres ouvriers faisant partie de la manufacture d'Amiens," Paris, August 23, 1666, article 132, in *Recueil des règlements généraux et particuliers concernant les manufactures du royaume*, p. 247.
53 See "Attribution aux maires et échevins des villes ... concernant les manufactures," August 1669, article 1, ibid., p. 1.
54 Scipion Dupleix, *La Curiosité naturelle rédigée en questions selon l'ordre alphabétique* (Paris, 1623), p. 52.
55 Jérôme Cardan, *De la subtilité et subtiles inventions* (Latin edn, 1550) (Paris, 1566), p. 428.
56 Ibid.
57 Leonardo da Vinci, *Traité de la peinture* (1651) (Paris, 1796), "Du mouvement de l'homme," p. 152.
58 André Félibien, *Entretiens sur les vies et sur les ouvrages des plus excellents peintres anciens et modernes* (1666) (Paris, 1725), vol. II, p. 540.
59 See above p. 10.
60 Galileo Galilei, *Le opere* (XVII century) (Milan, 1811), vol. II, p. 564.
61 Giovanni Alfonso Borelli, *De motu animalium* (Rome, 1680), p. 293.
62 Daniel Tauvry, *Nouvelle Anatomie raisonnée où l'on explique les usages de la structure du corps de l'homme* (Paris [1680] 1698), p. 395.
63 Philippe de La Hire, *Traité de mécanique* (Paris, [1695] 1729), p. 142.
64 See Hélène Daffos-Diogo, "Philippe de La Hire (1640–1718), précurseur de l'ergonomie," paper presented on March 28, 1987, at the Société française d'histoire de la médecine.
65 Ibid.
66 Michèle Virol, "La recherche d'une norme de productivité," in Virol, ed., *Les Oisivetés de Monsieur de Vauban* (Seyssel: Champ Vallon, 2007), p. 1634.
67 Louvois, letter to Vauban, February 7, 1685, quoted in Camille Rousset, *Histoire de Louvois et de son administration politique et militaire* (Paris, 1863), vol. III, p. 389.
68 Richelieu, letter to Cardinal de La Valette (1638), in *Lettres du cardinal duc de Richelieu* (Paris, 1696), vol. I, p. 178.
69 Virol, "La recherche d'une norme de productivité."
70 Ibid.
71 Louis de Rouvroy de Saint-Simon, *Mémoires complètes et authentiques* (Paris, 1829), vol. XIII, p. 88.
72 Virol, "La recherche d'une norme de productivité," p. 1633.
73 Ibid.
74 Ibid., p. 1634.
75 Sébastien Le Prestre de Vauban, "Règlement fait en Alsace pour le prix que les

entrepreneurs doivent payer aux soldats employés aux transports et remuement des terres de la fortification des places de Sa Majesté" (1690), in *Les Oisivetés de Monsieur de Vauban*, p. 1642.

76 Vauban, "Instruction pour servir au règlement du transport et remuement des terres" (1697), ibid., p. 1656.

77 Ibid.

78 Ibid.

Chapter 10 Diversifying Influences

1 Philippe de Villers, *Journal de voyage de deux jeunes Hollandais à Paris en 1656-1658*, ed. Armand-Prosper Faugère (Paris: Honoré Champion, 1899), p. 84.

2 François de Rabutin, *Commentaires des dernières guerres en la Gaule Belgique (1551–1559)*, in François Michaud and Jean-Joseph-François Poujoulat, eds, *Nouvelle Collection des mémoires pour servir à l'histoire de France* (Paris, 1836), series II, vol. VII, p. 412.

3 Pierre de L'Estoile, *Journal*, ibid., series II, vol. I, p. 24.

4 Ibid., p. 119.

5 Joseph Sevin de Quincy, *Mémoires du chevalier de Quincy* (Paris, 1898–1901), vol. I, p. 83.

6 Giorgio Baglivi, *Opera omnia, medico practica et anatomica* (Lugduni, 1710), p. 116. See also the quotation in Étienne Tourtelle, *Éléments de médecine théorique et pratique* (Strasbourg, 1798), vol. II, p. 306.

7 Michael Ernst Ettmüller, *Pratique générale de médecine et de tout le corps humain* (Paris, [1685] 1691), p. 292.

8 Lazare Rivière, *Observationes medicae et curationes insignes* (Paris, 1646). Trans. François Deboze (Lyon: 1688), p. 448.

9 Jean Fernel, *La Pathologie* (Paris: [1554] 1661), p. 389.

10 Ibid., p. 378.

11 Ibid., p. 320.

12 Giorgius Agricola, *De re metallica* (1541), quoted in Michel Angel, *Mines et fonderies au XVIe siècle* (Paris: Les Belles Lettres, 1989), p. 50.

13 François Ranchin, *Traité des maladies et accidents qui arrivent à ceux qui courent la poste* (Lyon, 1640), pp. 656–8.

14 See Bernardino Ramazzini, *Traité des maladies des artisans* (1700) (Paris, 1840).

15 Ibid., p. 112.

16 Ibid., p. 132.

17 *Un libertin dans L'Inde moghole: les voyages de François Bernier, 1656–1669* (Paris: Chandeigne, 2008), p. 400.

18 Robert Challe, *Journal d'un voyage fait aux Indes orientales, 1690–1691* (Paris: Mercure de France, 1979), p. 165.

19 Ibid., p. 192.

20 Mme de Sévigné, letter of June 18, 1677, in *Correspondance*, ed. Roger Duchêne (Paris: Gallimard, 1973), vol. II, p. 470.

21 Letter of April 23, 1690, ibid., vol. III, p. 869.

22 Letter of November 5, 1684, ibid., p. 152.

23 Letter of July 13, 1689, ibid., p. 640.

24 Letter of April 19, 1689, ibid., p. 580.

25 Letter of October 30, 1689, ibid., p. 740.

26 Letter of October 6, 1680, ibid., p. 33.

27 Théodore Agrippa d'Aubigné, *Sa vie à ses enfants* (XVI century), in *Œuvres*, ed. Henri Weber (Paris: Gallimard, 1969), p. 396.

28 Gédéon Tallement des Réaux, *Historiettes*, ed. Antoine Adam (Paris: Gallimard, 1960), vol. I, p. 215.

29 Marguerite de Navarre, *L'Heptaméron* (1559), in Pierre Jourda, ed., *Conteurs français du XVIe siècle* (Paris: Gallimard, 1965), p. 961.
30 Tallement des Réaux, *Historiettes*, vol. I, p. 273.
31 Robert de La Marck Fleuranges, *Mémoires*, in Joseph-François Michaud and Jean-Joseph-François Poujoulat, eds, *Nouvelle Collection des mémoires pour servir à l'histoire de France* (Paris, 1836), series I, vol. V, p. 45.
32 Antoine du Verdier, *Diverses leçons* (Lyon, 1592), p. 340.
33 Ibid.
34 Scipion Dupleix, *La Curiosité naturelle rédigée en questions selon l'ordre alphabétique* (Paris, 1623), p. 186.
35 Ibid.
36 Jacques-Auguste de Thou, *Mémoires* (XVI century), in *Nouvelle Collection des mémoires pour servir à l'histoire de France*, series I, vol. XI, p. 346.

Chapter 11 The Diversification of Remedies

1 Mme de Sévigné, letter of July 9, 1677, in *Correspondance*, ed. Roger Duchêne (Paris: Gallimard, 1973), vol. II, p. 485.
2 Letter of July 14, 1677, ibid., p. 485.
3 Robert Challe, *Journal d'un voyage fait aux Indes orientales, 1690–1691* (Paris: Mercure de France, 1979), p. 192.
4 Joseph Sevin de Quincy, *Mémoires du chevalier de Quincy* (Paris, 1898–1901), vol. II, p. 56.
5 Jean de Combe, *Hydrologie, ou discours des eaux* (Aix, 1645), pp. 50–1.
6 Jean de Combe is writing here about the "Greaux thermal springs"; his book focuses on spas.
7 See Georges Vigarello, *Le Propre et le sale: l'hygiène du corps depuis le Moyen Âge* (Paris: Seuil, 1987).
8 In François Rabelais' *Gargantua et Pantagruel* (1540) the tennis players do not bathe after their game but instead stand in front of the fireplace to dry their clothes and their humors. *Oeuvres complètes* (Paris: Gallimard, 1955), p. 55. Trans. Thomas Urquhart and Peter Anthony Motteux (London: Oxford University Press, 1934).
9 Françoise Lehoux, *Le Cadre de vie des médecins parisiens aux XVIe et XVIIe siècles* (Paris: Picard, 1976).
10 Charles Perrault, *La Querelle des anciens et des modernes en ce qui regarde les arts et les sciences* (Paris, 1688), vol. I, p. 80.
11 Laurent Joubert, *La Première et Seconde Partie des erreurs populaires touchant la médecine et le régime de santé* (Paris, 1587), part II, p. 18.
12 Benvenuto Cellini, *Mémoires* (XVI century) (Paris: Garnier, 1908), vol. II, p. 48. *The Memoirs of Benvenuto Cellini*, trans. Anne Macdonell (London: Dent, 1907).
13 Harlequin, *Nouveau Jardin des vertus et propriétez des herbes communes qui croissent aux jardins et se vendent ordinairement à la place* (Aix, 1624), p. 12.
14 See Ambroise Paré, *Oeuvres complètes* (1585), ed. Joseph-François Malgaigne (Paris, 1840), vol. I, p. 41.
15 Jacques-Auguste de Thou, *Mémoires*, in Joseph-François Michaud and Jean-Joseph-François Poujoulat, eds, *Nouvelle Collection des mémoires pour servir à l'histoire de France*, series I, vol. XI, p. 341.
16 Louis de Rouvroy de Saint-Simon, *Mémoires complètes et authentiques* (Paris, 1829), vol. XXVII, p. 183.
17 Martin Lister, *Voyage à Paris en MDCXCVIII* (Paris, 1873), p. 151.
18 Robert Challe, *Journal d'un voyage fait aux Indes orientales, 1690–1691* (Paris: Mercure de France, 1979), p. 82.

19 Nicolas Monardes, *Histoire des simples médicaments apportés de l'Amérique, desquels on se sert en médecine* (Lyon, [1588] 1619), p. 41.
20 Jean Le Royer de Prade, *Histoire du tabac, où il est traité particulièrement du tabac en poudre* (Paris, 1677), p. 127.
21 Pierre Pomet, *Histoire générale des drogues* (Paris, [1694] 1724), vol. I, p. 178. Translator's note: Pomet was pharmacist to Louis XIV and purveyor of "exotic" medicinal remedies, including sugar and coffee. *The General History of Drugs* was translated into English in 1712.
22 The first edition of Pierre Pomet's book focused on tobacco's effects on hunger and thirst and its use treating rashes and scabies. The number of remedies increased to several dozen in subsequent editions.
23 Humbert de Guillot de Goulat de La Garenne, *Les Bacchanales ou Lois de Bacchus* (Paris, 1667), p. 58.
24 Corneille Bontekoe, *Suite des nouveaux éléments de médecine* (Paris [1685] 1698), p. 112.
25 Henri-Auguste de Loménie Brienne, *Mémoires* (Amsterdam, 1719), vol. II, p. 104.
26 See above p. 62.
27 Jean Thévenot, *Voyages en Europe, Asie et Afrique* (Paris, [1689] 1727), vol. I, p. 103.
28 Nicolas de Blégny, *Secrets concernant la beauté et la santé* (Paris, 1688), vol. I, p. 685.
29 Saint-Simon, *Mémoires complètes et authentiques*, vol. XV, p. 242.
30 Louis de Mailly, *Les Entretiens des cafés de Paris et les différends qui y surviennent* (Paris, 1702), p. 2.
31 See Lucette Chabouis, *Le Livre du café* (Paris: Bordas, 1988), p. 31.
32 See Georges d'Avenel, *Histoire économique de la propriété, des salaires, des denrées, de tous les prix en général, depuis l'an 1200 jusqu'en l'an 1800* (Paris, 1898), vol. III, p. 522.
33 See Wolfgang Schivelbusch, *Histoire des stimulants* (Paris: Gallimard, 1991), p. 28.
34 Anonymous poem, 1674, excerpt quoted ibid., p. 28. See original complete English version in "A brief description of the excellent vertues of that sober and wholesome drink, called coffee, And its incomparable effects in preventing or curing most diseases incident to humane bodies," in *Early English Books Online*, www.english-corpora.org/eebo.
35 François Lebrun, "Le mariage et la famille," in Jacques Dupâquier, ed., *Histoire de la population française* (Paris: PUF, 1988), vol. II, p. 305.
36 Ibid.
37 Jean-Marc Moriceau, *La Population du sud de Paris au XVIe et XVIIe siècles*, MA thesis, Université Paris-I, 1978.
38 Denise Turrel, *Bourg-en-Bresse au XVIe siècle: les hommes et la ville* (Paris: Société de démographie historique, 1986), p. 203.
39 Lebrun, "Le mariage et la famille," p. 305.
40 Pierre Chaunu, *La Civilisation de l'Europe classique* (Paris: Arthaud, 1966), p. 190.
41 Ibid.

Chapter 12 Poverty and "Exhaustion"

1 See above p. 73.
2 Jean de La Bruyère, *Les Caractères* (1688) (Paris: Garnier, 1954), p. 295. *The "Characters" of Jean de La Bruyère*, trans. Henri Van Laun (London: Nimmo, 1885).
3 Michel-André Jubert de Bouville, chief steward of Limoges, letter to the comptroller general, January 12, 1692, in *Correspondance des contrôleurs généraux des finances avec les intendants de provinces* (Paris: Imprimerie nationale, 1874), vol. I: *1683–1699*, no. 1038.
4 "Les lieutenants, gens de conseil et échevins de Reims, au contrôleur général," January 13, 1694, ibid., no. 1272.
5 René Pillorget, "L'âge classique, 1661–1715," in Georges Duby, ed., *Histoire de la France* (Paris: Larousse, 1971), vol. II, p. 200.
6 See Jean Delumeau and Yves Lequin, eds, *Les Malheurs du temps* (Paris: Larousse, 1987).

7 Théodore Agrippa d'Aubigné, "Les Tragiques" (1615), in *Œuvres*, ed. Henri Weber (Paris: Gallimard, 1969), p. 28, verse 313.
8 Robert Castel, *Les Métamorphoses de la question sociale: une chronique du salariat* (Paris: Fayard, 1995), p. 166.
9 M. Marcillac, intendant of Rouen, letter to the comptroller general, May 29, 1685, *Correspondance des contrôleurs généraux des finances avec les intendants de province*, vol. I, no. 182.
10 Hyacinthe Serroni, bishop of Mende, letter to the comptroller general, May 4, 1699, ibid., no. 1859.
11 Louis de Bernage, intendant of Limoges, letter to the comptroller general, June 15, 1700, ibid., vol. II: *1699–1708*, no. 146.
12 Sébastien Le Prestre de Vauban, "Description géographique de l'élection de Vézelay" (1696) in Michèle Virol, ed., *Les Oisivetés de Monsieur de Vauban* (Seyssel: Champ Vallon, 2007), p. 435.
13 Ibid., p. 442.
14 Ibid.
15 Ibid., p. 443.
16 Le Prestre de Vauban, "Projet de dîme royale" (1694), ibid., p. 752.
17 Ibid., p. 795.
18 Ibid., p. 762.
19 "Mémoire sur la misère des peuples et les moyens d'y remédier" (1687), *Mémoires des intendants sur l'état de la généralité dressés pour l'instruction du duc de Bourgogne*, vol. I: *Mémoire de la généralité de Paris*, ed. Michel de Boislisle (Paris, 1881), appendix, p. 782.

Chapter 13 Feelings at Stake

1 See François-Marie Arouet de Voltaire, *Lettres philosophiques* (Amsterdam, 1734), letter 25, pp. 339–40. *Philosophical Letters or Letters Regarding the English Nation*, trans. Prudence L. Steiner, ed. John Leigh (Indianapolis: Hackett, 2007): "Man is born for action, as fire stretches above and stone below."
2 Jean Starobinski, *L'Invention de la liberté, 1700–1789* (Geneva: Skira, 1964), p. 12.
3 See above p. 28.
4 See John S. Spink, "Les avatars du 'sentiment de l'existence' de Locke à Rousseau," *Dix-huitième siècle*, no 10 (1978), pp. 269–98.
5 Victor de Sèze, *Recherches physiologiques et philosophiques sur la sensibilité ou la vie animale* (Paris, 1786), p. 156.
6 Jean Le Rond d'Alembert and Denis Diderot, *Encyclopédie, ou Dictionnaire raisonné des sciences, des arts et des métiers* (Paris, 1751–80), article "Existence." *The Encyclopedia of Diderot and d'Alembert*, University of Michigan, https://quod.lib.umich.edu/d/did/.
7 René Descartes, "I think, therefore I am." See *Discours de la méthode* (Leiden, 1637), part IV. *Discourse on Method*, trans. Richard Kennington, ed. Richard Kennington, Frank Hunt and Pamela Kraus (Indianapolis: Hackett, 2007).
8 Jacques-Henri Bernardin de Saint-Pierre, *Études de la nature* (Paris, 1784), quoted in Simone Goyard-Fabre, *La Philosophie des Lumières en France* (Paris: Klincksieck, 1972), p. 217.
9 Charlotte Burel, "Le corps sensible dans le roman du XVIIIe siècle," in Michel Delon and Jean-Christophe Abramovici, eds, *Le Corps des Lumières, de la médecine au roman* (Paris: Centre des sciences de la littérature, Université Paris-X, 1997), p. 105.
10 Ibid., p. 110.
11 Goyard-Fabre, *La Philosophie des Lumières en France*, p. 205.
12 Mme du Deffand, letter to Horace Walpole, March 13, 1771, in *Lettres (1742–1780)* (Paris: Mercure de France, 2002), p. 421.

13 Julie de Lespinasse, letter to Jacques-Antoine de Guibert, June 20, 1773, in *Lettres de Mlle de Lespinasse, suivies de ses autres oeuvres et des lettres de Mme du Deffand, de Turgot, de Bernardin de Saint-Pierre* (Paris: Charpentier, 1903), p. 14.
14 Mme d'Épinay, *Les Contre-Confessions: Histoire de Mme de Montbrillant* (1818) (Paris: Mercure de France, 1989), p. 1207.
15 Marguerite Staal de Launay, *Mémoires* (Paris, 1845), p. 127.
16 Henriette-Louise de Waldner de Freundstein, baroness of Oberkirch, *Mémoires sur la cour de Louis XVI et la société française avant 1789* (1782–6) (Paris: Mercure de France, 1982), p. 158.
17 See above p. 60.
18 Oberkirch, *Mémoires sur la cour de Louis XVI et la société française avant 1789*, p. 89.
19 Ibid., p. 151.
20 Ibid., p. 339.
21 Ibid., p. 246.
22 Ibid., p. 336.
23 Ibid., p. 155.
24 Ibid., p. 199.
25 Ibid., p. 206.
26 Ibid., p. 215.
27 Ibid., p. 272.
28 Ibid., p. 199.
29 Ibid.
30 André-Ernest-Modeste Grétry, *Mémoires, ou Essais sur la musique* (Brussels, [1789] 1829), vol. I, p. 39.
31 Ibid., p. 41.
32 George Anson, *Voyage autour du monde fait dans les années 1740, 1741, 1742, 1743, 1744* (Paris, 1750), vol. IV, p. 104. *A Voyage Round the World in the Years 1740, 1741, 1742, 1743, 1744* (Dublin: A. O'Neil, 1825), vol. III, p. 325.
33 Ibid.
34 Ibid., p. 107.
35 Ibid., p. 108.
36 Ibid., p. 111.
37 Ibid.
38 James Beresford, *Les Misères de la vie humaine, ou Les Gémissements et soupirs* (Paris, [1806] 1809), vol. II, p. 254.
39 Ibid., p. 163.
40 Ibid., p. 180.
41 Ibid., p. 105.
42 Ibid., p. 258.
43 Ibid., vol. I, p. 66.
44 Ibid., vol. II, p. 232.
45 *Lettres inédites de Napoléon Ier à Marie-Louise, écrites de 1810 à 1814* (Paris: Bibliothèques nationales de France, 1935), letter of September 14, 1811. *The Letters of Napoleon to Marie-Louise* (London: Hutchinson, 1935).
46 Ibid., letter of May 30, 1812.
47 Ibid., letter of September 6, 1812.
48 Ibid., letter of May 2, 1813.
49 Ibid., letter of May 10, 1813.
50 *Dictionnaire universel, français et latin, vulgairement appelé Dictionnaire de Trévoux* (Paris, 1743), entry "Commodité."
51 Jacques-François Blondel, *Architecture française, ou Recueil des plans* (Paris, 1752–6), vol. I, p. 239.

52 See Guillaume Janneau, *Le Mobilier français: le meuble d'ébénisterie* (Paris: Jacques Fréal, 1974).
53 Nicolas Gauger, *La Mécanique du feu, ou L'Art d'en augmenter les effets et d'en diminuer la dépense* (Paris, 1713).
54 William Ritchey Newton, *Derrière la façade: vivre au château de Versailles au XVIIIe siècle* (Paris: Perrin, 2008), p. 108.
55 Janneau, *Le Mobilier français: le meuble d'ébénisterie*, p. 74.
56 Ibid., p. 136.
57 Ibid., p. 173.
58 Jacques Cambry, *Promenades d'automne en Angleterre* (Paris, 1791), p. 44.
59 See above p. 52.
60 See Saint-Hilaire, *L'Anatomie du corps humain avec les maladies et les remèdes pour les guérir* (Paris, 1680).
61 François Boissier de Sauvages, *Nosologie méthodique* (Paris, [1763] 1770), vol. I, p. vii.
62 William Buchan, *Domestic Medicine, or A Treatise on the Prevention and Cure of Diseases by Regimen and Simple Medicines* (Paris, [1774] 1792), vol. IV, pp. 487–9.
63 See above p. 78.
64 Boissier de Sauvages, *Nosologie méthodique*, vol. II, p. 418.
65 William Buchan, *Domestic Medicine*, vol. IV, p. 487.
66 Joseph Lieutaud, *Précis de la médecine pratique* (Paris, 1761), p. 67.
67 See Georges Vigarello, *Le Sentiment de soi: histoire de la perception du corps, XVIe–XXe siècles* (Paris: Seuil, 2014), "La Sensation inédite d'un dedans," p. 22.
68 Charles-Auguste Vandermonde, *Dictionnaire portatif de santé* (Paris, [1770] 1777), vol. I, p. 368.
69 Ibid., p. 300.
70 Ibid., p. 216.
71 Ibid., vol. II, p. 495.
72 *Dictionnaire de Trévoux*, article "Epuisable," "Epuisement," "Epuiser."
73 Boissier de Sauvages, *Nosologie méthodique*, vol. II, pp. 290–364.
74 Ibid., p. 391.
75 Ibid.
76 Georges-Louis Leclerc Buffon, letter of November 21, 1759, in *Correspondance* (Paris, 1869), vol. I, p. 75.
77 Pierre-Augustin Caron de Beaumarchais, *Oeuvres complètes* (Paris, 1865), p. 206.
78 Charles-Joseph de Ligne, "De moi pendant le jour, de moi pendant la nuit" (1783), in Jeroom Vercruysse, ed., *Écrits sur la société* (Paris: Honoré Champion, 2010), p. 393.

Chapter 14 Nerves: From a Stimulus to a Whirlwind

1 François-Thomas-Marie de Baculard d'Arnaud, *Épreuves de sentiment, Sidney et Volsan* (1772) in Henri Coulet, ed., *Nouvelles du XVIIIe siècle* (Paris: Gallimard, 2002), p. 859.
2 Antoine-François Prévost, *Histoire du chevalier des Grieux et de Manon Lescaut* (1773) in René Étiemble, ed., *Romanciers du XVIIIe siècle* (Paris: Gallimard, 1966), vol. I, p. 1276. *Manon Lescaut*, trans. L. W. Tancock (London: Penguin, 1949).
3 See Nahema Hanafi, *Le Frisson et le baume: expériences féminines du corps au siècle des Lumières* (Rennes: Presses Universitaires de Rennes, 2017), p. 57.
4 Denis Diderot, *Éléments de physiologie* (1769) (Paris: Didier, 1964), pp. 63–6.
5 George Cheyne, *Règles sur la santé et sur les moyens de prolonger la vie* (1724) (Castanet: Michel d'Orions, 2002), pp. 131–2.
6 Daniel Delaroche, *Analyse des fonctions du système nerveux* (Geneva, 1778), vol. II, p. 180.
7 Ibid.
8 Joseph Priestley, *Histoire de l'électricité* (Paris, 1770), vol. I, p. xviii. *The History and*

Present State of Electricity, with Original Experiments (London: Dodley, Johnson & Cadell, 1767).

9 Ibid., p. xx.

10 See Pierre Bertholon, *De l'électricité du corps humain dans l'état de santé et de maladie* (Lyon, 1780), p. 263.

11 Priestley, *Histoire de l'électricité*, p. 253.

12 See Pierre Brunet, *Les Physiciens hollandais et la méthode expérimentale en France au XVIIIe siècle* (Paris: Blanchard, 1926); see p. 113 on the experiments by Abbé Nollet.

13 Pierre-Jean-Claude Mauduyt, "Sur l'électricité considérée relativement à l'économie animale et à l'utilité dont elle peut être en médecine," *Histoire de la société royale de médecine: ... avec les Mémoires de médecine et de physique médicale* (Paris, 1776), p. 509.

14 "Recherche sur les causes des affections hypocondriaques," *Journal de médecine*, March 1780, p. 196.

15 "L'Électricité augmente-t-elle la vitesse du pouls?" *Journal de médecine*, March 1782, p. 263.

16 See Bertholon, *De l'électricité du corps humain dans l'état de santé et de maladie*, p. 303.

17 Samuel Richardson, *Lettres anglaises, ou Histoire de Miss Clarisse Harlove*, trans. Abbé Prévost (Paris: Desjonquères, 1999), vol. I, p 553. *Clarissa, or The History of a Young Lady*, ed. Angus Ross (London: Penguin, 1985).

18 Prévost, *Histoire du chevalier des Grieux et de Manon Lescaut*, vol. I, pp. 1353 and 1365.

19 Julie de Lespinasse, *Lettres de Mlle de Lespinasse* (Paris: Charpentier, 1903), p. 75.

20 Louis-Sébastien Mercier, "Les vapeurs," in *Tableau de Paris* (1780) (Paris: Mercure de France, 1994), vol. I, p. 633.

21 Ibid.

22 Georges-Louis Leclerc Buffon, letter of August 12, 1781, in *Correspondance* (Paris, 1869), vol. II, p. 104.

23 *Journal d'un provincial à Paris, 25 juin – 1er août 1784, dédié à ma charmante amie* (Paris, 1784), p. 133.

24 Louis-Sébastien Mercier, "Les heures du jour," in *Tableau de Paris*, p. 873.

25 Jean-François Marmontel, *Mémoires* (1786), in *Oeuvres complètes* (Geneva: Slatkine, 1968), vol. I, p. 85.

26 Jean-Jacques Rousseau, *Émile, ou De l'éducation* (1761) (Paris: Garnier, 1951), p. 37. *Emile, or On Education*, trans. Allan Bloom (New York: Basic Books, 1979).

27 Louis-Sébastien Mercier, *Songe d'un hermite* (Paris, 1770), p. 4.

28 Nicolas-Edme Rétif de la Bretonne, *Tableaux de la bonne compagnie* (Paris, 1787). p. 27.

29 Ibid., p. 55.

30 Ulrich Bräker, *Le Pauvre Homme de Toggenbourg* (XVIII century), trans. Caty Dentan, (Lausanne: Éditions de l'Aire, 1978), p. 156.

31 Frédéric Hoffman, *Consultations de médecine* (Paris, 1754), vol. I, p. 165.

32 Samuel-Auguste Tissot, *L'Onanisme* (1760) (Paris: Éditions de la Différence, 1991), p. 48.

33 Ibid., pp. 50–1.

34 Ibid., p. 45.

35 Ibid., p. 47.

36 Hoffman, *Consultations de médecine*, vol. VII, pp. 328–30.

37 "Prix," *Journal de médecine, chirurgie, pharmacie*, July 1777, p. 92.

38 Samuel-Auguste Tissot, *Traité des nerfs et de leurs maladies* (1770–9), in *Oeuvres* (Paris, 1861), p. 60.

39 See John Brewer, *The Pleasures of the Imagination: English Culture in the Eighteenth Century* (Chicago: University of Chicago Press, 1997), "The Pleasures of the Imagination," p. 56.

40 Jean-Baptiste Louvet de Couvray, *La Fin des amours du chevalier de Faublas* (1790), in *Romanciers du XVIIIe siècle*, vol. II, p. 907.

41 Jacques-Antoine-Hippolyte de Guibert, *Essai général de tactique* (London, [1772] 1773), p. 15. *A General Essay on Tactics, with an Introductory Discourse upon the Present State of Politics* (London: J. Milan, 1791).
42 Jean Verdier, *Cours d'éducation à l'usage des élèves destinés aux premières professions et aux grands emplois de l'État* (Paris, 1772), pp. 9–10.
43 Tissot, *Traité des nerfs et de leurs maladies*, p. 159.
44 Ibid.
45 Jean-Baptiste Moheau, *Recherches et considérations sur la population de la France* (Paris, 1778), p. 122.
46 Ferdinando Galiani, letter to Diderot, September 5, 1772. See Denis Diderot, *Oeuvres complètes* (Paris: Le Club français du livre: 1971), vol. X, p. 951.
47 Jacques Ballexserd, Dissertation sur l'éducation physique des enfants, depuis leur naissance jusqu'á l'âge de la puberté (Paris, 1762) p. 25.
48 Jean Le Rond d'Alembert and Denis Diderot, *Encyclopédie, ou Dictionnaire raisonné des sciences, des arts et des métiers* (Paris, 1751–80), vol. XXV, entry "Proportions," p. 604. Collaborative Translation Project, *The Encyclopedia of Diderot and d'Alembert*, University of Michigan, https://quod.lib.umich.edu/d/did/.
49 Laurence Sterne, *Voyage sentimental à travers la France et l'Italie*, in *Voyages imaginaires, songes, visions et romans cabalistiques* (Amsterdam, 1789), vol. XXVIII, p. 104. *A Sentimental Journey and Other Writings*, ed. Ian Jack and Tim Parnell (Oxford: Oxford University Press, 1968), p. 607.
50 Ibid.
51 See Patrice Bourdelais, *Les Épidémies terrassées: une histoire de pays riches* (Paris: La Martinière, 2003), on "Reducing Deaths," p. 59.
52 See Isabelle Queval, *S'accomplir ou se dépasser: essai sur le sport contemporain* (Paris: Gallimard, 2004), on the "legibility of progress in the XVIII century," p. 125.
53 Jean-Charles Desessartz, *Traité de l'éducation corporelle des enfants en bas âge* (Paris, 1760), p. vi.
54 Charles-Augustin Vandermonde, *Essai sur la manière de perfectionner l'espèce humaine* (Paris, 1756), vol. II, p. 31.
55 Ibid., p. vii.
56 Patrice Bourdelais, ed., *Les Hygiénistes, enjeux, modèles pratiques, XVIIIe–XXe siècles* (Paris: Belin, 2001). See "The strategies of developing public health."
57 Léopold de Genneté, *Purification de l'air croupissant dans les hôpitaux, les prisons et les vaisseaux de mer* (Nancy, 1767), p. 3.

Chapter 15 Speaking of Strength

1 Pierre Rosanvallon, *L'État en France, de 1789 à nos jours* (Paris: Seuil, 1990), p. 45.
2 Georges-Louis Leclerc Buffon, *De l'homme* (1749), in *Oeuvres complètes* (Paris, 1836), vol. IV, p. 100.
3 See above p. 73.
4 Jean-Jacques Rousseau, *Discours sur l'origine de l'inégalité* (1755) (Paris: Flammarion, 1931), p. 93. *A Discourse upon the Origin and Foundation of the Inequality among Mankind* (London: Dodsley, 1761).
5 Isabelle Queval, *S'accomplir ou se dépasser: essai sur le sport contemporain* (Paris: Gallimard, 2004), p. 125.
6 See the first anthropological studies, Jean-Nicolas Démeunier, *L'Esprit des usages et des coutumes des différents peuples* (London, 1776), vol. I, p. v: "Le genre humain offrira désormais un spectacle monotone" [Stressing the diversity to be found in different human groups, Démeunier warned that "in the future humanity will be a monotonous sight."]

7 Buffon, *De l'homme*, vol. IV, p. 100.
8 Ibid.
9 Démeunier, *L'Esprit des usages et des coutumes des différents peuples*, vol. III, p. 66.
10 Jean-Théophile Désaguliers, *Cours de physique expérimentale* (Paris, [1717] 1751), vol. I, p. 259.
11 See above p. 88.
12 See Daniel Roche, "L'Encyclopédie et les pratiques du savoir au XVIIIe siècle," in Roland Schaer, ed., *Tous les savoirs du monde: encyclopédies et bibliothèques, de Sumer au XXIe siècle* (Paris: Bibliothèque nationale de France–Flammarion, 1996), p. 370.
13 Michel Delon, *L'Idée d'énergie au tournant des Lumières, 1770–1820* (Paris: PUF, 1988).
14 Ibid., p. 237.
15 Dominique Méda, *Travail: la révolution nécessaire* (La Tour-d'Aigues: Édition de l'Aube, 2013), p. 49.
16 Philippe Minard, *La Fortune du colbertisme: état et industrie dans la France des Lumières* (Paris: Fayard, 1998), p. 188.
17 See above p. 181.
18 See above p. 115.
19 See Hélène Vérin, *La Gloire des ingénieurs: l'intelligence technique du XVIe au XVIIIe siècle* (Paris: Albin Michel, 1993).
20 See above p. 89.
21 Jacques Proust, *L'Encyclopédie Diderot et d'Alembert: planches et commentaires* (Paris: EDDL, 2001), p. 14.
22 Jean Le Rond d'Alembert, "Discours préliminaire," in Diderot and d'Alembert, *Encyclopédie*, vol. I, p. xiii. See also the letter sent to subscribers (1751): "There are many things one learns only in a workshop."
23 See the 113 volumes published on this subject by the French Royal Academy of Sciences between 1761 and 1788.
24 Abbé Jaubert, *Dictionnaire raisonné universel des arts et métiers* (Paris, 1773), vol. I, p. xiv.
25 Henri-Louis Duhamel du Monceau, *Éléments d'agriculture* (Paris, 1763), vol. I, p. 376.
26 Duhamel du Monceau, *L'Art du couvreur* (1766), in *Descriptions des arts et métiers faites et approuvées par Messieurs de l'Académie royale des sciences* (Paris, 1761–89), p. 34.
27 Hulot père, *L'Art du tourneur mécanicien* (1775), ibid., p. 271.
28 Diderot and d'Alembert, *Encyclopédie*, entry "Rame."
29 Charles Coulomb, "Résultats de plusieurs expériences destinées à déterminer la quantité d'action que les hommes peuvent fournir par leur travail journalier," *Mémoires de mathématiques*, 6 ventôse an 6 [24 February 1798], p. 423.
30 *Règlement concernant l'exercice et les manoeuvres de l'infanterie* (Lille, 1791), pp. 28–9.
31 Jacques-Antoine-Hippolyte de Guibert, *Essai général de tactique* (London, [1772] 1773), p. 30.
32 Ibid., p. 31.
33 AD Calvados, C 3372, *Mémoire concernant la manutention des corvées dans la généralité de Caen* (1762), quoted in Anne Conchon, *La Corvée des grands chemins au XVIIIe siècle: économie d'une institution* (Rennes: Presses universitaires de Rennes, 2016), p. 61.
34 See above p. 114.
35 Yannick Fonteneau, "'Les ouvriers ... sont des espèces d'automates montés pour une certaine suite de mouvements': fondations d'une représentation mécanique du temps laborieux (1700–1750)," in Corine Maitte and Didier Terrier, eds, *Le Temps du travail: norms, pratiques, évolutions, XIVe–XIXe siècle* (Rennes: Presses universitaires de Rennes, 2014), p. 321.
36 Daniel Bernoulli, "Recherches sur la manière la plus avantageuse de suppléer à l'action

du vent sur les grands vaisseaux, soit en y appliquant les rames, soit en y employant quelqu'autre moyen que ce puisse être," *Recueil des pièces qui ont remporté les prix de l'Académie royale des sciences*, 7 (1769), p. 10.

37 See Barthélemy Durrive, "Deux ouvriers-machine, avant et après Taylor," *L'Homme et la société*, 3/205 (2017), p. 57.

38 François Vatin, "Le 'travail physique' comme valeur mécanique (XVIIIe–XIXe siècle)", *Cahiers d'histoire: revue d'histoire critique*, no. 110 (2009), p. 9.

39 See above p. 88 re Vauban.

40 Bernoulli, "Recherches sur la manière la plus avantageuse de suppléer à l'action du vent sur les grands vaisseaux," p. 4.

41 Ibid., p. 7.

42 Fonteneau, "'Les ouvriers ... sont des espèces d'automates montés pour une certaine suite de mouvements,'"p. 321.

43 Coulomb, "Résultats de plusieurs expériences destinées à déterminer la quantité d'action que les hommes peuvent fournir par leur travail journalier," p. 382.

44 See above chapter 15 re Bernoulli.

45 Coulomb, "Résultats de plusieurs expériences destinées à déterminer la quantité d'action que les hommes peuvent fournir par leur travail journalier," p. 382.

46 Ibid., p. 381.

47 Ibid., p. 388.

48 Ibid., p. 390.

49 See the discussion of Coulomb's project at the beginning of the twentieth century in Jules Amar, *Le Moteur humain et les bases scientifiques du travail professionel* (Paris: Dunod, 1914), p. 236.

50 Coulomb, "Résultats de plusieurs expériences destinées à déterminer la quantité d'action que les hommes peuvent fournir par leur travail journalier," p. 417.

51 Ibid.

52 See Amar, *Le Moteur humain et les bases scientifiques du travail professionel*, p. 237: Les expériences "de Coulomb, toujours tirées d'une observation unique et parfois empruntées à des observateurs peu sûrs, n'ont pas assez de poids, malgré l'autorité hors de pair du célèbre physicien" [Coulomb's experiments, always based on a single observation that was sometimes conducted by an unreliable observer, are of limited value, despite the unquestionable renown of this well-known engineer].

53 See above p. 118.

54 Fonteneau, "'Les ouvriers ... sont des espèces d'automates montés pour une certaine suite de mouvements,'" p. 312.

55 See François Dagognet, *Écriture et iconographie* (Paris: Vrin, 1973), pp. 87 and 89.

56 Antoine-Laurent de Lavoisier, "Expériences sur la respiration des animaux et sur les changements qui arrivent à l'air en passant dans les poumons" (1777), quoted in Vatin, "Le 'travail physique' comme valeur mécanique (XVIIIe–XIXe siècle)", p. 45.

57 Joseph Priestley, *Expériences et observations sur différentes espèces d'air* (1774) (Paris: 1777–80), vol. I, p. 126. *Experiments and Observations on Different Kinds of Air* (London: J. Johnson, 1774).

Chapter 16 Suffering from Fatigue: The Beginning of Compassion

1 See above p. 90.

2 Louis-Sébastien Mercier, "Portefaix," in *Tableau de Paris* (1780) (Paris: Mercure de France, 1994), vol. I, p. 789.

3 "Chaises à porteurs," ibid., p. 1312.

4 "Portefaix (femmes)," ibid., p. 791.

5 Antoine-René de Voyer d'Argenson de Paulmy, letter of October 1749, quoted in

François Cadilhon, ed., *La France d'Ancien Régime: textes et documents, 1484–1789* (Bordeaux: Presses universitaires de Bordeaux, 2002). p. 396.

6 Claude-François Berthelot, *La Mécanique appliquée aux arts, aux manufactures, à l'agriculture et à la guerre* (Paris, 1782), vol. I, p. 19.

7 Jean-Jacques Rousseau, *Émile, ou De l'éducation* (1761) (Paris: Garnier, 1951); see p. 61, "Que faut-il penser de cette éducation barbare qui charge un enfant de chaînes de toutes espèces?"

8 Cesare Beccaria, *Des délits et des peines* (1764) (Paris, 1766); see p. 125, "Qui ne frémirait d'horreur en voyant dans l'histoire les supplices barbares et inutiles inventés et appliqués froidement par des hommes qui se prétendent sages?" *On Crimes and Punishments*, trans. David Young (Indianapolis: Hackett, 1986).

9 Guillaume-Thomas Raynal, *Histoire philosophique et politique des établissements des entreprises et du commerce des Européens dans les deux Indes* (Paris, [1770] 1775), vol. IV, p. 150.

10 Antoine-Gabriel Jars, *Voyages métallurgiques* (Paris, 1774), vol. I, p. 268.

11 Claude Henrys, *Oeuvres, contenant son receuil d'ârrets, ses plaidoyers et harangues* (Paris, 1708), vol. I, p. 303.

12 See Jean-Baptiste Denisart, *Collections de décisions nouvelles et de notions relatives à la jurisprudence* (Paris [1754] 1775) entry "Corvées."

13 Louis-Philippe de Ségur, *Mémoires, ou Souvenirs et anecdotes* (Paris, [1824] 1827), vol. I, p. 230.

14 Pierre Goubert and Daniel Roche, *Les Français et l'Ancien Régime*, vol. II: *Culture et société* (Paris: Armand Colin, 1991), p. 338.

15 Paul Mantoux, *La Révolution industrielle au XVIIIe siècle: essai sur les commencements de la grande industrie en Angleterre* (Paris: Georges Bellais, 1906), p. 57.

16 Pierre Goubert and Daniel Roche, *Les Français et l'Ancien Régime*, p. 338

17 Ibid.

18 Denis Diderot, "La réfutation d'Helvétius" (1783), in *Oeuvres complètes* (Paris: Le Club français du livre: 1971), vol. XI, p. 458.

19 François Raymond, "Topographie médicale de Marseille," in *Histoire de la société royale de médecine* (Paris, 1777–8), p. 127.

20 Georges-Louis Leclerc Buffon, *De l'homme* (1749), in *Oeuvres complètes* (Paris, 1836), vol. IV, p. 353.

21 Ibid., pp. 293ff.

22 See above p. 126.

23 Jean-François d'Aubuisson, *Rapport XVIIIe siècle*, AN F14 7822.

24 Vincent-Marie Viénot Vaublanc, *Mémoires* (Paris, 1857), p. 353.

25 See Corine Maitte and Denis Woronoff, "Les mondes ouvriers," in Corine Maitte, Philippe Minard and Matthieu de Oliveira, eds, *La Gloire de l'industrie, XVIIe–XIXe siècle: faire de l'histoire avec Gérard Gayot* (Rennes: Presses universitaires de Rennes, 2012), p. 253.

26 Henri-Louis Duhamel Du Morceau, "Art de la draperie," *Descriptions des arts et métiers faites ou approuvées par Messieurs de l'Académie royale des sciences*, vol. XXIII (Paris, 1761) p. 111.

27 Gérard Gayot, "'Les ouvriers les plus nécessaires' sur le marché du travail des manufactures de draps aux XVIIe–XVIIIe siècles," in Philippe Minard and Gérard Gayot, eds, *Les ouvriers qualifiés de l'industrie (XVIe–XXe siècle): formation, emploi, migrations*. Villeneuve-d'Ascq: Revue du Nord, 2001.

28 Adam Smith, *An Inquiry into the Nature and Causes of the Wealth of Nations* (London: J. M. Dent, 1910), vol. I, pp. 5–6.

29 Ibid., p. 9.

30 See Jean-Pierre Séris, *Qu'est-ce que la division du travail?* (Paris: Vrin, 1994), p. 55.

31 Ibid., p. 91.
32 Mantoux, *La Révolution industrielle au XVIIIe siècle*, p. 392.
33 Samuel Smiles, *Lives of Boulton and Watt* (London, 1865), p. 482.
34 Mantoux, *La Révolution industrielle au XVIIIe siècle*, p. 426.
35 See Jean-Rodolphe Perronet, *Recueil des planches sur les sciences, les arts ...* (Paris, 1765), vol. IV, p. 52, who was concerned with the "fatigue caused by repeatedly performing the same actions constantly."
36 Samuel Smiles, *Josiah Wedgwood, F.R.S.: His Personal History* (London, 1894), quoted in Mantoux, *La Révolution industrielle au XVIIIe siècle*, p. 418.
37 Michel Beaud, *Histoire du capitalisme, 1500–2010* (Paris: Seuil, [1980] 2010), p. 105.
38 Jules Michelet, *Le Peuple* (Paris, 1846), p. 45.
39 Mantoux, *La Révolution industrielle au XVIIIe siècle*. p.398.

Chapter 17 Fatigue is in Demand: The Challenge Begins

1 Fatigue is no longer a "punishment or a route to salvation." See above p. 24.
2 Mme du Deffand, letter of June 26, 1771, in *Lettres (1742–1780)* (Paris: Mercure de France, 2002), p. 441.
3 Denis Diderot, letter to Mme Diderot, October 8, 1773, in *Oeuvres complètes* (Paris: Le Club français du livre: 1971), vol. X, p. 1079.
4 See above p. 66.
5 See above p. 36.
6 Diderot, letter of October 15, 1773, in *Oeuvres complètes*, vol. X, p. 1085.
7 See Jean-Baptiste Pressavin, *L'Art de prolonger la vie et de conserver la santé* (Paris, 1784), p. 154.
8 See "Tabouret d'équitation," *Affiches, annonces et avis divers* (1761), p. 185.
9 Jean Le Rond d'Alembert and Denis Diderot, *Encyclopédie* (Paris, 1751–80), entry "Équitation."
10 See above p. 67.
11 Henry Lee, *Historique des courses de chevaux, de l'Antiquité à ce jour* (Paris: Fasquelle, 1914), p. 89.
12 Louis-Sébastien Mercier, "Jockeys," in *Tableau de Paris* (1780) (Paris: Mercure de France, 1994), vol. II, p. 272.
13 Jean-Nicolas Dufort de Cheverny, *Mémoires* (XVIII century) (Paris: Perrin, 1990), p. 165.
14 Ibid.
15 See Edmond-Jean-François Barbier, *Chronique de la Régence et du règne de Louis XV* (Paris, 1858), vol. I, p. 230.
16 Ibid.
17 Emmanuel de Croÿ-Solre, *Journal inédit du duc de Croÿ (1718–1784)* (Paris: Flammarion, 1906–21), vol. I, p. 230.
18 Ibid., vol. II, p. 212. Translator's note: The race vehicle was a "berline," considered very maneuverable and lighter than older-style carriages.
19 See above p. 10.
20 See above p. 131.
21 Jeanne Beausoleil, ed., *Jean Brunhes autour du monde: regards d'un géographe, regards de la géographie* (Boulogne: Musée Albert-Kahn, 1993). See the introduction by Michel Lesourd, "Appropriation du monde," p. 17.
22 James Cook, *Voyage dans l'hémisphère austral et autour du monde, fait sur les vaisseaux du roi, L'Aventure et La Résolution, en 1772, 1773, 1774 et 1775* (Paris, 1778), introduction, p. vi. *A Voyage towards the South Pole, and around the World* (London: Strahan and Cadell, 1785).

23 Louis-Antoine de Bougainville, *Voyage autour du monde par la frégate du roi La Boudeuse et la flûte L'Étoile en 1766, 1767, 1768 et 1769* (Paris, 1771). See Bougainville's dedication to the king: "Under your auspices, Sire, we undertook this venture; challenges of all kinds awaited us at every step. We didn't lack patience or zeal."
24 Édouard Charton, "La Pérouse, navigateur français," in *Voyageurs anciens et modernes* (Paris, 1861), vol. IV, p. 440.
25 Yves-Joseph de Kerguelen de Trémarec, *Relation d'un voyage dans la mer du Nord, aux côtes d'Islande, de Groenland, de Ferro, de Schettland, des Orcades et de Norvège, fait entre 1767 et 1768* (Paris, 1771), p. v. *A General Collection of the Best and Most Interesting Voyages and Travels in All Parts of the World*, trans. John Pinkerton (London: Longman, Hurst, Rees & Orms, 1808), vol. I, pp. 715, 738–9.
26 Henri Wilson, *Relation des îles Pelew* (Paris, [1788] 1793), p. 2.
27 Anders Sparrman, *Voyage au cap de Bonne-Espérance et autour du monde avec le capitaine Cook* (Paris, 1787), vol. I, p. xxxv.
28 Marc Loriol, *Le Temps de la fatigue* (Paris: Anthropos, 2000), p. 60.
29 William Windham, letter dated 1741, in Henri Ferrand, *Premiers Voyages à Chamouni: lettres de Windham et de Martel* (Lyon, 1912), p. 17.
30 Marc-Théodore Bourrit, *Nouvelle Description des glacières et glaciers de Savoie, particulièrement de la vallée de Chamouni et du Mont-Blanc* (Geneva, 1785), p. 158.
31 Windham, letter dated 1741, in Ferrand, *Premiers Voyages à Chamouni*, pp. 41–2.
32 Horace-Bénédict de Saussure, *Voyages dans les Alpes* (Paris, 1787), vol. III, p. 147.
33 Bourrit, *Nouvelle Description des glacières et glaciers de Savoie*, p. 154.
34 Saussure, *Voyages dans les Alpes*, vol. III, p. 144.
35 Ibid., p. 147.
36 Ibid., p. 146.

Chapter 18 The Beginning of Training and the Review of Time

1 See above p. 106.
2 Louis Desbois de Rochefort, *Cours élémentaire de matière médicale* (Paris, 1789), vol. II, p. 27. Translator's note: See also Hisao Ishizuka's study *Fiber, Medicine and Culture in the British Enlightenment* (New York: Palgrave Macmillan, 2016) for a definition and discussion of fibers and "solids" (French "*solides*") in European medicine.
3 Antoine Baumé, *Éléments de pharmacie théorique et pratique* (Paris, [1762] 1770), p. 812.
4 Rochefort, *Cours élémentaire de matière médicale*, p. 35.
5 Joseph Lieutaud, *Précis de la matière médicale* (Paris, 1766), p. 173.
6 *L'Avant-Coureur*, February 18, 1760.
7 See Jean Le Rond d'Alembert and Denis Diderot, *Encyclopédie* (Paris, 1751–80), entries "Orange," "Menthe," Tartre," "Eau de carme," "Eau de Balaruc."
8 *Dictionnaire portatif de santé* (Paris, 1760), entry "Epuisement."
9 Charles-Philippe d'Albert de Luynes, *Mémoires sur la cour de Louis XV (1735–1758)* (Paris, 1860–5), vol. I, p. 137.
10 James Boswell, *Journal intime d'un mélancolique, 1762–1769* (Paris: Hachette, 1986), p. 116.
11 Emmanuel de Croÿ-Solre, *Journal inédit du duc de Croÿ (1718–1784)* (Paris: Flammarion, 1906–21), vol. II, p. 369.
12 Giacomo Casanova de Seingault, *Mémoires* (Brussels [1825], 1860), vol. VI, p. 10. *The Memoirs of Jacques Casanova de Seingault, 1725–1798*, trans. Arthur Machen (London: Elek Books, 1894).
13 Ibid., vol. V, pp. 60, 84.
14 See Eugen Duehren, "La prostitution et la vie sexuelle au XVIIIe siècle," in Michel Camus, ed., *Sade: Obliques*, nos. 12–13(1977), pp. 270–1.

15 Donatien Alphonse François de Sade, *L'Histoire de Juliette* (1797), in *Oeuvres complètes* (Paris: Tête de Feuilles, 1973), vol. VII, pp. 512–13.
16 Ibid., vol. IX, p. 508.
17 Eugen Duehren, "La prostitution et la vie sexuelle au XVIIIe siècle," pp. 270–1.
18 See John Davenport, *Aphrodisiacs and Anti-Aphrodisiacs: Three Essays on the Power of Reproduction* (London, 1869), p. 94.
19 Mme d'Épinay, *Les Contre-Confessions: Histoire de Mme de Montbrillant* (1818) (Paris: Mercure de France, 1989), p. 1282.
20 Dominique-Jean Larrey, *Relation historique et chirurgicale de l'expédition de l'armée d'Orient en Égypte et en Syrie* (Paris, 1803), p. 11.
21 See above p. 84.
22 Pierre Pomme, *Traité des affections vaporeuses des deux sexes* (Lyon, 1763), p. 18.
23 Charles-Augustin Vandermonde, *Essai sur la manière de perfectionner l'espèce humaine* (Paris, 1756), vol. I, p. 189.
24 Georges-Louis Leclerc Buffon, letter of July 14, 1783, in *Correspondance* (Paris, 1869), p. 167.
25 Louis-Sébastien Mercier, "Les vapeurs," in *Tableau de Paris* (1780) (Paris: Mercure de France, 1994), vol. I, p. 634.
26 Jean-Louis de Fourcroy, *Les enfants élevés dans l'ordre de la nature* (Paris, [1775] 1783), p. 96.
27 See *Une femme d'affaires au XVIIIe siècle: la correspondance de Mme de Maraise, collaboratrice d'Oberkampf* (Toulouse: Privat, 1981), p. 74.
28 William Buchan, *Le Conservateur de la santé des mères et des enfants* (Paris, 1805), p. 109.
29 Jean Pontas, *Dictionnaire des cas de conscience, ou Décisions des plus considérables difficultés touchant la morale et la discipline ecclésiastique* (rev. edn, Paris, [1715] 1743), entry "Danse."
30 See above p. 15.
31 François-Alexandre-Pierre de Garsault, *Le Nouveau Parfait Maréchal, ou La Connaissance générale et universelle du cheval* (Paris, [1741] 1755), p. 114.
32 *The art of manual defence or system of boxing* (London, 1789), in John Sinclair, *The Code of Health and Longevity* (Edinburgh, 1807), vol. II, appendix IV, p. 163. See also André Rauch, "La Notion de *training* à la fin de siècle des Lumières," *Travaux et recherches en EPS de l'INSEP*, no. 6 (1980), pp. 61–7.
33 Jean-Augustin Amar Du Rivier and Louis-François Jauffret, *La Gymnastique de la jeunesse* (Paris, 1803), p. 72.
34 Stéphanie-Félicité Du Crest, comtesse de Genlis, *Journal des princes* (Chantilly: Musée Condé).
35 Ibid.
36 John Pringle, *Observations sur les maladies des armées, dans les camps et dans les garnisons* (Paris [1753] 1771), vol. I, pp. 212–13.
37 Jourdan Lecointe, *La Santé de Mars* (Paris, 1793), p. 339.
38 Jacques-Antoine-Hippolyte de Guibert, *Essai général de tactique* (London, [1772] 1773), p. 39.
39 Jules-César Boissat, *Des causes physiques du perfectionnement de l'espèce humaine* (Paris, 1800), p. 5.

Part IV The Nineteenth Century and the Challenge of Numbers

1 Honoré de Balzac, *La Comédie humaine*, ed. Marcel Bouteron (Paris: Gallimard, 1969), p. 12. See Foreword to *The Human Comedy*, trans. George Saintsbury.
2 See above p. 91.

Chapter 19 The Steadfast Citizen

1 Giovanna Procacci, *Gouverner la misère: la question sociale en France (1789–1848)* (Paris: Seuil, 1993), p. 233.
2 *Les Français peints par eux-mêmes: encyclopédie morale du dix-neuvième siècle*, 9 vols (Paris, 1840).
3 "L'avocat," ibid., vol. II, pp. 67–8.
4 "La journée d'un médecin," ibid., vol. IX, p. 179.
5 "Le pharmacien," ibid., vol. III, p. 319.
6 "Le commissaire de police," ibid., vol. III, p. 349.
7 "Le gendarme," ibid., vol. II, p. 50.
8 "Le garde du commerce," ibid., vol. III, p. 262.
9 "L'herboriste," ibid., vol. II, p. 232.
10 "Les maraîchers," ibid., vol. V, p. 325.
11 'L'épicier," ibid., vol. I, p. 3.
12 "Le chiffonnier," ibid., vol. III, p. 335.
13 "L'homme à tout faire," ibid., vol. II, p. 257.
14 "La dévote," ibid., vol. IV, p. 133.
15 "Le compositeur typographe," ibid., vol. II, p. 272.
16 Alexandre de Saillet, *Les Enfants peints par eux-mêmes: sujets de composition donnés á ses élèves* (Paris: Desesserts, 1841), p. 69. Translator's note: The book cover describes the author as a boarding-school teacher (*maître de pension*).
17 Victor Hugo, "À l'obéissance passive," in *Les Châtiments* (Paris, 1853), p. 82.
18 See above p. 98.
19 Sergent Bourgogne, *Mémoires, 1812–1813*, ed. Paul Cottin (Paris: Hachette, 1909), p. 206.
20 Ibid., p. 205.
21 Ibid., p. 213.
22 See above p. 97.
23 See above p. 60.
24 See above pp. 130ff.
25 Gustave des Essards, *Vertu et travail* (Paris: Louis Janet, 1840).
26 Ibid., p. 116.
27 Ibid.
28 Ibid., p. 117.
29 Ibid., p. 229.
30 See *Le Fabricant: journal du maître et de l'ouvrier*, March 19 and June 11, 1842.
31 "Antoine-Jean Beauvisage," in *Portraits et histoire des hommes utiles* (Paris, 1837–8), p. 369.
32 Ibid., p. 370.
33 Ibid., p. 368.
34 Ibid., p. 370.
35 Ibid.
36 Honoré de Balzac, *Le Médecin de campagne*, in *La Comédie humaine*, ed. Marcel Bouteron (Paris: Gallimard, 1969), vol. VIII, p. 352.
37 Ibid., p. 359.
38 Balzac, *La Maison Nucingen*, ibid., vol. V, p. 618.
39 Balzac, *Albert Savarus*, ibid., vol. I, p. 766.
40 Ibid., p. 814.
41 Ibid.
42 Ibid., p. 819.
43 See above p. 107.

44 Balzac, *La Fille aux yeux d'or*, in *La Comédie humaine*, vol. V, p. 257.
45 See above p. 50.
46 Claude-Ignace Busson, *Instructions et conseils aux filles de service et à tous les domestiques en général* (Paris, 1842), p. 168.
47 Pierre Guiral and Guy Thuillier, *La Vie quotidienne des domestiques au XIXe siècle* (Paris: Hachette, 1978), p. 27.
48 See above p. 145.
49 Gustave Planche, "La journée d'un journaliste," *Paris, ou Le Livre des cent et un* (Paris, 1832), vol. VI, p. 145.
50 Émile de la Bédollière, *Les Industriels: métiers et professions en France* (Paris, 1842), pp. 19–20.
51 Étienne de Jouy, *L'Hermite de la Chaussée-d'Antin, ou Observations sur les moeurs et les usages parisiens au commencement du XIXe siècle* (Paris, [1812] 1816), vol. V, pp. 156ff.
52 "L'employé," *Les Français peints par eux-mêmes*, vol. I, p. 306.
53 "Philosophie du peuple," *Le Fabricant: journal du maître et de l'ouvrier*, June 18, 1842.
54 Marc-Antoine Jullien, *Essai sur une méthode qui a pour objet de bien régler l'emploi du temps, premier moyen d'être heureux* (Paris, 1808), p. 28.
55 Julien-Joseph Virey, *De la puissance vitale considérée dans ses fonctions physiologiques chez l'homme et tous les êtres organisés* (Paris, 1823), p. 423.
56 Constant Le Tellier, *Manuel mythologique de la jeunesse, ou Instruction sur la mythologie par demandes et réponses* (Paris, 1812), p. 392.
57 Balzac *Les Illusions perdues* (Paris, 1837–43). *Lost Illusions*, trans. Kathleen Raine (New York: Modern Library, 2001).
58 See Eugénie de Keyser, *L'Occident romantique, 1789–1850* (Geneva: Skira, 1965), p. 9: "La souveraineté de l'argent alourdit la marche des hommes."
59 Ibid.
60 Alfred Musset, "La Nuit de mai" (1835), in *Les nuits* (Paris: Meynial, 1911), p. 31. "The May Night," American Verse Project, p. 240, https://quod.lib.umich.edu/amverse/BAK3042.0001.001.1:29?rgn=div1;view=fulltext.
61 Balzac, *La Peau de chagrin*, in *La Comédie humaine*, vol. IX, p. 243. *The Magic Skin*, trans. Ellen Marriage, www.gutenberg.org/files/1307/1307-/1307-h.htm 2016.
62 Ibid., p. 91.
63 Balzac, "Les Souffrances de l'inventeur," ibid., vol. IV, p. 883.
64 Alfred de Vigny, *Journal*, in *Oeuvres*, ed. Fernand Baldensperger (Paris: Gallimard, 1955), vol. II, p. 990.
65 This work also described the "new citizen" and his exertions for the benefit of all. See above pp. 145ff.
66 Pierre-François Tissot, "La jeunesse depuis cinquante ans," in *Les Français peints par eux-mêmes*, vol. II, p. xvii.
67 Maurice Alhoy, Louis Huart and Charles Philipon, *Les Cent et un Robert-Macaire, composés et dessinés par M. Henri Daumier sur les idées et les légendes de M. Charles Philipon* (Paris, 1839), "Robert Macaire et ses élèves," no. 75, p. 3.
68 Louis Reybaud, *Jérôme Paturot à la recherche d'une position sociale* (Paris, [1842] 1846).
69 Ibid., p. 453.
70 See Jean-Auguste Boyer-Nioche, *Coup d'oeil médico-philosophique sur l'influence de la civilisation dans la production des maladies nerveuses* (Paris, 1818), p. 8.
71 J. Paul-R. Cuisin, *Les Bains de Paris et des principales villes des quatre parties du monde* (Paris, 1822), p. 94.
72 P. J. Marie de Saint-Ursin, *L'Ami des femmes, ou Lettres d'un médecin concernant l'influence de l'habillement des femmes sur leurs moeurs et leur santé, … suivi d'un appendice contenant les recettes cosmétiques* (Paris, 1804), p. 136.

73 Ibid., p. 95.
74 Ibid., p. 49.
75 Ibid., pp. 50–1.
76 Joseph-Henri Réveillé-Parise, *Une saison aux eaux minérales d'Enghien* (Paris, 1842), p. 99.
77 F. Damien, *Aperçu topographique et médical sur les eaux minerales sulfureuses d'Enghien* (Paris, 1821), p. 55.
78 Jean-Charles Chenu, *Essai sur l'action thérapeutique des eaux ferrugineuses de Passy* (Paris, 1841), p. 2.
79 Michel Bertrand, *Recherches sur les propriétés physiques, chimiques, et médicinales des eaux du Mont-d'Or* (Paris, [1810] 1823), p. xxiv.
80 Stendhal, *Voyages en Italie* (1817–26), ed. Victor Del Litto (Paris: Gallimard, 1973), p. xxxv: "Je suis de plus en plus content des voyages" [I am more and more satisfied with travel].
81 Jules Janin, *Les Catacombes* (Paris, 1839), vol. II, p. 90: "Mon voyage à Brindes."
82 Ibid., p. 91.
83 Ibid.

Chapter 20 A World of Numbers: From Mechanics to Energy

1 See above pp. 98 and 124.
2 *Journal de l'École polytechnique*, no.1 (1794), p. iii.
3 Françoise Mayeur, "De la Révolution à l'école républicaine, 1789–1930," in Louis-Henri Parias, ed., *Histoire générale de l'enseignement et de l'éducation en France* (Paris: Nouvelle Librairie de France, 1981), vol. III, p. 442.
4 René Taton, "Les conditions du progrès en Europe occidentale," in Louis-Henri Parias, ed., *Histoire générale des sciences* (Paris: PUF, 1961), vol. III, pt 1: *Le XIXe siècle*, p. 617.
5 See ibid., p. 618.
6 Edme Regnier, "Description et usage du dynamomètre," *Journal de l'École polytechnique*, vol. VI, p. 163.
7 Ibid., p. 166.
8 See "les banquistes" [The circus performers], in *Les Français peints par eux-mêmes: encyclopédie morale du dix-neuvième siècle*, 9 vols (Paris, 1840), vol. V, p. 133.
9 Adolphe Quetelet, *Sur l'homme et le développement de ses facultés, ou Essai de physique sociale* (Paris, 1835), p. 72. *A Treatise on Man and the Development of his Faculties*, trans. R. Knox (Edinburgh: William and Robert Chambers, 1842), p. 69.
10 *Sur l'homme*, p. 79; *A Treatise on Man*, p. 76.
11 See above p. 241.
12 Peter Heinrich Clias, *Gymnastique élémentaire, ou Cours analytique et gradué d'exercices propres à developper et à fortifier l'organisation humaine* (Berne, 1819), quoted in Philippe-Joseph-Benjamin Buchez and Ulysse Trélat, *Précis élémentaire d'hygiène* (Paris, 1825), p. 306.
13 Francisco Amoros, *Manuel d'éducation physique, gymnastique et morale* (Paris, 1834), vol. I, p. 67.
14 Gérard-Joseph Christian, *Traité de mécanique industrielle* (Paris, 1822), vol. I, p. 1.
15 Charles Dupin, *Géométrie et mécanique des arts et métiers et des beaux-arts: Cours normal professé au conservatoire royal des arts* (Paris, 1826), vol. I, p. v: "I saw scientists and political leaders uniting their efforts to provide English, Scottish and Irish workers with a new kind of education that makes men more capable, comfortable and prudent."
16 The decree authorized the National Conservatory of Arts and Trades in 1819 to provide "public and free education in the practical application of science in the industrial arts." See Eugène-Oscar Lami, ed., *Dictionnaire encyclopédique et biographique de l'industrie et des arts industriels* (Paris, 1881–3), entry "Conservatoire national des arts et métiers."

17 See Dupin, *Géométrie et mécanique des arts et métiers et des beaux-arts.*
18 Claude-Lucien Bergery, *Économie industrielle, ou Science de l'industrie*, 3 vols (Metz: 1829–31).
19 Ibid., vol. I, p. 2.
20 Ibid., vol. I, p. 4.
21 Christian, *Traité de mécanique industrielle*, pp. 112–13.
22 Ibid.
23 See Raymond Queneau, *Aux confins des ténèbres: les fous littéraires français du XIXe siècle* (Paris: Gallimard, 2002).
24 See P. F. Lutterbach, *Révolution dans la marche, ou Cinq Cents Moyens naturels et utiles pour trouver le confortable dans les différentes manières de marcher* (Paris, 1850), pp. 520ff.
25 See especially the superb illustrations by Charles Delaunay, *Cours élémentaire de mécanique théorique et pratique* (Paris, 1851).
26 Jean Duplessi-Bertaux, *Recueil de cent sujets de divers genres composés et gravés à l'eau-forte* (Paris, 1820).
27 Christian, *Traité de mécanique industrielle*, p. 111.
28 See above p. 118.
29 Jean-Victor Poncelet, *Introduction à la mécanique industrielle, physique ou expérimentale* (Paris, [1828] 1841), p. 239. Translator's note: The treadmill had interior steps set into two cast-iron wheels.
30 Joseph Laisné, *Aide-mémoire portatif des officers du génie* (Paris, 1837), p. 42.
31 Ibid.
32 Dupin, *Géométrie et mécanique des arts et métiers et des beaux-arts*, p. 75.
33 See Charles-François Bailly de Merlieux, ed., *Maison rustique du XIXe siècle* (Paris, 1834), vol. IV, pp. 510–12.
34 André Guenyveau, *Essai sur la science des machines* (Paris, 1810), p. 256.
35 See above pp. 99 and 118.
36 Christian, *Traité de mécanique industrielle*, p. 67.
37 Ibid., p. 64.
38 Guenyveau, *Essai sur la science des machines*, p. 254.
39 See above pp. 118–20.
40 Bailly de Merlieux, *Maison rustique du XIXe siècle*, p. 389.
41 Gabriel Andral and Jules Gavarret, "Recherches sur la quantité d'acide carbonique exhalé par le poumon dans l'espèce humaine," *Comptes rendus hebdomadaires de l'Académie des sciences* (1843), p. 119.
42 Jules Gavarret, *Physique médicale: de la chaleur produite par les êtres vivants* (Paris, 1855), p. 349.
43 Henri-Victor Regnault and Jules Reiset, "Recherches chimiques sur la respiration des animaux de diverses classes," *Annales de chimie et physique*, vol. 26 (1849), p. 514.
44 Gustave-Adolphe Hirn, *Théorie mécanique de la chaleur: conséquences philosophiques et métaphysiques de la thermodynamique* (Paris, 1868), p. 30.
45 Ibid., p. 35.
46 Ibid., p. 41.
47 Edgar Saveney, "De l'équivalence de la chaleur et du travail mécanique," *Revue des deux mondes*, vol. 45 (1863), p. 40.
48 Gustave-Adolphe Hirn, *Recherches sur l'équivalent mécanique de la chaleur* (Colmar, 1858), p. 67.
49 Hirn, *Théorie mécanique de la chaleur*, p. 42.
50 See above pp. 105–6.
51 Anson Rabinbach, *Le Moteur humain: l'énergie, la fatigue et les origines de la modernité* (Paris: La Fabrique, [1992] 2004), p. 91.

52 Hirn, *Théorie mécanique de la chaleur*, p. 40.
53 Gabriel Andral, Cours de médecine clinique (Paris, 1823), "Maladies de la poitrine," vol. I, pp. 1ff.
54 Gabriel Andral, "Cours d'hygiène," 1828, MS, Paris, Faculté de médecine, notes taken by a student, private collection.
55 See Michel Lévy, *Traité d'hygiène publique et privée* (Paris, 1844), vol. I, p. 236.
56 Eugène-Joseph Woillez, *Recherches pratiques sur l'inspection et la mensuration de la poitrine considérées comme moyens diagnostiques complémentaires de la percussion et de l'auscultation* (Paris, 1838).
57 Louis-Théodore Laveran, "De la mensuration vertical du thorax," *Gazette médicale de Paris*, February 8, 1846, p. 82.
58 P. F. Lutterbach, *Art de respirer, moyen positif pour augmenter agréablement la vie* (Paris, 1852).
59 See John Hutchinson, "Lecture on vital statistics, embracing an account of a new instrument for detecting the presence of disease in the respiratory system," *The Lancet*, no. 1 (1844), pp. 567–70.
60 Michel Lévy, *Traité d'hygiène publique et privée* (Paris, 1850), vol. I, p. 241.
61 Albrecht Thaër, *Principes raisonnés d'agriculture* (Paris, 1830), pp. 149–50.
62 Lévy, *Traité d'hygiène publique et privée*, 1844, vol. II, p. 408.
63 Justus von Liebig, *Chimie organique appliquée à la physiologie animale et à la pathologie* (Paris [1837] 1842), p. 24.
64 Ibid.
65 Lévy, *Traité d'hygiène publique et privée* (Paris, 1857), vol. I, p. 700.
66 Adolphe d'Angeville, *Essai sur la statistique de la population française, considérée sous quelques-uns de ses rapports physiques et moraux* (Bourg, 1836), p. 49. Translator's note: The original report uses the metric unit hectoliter, which equals 2.88 bushels.
67 Honoré de Balzac, *Le Médecin de campagne*, in *La Comédie humaine*, ed. Marcel Bouteron (Paris: Gallimard, 1969), vol. VIII, p. 7.
68 Ibid., p. 12.
69 John Sinclair, *L'agriculture pratique et raisonnée* (Paris, 1825), p. 208. *The Code of Agriculture, including Observations on Gardens, Orchards, Woods and Plantations* (London: Sherwood, Neely & Jones, 1819).
70 Pierre-Honoré Bérard, *Rapport sur le régime alimentaire des lycées de Paris* (1852). See Ambroise Tardieu, *Dictionnaire d'hygiène publique et de salubrité* (Paris, 1852), entry "Lycées."
71 See ibid., entry "Militaire (hygiène)."
72 Jean-Baptiste Fonssagrives, *Hygiène alimentaire des malades, des convalescents et des valétudinaires, ou Du régime envisagé comme moyen thérapeutique* (Paris, 1867), p. 94.
73 See above p. 47.
74 *Dictionnaire de médecine et de chirurgie pratique* (Paris, 1830), entry "Constitution."
75 Lévy, *Traité d'hygiène publique et privée*, 1844, vol. I, p. 232.
76 Ibid., 1850, vol. I, p. 241.
77 Ibid., p. 232.
78 Gabriel Andral, *Essai d'hématologie pathologique* (Paris, 1843), p. 183.
79 A. E. Coche, *De l'opération médicale du recrutement et des inspections générales* (Paris, 1829), p. 62.
80 Pierre-Jean Moricheau-Beaupré, *Mémoire sur le choix des hommes propres au service militaire de l'armée de terre, et sur leur visite devant les conseils de révision présenté á … Mgr le marquis de Latour-Maubourg* (Paris, 1820), p. 13.
81 Valentin Cazeneuve, *Recrutement de l'armée, contingent de la classe de 1840, département du Nord, année 1841, addressé à M. le préfet du Nord* (Lille, 1842), p. 17.

82 See ibid., pp. 20–3.
83 Ibid., p. 18.
84 "Les vidangeurs," in *Les Français peints par eux-mêmes*, vol. III, p. 194.
85 James Cowles Prichard, *Histoire naturelle de l'homme* (Paris, [1836] 1845), vol. II, p. 180. Prichard is describing the mountain people of the South American Andes as typical mountaineers.
86 Louis Maigron, *Le Romantisme et la mode* (Paris: Honoré Champion, 1911), p. 69.
87 Alexandre Dumas, Théophile Gautier, Arsène Houssaye, Paul de Musset, Louis Énault and G. Du Fayl, *Paris et les Parisiens au XIXe siècle* (Paris, 1856), p. 439.
88 Guillaume Compaing, *L'art du tailleur* (Paris, 1828).
89 J. Coutts, *Guide pratique du tailleur* (Paris, 1848), illustration 11.
90 Jean-Jacques Grandville, *Cent Proverbes* (Paris, 1845), p. 225.

Chapter 21 A Universe under Threat: The Poverty of the Workers

1 See above pp. 127–9.
2 Edward P. Thompson, *La Formation de la classe ouvrière anglaise*, trans. Gilles Dauvé, Mireille Golaszewski and Marie-Noëlle Thibault (Paris: Seuil, 2012), p. 368. *The Making of the English Working* Class (New York: Random House, 1964).
3 Édouard Ducpetiaux, *De la condition physique et morale des jeunes ouvriers et des moyens de l'améliorer* (Brussels, 1843), "Introduction," p. 1.
4 See Philippe-René Marchand, *Du paupérisme* (Paris, 1845).
5 Michelle Perrot, *Enquêtes sur la condition ouvrière en France au XIXe siècle* (Paris: Microéditions Hachette, 1972), p. 10.
6 Honoré de Balzac, *La Fille aux yeux d'or* (1835), in *La Comédie humaine*, ed. Marcel Bouteron (Paris: Gallimard, 1969), vol. V, p. 256.
7 Ibid., p. 257.
8 Thomas Fouilleron, *Des princes en Europe: les Grimaldi de Monaco, des Lumières au printemps des peuples* (Paris: Honoré Champion, 2012), p. 716. See "Interpreter le pauperisme," pp. 708ff.
9 See Louis Chevalier, *Classes laborieuses et classes dangereuses à Paris pendant la première moitié du XIXe siècle* (Paris: Plon, 1958).
10 Alexandre Lesguilliez, *Notice historique, topographique et statistique sur la ville de Darnétal* (Rouen, 1835), p. 324.
11 Louis Blanc, *Histoire de dix ans, 1830–1840* (Lausanne, [1841–4] 1850), vol. III, p. 44.
12 *Rapport fait et présenté à M. le Président du Conseil des ministres, sur les causes générales qui ont amené les événements de Lyon par deux chefs d'atelier* (Lyon, 1832), p. 2.
13 Claude Fohlen, *Qu'est-ce que la révolution industrielle?* (Paris: Robert Laffont, 1971), p. 177.
14 Brinley Thomas, *Migration and Economic Growth: A Study of Great Britain and the Atlantic Economy* (Cambridge: Cambridge University Press, 1954), p. 158.
15 The word "pauperism" appears in 1823. See Alain Rey, *Dictionnaire historique de la langue française* (Paris: Robert, 1994), entry "Pauperisme."
16 Perrot, *Enquêtes sur la condition ouvrière en France au XIXe siècle*, p. 10.
17 Ducpetiaux, *De la condition physique et morale des jeunes ouvriers*, p. 4.
18 François Jarrige, "Grandeur et misère du progrès technique," *Vivre avec les machines: les textes fondamentaux*, *Le Point*, November 2018, p. 48. See also Jarrige, *Au temps des 'tueuses de bras': les bris de machines à l'aube de l'ère industrielle, 1780–1860* (Rennes: Presses universitaires de Rennes, 2009).
19 Ibid.
20 See Blanc, *Histoire de dix ans*, p. 54.
21 Fernand Rude, *C'est nous les canuts...* (Paris: Maspero, 1977), p. 194.

22 Statements made by a parliamentary deputy, quoted ibid., p. 222.
23 Charles Béranger, prolétaire, ouvrier horloger, "Pétition d'un prolétaire à la Chambre des députés," *Le Globe*, February 3, 1831.
24 Grignon, ouvrier tailleur, *Réflexions d'un ouvrier tailleur sur la misère des ouvriers en général, la durée des journées de travail, le taux des salaires, les rapports actuellement établis entre les ouvriers et les maîtres d'ateliers, la nécessité des associations d'ouvriers comme moyen d'améliorer leur condition* (Paris, 1833), p. 2.
25 Jean-Louis Ferrien, garçon tailleur, *Première Épître aux Parisiens et aux membres de la République dispersée* (Paris, 1831), p. 8.
26 Ibid., p. 1.
27 Béranger, "Pétition d'un prolétaire à la Chambre des députés."
28 See Jacques Rancière, *Gabriel Gauny, le philosophe plébéien* (Paris: La Fabrique, [1983] 2017), p. 53.
29 Ibid.
30 Ibid., p. 54.
31 Ibid.
32 Ibid., p. 53.
33 Ibid., p. 55.
34 Ibid.
35 See above p. 136.
36 Eugène Sue, *Le Juif errant* (Brussels, [1844] 1845), p. 118.
37 Friedrich Engels, *La Situation de la classe ouvrière en Angleterre* (Paris: Éd. Science marxiste, 2011), p. 145. *The Condition of the Working Class in England in 1844* (London: George Allen & Unwin, 1845), p. 157.
38 See the *New Monthly Magazine*, quoted by Alban de Villeneuve-Bargemont, *Économie politique chrétienne* (Paris, 1838), p. 318.
39 Louis-René Villermé, *Tableau de l'état physique et moral des ouvriers employés dans les manufactures de coton, de laine et de soie* (Paris, 1840), vol. I, p. v.
40 Ibid., p. 30.
41 Ibid., p. 87n.
42 Ibid., p. 312.
43 Jean Fourastié, "Doctrine et réalité," *Arguments*, nos. 27–8 (1962), p. 59.
44 Ibid. See also p. 79.
45 François Foy, *Choléra-morbus: premiers secours à donner aux cholériques avant l'arrivée du médecin* (Paris, 1849), p. 45.
46 Classical medical texts focused on diseases of part of the body (head, neck, chest, stomach, legs, etc.) See Saint-Hilaire, *L'Anatomie du corps humain avec les maladies et les remèdes pour les guérir* (Paris, 1680). In the eighteenth century medical texts began to be organized by type: fevers, inflammations, convulsions, shortness of breath, etc. See François Boissier de Sauvages, *Nosologie méthodique* (Paris, [1763] 1770).
47 See above p. 79.
48 Bernandino Ramazzini, *Traité des maladies des artisans* (Paris, 1840), p. 94.
49 Émile-Auguste Bégin, *Le Buchan français: nouveau traité complet de médecine usuelle et domestique* (Paris, 1839).
50 Ramazzini, *Traité des maladies des artisans*, p. 45.
51 Bégin, *Le Buchan français*, vol. I, p. 320.
52 Ibid.
53 Ibid., p. 321.
54 Ibid.
55 Édouard Ducpetiaux, "Travail du mineur," *Annales d'hygiène publique et de médecine légale*, XXIX (1843), p. 147.

56 Jean Bouillaud, *Traité clinique des maladies du coeur* (Paris, [1835] 1841), vol. II, p. 584. Jean-Nicolas Corvisart was the first to warn of this, in his *Essai sur les maladies et lésions organiques du coeur et des gros vaisseaux* in 1806, citing "exertions of all kinds," p. 355.
57 Maurice Alhoy, *Les Bagnes: histoire, types, moeurs, mystères* (Paris, 1845), p. 92.
58 Hubert Lauvergne, *Les Forçats*, ed. André Zysberg (Grenoble, Jerôme Millon, [1841] 1992), p. 260.
59 Alhoy, *Les Bagnes*, p. 93.
60 Ibid., p. 101.
61 Villermé, *Tableau de l'état physique et moral des ouvriers employés dans les manufactures de coton, de laine et de soie*, vol. II, p. 91.
62 Flora Tristan, *Promenades dans Londres* (Paris, 1840), p. 103.
63 Valentin Cazeneuve, *Recrutement de l'armée, contingent de la classe de 1840, département du Nord, année 1841, addressé à M. le préfet du Nord* (Lille, 1842), p. 37.
64 Eugène Buret, *De la misère des classes laborieuses en Angleterre et en France* (Brussels, 1842), vol. II, p. 108.
65 Villermé, *Tableau de l'état physique et moral des ouvriers employés dans les manufactures de coton, de laine et de soie*, vol. II, p. 222.
66 Buret, *De la misère des classes laborieuses en Angleterre et en France*, vol. II, p. 117.
67 Ange Guépin and Eugène Bonamy, *Nantes au XIXe siècle: statistique topographique, industrielle, et morale, faisant suite à l'histoire des progrès de Nantes* (Nantes, 1835), p. 485.
68 Buret, *De la misère des classes laborieuses en Angleterre et en France*, p. 239.
69 Ibid., p. 243.
70 Ibid., p. 248.
71 Villermé, *Tableau de l'état physique et moral des ouvriers employés dans les manufactures de coton, de laine et de soie*, vol. I, p. 27.
72 Norbert Truquin, *Mémoires et aventures d'un prolétaire à travers la Révolution: l'Algérie, la République argentine et le Paraguay* (Paris: Maspero, 1977), pp. 128–9.
73 Sue, *Le Juif errant*, p. 119.
74 Guépin and Bonamy, *Nantes au XIXe siècle*, p. 489.
75 The term "dépérissement" is used by Eugène Schneider d'Autun in his *Rapport présenté au nom de la commission chargée d'examiner la loi du 22 mars 1841 sur le travail des enfants dans les manufactures* (Paris, 1846), p. 15. Translator's note: "dépérissement" is rendered here as "decline" or "chronic wasting."
76 Frederick Morton Eden, *The State of the Poor: A History of the Labouring Classes in England* (London: J. Davis, 1797), vol. I, p. 61. See also Buret, *De la misère des classes laborieuses en Angleterre et en France*, p. 48.
77 Pierre-Auguste-Rémi Mimerel, quoted by Michel Beaud, *Histoire du capitalisme, 1500–2010* (Paris: Seuil, [1980] 2010), p. 155.
78 Thomas-Robert Bugeaud, quoted ibid., p. 156.
79 Karl Marx, *Capital: A Critique of Political Economy* (New York: Modern Library, 1906); see Part 3: "The labour process and the process of creating surplus-value" and "The degree of exploitation of labour power."
80 Beaud, *Histoire du capitalisme*, p.167.
81 Ibid.
82 Marx, *Capital*, Part 3.
83 See ibid., vol. I, ch. 10.
84 Ibid., Part 3, "The labour process and the process of creating surplus-value."
85 Ibid., Part 4, "The concept of relative surplus-value."
86 Ibid.
87 Ibid.
88 Ibid.

89 Ibid.
90 Ibid., Annexe I, "The workday," p. 281.
91 Ibid.
92 Ibid., p. 268.
93 *Recueil général des lois et ordonnances*, vol. II, 1841: Loi relative au travail des enfants, rapport lu à la Chambre des députés par Augustin-Charles Renouard, député de la Somme, 25 mai 1840, discussion les 21, 22, 23, 24, 26, 28, 29 décembre.
94 Patrice Bourdelais, "L'intolérable du travail des enfants, son émergence et son évolution entre compassion et libéralisme, en France et en Angleterre," in Bourdelais and Didier Fassin, eds, *Les Constructions de l'intolérable, études d'anthropologie et d'histoire sur les frontières de l'espace moral* (Paris: La Découverte, 2005), p. 95.
95 Jules Michelet, quoted ibid., p. 91.
96 Jean-Charles-Léonard Simonde de Sismondi, *Nouveaux Principes d'économie politique* (Paris, 1819), vol. I, p. 353: "Since children have started earning wages, the fathers' salary can be reduced," resulting in "an increase in work."
97 Marx, *Capital*, Part 4.
98 Charles d'Haussez, *La Grande-Bretagne en mille huit cent trente-trois* (Paris, 1834), vol. II, p. 92.
99 Honoré de Balzac, *Splendeurs et misères des courtisanes* (1838), in *La Comédie humaine*, vol. V, p. 807.
100 See Suzanne Touren, *La Loi de 1841 sur le travail des enfants dans les manufactures* (Paris, 1931), thesis, Law Faculty, p. 21.
101 See especially Françoise Mayeur, "De la Révolution à l'école républicaine, 1789–1930," in Louis-Henri Parias, ed., *Histoire générale de l'enseignement et de l'éducation en France* (Paris: Nouvelle Librairie de France, 1981), p. 105.
102 See George Sand, *La Petite Fadette* (Paris, 1849).
103 Charles Dickens, *The Personal History, Adventures, Experience and Observation of David Copperfield the Younger*, 3 vols (London, 1849–50).
104 Suzanne Touren, *La Loi de 1841 sur le travail des enfants dans les manufactures*, p. 14.
105 Arnould Frémy, "L'Enfant de fabrique," *Les Français peints par eux-mêmes: encyclopédie morale du dix-neuvième siècle*, 9 vols (Paris, 1840), vol. X, p. 258.
106 See Suzanne Touren, *La Loi de 1841 sur le travail des enfants dans les manufactures*, p. 51.
107 See Francis Hordern, *La Loi de 1841 sur le travail des enfants: point de départ de la législation sociale* (Aix-en-Provence: Institut régional du travail, 1980), p. 4.
108 Factory Inquiry, First Report, 1840, quoted in Ducpetiaux, *De la condition physique et morale des jeunes ouvriers et des moyens de l'améliorer*, p. 56.
109 Ibid., p. 62.
110 Ibid., p. 61.
111 Ibid., p. 59.
112 Ibid.
113 Louis-René Villermé, "Sur la durée trop longue du travail des enfants dans beaucoup de manufactures," *Annales d'hygiène et de médecine légale*, XVIII (1837), public lecture at the Institut de France, May 2, 1837, p. 168.
114 Peter Gaskell, *The Manufacturing Population of England* (London, 1833), p. 7.
115 See "Nouvelle loi rendue par le Parlement britannique, le 29 août 1833, pour régler le travail des enfants …," *Bulletin de la société industrielle de Mulhouse*, VIII (1835), p. 53.
116 See Hordern, *La Loi de 1841 sur le travail des enfants*, p. 16.
117 Ibid., p. 1.
118 Ibid.
119 Louis-René Villermé, *Enquête sur le travail et la condition des enfants et des adolescents dans les mines de la Grande-Bretagne* (Paris, 1843), p. 5.

120 Ibid.
121 Ibid. p. 3.
122 Edward P. Thompson, *La Formation de la classe ouvrière anglaise,* trans. Gilles Dauvé, Mireille Golaszewski and Marie-Noëlle Thibault (Paris: Seuil, 2012), p. 395. *The Making of the English Working* Class (New York: Random House, 1964).
123 Karl Marx, *Selected Works* (London: Lawrence & Wishart, 1942), vol. II, p. 439.
124 Thompson, *La Formation de la classe ouvrière anglaise*, p. 41.
125 See Georges Duveau, *La Vie ouvrière en France sous le Second Empire* (Paris: Gallimard, 1946), p. 93.
126 Ibid., p. 80.
127 Ibid., p. 93.
128 Ibid.
129 See Nicole Samuel, *Étapes de la conquête du temps libre en France, 1780–1980* (Paris: ADRAC, 1981), p. 11.
130 *La Réforme sociale*, 17 (1889), p. 81.
131 Duveau, *La Vie ouvrière en France sous le Second Empire*, p. 237.

Chapter 22 The World of Output

1 Eugène-Oscar Lami, ed., *Dictionnaire encyclopédique et biographique de l'industrie et des arts industriels* (Paris, 1881–3), entry "Rendement." Translator's note: "Rendement" is "yield," "output" or "return on investment."
2 "Établissements Dollfus-Mieg et Cie," in Julien Turgan, *Les Grandes Usines de France* (Paris, 1860), vol. IV, p. 8.
3 "Les Omnibus de Paris," ibid., vol. III, p. 51.
4 Léon Poincaré, *Traité d'hygiène industrielle à l'usage des médecins et des membres des conseils d'hygiène* (Paris, 1886), pp. 240–1.
5 Jules Amar, *Le Moteur humain et les bases scientifiques du travail professionnel* (Paris: Dunod, 1914), p. 575.
6 Émile Zola, *Germinal*, in Armand Lanoux and Henri Mitterand, eds, *Les Rougon-Macquart (1872–1893)* (Paris: Gallimard, 1964), vol. III, p. 1174; trans. Havelock Ellis (London: J. M. Dent, 1885), p. 43.
7 Ibid., p. 1428.
8 Ibid., p. 1174.
9 "Le travail national et la réglementation," *La Réforme sociale*, 19 (1890), p. 754.
10 Charles Virmaître, *Paris-boursicotier* (Paris, 1888), p. 97.
11 See Michelle Perrot, *Les Ouvriers en grève: France, 1871–1890* (Paris: Mouton, 1973), vol. I, pp. 260ff.
12 See Donat Béchamp, "Un groupe d'usines de la vallée de Masevaux (Alsace-Lorraine)," *La Réforme sociale*, 6 (1883), p. 114.
13 See Émile Levasseur, *Questions ouvrières et industrielles en France sous la Troisième République* (Paris: Arthur Rousseau, 1907), pp. 650–1.
14 Quoted ibid., p. 651.
15 See above p. 161.
16 See above p. 164.
17 Anson Rabinbach, *Le Moteur humain: l'énergie, la fatigue et les origines de la modernité* (Paris: La Fabrique, [1992] 2004), p. 121.
18 See above p. 196.
19 Armando Maggiora, "Les Lois de la fatigue étudiées dans les muscles de l'homme," *Archives italiennes de biologie* (1890), p. 129.
20 Angelo Mosso, *La Fatigue intellectuelle et physique* (Paris: Alcan, 1894), p. 91.
21 Ibid., p. 61.

22 Ibid., p. 63.
23 See the observations of Jules Lefèvre, *Chaleur animale et bioénergétique* (Paris: Masson, 1911), p. 773.
24 See Maggiora, "Les Lois de la fatigue étudiées dans les muscles de l'homme," pp. 187ff.
25 Mosso, *La Fatigue intellectuelle et physique*, p. 91. "Two hours of rest is necessary before all signs of fatigue are gone from the muscles that flex the finger."
26 Ibid., pp. 91–2.
27 Ibid., p. 92.
28 Charles Féré, *Les Variations de l'excitabilité dans la fatigue* (Paris: Reinwald, 1901), p. 69.
29 Ibid., p. 78.
30 Ibid., p. 83.
31 Marco Saraceno, *De la mesure du corps à la politique des corps: une histoire des sciences du travail (1880–1920)*, thesis, University of Pisa, 2013, p. 171.
32 Mosso, *La Fatigue intellectuelle et physique*, p. 180. Quoted in Saraceno, *De la mesure du corps*.
33 See p. 198.
34 See above p. 183.
35 Henry Le Chatelier, preface to the French edition of Frederick Winslow Taylor, *Principes d'organisation scientifique des usines* (Paris: Dunod, [1918] 1927), p. 2.
36 Taylor, *The Principles of Scientific Management* (New York: Harper & Brothers, 1911), p. 7: "the greatest permanent prosperity for the workman, coupled with the greatest prosperity for the employer … with the smallest combined expenditure of human effort …"
37 See above pp. 161–2.
38 See above pp. 116–18.
39 Taylor, *The Principles of Scientific Management*, p. 65.
40 Ibid., p. 41: "one type of man … whose speciality under scientific management … is needed to plan ahead and an entirely different type to execute the work."
41 Ibid.
42 Ibid., "a true science," p. 126.
43 See above p. 161.
44 Alain Corbin, "La fatigue, le repos et la conquête du temps," in Corbin, ed., *L'Avènement des loisirs, 1850–1960* (Paris: Aubier, 1995), p. 280.
45 Jean-Maurice Lahy, *Le système Taylor et la physiologie du travail professionnel* (Paris: Gauthier-Villars, [1916] 1921), p. 62.
46 Taylor, *The Principles of Scientific Management*, p. 87: "lowering the pay of those who did indifferent work and discharging others who proved incorrigibly slow or careless …"
47 See above p. 197.
48 Alphonse Merrheim, "Le système Taylor," *La vie ouvrière*, February 20, 1913, pp. 214–15 and 224.
49 Henry Ford with Henry Crowther, *Ma vie et mon oeuvre* (Paris: Payot, [1923] 1930), pp. 90–3.
50 Ibid., p. 94.
51 Ibid., p. 100.
52 Ibid., pp. 93–4.
53 Thierry Pillon, *Lire Georges Friedmann. Problèmes humains du machinisme industriel: le débuts de la sociologie du travail* (Paris: Ellipses, 2009), p. 330.
54 See https://en.wikipedia.org/wiki/Henry_Ford.
55 Louis-Ferdinand Céline, *Voyage au bout de la nuit* (Paris: Gallimard, 1932). See also Céline, "Voyage aux usines Ford," *Le Un*, "Le travail nuit grave," June 10, 2015, p. 3.

56 See above p. 177.
57 See above pp. 121–2.
58 See above p. 166.
59 See Wilbur Olin Atwater and Edward B. Rosa, "A new respiration calorimeter and experiments on the conservation of energy in the human body," *Physical Review*, 9/214 (1899).
60 Lefèvre, *Chaleur animale et bioénergétique*, p. 165.
61 Armand Gautier, *L'Alimentation et les régimes chez l'homme sain et chez les malades* (Paris: Masson, 1904), p. 83.
62 See Georges Vigarello, *Les Métamorphoses du gras: histoire de l'obésité* (Paris: Seuil, [2010] 2013), p. 218: "La diffusion des pesées."
63 Constantin Miculescu, "L'équivalent mécanique de la calorie," *Annales de chimie et de physique* (1892).
64 See above p. 169.
65 Jules Lefèvre, "Dépense et besoin d'énergie: introduction critique et expérimentale à l'étude des bilans d'Atwater," *Paris, I Congrès international d'hygiène alimentaire*, 1904, p. 5.
66 See above p. 170.
67 See above p 169.
68 Quoted by Marcel Labbé, *Régimes alimentaires* (Paris: Baillière, 1910), p. 11.
69 See Russell Henry Chittenden, *Physiological Economy in Nutrition* (London: Heinemann, 1907), quoted by Labbé, *Régimes alimentaires*, p. 12.
70 Josefa Ioteyko and Varia Kipiani, *Enquête scientifique sur les végétariens de Bruxelles: leur résistance à la fatigue étudiée à l'ergographe* (Brussels: Lamertin, 1907), p. 50.
71 Lefèvre, "Dépense et besoin d'énergie: introduction critique et expérimentale à l'étude des bilans d'Atwater," p. 20.
72 Ibid., p. 21.
73 See above p. 166.
74 See Barthélemy Durrive, "Deux ouvriers-machine, avant et après Taylor," *L'Homme et la société*, 3/205 (2017), pp. 53–86. Hirn prioritized respiration; see p. 65. "Because, if we intend to measure in humans the mechanical equivalent of heat, since any direct measurement of nutritional input is impossible, we have to believe that everything functions like a steam engine."
75 Jules Amar, *Le Moteur humain et les bases scientifiques du travail professionel*, p. 469. See "le travail professional," pp. 439ff.
76 Ibid., p. 491.
77 See Étienne-Jules Marey, *La Méthode graphique dans les sciences expérimentales et principalement en physiologie et en médecine* (Paris, 1878). The invention of recording devices in the 1870s enabled investigators to see physiological functions and actions represented in waves, diagrams, tables or systems. The internal translated into the external. See also Christian Pociello, *La Science en mouvement: Étienne Marey et Georges Demenÿ (1870–1920)* (Paris: PUF, 1999).
78 Amar, *Le Moteur humain et les bases scientifiques du travail professionnel*, p. 531.
79 Ibid., p. 546.
80 Ibid., p. 552.
81 See Durrive, "Deux ouvriers-machine, avant et après Taylor," p. 74: "For Amar, it is crucial that the work task that is measured (in kilogram-meters) corresponds as closely as possible to a specific occupation."
82 Amar, *Le Moteur humain et les bases scientifiques du travail professionnel*, p. 536.
83 Ibid., p. 547.
84 Ibid., p. 551.

85 Ibid., p. 594. See Robert Tigerstedt, *Physiologische Übungen und Demonstrationen* (Leipzig: S. Hirzel, 1913).
86 Amar, *Le Moteur humain et les bases scientifiques du travail professionel*, p. 595.
87 Ibid., p. 583.
88 Armand Imbert, *Mode de fonctionnement économique de l'organisme* (Évreux: Hérissey, 1902), p. 13.
89 See the important work by Jacqueline Carroy, Annick Ohayon and Régine Plas, *Histoire de la psychologie en France, XIXe–XXe siècles* (Paris: La Découverte, 2006).
90 Lahy, *Le système Taylor et la physiologie du travail professionnel*, p. 210.
91 Alfred Binet and Victor Henri, *La Fatigue intellectuelle* (Paris: Schleicher Frères, 1898), quoted in Marc Loriol, *Le Temps de la fatigue* (Paris: Anthropos, 2000), p. 74.

Chapter 23 The World of "Mental Fatigue"

1 Angelo Mosso, *La Fatigue intellectuelle et physique* (Paris: Alcan, 1894), p. 93.
2 Paul Dupuy, *De la fatigue musculaire* (Paris, 1869), p. 3.
3 See above p. 59.
4 See above p. 98.
5 See above p. 176.
6 Pierre Loti, *Ramuntcho* (Paris: 1897) pp. 25–6; trans. Henri Pène du Bois (New York: Brentano's, 1917), p. 25.
7 Émile Zola, *Germinal*, in Armand Lanoux and Henri Mitterand, eds, *Les Rougon-Macquart (1872–1893)* (Paris: Gallimard, 1964), vol. III, p. 1406; trans. Roger Pearson (London: Penguin, 2004), p. 317.
8 Ibid., pp. 1406–7; trans. Roger Pearson, pp. 317–18.
9 Victor Hugo, *Les Travailleurs de la mer* (Paris, 1866), p. 308.
10 Philippe Tissié, *La Fatigue et l'entraînement physique* (Paris, 1897), pp. 44–6.
11 Mona Ozouf, ed., *La Classe ininterrompue: cahiers de la famille Sandre, enseignants, 1780–1960: Bertrand, Baptiste, Joseph, Marie Sandre* (Paris: Hachette, 1979), pp. 414–15.
12 Ned Pearson, *Dictionnaire du sport français* (Paris, 1872) entry "Surmener."
13 Émile Littré, *Dictionnaire de la langue française* (Paris, 1863–1872), vol. IV (1870), entry "Surmener."
14 Henry Lee, *Historique des courses de chevaux, de l'Antiquité à ce jour* (Paris: Fasquelle, 1914), p. 270.
15 Charles Dessalines d'Orbigny, ed., *Dictionnaire universel d'histoire naturelle* (Paris, 1861), entry "Cheval."
16 A myriameter is the equivalent of a kilometer.
17 "Le Derby d'Epsom," *Almanach du magasin pittoresque* (1883).
18 Pearson, *Dictionnaire du sport français*, entry "Voler." "The supple action makes it resemble a bird in flight."
19 Marie de Manacéine, *Le Surmenage mental dans la civilisation moderne: effets, causes, remèdes* (Paris, 1890), p. 134.
20 Alain Beltran and Patrice A. Carré, *La Fée et la servante: la société française face à l'électricité, XIXe–XXe siècle* (Paris: Belin, 1991), p. 64.
21 Manacéine, *Le Surmenage mental dans la civilisation moderne*, p. 134.
22 Jules Claretie, *La Vie à Paris, 1905* (Paris: Eugène Fasquelle, 1906), p. 368.
23 Eugène-Oscar Lami, ed., *Dictionnaire encyclopédique et biographique de l'industrie et des arts industriels* (Paris, 1881–3), entry "Vitesse."
24 Albert Mathieu, *Neurasthénie (épuisement nerveux)* (Paris, 1892) p. 17.
25 See above pp. 107–8.
26 See above p. 57.
27 Tissié, *La Fatigue et l'entraînement physique*, p. 108.

28 Maurice du Seigneur, *Paris, voici Paris* (Paris, 1889), pp. 1–2.
29 See the title of Beltran and Carré's book: *La Fée et la servante: la société française face à l'électricité, XIXe–XXe siècle*.
30 Émile Zola, *Au bonheur des dames* (Paris: Garnier-Flammarion, [1883] 1971), p. 65. *The Ladies' Paradise* (London: Vizetelly, 1886), p. 17.
31 Émile Verhaeren, *Les Villes tentaculaires* (Paris, 1895), p. 60.
32 Aimé Riant, *Hygiène du cabinet de travail* (Paris, 1883), p. 116.
33 Manacéine, *Le Surmenage mental dans la civilisation moderne*, p. 157.
34 Ibid., p. 145.
35 Ibid., p. 170.
36 J. A. Conelli, *La Neurasthénie: histoire, symptômes, pathogénèse, traitement* (Turin, 1895), p. 34.
37 Émile Zola, preface to Charles Chincholle, *Les Mémoires de Paris* (Paris, 1889).
38 Aimé Riant, *Le Surmenage intellectuel et les exercices physiques* (Paris, 1889).
39 Paul de Rousiers, *La vie américaine* (Paris, 1892), p. 380.
40 Louis-Laurent Simonin, *Le Monde américain: souvenirs de mes voyages aux États-Unis* (Paris, 1876), p. 36.
41 Theodore Roosevelt, *The Strenuous Life: Essays and Addresses* (New York: Century, 1900).
42 See Ralf Wichmann, *Die Neurasthenie und ihre Behandlung: ein Ratgeber für Nervenkranke* (Berlin, 1899), p. 5.
43 Émile Zola, *Au Bonheur des dames*, p. 264; *The Ladies' Paradise*, pp. 69–70.
44 Ibid., p. 269; *The Ladies' Paradise*, p. 70.
45 Mathieu, *Neurasthénie (épuisement nerveux)*, p. 17.
46 Yvette Conry, *L'Introduction du darwinisme en France au XIXe siècle* (Paris: Vrin, 1974), pp. 39 and 310.
47 Manacéine, *Le Surmenage mental dans la civilisation moderne: effets, causes, remèdes*, p. 134.
48 See Pierre de Coubertin's *Lettre aux électeurs de l'arrondissement du Havre* of 1898, where he cites the "struggle for life" and claims that sports will enhance resilience and strength.
49 Conelli, *La Neurasthénie: histoire, symptômes, pathogénèse, traitement*, p. 34.
50 See Yves Lequin, ed., *Histoire des Français, XIXe–XXe siècles* (Paris: Armand Colin, 1983–4), vol. II, p. 329.
51 Zola, *Au bonheur des dames*, p. 190; *The Ladies' Paradise*, p. 143.
52 See above p. 148.
53 Adrien Proust and Gilbert Ballet, *Hygiène du neurasthénique* (Paris, 1900), p. 10.
54 Léon Bouveret, *La Neurasthénie: épuisement nerveux* (Paris, 1890), p. 14.
55 Manacéine, *Le Surmenage mental dans la civilisation moderne: effets, causes, remèdes*, preface, p. ix.
56 Mosso, *La Fatigue intellectuelle et physique*, p. 77.
57 Tissié, *La Fatigue et l'entraînement physique*, p. 122.
58 Francisque Sarcey, "Les illettrés au régiment," *Le Petit Journal*, April 4, 1895.
59 Émile Zola, "La littérature et la gymnastique," in *Mes haines* (Paris: Charpentier, [1866] 1879), p. 57.
60 Tissié, *La Fatigue et l'entraînement physique*, pp. 34–5.
61 *Encyclopédie des gens du monde*, 22 vols (Paris, 1833–43).
62 *Encyclopédie moderne*, 26 vols (Paris, 1823–33).
63 *Encyclopédie des connaissances utiles*, 19 vols (Paris, 1832–7).
64 *Encyclopédie domestique: recueil des procédés et de recettes concernant les arts et métiers, l'économie rurale et domestique*, 3 vols (Paris, 1822).

65 *Encyclopédie catholique: répertoire universel et raisonné des sciences, des lettres, des arts, et des métiers, formant une bibliothèque universelle*, 4 vols (Paris, 1839).
66 *Petite Encyclopédie des enfants* (Paris, 1825).
67 *Nouvelle Encyclopédie de la jeunesse, ou Abrégé de toutes les sciences* (Paris, 1822).
68 Léon Rénier, ed., *Encyclopédie moderne*, 44 vols (2nd edn, Paris, 1846).
69 Pierre Larousse, preface, *Grand Dictionnaire universel du XIXe siècle*, 17 vols, vol. I (Paris, 1866), p. lxiv.
70 Cited by Gustave Lagneau, *Du surmenage intellectuel et de la sédentarité dans les écoles* (Paris, 1886).
71 Victor de Laprade, *L'Éducation homicide: plaidoyer pour l'enfance* (Paris, 1868), p. 65.
72 Jean-Marie Guyau, *Éducation et hérédité: étude sociologique* (Paris, 1889), p. 96.
73 See the *Medical Times and Gazette*, July 21, 1883, pp. 74 and 94.
74 See Niels Theodor Axel Hertel, *Overpressure in High Schools in Denmark* (London, 1885).
75 See the *Rapport sur les écoles publiques supérieures d'Alsace-Lorraine* (Gex, 1884), p. 11.
76 Jean-Baptiste Fonssagrives, *L'Éducation physique des garçons* (Paris, 1870), p. 144.
77 Gustave Lagneau, *Du surmenage intellectuel et de la sédentarité dans les écoles*, p. 39.
78 *Le Parisien*, December 21, 1881.
79 Eugène Dally, "De l'exercice méthodique de la respiration dans ses rapports avec la conformation thoracique et la santé mentale," *Bulletin général de thérapeutique*, September 15, 1881, p. 20.
80 Georges Dujardin-Beaumetz, *Compte rendu de la séance de l'Académie de médecine*, September 14, 1886.
81 See the minutes of the Académie des sciences morales, 1864, p. 11.
82 Alphonse de Candolle, *Histoire des sciences et des savants depuis deux siècles* (Lyon, 1873), p. 392n.
83 See *Medical Times and Gazette*, July 21, 1883.
84 Ibid., June 21, 1884.
85 Gustave Lagneau, *Du surmenage intellectuel et de la sédentarité dans les écoles*, p. 760.
86 Maurice de Fleury, *Le Corps et l'âme de l'enfant* (Paris: Armand Colin, 1899), p. 196.
87 Bouveret, *La Neurasthénie: épuisement nerveux*, p. 13.
88 Ludwig Hirt, *Pathologie et thérapeutique des maladies du système nerveux* (Paris, 1894), p. 184.
89 The word was used for the first time in 1869. See George M. Beard, "Neurasthenia, or Nervous Exhaustion," *Boston Medical and Surgical Journal*, April 29, 1869, pp. 217–21.
90 Virgile Borel, *Nervosisme ou neurasthénie: la maladie du siècle et les divers moyens de la combattre* (Lausanne, 1894), pp. 98–100.
91 The *Journal de médecine et de chirurgie* included several articles on it every year by the end of the 1880s.
92 Charles Féré, *La Famille névropathique: théorie tératologique de l'hérédité et de la prédisposition morbide et de la dégénérescence* (Paris: Alcan, 1894), p. 105. See also Henry Meige, *Étude sur certains névropathes voyageurs: le juif errant à la Salpêtrière* (Paris, 1893).
93 Joris-Karl Huysmans, *À Rebours* (Paris: Gallimard, 2012), p. 166. *Against the Grain*, trans. John Howard (New York: Lieber & Lewis, 1922), pp. 130–1.
94 Pierre-Henri Castel, *Âmes scrupuleuses, vie d'angoisse, tristes obsédés: obsessions et contrainte intérieure de l'Antiquité à Freud* (Paris: Ithaque, 2017), p. 227.
95 Guy de Maupassant. "La Nuit: Cauchemar" (1887), in Brigitte Monglond (ed.), *Contes et nouvelles* (Paris: Robert Laffont, 1998), vol. I, p. 600.
96 Pierre de Coubertin, *Essais de psychologie sportive* (Grenoble: Jérôme Millon, [1913] 1992), p. 183.
97 Richard von Krafft-Ebing, *Über Nervosität* (Graz, 1884), preface.

98 Octave Mirbeau, "Mémoire pour un avocat" (1894), in *Contes cruels* (Paris: Librairie Séguier, 1990), vol. I, p. 112.
99 Alain Corbin, *L'Harmonie des plaisirs: les manières de jouir du siècle des Lumières à l'avènement de la sexologie* (Paris: Perrin, 2008), p. 117.
100 See Beard, "Neurasthenia, or Nervous Exhaustion." See also Beard, *American Nervousness: Its Causes and Consequences. A Supplement to Nervous Exhaustion* (New York, [1869] 1881), p. 98.
101 See ibid., p. 99: "Like the steam engine, its force is limited although it cannot be mathematically measured."
102 See the title of Bouveret, *La Neurasthénie: épuisement nerveux.*
103 See the title of Beard, *American Nervousness.*
104 Hirt, *Pathologie et thérapeutique des maladies du système nerveux*, p. 483.
105 Fernand Levillain, *Essais de neurologie clinique, neurasthénie de Beard et états neurasthéniformes* (Paris, 1896), p.10.
106 Castel, *Âmes scrupuleuses, vie d'angoisse, tristes obsédés: obsessions et contrainte intérieure de l'Antiquité à Freud*, p. 228.
107 See above p. 61.
108 Jules Dejerine and Emmanuel Gauckler, *Les Manifestations fonctionelles des psychonévroses* (Paris: Masson, 1911), pp. 370–2.
109 Coubertin, *Essais de psychologie sportive*, p. 183.
110 Dr Angelvin, La *neurasthénie, mal social* (Paris, 1905), p. 20.
111 Charles Fiessinger, *Erreurs sociales et maladies morales* (Paris: Perrin, 1909), p. 284.
112 Friedrich Nietzsche, *La Volonté de puissance* (1903). Trans. in James Miller, *History and Human Existence: From Marx to Merleau-Ponty* (Berkeley: University of California Press, 1979), p. 141. See Fiessinger, *Erreurs sociales et maladies morales*, p. 284.
113 Fulgence Raymond and Pierre Janet, *Les Obsessions et la psychasthénie* (Paris: Alcan, 1903), vol. II, p. 352.
114 Ibid., p. 353.
115 See above p. 213.
116 Fernand Lagrange, *Physiologie des exercices du corps* (Paris, 1888), p. 55.
117 Ibid.
118 See Théodule Ribot, *Psychologie de l'attention* (Paris, 1889).
119 See Binet and Henri, *La Fatigue intellectuelle*, p. 82.
120 See Guyot-Daubès, *Physiologie et hygiène du cerveau et des fonctions intellectuelles* (Paris: 1890).
121 Mosso, *La Fatigue intellectuelle et physique*, p. 82.
122 Ibid., p. 123.
123 Ribot, *Psychologie de l'attention*, p. 161.
124 Binet and Henri, *La Fatigue intellectuelle*, p. 328.
125 Mosso, *La Fatigue intellectuelle et physique*, p. 74.
126 Ibid., p. 122.
127 Ibid., p. 126.
128 Ibid., p. 140.
129 Jean-Martin Charcot, *Leçons sur les maladies du système nerveux faites à la Salpêtrière* (Paris, 1887), vol. III, p. 251.
130 Henri Huchard, *Traité clinique des maladies du cœur et de l'aorte* (Paris, 1899), vol. I, p. 186.
131 Ibid., p. 189.
132 Tissié, *La Fatigue et l'entraînement physique*, pp. 40–1.
133 Sigmund Freud and Josef Breuer, *Études sur l'hystérie* (Paris: PUF, [1895] 1956), p. 112. *Studies in Hysteria*, trans. Nicola Luckhurst (London: Penguin, 2004).
134 Ibid., p. 120.

Chapter 24 Resistance and Growth

1 Alfred Picard, *Le Bilan d'un siècle, 1801–1900*, vol. IV: *Mines et métallurgie, industries de la décoration et du mobilier, chauffage et ventilation, éclairage non électrique, fils, tissus, vêtements* (Paris: Imprimerie nationale, 1906), pp. 1–22.

2 Alain Corbin, "La fatigue, le repos et la conquête du temps," in Corbin, ed., *L'Avènement des loisirs, 1850–1960* (Paris: Aubier, 1995), p. 288.

3 Émile Levasseur, *Questions ouvrières et industrielles en France sous la Troisième République* (Paris: Arthur Rousseau, 1907), p. 442.

4 Picard, *Le Bilan d'un siècle, 1801–1900*, vol. V: *Industrie chimique, industries diverses économie sociale* (Paris: Imprimerie nationale, 1906), p. 280.

5 See Émile Bottigelli, ed., *La Naissance du Parti Ouvrier français: correspondance inédite de Paul Lafargue, Jules Guesde, José Mesa, Paul Brousse, Benoît Malon, Gabriel Deville, Victor Jaclard, Léon Camescasse et Friedrich Engels* (Paris: Éditions sociales, 1981).

6 Émile Cheysson, "La réglementation internationale du travail," *La Réforme sociale*, 19 (1890), p. 91.

7 Arnold t'Kint de Roodenbeke, "La réglementation internationale du travail et la conférence internationale de Berlin," *La Réforme sociale*, 20 (1890), p. 155.

8 Jules Arnould, *Nouveaux Éléments d'hygiène* (Paris: Baillière, [1881] 1907), p. 790.

9 See Yves Tyl, *Les Enfants au travail dans les usines au XIXe siècle* (Paris: Institut coopératif de l'école moderne, 1984); www.icem-pedagogie-freinet.org/sites/default/files/172_Travail_Enfants.pdf.

10 Ibid.

11 See "Règlement général pour le service des cantonniers," Département de Seine-et-Oise, 1853, pp. 15–16.

12 See Thierry Tauran, "Les initiatives ponctuelles de l'État (1604–1853)," in Tauran, ed., *La Sécurité sociale: son histoire à travers les textes*, vol. VII: *Les Régimes spéciaux de sécurité sociale* (Paris: Association pour l'étude de la Sécurité sociale, 2015).

13 Léon Say, ed., *Nouveau Dictionnaire d'économie politique* (Paris, 1892), entry "Retraites."

14 See "Présentation de la loi sur les pensions civiles du 9 juin 1853," in Adrien Carpentier, *Codes et lois pour la France, l'Algérie et les colonies* (Paris: Marchal & Brillard, 1908), p. 491.

15 See Robert Fonteneau, ed., *La Protection sociale minière du XVIIIe siècle à nos jours* (Paris: Association pour l'étude de l'histoire de la sécurité sociale, 2009), pp. 97 and 127.

16 See Leyla Dakhli, "Histoire des régimes spéciaux de retraite," Le Mouvement social, 2007; Roundtable discussion, November 22, 2007.

17 See Tauran, *La Sécurité sociale: son histoire à travers les textes*, vol. VII: *Les Régimes spéciaux de sécurité sociale*, p. 64.

18 See Maxime Tellier, "À l'origine, le régime spécial des cheminots a été une volonté patronale," *France culture*, December 5, 2019; www.franceculture.fr/histoire/a-lorigine-le-regime-special-des-cheminots-a-ete-une-volonte-patronale.

19 Paul Lafargue, *Le Droit à la paresse: réfutation du droit au travail de 1848* (Paris, 1883), p. 21. *The Right to Be Lazy, Being a Refutation of the "Right to Work" of 1848*, trans. Harriet E. Lothrop (New York: International, 1898), p. 34.

20 Lafargue, *Le Droit à la paresse*, p. 26.

21 Ibid.

22 "Miracles industriels," *Almanach du Père Peinard pour 1897*, p. 26.

23 Arnould, *Nouveaux Éléments d'hygiène*, p. 792.

24 Illustration by Paul Guillaume, *L'Illustré national*, November 23, 1902.

25 See Levasseur, *Questions ouvrières et industrielles en France sous la Troisième République*, p. 442.

26 Robert Beck, *Histoire du dimanche: de 1700 à nos jours* (Paris: Éditions de l'Atelier, 1997), p. 321.

27 Fernand Boulard, *Premiers Itinéraires en sociologie religieuse* (Paris: Éditions ouvrières, 1966), p. 27.
28 Bruno Béthouart, "Les syndicats chrétiens et le repos du dimanche (1887–1964)," *Histoire, économie et société*, no. 3 (2009), pp. 99–108.
29 Ibid.
30 Say, *Nouveau Dictionnaire d'économie politique*, entry "Dimanche et jours fériés."
31 Béthouart, "Les syndicats chrétiens et le repos du dimanche."
32 Corbin, "La fatigue, le repos et la conquête du temps," p. 289.
33 Confédération générale du travail, *XVIIIe Congrès national corporatif, compte rendu des travaux* (Le Havre: L'Union, 1912), pp. 22–4.
34 See Beck, *Histoire du dimanche: de 1700 à nos jours*, p. 324.
35 Augustin-Fabien Declercq, "Le vocabulaire de Rerum novarum dans les hymnes populaires de la CFTC," *Revue du Nord*, 73/290–1 (1991), p. 431.
36 Anson Rabinbach, *Le Moteur humain: l'énergie, la fatigue et les origines de la modernité* (Paris: La Fabrique, [1992] 2004), p. 127.
37 See Eugen Weber, *La Fin des terroirs: la modernisation de la France rurale, 1870–1914* (Paris: Fayard, 1983).
38 See Georges Vigarello, *Du jeu ancien au show sportif: la naissance d'un mythe* (Paris: Seuil, 2002), p. 94: "La naissance des grands spectacles."
39 Pierre de Coubertin, "La bataille continue ..." *Bulletin du Bureau international de pédagogie sportive*, no. 5 (1931), p. 7.
40 Pierre de Coubertin, "L'éducation athlétique," Association française pour l'avancement des sciences, compte rendu de la 18e session (Paris: Masson, 1889) in *Pierre de Coubertin: textes choisis*, ed. Norbert Muller (Zurich: Weidmann, 1986), vol. I, p. 168.
41 See above pp. 135–6.
42 See Isabelle Queval, *S'accomplir ou se dépasser: essai sur le sport contemporain* (Paris: Gallimard, 2004).
43 Coubertin, *Pédagogie sportive* (1921), in *Pierre de Coubertin: textes choisis*, p. 571.
44 J. H. Rosny, *Les Joies du sport* (1910), in Gilbert Prouteau, *Anthologie des textes sportifs de la littérature* (Paris: Défense de la France, 1948), p. 359.
45 Colette, "Dans la foule: la fin d'un Tour de France, July 28, 1912," in *Oeuvres*, vol. II (Paris: Gallimard, 1986), p. 622.
46 See above p. 169.
47 See above p. 141.
48 See above p. 197.
49 Philippe Tissié, *La Fatigue et l'entraînement physique* (Paris, 1897), p. 3.
50 Fernand Lagrange, *Physiologie des exercices du corps* (Paris, 1888), p. 195.
51 "L'hygiène des sports," *Annuaire général des sports illustré: encyclopédie universelle du tourisme, de tous les sports et jeux de plein air, commerce et industrie sportive*, 2 (1905–6), p. 127.
52 Tissié, *La Fatigue et l'entraînement physique*, p. 2.
53 Georges Hébert, *Ma leçon-type d'entraînement complet et utilitaire* (Paris: Vuibert, 1913).
54 Eugen Sandow, *Strength and How to Obtain It* (London, 1897), p. 28: "Sandow's Charts of Measurements."
55 Bernarr Macfadden, *Muscular Power and Beauty* (New York, 1906), p. 21.
56 See Bernard Maccario, *Jean Bouin: héros du sport, héros de la Grande Guerre* (Paris: Chistera, 2018), pp. 111ff.: "Une conception novatrice de l'entraînement."
57 Lagrange, *Physiologie des exercices du corps*, p. 195.
58 Raoul Fabens, *Le Sport pour tous* (Paris: Armand Colin, 1905), p. 44.
59 *La vie au grand air*, March 14, 1914. See also on this topic Alfred Wahl, *Les Archives du football: sport et société en France, 1880–1980* (Paris: Gallimard, 1989), pp. 140–1.

60 Tissié, *La Fatigue et l'entraînement physique*, p. 1.
61 Ibid., p. 24.
62 Ibid.
63 Pierre M. Besse and Jean Anex, "L'alimentation dans l'entraînement et l'entraînement dans l'alimentation," Congrès international d'éducation physique, Paris, March 17–20, 1913, conference report (Paris: Baillière, 1913), vol. III, p. 167. See also in the same conference Édouard Maurel, "L'alimentation dans les sports," p. 162.
64 Tissié, *La Fatigue et l'entraînement physique*, p. 16.
65 See Daniel Mérillon, ed., *Concours internationaux d'exercices physiques et de sports: exposition universelle internationale de 1900 à Paris: rapports*, 2 vols (Paris: Imprimerie nationale, 1901–2).
66 Félix Régnault, "Les types humains d'après les principales proportions du corps," *Revue scientifique*, no. 22, May 28, 1910.
67 Claude Sigaud, *La forme humaine*, vol. I : *Sa signification* (Paris: Maloine, 1914).
68 Marco Saraceno, *De la mesure du corps à la politique des corps: une histoire des sciences du travail (1880–1920)*, thesis, University of Pisa, 2013, p. 128.
69 Léon Mac-Auliffe and Auguste Chaillou, *Morphologie médicale: étude des quatre types humains: applications à la clinique et à la thérapeutique* (Paris: Doin, 1912). Translator's note: In the photographs the women were nude, but the men were not.
70 Pierre-Joseph Bonnette, *Du choix des conscrits: indices de robusticité physique, utilisation méthodique du contingent, service armé, service auxiliaire: dépôts de viriculture, extra-régimentaires pour les malingres* (Paris: Doin, 1910), pp. 4–5.
71 Anne-Marie Sohn, *La Fabrique des garçons: l'éducation des garçons de 1820 à aujourd'hui* (Paris: Textuel, 2015), p. 86.
72 See, among others, Alphonse Laveran, *Traité d'hygiène militaire* (Paris, 1896).
73 See Eugène-François Ravenez, *La Vie du soldat au point de vue de l'hygiène* (Paris: Baillière, 1889), p. 25.
74 Maurice-Charles-Joseph Pignet, "Valeur numérique de l'homme," *Archives médicales d'Angers*, 1900, p. 346.
75 Ibid., p. 347.
76 Ibid., p. 351.
77 Marcel Craponne, *Les Neurasthéniques aux villes d'eaux* (Paris, 1914), p. 4.
78 Septimus Piesse, *Des odeurs, des parfums et des cosmétiques* (Paris, [1865] 1877), p. 172.
79 Ibid., p. 207.
80 Ibid., p. 203.
81 See Michel Hautefeuille and Dan Véléa, *Les Drogues de synthèse* (Paris: PUF, 2002).
82 Gustave Geley, "La cocaine contre la neurasthénie," *Journal de médecine et de chirurgie* (1894), p. 860.
83 "Traitement de la céphalée des neurasthéniques," ibid., p. 116.
84 See the advertisements in the *Journal de la santé publique: annales de l'hydrothérapie scientifique* in the 1880s.
85 A prominent advertisement in the *Guides pratiques Conty: la Méditerranée* (Paris, 1908).
86 Ibid.
87 "Transfusion nerveuse pour combattre la neurasthénie," *Journal de médecine et de chirurgie* (1894), p. 201.
88 *Les Annales du bioscope, de la bioscopie et de la biothérapie pendant la cure thermale de Vichy* (Vichy, 1903), p. 3.
89 Craponne, *Les Neurasthéniques aux villes d'eaux*, p. 9.
90 Hugh Campbell, *Nervous Exhaustion and the Diseases Induced by It* (London, 1873).
91 "Le bicycle dans le traitement des maladies nerveuses," *Journal de médecine et de*

chirurgie pratiques (1892), p. 578. See also the *Journal of Nervous and Mental Disease* (1892).
92 Ibid.
93 Octave Mirbeau, "En traitement" (1897), in *Contes cruels* (Paris: Librairie Séguier, 1990), vol. I, p. 222.
94 Craponne, *Les Neurasthéniques aux villes d'eaux*, p. 10.
95 Fernand Lagrange, *La Médication par l'exercice* (Paris, 1894), p. 254.
96 Ibid. See the map of a spa town, p. 260.
97 See above p. 156.
98 Craponne, *Les Neurasthéniques aux villes d'eaux*, p. 10.
99 Alfred Guillon, "Aux Eaux," a one-act play (Paris, 1886), p. 11.
100 See the analysis of Pierre-Henri Castel in *Âmes scrupuleuses, vie d'angoisse, tristes obsédés: obsessions et contrainte intérieure de l'Antiquité à Freud* (Paris: Ithaque, 2017), p. 228.
101 Théodule Ribot, *Les Maladies de la personnalité* (Paris, 1885), p. 93.
102 Henry Maudsley, *The Physiology and Pathology of the Mind* (New York: Appleton, 1867).
103 Sebastien Kneipp, *Ma cure d'eau, ou Hygiène et médication pour la guérison des maladies et la conservation de la santé* (Strasbourg, 1890), p. 393.
104 Jules Rengade, *Les Besoins de la vie et les éléments du bien-être* (Paris, 1887), p. 550.
105 See Georges Vigarello, "Le fauteuil," in Pierre Singaravélou and Sylvain Venayre, eds., *Histoire du monde au XIXe siècle* (Paris: Fayard, 2017).
106 Alain Rey finds the new word in use in the second half of the nineteenth century. See Rey, *Dictionnaire historique de la langue française* (Paris: Robert, 1994), entry "Détendu attesté dans la deuxième moitié du XIXe siècle."
107 Joris-Karl Huysmans, *Là-Bas* (1891) (Paris: Gallimard, 1985), p. 84. *Down There*, trans. Keene Wallace, privately pubd, 1928, chapter V.
108 See Percy MacKaye, *Epoch: The Life of Steele MacKaye, Genius of the Theatre, in Relation to His Times and Contemporaries* (New York: Boni & Liveright, 1927). See also Annie Suquet, *L'Éveil des modernités: une histoire culturelle de la danse, 1870–1945* (Pantin: Centre national de la danse, 2012), p. 151.
109 See above p. 228.
110 Eustace Miles, *Cassell's Physical Educator* (London: Cassell, 1904), p. 159.
111 Ibid., p. 651.
112 Ibid., pp. 652–3.
113 Willibald Gebhardt, *L'Attitude qui en impose et comment l'acquérir* (Paris, 1900).
114 See the important work of Hervé Guillemain, *La Méthode Coué: histoire d'une pratique de guérison au XXe siècle* (Paris: Seuil, 2010).
115 Gebhardt, *L'Attitude qui en impose et comment l'acquérir*, p. 131.
116 Philippe Tissié, "La fatigue dans l'entraînement physique," in Tissié, ed., *L'Éducation physique* (Paris: Larousse, 1901), p. 17.
117 Paul-Émile Lévy, *L'Éducation rationnelle de la volonté: son emploi thérapeutique* (Paris: Alcan, [1898] 1907), p. 79.
118 Frédéric Rauh and Gabriel Revault d'Allonnes, *Psychologie appliquée à la morale et à l'éducation* (Paris, 1900), p. 303.
119 Lévy, *L'Éducation rationnelle de la volonté*, p. 147.
120 Ralph Waldo Emerson's analysis was first published in 1841 and later translated into French. See Emerson, *The Essay on Self-Reliance* (East Aurora, NY: Roycrofters, 1908).
121 J. de Lerne, *Comment devenir plus fort* (Paris, 1902).
122 Silvain Roudès, *Pour faire son chemin dans la vie: moyens et qualités qui permettent d'arriver au succès et à la fortune* (Paris, 1902).
123 Macfadden, *Muscular Power and Beauty*. See the advertisement "Vitality Supreme for Men and Women" at the end of the book.

Part V The Twentieth and Twenty-First Centuries and the Challenge of Psychology

1 Élisabeth Roudinesco, "Les prédateurs sexuels sont aujourd'hui considérés comme des malades," *Le Monde*, February 28, 2020.
2 See Madeline Aveline, *Des remèdes à l'anxiété et à l'angoisse modernes* (Geneva: Farnot, 1979).
3 Daniel Cohen, "Où va le travail humain?" in Cohen, Raymond Depardon, Jacques Donzelot, Antoine Garapon et al., *France: les révolutions invisibles* (Paris: Calmann-Lévy, 1998), p. 117.
4 Pierre Rosenvallon, *Le Sacre du citoyen: histoire du suffrage universel en France* (Paris: Gallimard, 1992), pp. 14–15.
5 Pierre Rosenvallon, "Les utopies régressives de la démocratie," in Cohen et al., *France: les révolutions invisibles*, p. 210.

Chapter 25 Revealing the Psyche

1 Anne Duménil, "Le combattant," in Stéphane Audoin-Rouzeau and Jean-Jacques Becker, eds, *Encyclopédie de la Grande Guerre, 1914–1918: histoire et culture* (Paris: Bayard, 2004), p. 322.
2 Stéphane Audoin-Rouzeau, "Massacres, le corps et la guerre," in Alain Corbin, Jean-Jacques Courtine and Georges Vigarello, eds, *Histoire du corps*, vol. III: *Les Mutations du regard: le XXe siècle* (Paris: Seuil, 2006), p. 293.
3 Antoine Prost, "Le bouleversement des sociétés," in *Encyclopédie de la Grande Guerre, 1914–1918*, p. 1178.
4 Stéphane Audoin-Rouzeau, "Les tranchées," ibid., p. 250.
5 Audoin-Rouzeau, "Massacres, les corps et la guerre," p. 284.
6 Erich Maria Remarque, *À l'ouest rien de nouveau* (1929), in *1914–1918, Français et Allemands dans les tranchées* (Paris: Le Livre de Poche, 2013), p. 621. *All Quiet on the Western Front*, trans. A. W. Wheen (New York: Little, Brown, 1929).
7 Audoin-Rouzeau, "Les tranchées," p. 249.
8 Duménil, "Le combattant," p. 325.
9 Remarque, *À l'ouest rien de nouveau*, p. 606.
10 Émile Galitier-Boissière, ed., *Larousse médical illustré de la guerre* (Paris: Larousse, 1916), entry "Maladies nerveuses."
11 Maurice Boigey, *Manuel scientifique d'éducation physique* (Paris: Payot, 1923), p. 432: "the loss of energy was observed by many officers."
12 Victor Dhers, *Essai de critique théorique des tests de fatigue*, thesis, Paris, 1924, p. 6.
13 Gabriel Chevallier, *La Peur* (1930), in *Français et Allemands dans les tranchées*, p. 929.
14 Ibid., p. 790.
15 André Pézard, *Nous autres à Vauquois, 1915–1916* (Paris: La Table ronde, [1918] 2016), p. 214.
16 Chevallier, *La Peur*, p. 906.
17 Charles S. Myers, *Industrial Psychology in Great Britain* (London: Jonathan Cape, [1926] 1933), p. 45.
18 Paul Sédallian and Roger Sohier, *Précis d'hygiène et d'épidémiologie* (Paris: Masson, 1949), p. 112.
19 Arthur Van Gehuchten, *Les Maladies nerveuses* (Louvain: Uystpruyst, 1920), p. 627.
20 Georges Friedmann, *Machine et humanisme: problèmes humains du machinisme industriel* (Paris: Gallimard, 1946), p. 66.
21 Kurt Goldstein, *La Structure de l'organisme: introduction à la biologie à partir de la pathologie humaine* (Paris: Gallimard, [1934] 1983), p. 224.
22 Boigey, *Manuel scientifique d'éducation physique*, pp. 443–8.
23 Friedmann, *Machine et humanisme*, p. 72.

24 Elliott Dunlap Smith, *Psychology for Executives: A Study of Human Nature in Industry* (New York: Harper, 1928), pp. 101–2.
25 Morris S. Viteles, *Industrial Psychology* (New York: W. W. Norton, 1932), p. 440.
26 See Camille Simonin, "Évolution de la protection médicale des travailleurs," in Simonin, *Médecine du travail* (Paris: Maloine, [1950] 1956), p. 770.
27 See https://en.wikipedia.org/wiki/Occupational_medicine.
28 See Myers, *Industrial Psychology in Great Britain*, p. 50: "all conflicting nervous impulses must be inhibited." Translator's note: Tonic and clonic are used to describe seizures; tonic is characterized by a stiffening of the muscles and clonic by convulsions, jerking and twitching.
29 Ibid., p. 42: "blocking the path of outgoing impulses."
30 Friedmann, *Machine et humanisme*, p. 79.
31 Ibid., p. 77.
32 Myers *Industrial Psychology in Great Britain*, p. 51.
33 See Ibid., pp. 40ff.
34 Friedmann, *Machine et humanisme*, p. 79.
35 See above p. 187.
36 Myers, *Industrial Psychology in Great Britain*, p. 51.
37 Friedmann, *Machine et humanisme*, p. 79.
38 See above p. 80.
39 Ralph Mosser Barnes, *Études des mouvements et des temps* (Paris: Éditions d'Organisation, [1937] 1949), p. 191.
40 See above p. 203.
41 Jean-Maurice Lahy, "L'influence de l'éclairage sur le rendement," *Mon Bureau*, September 1927.
42 *Mon Bureau*, advertisement for Ilrin, March 1930.
43 See L. Blumenthal, "Organisation de l'entreprise, le bruit et le rendement," *Mon Bureau*, July 1934.
44 Friedmann, *Machine et humanisme*, p. 87.
45 *Mon Bureau*, advertisement for Moderny, March 15, 1921.
46 Ibid., advertisement for Chauvin, February 1934.
47 Ibid., advertisement for Strafor, March 15, 1922.
48 Ibid., advertisement for Le Porin, March 1937.
49 Ibid., "Le machinisme dans le bureau," March 1938.
50 See R. M. Blakelock, "Micromotion Study Applied to the Manufacture of Small Parts," *Factory and Industrial Management*, 80 (October 1930).
51 Barnes, *Études des mouvements et des temps*.
52 Ibid., p. 240.
53 Ibid., p. 230.
54 Ibid., p. 183.
55 See Archibald Vivian Hill, *Living Machinery* (New York, 1927).
56 Bernard Metz, "Aspects physiologiques et psychologiques de la fatigue," in Simonin, *Médecine du travail*, p. 158.
57 Myers, *Industrial Psychology in Great Britain*, p. 45.
58 Ibid., p. 47.
59 Edward David Jones, *The Administration of Industrial Enterprises* (New York: Longmans, 1919), p. 221.
60 Harold Ernest Burtt, *Psychology and Industrial Efficiency* (New York: Appleton, 1931), p. 174.
61 J. Ramsay and R. E. Rawson, *Rest Pauses and Refreshments in Industry* (London: National Institute of Industrial Psychology, 1939), pp. 5 and 42.

62 Burtt, *Psychology and Industrial Efficiency*, p. 191.
63 Elton Mayo, "Revery and industrial fatigue," *Journal of Personnel Research*, 3/8 (1924), p. 273.
64 Jean-Maurice Lahy, "Recherches expérimentales sur des activités simultanées de force et de précision," *Le Travail humain*, 8/1 (1940), p. 45.
65 Jean-Maurice Lahy, "Les conducteurs de 'poids lourds,' analyse du métier, étude de la fatigue et organisation du travail," ibid., 5/1 (1937), p. 35.
66 Ibid., p. 38.
67 A. H. Ryan and Mary Warner, "The effect of automobile driving on the reactions of the driver," *American Journal of Psychology*, 48/3 (1936).
68 See the category "Physiologie du travail et psychotechnique" in the journal *Le Travail humain*.
69 See Anson Rabinbach, *Le Moteur humain: l'énergie, la fatigue et les origines de la modernité* (Paris: La Fabrique, [1992] 2004), p. 445. Or Marc Loriol, *Le Temps de la fatigue* (Paris: Anthropos, 2000), p. 68.
70 Henri Mignet, *Le Sport de l'air* (Paris: Taffin-Lefort, 1934), p. 21.
71 Charles Lindbergh, *Trente-Trois Heures pour Paris* (Paris: Presses de la Cité, 1953), p. 287. English version: www.mnhs.org/lindbergh/learn/timeline.
72 Ibid., p. 212.
73 Ibid., p. 213.
74 Ibid., p. 389.
75 Ibid., p. 214.
76 Elton Mayo, *The Social Problems of an Industrial Civilization* (Boston: Harvard University, 1945).
77 See the comprehensive analysis of the Hawthorne experiment by Thomas North Whitehead, *The Industrial Worker: A Statistical Study of Human Relations in a Group of Manual Workers* (Cambridge, MA: Harvard University Press, 1938), vol. 1, p. 198: "negative correlations"; or p. 215: "neighbor relations and distant relations."
78 Ibid., p. 139: "marriage, attitude towards."
79 Fritz Jules Roethlisberger and William J. Dickson, *Management and the Worker: An Account of a Research Program Conducted by the Western Electric Company* (Cambridge, MA: Harvard University Press, 1939), p. 160.
80 M. L. Lipman, "Improving employee relations," *Personnel Journal*, no. 8 (1930), p. 325.
81 See Friedmann discussing Elton Mayo's experiment in *Machine et humanisme*, p. 299.
82 See "proportional salary" and remuneration based on business profits in Eugène Schueller, *La Révolution de l'économie* (Paris: Denoël, 1941) and also the possible role of "workers' councils" Gérard Bardet, "Une expérience de collaboration ouvrière à la direction d'une usine," quoted in Jean Coutrot, *L'Humanisme économique* (Paris: Éditions du Centre polytechnicien d'études économiques, 1936), p. 38.
83 See above p. 222.
84 See Whitehead, *The Industrial Worker*, vol. I, p. 108: "The establishment of routines and sentiments."
85 See above p. 267.
86 Michel-P. Hamelet, *Le Figaro*, April 23–6, 1946.
87 See Friedmann's discussion of Elton Mayo's experiment in *Machine et humanisme*, p. 305.
88 "Les métiers du fer," *La France travaille* (Paris: Éditions des Horizons de France, 1932), vol. I, p. 130.
89 All of the photographs are found in the two volumes of *La France travaille* published in 1932 and 1934. This was the only major photographic study undertaken in France in the interwar period.

90 See above p. 179.
91 *La France travaille.*
92 Ibid.
93 Ibid., p. 192.
94 Ibid., p. 199.
95 Ibid., p. 31.
96 Ibid., p. 140.
97 *Floréal: l'hebdomadaire illustré du monde du travail*, 1920–3.
98 "Le monde du travail: les terrassiers," ibid., February 20, 1921.
99 Frédéric Bordas, *La Prophylaxie de la fatigue et ses avantages sociaux* (Paris: Institut général de psychologie, 1927), p. 5.
100 Constant Malva, *Ma Nuit au jour le jour* (Paris: Maspero, [1937] 1978), p. 41. Many of the examples that follow are taken from the ground-breaking book by Thierry Pillon, *Le Corps à l'ouvrage* (Paris: Stock, 2012).
101 Maurice Alline, *Quand j'étais ouvrier, 1930–1948* (Rennes: Éditions Ouest-France, 2003), p. 118.
102 Albert Soulillou, *Les Temps promis: Élie ou Le Ford-France 580* (Paris: Gallimard, 1933), p. 41.
103 Simone Weil, *La Condition ouvrière* (Paris: Gallimard, 1951), p. 121.
104 Georges Navel, *Travaux* (Paris: Gallimard, [1945] 1979), p. 69.
105 See above p. 213.
106 See above p. 228.
107 See above p. 257.
108 See above p. 107.
109 Alline, *Quand j'étais ouvrier, 1930–1948*, p. 73.
110 Claude Pigi, *La Fatigue de Marie Tavernier* (Paris: Les Livres nouveaux, 1938).
111 Ibid., p. 11.
112 Ibid.
113 Ibid., p. 117.
114 *Marie Claire*, March 12, 1937.

Chapter 26 From Hormones to Stress

1 Mathias Duval and Eugène Gley, *Traité élémentaire de physiologie* (Paris: Baillière, 1906, p. 617.
2 Léopold Lévi, *Le Tempérament et ses troubles: les glandes endocriniens* (Paris: J. Oliven, 1929), p. xvi. *Organotherapy in General Practice*, no. 3: *Asthenia, hypothyroidism, hypoadrenia, senility* (New York: G. W. Carnrick, 1922), pp. 16–20.
3 *Le Tempérament et ses troubles*, p. 10.
4 Ibid., p. xv.
5 Ibid., p. 110.
6 Ibid., p. 91.
7 Ibid., p. 74.
8 Ibid., pp. 73–118.
9 Ibid., p. x.
10 Serge Voronoff, *Les Sources de la vie* (Paris: Fasquelle, 1933), p. 1.
11 See Charles-Édouard Brown-Séquard, "On a new therapeutic method consisting in the use of organic liquids extracted from glands and other organs," *British Medical Journal*, June 1893, pp. 1145–7.
12 Serge Voronoff, *Quarante-Trois Greffes du singe à l'homme* (Paris, Octave Doin, 1924), pp. 48 and 51.
13 Ibid., p. 91.

14 Ibid., p. 117.
15 Ibid., p. 98.
16 René Prédal, *L'Étrange Destin du docteur Voronoff: en quête d'une jeunesse éternelle?* (Paris: L'Harmattan, 2017), p. 135.
17 *L'Illustration* November 22, 1924.
18 See Jean Real, *Voronoff* (Paris: Stock, 2001), p. 205.
19 See https://en.wikipedia.org/wiki/Serge_Voronoff.
20 See "Medical monkey business," *Cincinnati-Kentucky Post*, November 5, 1998, p. 22.
21 Prédal, *L'Étrange Destine du docteur Voronoff*, p. 148.
22 Blaise Cendrars, *L'Amiral* (Paris: Gallimard, [1935] 2014), p. 75.
23 See above p. 276.
24 See G. Alles, G. Pines and H. Miller, *Journal of the American Medical Association*, 1930.
25 See http://en.wikipedia.org/wiki/Amphetamine.
26 Seewww.theatlantic.com/health/archive/2012/04/the-lost-world-of-benzedrine/255904/.
27 Norbert Wiener, *I Am a Mathematician: The Later Life of a Prodigy* (New York: Doubleday, 1956).
28 Norman Ohler, *L'Extase totale: le IIIe Reich, les Allemands et la drogue*, trans. Vincent Platini (Paris: La Découverte, [2015] 2018), p. 47.
29 Ibid., p. 46.
30 Jean-Pierre de Mondenard, *Dictionnaire du dopage: substances, procédés, conduites, dangers* (Paris: Masson, 2004), p. 750.
31 Ibid., p. 754.
32 Ohler, *L'Extase totale*, p. 110.
33 Ibid., p. 67.
34 Leonardo Conti, "An die ehrenamtlichen Mitglieder der früheren RfR," October 19, 1939, BArch-Berlin R36/1360, quoted in Ohler, ibid., p. 79.
35 Ohler, ibid., p. 125.
36 Norbert Wiener, *I Am a Mathematician*.
37 Ohler, *L'Extase total*e, p. 62.
38 Heinrich Böll, *Lettres de guerre, 1939–1945*, trans. Jeanne Guérout (Paris: L'Iconoclaste, [2001] 2018).
39 Ohler, *L'Extase total*e, p. 84.
40 Quoted in Karl-Heinz Frieser, *Le Mythe de la guerre-éclair*, trans. Nicole Thiers (Paris: Belin, [1995] 2003), p. 209.
41 Quoted in *La Pilule de Göring*, a documentary film by Sönke el Bitar, Arte, 2010.
42 See *Alliés et nazis sous amphétamines*, a documentary film by Steven Hoggard, 2018.
43 See Mondenard, *Dictionnaire du dopage: substances, procédés, conduites, dangers*, p. 752.
44 Hans Selye, "A syndrome produced by diverse nocuous agents," *Nature*, July 4, 1936, p. 32.
45 Ibid.
46 See Herbert Fisher Moore and Glen N. Krouse, "Repeated stress (fatigue) testing machines used in the materials testing laboratory of the University of Illinois," *University of Illinois Bulletin*, 31/30 (1934).
47 See above pp. 258–9.
48 Walter B. Cannon, *The Wisdom of the Body* (New York: W. W. Norton, [1932] 1989). See p. xiii: "the overall effect of a traumatic shock."
49 Hans Selye, *Le Stress de la vie: le problème de l'adaptation*, trans. Pauline Verdun, (Paris: Gallimard, [1956] 1962), p. 229.
50 Ibid., p. 151.
51 Hans Selye, *L'Histoire du syndrome général d'adaptation*, trans. Dr Tchekoff and Pierre-Jean Caplier (Paris: Gallimard, [1952] 1954), p. 34. See Mark Jackson, "Evaluating

the role of Hans Selye in the modern history of stress," in D. Cantor and E. Ramsden, *Stress, Shock, and Adaptation in the Twentieth Century* (Rochester, NY: University of Rochester Press, 2014), chapter 1.

Chapter 27 From the "New Man" to Tragedy

1 See Marcel Gauchet, *La Condition historique* (Paris: Stock, 2003), p. 303.
2 Ibid.
3 Hannah Arendt, *Les Origines du totalitarisme* (1951), trans. Pierre Bouretz, Micheline Pouteau and Martine Leiris (Paris: Gallimard, 2002), p. 624. *The Origins of Totalitarianism* (New York: Harcourt, 1951).
4 Pierre Milza, *Mussolini* (Paris: Fayard, 1999). See p. 781: "le mythe de l'homme nouveau."
5 Illustration by Boris Koustodiev. The magazine, edited by Grigori Zinoviev, was published in Moscow in Russian, French, German and English versions.
6 Thierry Pillon, "Virilité ouvrière," in Alain Corbin, Jean-Jacques Courtine and Georges Vigarello, eds, *Histoire de la virilité* (Paris: Seuil, 2011), vol. III, p. 308.
7 Pierre Milza, "Mussolini, figure emblématique de 'l'homme nouveau,'" in Milza and Marie-Anne Matard-Bonucci, eds, *L'Homme nouveau, dans l'Europe fasciste (1922–1945): entre dictature et totalitarisme* (Paris: Fayard, 2004), p. 77.
8 Adolf Hitler, speech at Nuremberg, September 14, 1935, quoted by Éric Michaud, "L'homme nouveau et son autre dans l'Allemagne national-socialiste," ibid., p. 307.
9 Michaud, "'L'homme nouveau et son autre dans l'Allemagne national-socialiste," p. 314.
10 Jacques Doriot, *Le Mouvement et les hommes* (1942), in Bernard-Henry Lejeune, *Historisme de Jacques Doriot et du Parti populaire français* (Amiens: Les Nouveaux Cahiers du CERPES, 1977), vol. I, pp. 68–9.
11 Arendt, *Les Origines du totalitarisme*, p. 767.
12 Pillon, "Virilité ouvrière," p. 311.
13 See Jean-Paul Depretto, "La réalité du stakhanovisme ou Staxanov par lui-même," *Revue des études slaves*, 3/54 (1982), p. 348.
14 Ibid.
15 Anne Applebaum, *Rideau de fer: l'Europe de l'Est écrasée*, trans. Pierre-Emmanuel Dauzat (Paris: Grasset, 2014). *Iron Curtain: The Crushing of Eastern Europe, 1944–1956* (New York: Doubleday, 2012), chapter 13: "Homo Sovieticus."
16 See www.histoire-fr.com/mensonges_histoire_stakhanov.htm.
17 Georges Friedmann, "La civilisation technicienne," *Arguments*, no. 27–8 (1962), p. 50.
18 See Éric Vigne, "Stakhanov, ce héros normatif," *Vingtième siècle*, no. 1 (1984), p. 26: "Histoires de l'avenir: 1984 au rendez-vous d'Orwell."
19 See www.histoire-fr.com/mensonges_histoire_stakhanov.htm.
20 Arendt, *Les Origines du totalitarisme*, p. 632.
21 Applebaum, *Rideau de fer: l'Europe de l'Est.*
22 Eugen Kogon, *L'Enfer organisé: le système des camps de concentration* (Paris: La Jeune Parque, 1947), p. 118.
23 Joël Kotek, "Camps et centres d'extermination au XXe siècle: essai de classification," *Les Cahiers de la Shoah*, 1/7 (2003). See "Trois types de camps."
24 Ibid. See "À quoi sert un camp?"
25 Hermann Langbein, *Hommes et femmes à Auschwitz*, trans. Denise Meunier (Paris: UGE, [1980] 1994).
26 See Wolfgang Sofsky, *L'Organisation de la terreur: les camps de concentration*, trans. Olivier Mannoni (Paris: Calmann-Lévy, 1995), p. 55.
27 Alexandre Soljenitsyne, *L'Archipel du Goulag* (1973), trans. Geneviève Johannet (Paris:

Seuil, 1974). Alexander Solzhenitsyn, *The Gulag Archipelago: An Experiment in Literary Investigation* (New York: Harper & Row, 1976).

28 Juliette Cadiot and Marc Élie, *Histoire du Goulag* (Paris: La Découverte, 2017).

29 Among the many survivors' accounts, see Georges Snyders, in "Grands Entretiens," INA, https://entretiens.ina.fr/memoires-de-la-shoah/Snyders/georgessnyders/transcription/3. See also Jan Sehn et al., *German Crimes in Poland* (London, 1946), vol. I, p. 53.

30 Raul Hilberg, *La Destruction des Juifs d'Europe* (1985), trans. Marie-France de Paloméra and André Charpentier (Paris: Gallimard, 1991), vol. II, p. 806.

31 Christian Ingrao, *Croire et détruire: les intellectuels dans la machine de guerre SS* (Paris: Pluriel, 2011).

32 Norman Ohler, *L'Extase totale: le IIIe Reich, les Allemands et la drogue*, trans. Vincent Platini (Paris: La Découverte, [2015] 2018), p. 243.

33 H.-J. Richter, *Journal de guerre*, quoted ibid., p. 246.

34 A Nazi attorney's comments, reported by Jean-Claude Richez and Léon Strauss, "Un temps nouveau pour les ouvriers: les congés payés (1930–1960)," in Alain Corbin, ed., *L'Avènement des loisirs, 1850–1960* (Paris: Aubier, 1995), p. 387.

35 The phrase is attributed to Hitler and quoted ibid., p. 388.

36 International Labor Conference, October–November, 1919, sponsored by the International Labor Organization and the League of Nations, report prepared by the organizing committee of the Conference, Washington, DC, 1919. See "History of the ILO," www.ilo.org/global/about-the-ilo/history/lang--en/index.htm.

37 Roger-Henri Guerrand, *La Conquête des vacances* (Paris: Les Éditions ouvrières, 1963), p. 54.

38 Richez and Strauss, "Un temps nouveau pour les ouvriers," p. 403.

39 See https://en.wikipedia.org/wiki/Strength_Through_Joy.

40 Anne-Marie Thiesse, *La Création des identités nationales: Europe, XVIIIe-XXe siècle* (Paris: Le grand Livre du mois, 1999). See also Thiesse, "Organisation des loisirs des travailleurs et temps dérobés (1880–1930)," in Corbin, ed., *L'Avènement des loisirs*, especially "Organisations officielles soumises à une mystique nationale," p. 316.

41 Janine Larrue, "Loisirs ouvriers: chez les métallurgistes toulousains," *Esprit*, June 1959, p. 955, quoted by André Rauch, *Vacances en France de 1830 à nos jours* (Paris: Hachette, 1996), p. 100.

42 Ibid.

43 Madeleine Léo-Lagrange, "1936, an I du bonheur," *Janus: l'homme, son histoire et son avenir*, no. 7, "La révolution du loisir," June 1965.

44 Joseph Daniel, "Semaines sociales de Rouen, 1938," quoted by Jean-Victor Parant, *Le Problème du tourisme populaire: emploi des congés payés et institutions de vacances ouvrières en France et à l'étranger* (Paris: Librairie générale de droit et de jurisprudence, 1939), p. 37.

45 A worker, quoted by Rolande Trempé and Alain Boscus, "Les premiers congés payés à Decazeville et Mazamet," *Le Mouvement sociale*, no. 150 (1990), p. 72.

46 Simone Weil, quoted by Françoise Cribier, *La Grande Migration d'été des citadins en France* (Paris: Éditions du CNRS, 1969), p. 48.

47 Krsto Hegedušić, *The Dawn* (1936), private collection.

48 Fernand Léger, *Les Loisirs: hommage à Louis David* (1948–9), Centre Pompidou, Paris.

Chapter 28 The Promise of Wellbeing?

1 Jean Baudrillard, *La Société de consommation: ses mythes, ses structures* (Paris: SGPP, 1970), p. 208. *The Consumer Society: Myths and Structures*, trans. George Ritzer (London: Sage, 1998), p. 49.

2 See Conseil National de la Résistance, "Plan complet de sécurité sociale," www.voltairenet.org/article14072.html.

3 See the recommendations Silo-Agora des pensées critiques, https://silogora.org/une-histoire-de-lordonnance-4-octobre-1945/.
4 See Institut de recherche et documentation en économie de santé, www. irdes.fr/EspaceEnseignement/ChiffresGraphiques/Cadrage/IndicateursEtatSante/EsperanceVie.htm.
5 Order of October 4, 1945, article 64.
6 Ibid.
7 Frédéric Buffin and Thierry Tauran, "La consolidation des régimes spéciaux, 1945 à nos jours," in Tauran, ed., *La Sécurité sociale: son histoire à travers les textes*, vol. VII: *Les Régimes spéciaux de sécurité sociale* (Paris: Association pour l'étude de la Sécurité sociale, 2015), p. 218.
8 Ibid., p. 219.
9 Bastien Urbain, *Le Système de retraite à l'épreuve de son financement* (Issy-les-Moulineaux: LGDJ, 2019), p. 124.
10 Order no. 53-711, August 9, 1953, on the retirement system.
11 See above p. 237.
12 Alain Grangé, "Le régime spécial à la SNCF," in Tauran, *La Sécurité sociale, son histoire à travers les textes*, p. 234.
13 Jacques Doublet, "Âge de la retraite et prolongation de la vie humaine," *Droit social*, 1961, p. 172.
14 Bastien Urbain, *Le Système de retraite à l'épreuve de son financement*, p. 61.
15 See "L'apparition de la vignette," www.caradisiac.com/L-apparition-de-la-vignette-51019.htm.
16 Camille Simonin, "Pathologie générale," in Simonin, *Médecine du travail* (Paris: Maloine, [1950] 1956), p. 171.
17 See ibid.
18 See https://en.wikipedia.org/wiki/Occupational_medicine.
19 Camille Simonin, "Évolution de la protection médicale des travailleurs," in Simonin *Médecine du travail*, p. 774.
20 Camille Simonin, "Fonctionnement des services médicaux du travail," ibid., p. 785.
21 Ibid.
22 See Antoine Laville, *L'Ergonomie* (Paris: PUF, 1976), p. 5.
23 See W. F. Floyd and A. T. Welford, eds, *Symposium on Fatigue* (London: H. K. Lewis, 1953), p. 1.
24 See above p. 72.
25 See above p. 162.
26 See above p. 207.
27 Laville, *L'Ergonomie*, p. 12.
28 Étienne Grandjean, *Précis d'ergonomie: organisation physiologique du travail* (Paris: Dunod, 1969), p. 33.
29 Ibid., p. 27.
30 Ibid., p.28.
31 See Frans Thomas Kellermann et al., *Vademecum d'ergonomie destiné à l'industrie* (Paris: Dunod, 1964), p. 67.
32 Wesley E. Woodson, Peggy Tillman and Barry Tillman, *Human Factors Design Handbook: Information and Guidelines for the Design of Systems, Facilities, Equipment and Products for Human Use* (1966), quoted in Henri de Frémont and Michel Valentin, *L'Ergonomie: l'homme et le travail* (Paris: Dunod, 1970), p. 8.
33 See Camille Simonin, "Prévention de la fatigue," in Simonin, *Médecine du travail*, pp. 1024–5.
34 See Kellermann et al., *Vademecum d'ergonomie destiné à l'industrie*, p. 74.

35 Pierre Bugard, *La Fatigue: physiologie, psychologie, et médecine sociale* (Paris: Masson, 1960), p. 20. Translator's note: Dehydrogenation is the process by which hydrogen is removed from an organic compound. An example is the conversion of saturated into unsaturated compounds.
36 See Bernard Metz, "Principes physiologiques d'alimentation des travailleurs," in Simonin, *Médecine du travail*, p. 129.
37 See above p. 205.
38 Jean Scherrer and Hugues Monod, "Point de vue physiologique sur la fatigue," in Léon Chertok and Michel Sapir, eds, *La Fatigue*, IIIe Congrès international de médecine psychosomatique (Toulouse: Privat, 1967), p. 18.
39 See *Encyclopedia universalis* (Paris, 1968) entry "Hormones."
40 Georges Bresse, *Morphologie et physiologie animales* (Paris: Larousse, 1953), p. 784.
41 Ibid., p. 809.
42 Ibid., pp. 460–1.
43 See Henri Coutière, *Connais tes outils: diastases, vitamines, hormones* (Paris: Béranger, 1943), p. 79.
44 Ibid.. p. 69.
45 Ibid.. p. 99.
46 National Research Council, *Reprint no. 122* (Washington, DC: Office of Medical Information, 1945).
47 See above p. 170.
48 Bugard, *La Fatigue*, p. 265.
49 Pierre Bugard, *L'Usure par l'existence* (Paris : Masson, 1964), p. 17.
50 Ibid.
51 Bernard Metz, "Aspects physiologiques et psychologiques de la fatigue," in Simonin, *Médecine du travail*, p. 132.
52 Ibid.
53 Bugard, *L'Usure par l'existence*, p. 22.
54 See above p. 281.
55 Bugard, *L'Usure par l'existence*, "Avant-propos."
56 Henri Desoille, "Introduction," in Chertok and Sapir, *La Fatigue*, p. 7.
57 Bugard, *L'Usure par l'existence*, p. 13.
58 Ibid., p. 46.
59 Desoille, "Introduction," p. 12.
60 Michel Sapir, M.-J. Flouest and Françoise Lugassy, "La fatigue du cadre supérieur, de l'ouvrier spécialisé et de l'étudiant," in Chertok and Sapir, *La Fatigue*, p. 251.
61 See above pp. 280–1.
62 See Michel Duc, H. Viniaker and Dominique Barrucand, "La fatigue symptôme et la fatigue syndrôme, leur diagnostic différentiel en milieu hospitalier," in Chertok and Sapir, *La Fatigue*, p. 65.
63 See above p. 267.
64 R. A. McFarland, "Operational fatigue in aviation," paper given at the Aero Medical Association meeting, Washington, DC, March 24, 1958, quoted in Bugard, *La Fatigue*, p. 185.
65 Jacques Fessard and Christian David, "Fatigue et accidentiéisme routier," in Chertok and Sapir, *La Fatigue*, p. 195.
66 Bugard, *La Fatigue*, pp. 171ff.
67 Claude Veil, "Les états d'épuisement" (1958), in *Vulnérabilités au travail: naissance et actualité de la psychopathologie du travail* (Toulouse: Érès, 2012), p. 178.
68 See Samuel Howard Bartley and Eloise Chute, *Fatigue and Impairment in Man* (New York: McGraw-Hill, 1947), especially pp. 324ff.: "Personal factors in the work situation."

69 Ibid., p. 331.
70 Ibid., p. 336.
71 Ibid., see p. 337: "Job Analysis," "The worker is viewed holistically."
72 Claude Nègre, *La Fatigue en régions polaires* (Paris: Publication des expéditions polaires françaises, 1961).
73 François Dubet, *Le Temps des passions tristes* (Paris: Seuil, 2019), p. 22.
74 See "Travailleuses et travailleurs immigrés en France," in Marie-Christine Bureau, Antonella Corsani, Olivier Giraud and Frédéric Rey, eds, *Les Zones grises des relations de travail et d'emploi* (Buenos Aires: Teseo, 2019); www.teseopress.com/dictionnaire/chapter/229/.
75 See Musée de l'Histoire de l'immigration, Paris, https://histoire-immigration.fr/.
76 See "Travailleuses et travailleurs immigrés en France."
77 E. Elser-Falik and H. M. Raveau, "Fatigue-symptôme de l'acculturation des Africains en France," in Chertok and Sapir, *La Fatigue*, p. 173.
78 Ibid., p. 177.
79 Pierre Bugard and Pierre Bernachon, "Étude psychosomatique d'une asthénie au long cours," in Chertok and Sapir, *La Fatigue*, p. 180.
80 Georges Friedmann, *Le Travail en miettes: spécialisation et loisirs* (Paris: Gallimard, [1956] 1964), p. 32.
81 The manager of a car factory in Britain, quoted ibid.
82 Ibid., pp. 33–48.
83 See above pp. 23–6.
84 See above p. 269.
85 Friedmann, *Le Travail en miettes*, pp. 248–50.
86 Simonin, "Examens médicaux périodiques," in *Médecine du travail*, p. 869.
87 Peter R. Drucker, *La Pratique de la direction des entreprises*, trans. Bureau des temps élémentaires (Paris: Éditions d'Organisation, 1957). *The Practice of Management* (New York: Harper & Bros., 1954).
88 Bugard, *La Fatigue*, p. 56.
89 Marie-France Bied-Charreton, *Usine de femmes* (Paris: L'Harmattan, [1978] 2003), p. 162.
90 Tommaso Di Ciàula, *Tuta blu* (Paris: Actes Sud, [1978] 2002), p. 29.
91 Nicolas Dubost, *Flins sans fin* (Paris: Maspero, 1979), p. 40.Translator's note: Flins is the location of the first Renault factory.
92 See "La Nouvelle Belle Époque," *Paris Match*, January 12, 1963.
93 Bernard Cazes and Edgar Morin, "La question du bien-être," *Arguments*, no. 22 (1961) p. 1.
94 Jean Baudrillard, *Le Système des objets* (1968) (Paris: Gallimard, 1975), p. 7. *The System of Objects*, trans. James Benedict (London: Verso, 1996), p. 5.
95 See Jim Heimann, ed., *50s: All-American Ads* (New York: Taschen, 2001), p. 398.
96 Ibid., p. 402. See also Susan Strasser, *Never Done: A History of American Housework* (New York: Pantheon Books, 1982).
97 See above pp. 161 and 263.
98 See above p. 271.
99 "Editorial," *Paris Match*, January 13, 1963.
100 Jean Baudrillard, *Le Système des objets*, p. 62; *The System of Objects*, p. 57.
101 Philippe Perrot, "De l'apparat au bien-être: les avatars d'un superflu nécessaire," in Jean-Pierre Goubert, ed., *Du luxe au confort* (Paris: Belin, 1988), p. 46.
102 Michel Crozier, "Défense du bien-être," *Arguments*, no. 22 (1961), p. 47.
103 Alain Ehrenberg, *La Fatigue d'être soi: dépression et société* (Paris: Odile Jacob, 1998).
104 Georges Perec, *Les Choses* (1965), in *Oeuvres*, ed. Christelle Reggiani (Paris: Gallimard,

2017), vol. I, p. 126. *Things: A Story of the Sixties*, trans. David Bellos (Boston: Godine, 1990), p. 35.

105 Cazes and Morin, "La question du bien-être," p. 2.

106 Michel Drancourt, "Les femmes de la bourgeoisie vivent-elles mieux que leurs grand-mères?" *Réalités*, no. 191 (December 1961).

107 See above p. 150.

108 See above p. 220.

109 The quotations from Chris Marker's documentary *Le Joli Mai* (1963) were published in *L'Express*, April 11, 1963.

110 "L'ouvrier de la prospérité," *L'Express*, May 29, 1963.

111 Ibid.

112 Sapir, Flouest and Lugassy, "La fatigue du cadre supérieur, de l'ouvrier spécialisé et de l'étudiant," p. 262.

113 Ibid., p. 253.

114 Ibid., p. 263.

Chapter 29 From Burn Out to Identity

1 Herbert J. Freudenberger, *L'Épuisement professionnel: "La brûlure interne"*, trans. Marc Pelletier (Boucherville: Gaëtan Morin, [1980] 1987), p. 22.

2 Ibid.

3 See above p. 298.

4 See "Un syndrome de fatigue démocratique," *Le Un*, June 4, 2014.

5 See Daniel D. Jacques, *La Fatigue politique du Québec français* (Montreal: Boréal, 2019).

6 Charles de Montalembert, see https://archive.org/stream/mdemontalemberte00mont/mdemontalemberte00mont_djvu.txt.

7 See Bruno Tilliette, "Fatigue administrative," Place publique, January 8, 2013, www.place-publique.fr/index.php/le-magazine-2/articlefatigue-administrative/?highlight=fatigue.

8 See www.linguee.fr/francais-anglais/traduction/fatigue+institutionnelle.html.

9 See https://en.wikipedia.org/wiki/Tertiary_sector_of_the_economy.

10 See Jean-Yves Nau, "Les 'troubles musculo-squelettiques': des pathologies liées au productivisme," *Le Monde*, December 19, 2005.

11 See *Ergonomie aux postes de travail: la prévention des troubles musculo-squelettiques (TMS)* (Paris: Cetim, 2012), p. 12.

12 See *Le Rapport annuel 2018 de l'Assurance Maladie: risques professionnels* (Paris: CNAM, 2018).

13 See *Ergonomie aux postes de travail*, p. 9.

14 See *Le Rapport annuel 2018 de l'Assurance Maladie*.

15 Ibid.

16 "Troubles musculo-squelettiques: qu'est-ce que c'est?" https://sante.lefigaro.fr/sante/maladie/troubles-musculo-squelettiques/quest-ce-que-cest.

17 See Nau, "Les 'troubles musculo-squelettiques.'"

18 See Marilyne Becque, Aimée Kingsada and Amélie Mauroux, "Contraintes physiques et intensité du travail," *Synthèse Stat'*, no. 24 (February 2019), p. 10.

19 Nau, "Les 'troubles musculo-squelettiques.'"

20 Becque, Kingsada and Mauroux, "Contraintes physiques et intensité du travail," p. 154.

21 Marie-Grenier-Pezé, "La maladie du geste de travail," *Performances*, no. 3 (2002), repr. in *Les Cahiers de Préventique*, no. 7 (2006), p. 14.

22 Ibid.

23 Ibid. Translator's note: The brachial plexus is the network of nerves in the shoulder that carries movement and sensory signals to the arms and hands.

24 See above p. 303.

25 Yves Clot, "Les TMS: hyper-sollicitation ou hypo-sollicitation?" in *Les Cahiers de Préventique* no. 7 (2006), p. 23. Translator's note: "Hypostress" is characterized by boredom, restlessness and lack of motivation.
26 See above p. 308.
27 Nau, "Les 'troubles musculo-squelettiques.'"
28 F. Bourgeois et al., *Troubles musculosquelettiques et travail: quand la santé interroge l'organisation* (Paris: ANACT, [2000] 2006), p. 90.
29 See above p. 294.
30 See Paul Robert, *Dictionnaire alphabétique et analogique de la langue française* (Paris: Société du Nouveau Littré, 1962), entry "Pénible."
31 Annie Jolivet, "Pénibilité du travail: la loi de 2010 et ses usages par les acteurs sociaux," *Revue de l'IRES*, 3/70 (2011) pp. 33–60.
32 See ibid.
33 Ibid.
34 See Gérard Lasfargues, *Départs en retraite et "travaux pénibles": l'usage des connaissances scientifiques sur le travail et ses risques à long terme pour la santé* (Paris: Centre d'études de l'emploi, 2005).
35 See above p. 79.
36 Lasfargues, *Départs en retraite et "travaux pénibles"*, p. 19.
37 Ibid., pp. 25–8.
38 Ibid., p. 16.
39 Decree no. 2011-354 of March 30, 2011, regarding the definition and prevention of hardship-related injuries and the right to early retirement.
40 See "Le compte professionnel de prévention: définition, principes et calcul des points," November 14, 2019.
41 Lasfargues, *Départs en retraite et "travaux pénibles"*, p. 12.
42 Ibid.
43 Ibid.
44 See above p. 311.
45 See above p. 314.
46 Francis Marion, "On ne peut faire l'économie d'évaluer tant l'usure physique que la fatigue psychologique," *Le Monde*, February 17, 2020.
47 Antonio A. Casilli, *En attendant les robots: enquête sur le travail du clic* (Paris: Seuil: 2019), p 187.
48 See Mireille Weinberg, "Retraite et pénibilité au travail: les quatre critères de la discorde," *L'Opinion*, December 26, 2019.
49 See "La pénibilité au travail: ce qui change en 2018," January 16, 2018, https://atworkconseil.fr/la-prevention-de-la-penibilite-en-2018/.
50 Ibid.
51 Ibid.
52 See Valentine Pasquesoone, "Je ne pense pas tenir jusqu'à soixante-cinq ans: l'inquiétude des salariés concernés par la réforme du compte pénibilité," France Info, July 12, 2017.
53 Ibid.
54 See Maly Drazkami, "Pénibilité au travail: les femmes sont les plus touchées, et les moins reconnues," December 5, 2017, www.revolutionpermanente.fr/penibilite-au-travail-les-femmes-sont-les-plus-touchees-et-les-moins-reconnues.
55 Jérôme Lefilliâtre, "Grève: à la RATP, 'il faut que ce soit pire lundi,'" *Libération*, December 5, 2019.
56 Jean-Pierre Daviet, "La grande entreprise: professions et culture," in Louis-Henri Parias, ed., *Histoire générale du travail* (Paris: Nouvelle Librairie de France, 1996), vol. IV, p. 292.

57 Ibid., p. 296.
58 Thierry Pillon and François Vatin, *Traité de sociologie du travail* (Toulouse: Octares, 2003), p. 221.
59 The term "Ergonomic" was first used in 1949 in the name "Ergonomic Research Society." The emphasis on ease and efficiency justifies its invention: "It is a comprehensive collection of scientific knowledge related to humans, essential for designing tools, equipment and strategies that can be used with a maximum of ease, safety and efficiency." Antoine Laville, *L'Ergonomie*, p. 12.
60 See Maurice de Montmollin, ed., *Vocabulaire de l'ergonomie* (Toulouse: Octares, 1995).
61 Pierre Bugard, *Stress, fatigue, dépression: l'homme et les agressions de la vie quotidienne* (Paris: Doin, 1974), p. 174.
62 Johan Wilhelm Hendrik Kalsbeek, "Standards of acceptable load in ATC tasks," *Ergonomics*, 14/5 (1971), pp. 641–50.
63 T.-M. Fraser, *Stress et satisfaction au travail: étude critique* (Geneva: Bureau international du travail, 1983).
64 Jacqueline M. Atkinson, *Coping with Stress at Work* (Wellingborough: Thorsons, 1988).
65 See above pp. 207–9.
66 See Claude Veil, *Vulnérabilités au travail: naissance et actualité de la psychopathologie du travail* (Toulouse: Érès, 2012).
67 Suzanne Peters and Patrick Mesters, *Vaincre l'épuisement professionnel: toutes les clés pour comprendre le burn out* (Paris: Robert Laffont, 2007).
68 Cercle Sésame, *2012–2017: ce que veulent les Français* (Paris: Éditions d'Organisation Groupe Eyrolles, 2011), p. 196.
69 Christophe Dejours, *Souffrance en France: la banalisation de l'injustice sociale* (Paris: Seuil, 1998), p. 28.
70 See above p. 258.
71 See Marie Pezé, *Ils ne mouraient pas tous mais tous étaient frappés: journal de consultation "Souffrance au travail," 1997–2008* (Paris: Pearson, 2008).
72 See *Le Parisien* newspaper using the term "employee" for "someone who performs a job for someone else in order to earn a wage."
73 Marie Pezé, *Ils ne mouraient pas tous mais tous étaient frappés*, pp. 33–44.
74 Ibid., pp. 151–7.
75 Dejours, *Souffrance en France*, p. 30.
76 Article 222-33-2 of the Criminal Code, January 27, 2002.
77 Mathilde Goanec, "De jeunes vendeuses bataillent contre l'apprentissage de l'humiliation," *Mediapart*, July 26, 2019.
78 See https://en.wikipedia.org/wiki/Harassment.
79 Report by Snesup in Évry, published July 11, 2010.
80 Marie-France Hirigoyen, "Des cas de plus en plus graves de harcèlement au travail," *Mediapart*, March 5, 2014.
81 See "Épuisement professionnel ou burnout," https://inrs.fr/risques/epuisement-burnout/ce-qu-il-faut-retenir.html.
82 Freudenberger, *L'Épuisement professionnel*, p. 25.
83 Ibid., p. 29.
84 Ibid., p. 32.
85 Ibid., p. 133.
86 See "Syndrome de burn out: c'est quoi?," www.burnout-info.ch/fr/burnout_c_est_quoi.htm.
87 Ibid.
88 Jean-Pierre Olié and Patrick Légeron, "Rapport sur le burn out," *Bulletin de l'Académie nationale de médecine*, meeting of February 23, 2016.

89 See Philippe Zawieja, *Le Burn out* (Paris: PUF, 2015), p. 3: "The Old Testament gives at least two examples of professional burn out." See also the very useful *Dictionnaire de la fatigue* (Geneva: Droz, 2016).
90 See "Épuisement professionnel ou burnout,".
91 See Cercle Sésame, *2012–2017: ce que veulent les Français*, p. 209.
92 "Les algorithmes chassent tout rapport humain," *TAF: Travailler au futur*, no. 1 (2020), p. 57.
93 Casilli, *En attendant les robots*, p. 263.
94 Julien Palleja, "SNCF: une déhumanisation lourde de conséquences," *TAF*, no. 1 (2020), p. 53.
95 Marc Loriol, "Numérisation de l'économie et transformation du travail," *Cahiers français*, no. 398 (2017), pp. 2–7.
96 See Helene Riffaudeau, "Les nouveaux esclaves du numérique," *Téléobs*, September 21–7, 2019.
97 See "Deliveroo, une forme d'esclavage moderne," *TAF*, no.1 (2020), p. 44.
98 The word "juice" means electricity; in this case, power to recharge the scooters.
99 See Gurvan Kristanadjaja, "'Juicers': la course aux clopinettes électriques," *Libération*, May 10, 2019.
100 See Cercle Sésame, *2012–2017: ce que veulent les Français*, p. 203.
101 See Riffandeau, "Les nouveaux esclaves du numérique." "This model is a step backward for thousands of workers."
102 See Éric Favereau, "À l'hôpital un médecin sur deux se dit épuisé," *Libération*, December 2, 2019.
103 Natalie Raulin, "Hôpital: Agnès Hartemann, en unité de resistance," *Libération*, February 14, 2020.
104 See Favereau, "À l'hôpital un médecin sur deux se dit épuisé."
105 Dominique Méda, "Le grand fossé," *Le Un*, April 29, 2020.
106 See Cécile Amar and David Le Bailly, "Santé publique, qui a désarmé l'hôpital?" *L'Obs*, April 9–15, 2020. See also Stéphane Velut, *L'hôpital, une nouvelle industrie: le langage comme symptôme* (Paris: Gallimard, 2020).
107 See Fiodor Rilov with Alexia Eychenne, *Qui a tué vos emplois?* (Paris: Don Quichotte–Seuil, 2019).
108 Laurie Moniez, "L'annonce de la fusion entre Bombardier et Alstom inquiète leurs salariés des Hauts-de-France," *Le Monde*, February 21, 2020.
109 See Cercle Sésame, *2012–2017: ce que veulent les Français*, p. 208.
110 Alain Supiot, "Le travail humain 'au-delà de l'emploi,'" *TAF*, no. 1 (2020), p. 31.
111 See "Les témoignages marquants des premières semaines du procès France Télécom," *France Info*, May 25, 2019.
112 Ibid.
113 Ibid.
114 "France Télécom, ils ont joué avec nos vies," *Libération*, August 9, 2018.
115 See https://francetvinfo.fr/economie/telecom/suicides-a-france-telecom/.
116 Ibid.
117 "France Télécom, ils ont joué avec nos vies."
118 Ibid.
119 See Jean-Christophe Vuattoux, "Les suicides cachent la forêt qu'est la souffrance au travail, laquelle n'est pas encore imputée aux organisations," *Slate*, December 28, 2019.
120 Ibid.
121 Alexandra Anders, "L'empowerment au coeur du nouveau management," *Cornerstone Blog*, October 18, 2019; www.gpomag.fr/web/tribunes-libres/l-empowerment-au-coeur-du-nouveau-management.

122 Arnaud Hautesserres, "Management, quelles tendances pour l'année 2019?" *Focus RH*, December 12, 2018.
123 Ibid.
124 Amélie Petitdemange, "Management, guide complet," *Les Échos Start*, December 18, 2018.
125 See Agathe Ranc, "J'étais un mauvais chef," *L'Obs*, February 13–19, 2020.
126 See the blog "Le réveil de la conscience."
127 Annika Rose, "Prenez soin de vous," *In the Moment*, May 2018.
128 Jean Baudrillard, *La Société de consommation: ses mythes, ses structures* (Paris: SGPP, 1970), p. 201.
129 Robert Castel and Claudine Haroche, *Propriété privée, propriété sociale, propriété de soi: entretiens sur la construction de l'individu moderne* (Paris: Fayard, 2001), p. 128.
130 Marcel Gauchet, "Essai de psychologie contemporaine: un nouvel âge de la personnalité," *Le Débat*, 2/99 (1998), p. 177.
131 Michel Houellebecq, *Sérotonine* (Paris: Flammarion, 2019), p. 181. *Serotonin*, trans. Shaun Whiteside and Michel Houellebecq (New York: Farrar, Straus, Giroux, 2019).
132 See https://en.wikipedia.org/wiki/Loreal.
133 See Cercle Sésame, *2012–2017: ce que veulent les Français*, pp. 199–200.
134 See Élisabeth Pineau, "Le burn out, un mal tabou chez les sportifs de haut niveau," *Le Monde*, January 29, 2020.
135 Ibid.
136 See "Burn out amoureux: les signes qui doivent vous alerter," *Femme actuelle*, October 2, 2018.
137 See "Le burn out familial, signes et conséquences, comment l'éviter?" www.coolparentsmakehappykids.com/burn-out-familial-signes-consequences-comment-eviter/.
138 See Gaëlle Dupont, "Quand la 'charge mentale' du foyer pèse sur les femmes," *Le Monde*, May 16, 2017.
139 Ibid.
140 See "Fallait demander," emmaclit, May 9, 2017, https://emmaclit.com/2017/05/09/repartition-des-taches-hommes-femmes/.
141 Michael Delisle, *Le Palais de la fatigue* (Montreal: Nouvelles Boréal, 2017), p. 76.
142 Houellebecq, *Sérotonine*, p. 148.
143 Jean Clair, *Le voyageur égoïste* (Paris: Petite Bibliothèque Payot, [1989] 2010).
144 See above p. 96.
145 "Pourquoi sommes-nous si fatigués?" *Philosophie Magazine*, no. 134 (November 2019).
146 See Nicole Aubert, ed., *@ la recherche du temps: individus hyperconnectés, société accélérée: tensions et transformations* (Toulouse: Érès, 2018).
147 See Laurent Muller, "Enjeux d'une quête anomique en des temps d'effervescence," ibid., p. 143.
148 See David Le Breton, *Tenir: douleur chronique et réinvention de soi* (Paris: Métailié, 2017).
149 Michel Eltchaninoff, "Fatigo ergo sum," *Philosophie Magazine*, no. 134 (November 2019), p. 46.
150 Clara Malraux, *Nos vingt ans* (Paris: Grasset, 1966), p. 147.
151 Emmanuel Levinas, *Totalité et infini: essai sur l'extériorité* (La Haye: Martinus Nijhoff, 1971). See Henri Duthu, "Au-delà du sens commun: avec Emmanuel Levinas," *Espace éthique*, October 23, 2005, http://espacethique.free.fr/articles.php?lng=fr&pg=123.
152 See above p. 328.
153 "En finir avec la fatigue," *Ça m'intéresse: Santé*, 9 December 2019, www.caminteresse.fr/sante/en-finir-avec-la-fatigue-avec-ca-minteresse-sante-127567/.

154 See Olivier Monod, "La France, fait-elle partie des plus gros consommateurs de médicaments dans le monde?" *Libération*, July 29, 2019.
155 *300 Médicaments pour se surpasser physiquement et intellectuellement* (Paris: Balland, 1988), pp. 15–16.
156 See Jean-François Bourg, *Le Dopage* (Paris: La Découverte, 2019). See also Georges Vigarello, "Le sport dopé," *Du jeu ancien au show sportif: la naissance d'un mythe* (Paris: Seuil, 2002), pp. 169–89.
157 *Respire: créer du temps pour soi*, no. 1, February 15, 2017.
158 *In the moment: parce qu'être soi n'attend pas*, no. 1, January 2018.
159 *ADN: les essentiels*, no. 1, March 14, 2017.
160 *Sens et santé: le corps, l'esprit, le monde*, no. 1, May 2017.
161 See above p. 329.
162 Cédric Villani, "Je mets mon cerveau en roue libre," *Clés*, December 2014, p. 56.
163 Anaïs Vanel, "J'ai tout quitté pour aller faire du surf," *Ça m'intéresse: Santé*, December 2019. See also Vanel, *Tout quitter* (Paris: Flammarion, 2019).
164 "Vaincre la fatigue, c'est d'abord savoir écouter les signaux du corps," *Ça m'intéresse: Santé*, December 2019, p. 57.
165 "Perception du stress," *ADN: les essentiels*, no. 6, December 2019, p. 50.
166 "Libérez votre esprit en dix étapes," *Respire*, no. 1, p. 8.
167 "Cinq façons d'écouter vos émotions," *Respire*, no. 5, p. 27.
168 "Évacuer le stress," *Sens et Santé*, no. 2, p. 25.
169 "Moment de sérénité," *Respire*, no. 19, p. 121.
170 See above pp. 249–50.
171 *My Switzerland: la nature te veut*, tourist pamphlet, Geneva, 2019, p. 73.
172 Gérard Bruant, *Anthropologie de l'effort: expériences vécues et représentation du monde* (Paris: L'Harmattan, 2017), p. 69.
173 Olivier Bessy, *Le Grand Raid de la Réunion: à chacun son extrême et un emblème pour tous* (La Réunion: Océan Éditions, 2002), p. 19.
174 See Carla de Silva, "Philippe Richet, adepte des raids extrêmes," *France Bleu*, January 15, 2020.
175 This is the subtitle of Mike Horn, *Latitude zéro: 40,000 km pour partir à la recherche du monde* (Paris: XO Éditions, 2001).
176 See Reto Lenherr et al., "From double iron to double deca iron ultra-triathalon: a retrospective data analysis from 1985 to 2011," *Physical Culture and Sport: Studies and Research*, 54 (2012), pp. 55–67. See also Raphaël Verchère, *Philosophie du triathlon, ou Les joies et les souffrances de l'Hercule moderne* (Le Crest: Éditions du Volcan, 2020), p. 113.
177 See above pp. 98–9.
178 Éric Fiat, "La fatigue permet un autre rapport au monde," *Ça m'intéresse: Santé*, December 2019. See also Fiat, *Ode à la fatigue* (Paris: Éditions de l'Observatoire, 2018), p. 398: "a herb garden of fatigues is part of the human condition, and we can make them our allies if we assimilate them."

Chapter 30 Surprises and "Viral" Dangers

1 See above p. 12.
2 See above p. 201.
3 Éric Favereau, ""À l'hôpital un médecin sur deux se dit épuisé," *Libération*, December 2, 2019. See also above p. 324.
4 Account of a doctor working in a hospital, "La fatigue et la trouille," *Le Monde*, April 2, 2020.
5 "Journal de crise des blouses blanches," entry 15, *Le Monde*, April 7, 2020.
6 See "Coronavirus: les soignants sont épuisés," *France Info*, April 5, 2020.

7 "Soignants: je pense Covid, je mange Covid, je dors Covid," *Libération*, April 5, 2020.
8 Jean-Paul Mari, "À l'hôpital, vague de fatigue et vague à l'âme," *Libération*, April 20, 2020.
9 "Journal de crise des blouses blanches," entry 14, *Le Monde* April 9, 2020.
10 Ibid., entry 9, March 31, 2020.
11 "Épuisement professionnel ou burnout," https://inrs.fr/risques/epuisement-burnout/ce-qu-il-faut-retenir.html.
12 Raphaëlle Rérolle, "Les jours sans répit d'un urgentiste parisien," *Le Monde*, April 4, 2020.
13 "Soignants: je pense Covid, je mange Covid, je dors Covid."
14 Sandrine Blanchard, "Journal de bord d'un médecin de campagne victime de coronavirus," *Le Monde*, April 2, 2020.
15 See also Thierry Philip and Jacques Leglise, "C'est l'ensemble du système hospitalier qui nécessite une réforme," *Le Monde*, June 17, 2020.
16 See Aurélie Lebelle, "Coronavirus: le palmarès des emplois les plus vulnérables," *Le Parisien*, April 28, 2020.
17 See the report by LCI, March 27, 2020.
18 See the order no. 2020-323 of March 25, 2020, that enacted emergency rules for paid leave, work schedules, and time off.
19 Yves Veyrier, general secretary of the labor union Force Ouvrière, *La Croix*, March 25, 2020.
20 "Commerces, usines, transports: ces Français qui vont travailler 'la boule au ventre,'" *Mediapart*, April 4, 2020.
21 "Avec la crise sanitaire, les travailleurs invisibles sortent de l'ombre," *Le Monde*, April 1, 2020.
22 Ibid.
23 Ibid.
24 Laurence Defranoux, "Auxiliaires de vie: 'on est basse classe, celle dont on ne parle pas,'" *Libération*, April 24, 2020.
25 Ibid.
26 Ibid.
27 Claire Legros, "Le souci de l'autre, un retour de l'éthique du 'care,'" *Le Monde*, May 1, 2020.
28 Lucie Delaporte, "Les ouvriers de la logistique sont devenus les 'caryatides du monde moderne,'" *Mediapart*, April 4, 2020.
29 Alexandre Piquard, "La controverse politique rattrape à nouveau Amazon aux États-Unis," *Le Monde*, May 6, 2020.
30 "Avec la crise sanitaire, les travailleurs invisibles sortent de l'ombre."
31 See Bertrand Bissuel, "Une conversion au télétravail plutôt réussie," *Le Monde*, May 1, 2020.
32 Ibid.
33 See Amandine Cailhol, "Télétravail: le boulot compresseur," *Libération*, April 29, 2020.
34 Ibid.
35 Danièle Linhart, "L'activité se retrouve déconnectée de sa finalité sociale," *Libération*, April 29, 2020.
36 Ibid.
37 See Cailhol, "Télétravail: le boulot compresseur."
38 "Journal de crise des blouses blanches," entry 9.
39 Annick Cojean, "La croisière à la dérive," *Le Monde*, April 16, 2020.
40 Doan Bui and David Le Bailly, "Covid Stories," *L'Obs*, May 7–13, 2020.
41 "Les conseils d'un psychiatre pour bien vivre le confinement," RFI, March 24, 2020.

42 See "Le confinement, reflet des inégalités sociales liées au logement et au niveau de revenu des Français," *Le Monde*, April 21, 2020.
43 Marie Duru-Bellat, "Cette crise met en évidence les conditions de vie très inégales des Français," *Le Monde*, April 1, 2020.
44 David Le Breton, "L'exposition au bruit et au silence est très inégalitaire," *Le Monde*, March 28, 2020.
45 "Rebelles au confinement," *Libération*, April 28, 2020.
46 Christophe Honoré, "Ce temps imposé est un temps empoisonné," *Le Monde*, May 1, 2020.
47 "Cohabiter avec le coronavirus dans la durée," *Le Monde*, April 7, 2020.
48 David Larousserie, "Coronavirus, comment sont élaborées les modélisations épidémiologiques," *Le Monde*, May 7, 2020.
49 "L'Enfer à la maison," *L'Obs*, April 9–15, 2020.
50 Catherine Mallaval and Sylvain Mouillard, "Familles confinées," *Libération*, April 22, 2020.
51 ZEP, "Moi jeune," *Libération*, April 22, 2020.
52 See above p. 328.
53 Virginie Ballet, "Les foyers pas vaccinés contre la charge mentale," *Libération*, April 22, 2020.

Index